Benjamin FRANKLIN
1721-1906

a reference guide

A
Reference
Publication
in
Literature

Everett Emerson
Editor

Benjamin FRANKLIN
1721-1906

a reference guide

MELVIN H. BUXBAUM

G.K. HALL & CO.

70 LINCOLN STREET, BOSTON, MASS.

Library of Congress Cataloging in Publication Data

Buxbaum, Melvin H.
  Benjamin Franklin, 1721-1906.

  Includes index.
  1. Franklin, Benjamin, 1706-1790—Bibliography.
I. Title.
Z8313.B89   1983   016.9733′092′4   82-12144
[E302.6.F8]
ISBN 0-8161-7985-9

This publication is printed on permanent/durable acid-free paper
MANUFACTURED IN THE UNITED STATES OF AMERICA

To the memory of my father and mother

Contents

The Author

Melvin H. Buxbaum was awarded the Ph.D. from the University of Chicago. He has taught at the University of Illinois in Chicago, the City University of New York, the University of Houston and, since 1978, has been Professor of English at the University of Colorado, Boulder. He has served on the editorial boards of Enlightenment Essays and English Language Notes. In addition to having written shorter works for journals and magazines, he is the author of Benjamin Franklin and the Zealous Presbyterians, which was published in 1975 by the Pennsylvania State University Press.

Preface

About six years ago, Professor Everett Emerson asked me to undertake this project. I knew at the time that there was a need for a comprehensive annotated bibliography of works on Benjamin Franklin, but in my innocence, my almost incredible naïveté, I did not realize what I was letting myself in for by agreeing to do the work. Obviously, many of the pieces would be minor, some downright trivial and perhaps best forgotten. But who was I to judge what might be interesting or useful to someone in the future? So I would sin in the direction of providing too much rather than too little: I would be very nearly complete!

The work in your hands is not that anticipated monument to Franklinian industry. In fact, I shudder to think how many items I have missed. The original plan was to deal with all published works, other than simple reviews, but also to include theses and dissertations that remain unpublished. An increasing sense of realism resulting from a frustrating summer in the Rare Books Room and microfilm reading room of the New York Public Library made poignantly clear the foolishness of going page by page through unindexed newspapers looking for Franklin items. After consulting with colleagues and friends, whose opinion was unanimous, I decided to eliminate all newspaper accounts rather than to annotate only those that were indexed or that I happened upon by accident. I believe that a systematic and thorough search of newspapers from throughout the world will turn up quite interesting and valuable material; however, this is a job for a small army of dedicated researchers.

In general, the work has proceeded according to the initial plan. Given Franklin's great stature, it seemed appropriate to try to suggest how he has been thought of throughout the world at different times. It was therefore necessary to arrange the writings according to the date of first publication. I have tried in every case to see the earliest published version. When I could see only a later printing or edition, I have supplied two entries, one for the first version and a second for the work I actually used. In such cases I place an asterisk next to the earlier work, thus indicating I have not seen this printing. I then provide the bibliographical information for this work and a cross-reference to the later printing which is annotated. Some unseen pieces have been annotated from secondary sources. In all cases, I indicate the source used. Many Franklin items defy positive dating. Instead of bunching all such works together at the end of the second volume, I have tried to determine whether an individual item was written before or after the cutoff date for the first volume, 31 December 1906. For this reason, there are undated listings at the end of the first volume, and there will also be others at the end of the second.

The underlying principle and the informing, passionate desire behind this book is that it be useful. Indeed, the promise that it might help many people for years to come is what probably saved my sanity! I have therefore sacrificed some bibliographic conventions to clarity when it seemed necessary to do so, and I have sincerely endeavored to make this work readable.

Acknowledgments

I have mixed feelings about thanking the people who have so far helped me. I am deeply in their debt and do wish to express my gratitude; yet, there are literally hundreds of persons from throughout the world, most of whom I do not know, who have helped. Even in naming those I have pestered most, I am sure to forget some. To all these unsung friends, my apologies and thanks now. As for those I do know, I want to thank the wonderful staff of the New York Public Library in the main reading room, the Rare Books Room, the various divisions, and the stacks. A very special thanks is due to Tom Bourke, formerly of the main reading room of the New York Public Library--if he cannot find a work, it no longer exists. My sincere appreciation, too, to the librarians at Columbia University, New York University, several specialized libraries in New York, and to Jean Longland of the Hispanic Society of America, who helped with some unusually difficult problems.

Anyone working seriously on Franklin is going to make his pilgrimages to Yale University and its splendid Franklin Collection. Here he will be greeted by the remarkable Dorothy Bridgwater, who made it possible for me to work through the Collection, who sped duplicated materials to me wherever my home base was and, finally, who gave me the benefit of her vast knowledge of Franklin and the Collection. My friends Claude-Anne Lopez and Jonathan Dull provided solid information and convivial support. To the wonderful people, past and present, at the interlibrary loan office of the Sterling Library, thank you for handling quickly and efficiently my hundreds of requests. And my best wishes for your good health--for I am not yet finished!

In addition to New York and New Haven, there is Philadelphia and the American Philosophical Society, which I wish to thank for a much needed grant. To my friend Roy Goodman of the Library of the American Philosophical Society, I owe a debt of gratitude I cannot repay. I want to extend to him my appreciation for the many, many times he responded to my desperate phone calls and letters or, when I was in Philadelphia, for the days he found things to do after closing time so that I could get more work done. Before leaving Philadelphia, I want to thank Dr. Westlake of Special Collections at the Van Pelt

Acknowledgments

Library of the University of Pennsylvania. One of her virtues is finding works everyone else thought were lost.

Chicago friends have also helped in a number of ways. Gwin J. Kolb of the University of Chicago, George Christakes, and Karen Skubish have all found and duplicated items for me. I was equally fortunate during the year I spent at the University of Houston. Here two extraordinary librarians, Jean Jackson and Lynn Sterba, did the seemingly impossible for me as a matter of course. And my assistant, Philip Montgomery, worked with genuine dedication and enthusiasm. For four years now, I have been at the University of Colorado at Boulder and have been helped greatly by Mary Kay, now of the University of Kansas, and by Sue Rusk. Boulder colleagues have also aided me, and I want to express my gratitude here to Professors Richard Schoeck, Marshall and Jane Brown, and Sophia Morgan.

It has been my good fortune to have served under a number of special administrators who have helped with time off, money for travel and research expenses, and encouragement. Bill Monat, formerly of the City University of New York and now president of Northern Illinois University, was instrumental in keeping alive the importance of scholarship during the financial disaster that beset the City University. Chancellor Barry Munitz of the University of Houston provided money and an assistant. At the University of Colorado, the former president, Roland Rautenstraus, was very generous, as were the former Dean of Arts and Science, Bill Briggs, and the Council on Research and Creative Work.

Finally, I want to thank Douglas Dix, who did a good deal of the typing, my daughters, Julie and Laurie, for helping with the proofreading and suspending their quarrels when the going was rough, and, most of all, my wife, Maxine, who typed, retyped, proofread, despaired, rejoiced, and counted the hours until we were through. Thank you all.

Introduction

One who undertakes to devote many years of his life to reading
and describing all works he can find in all languages and fields that
are entirely or substantially on Benjamin Franklin must have in mind
some overriding goal that can compensate for the tedium and frustra-
tion inherent in such a project. I do not mean to imply that there
are no intellectual compensations in doing an annotated bibliography
of writings on Franklin, for there are: one does learn a good deal
about Franklin, eighteenth-century science and social history (to use
a term that will cover at least most of the fields in which Franklin
was involved). Yet there are surely more congenial ways to learn,
and so one must look beyond himself to justify the endeavor. There
are at least two major rationales for the present study. For one,
Franklin is one of the most intriguing and important men in American
history. His great abilities and unmatched versatility have made his
biography and career almost endlessly fascinating. Poor Richard in-
nocently anticipated the future when, in 1738, he wrote: "If you
would not be forgotten as soon as you are dead and rotten, either
write things worth reading or do things worth the writing." His
creator has certainly done both. The second justification for the
time and labor that have gone into this work is that it should prove
useful to the many people who study Franklin and the events he helped
shape.

To be more specific, I hope these volumes will be helpful in several ways. First, a substantial number of writings on Franklin, especially those done in the nineteenth century, are in deplorable
condition. If there is money, some can be filmed and therefore saved;
however, too many simply disintegrate when handled and so cannot be
photoduplicated. This bibliography will at least preserve for us and
future students the main ideas in such items.

Another of its intended uses, of course, is to make available
works on Franklin that often would have been difficult to come by or
have been inaccessible to all but a few people. Many of the items
that are described here are indeed housed in the great libraries in
Cambridge, New Haven, New York, Philadelphia, Washington, Ann Arbor,
Chicago, and Berkeley. Hundreds of other works, though, were located,

sometimes serendipitously, in smaller repositories that seemed on the surface unlikely to have rare or obscure pieces on Franklin. Still other items are in Europe or Asia. (Interestingly, communist writers study Franklin not only as a scientist and political liberator, but as an economist whose ideas and maxims merit serious consideration. After all, it is better to be a relatively prosperous communist than a poor one!) No single library has all of these works; therefore, the present bibliography will make it possible for researchers to have easy access to the ideas in articles, essays, monographs, and books that they might not even know about, much less have at hand. Of course, using the annotations is not the same as seeing the originals. Ideally, one should be able to examine the writings and judge for himself what they say and how they say it. These annotations, though, should provide a reasonable and practical alternative for those who cannot see all the originals.

It is also my hope that users of this bibliography will have the opportunity to gain a better understanding and more balanced view of Franklin from having before them not only familiar but frequently unfamiliar writings about him. There are, for example, more than 270 annotations for the eighteenth century and, judging from citations in modern studies of Franklin, a good number of these pieces are generally unknown today. Yet some of them are important either in themselves or because, taken with others of the period, they express widely held opinions. The same point, moreover, can be made of nineteenth-century works, which are indeed numerous. If, as has been often thought, Franklin's reputation declined soon after his death, then this decline was surely limited chiefly to people whose noses and blood were both blue. Franklin apparently did not suffer any great loss of popularity at least among most of his fellow Americans or people abroad. Furthermore, those who have written on Franklin cover rather well the spectrum of abilities, taste, reputation, and areas of interest.

The fourth way in which this bibliography should prove useful is in revealing what those who have written on Franklin have had to say not only about their immediate subject, but also, sometimes unconsciously, about themselves and the attitudes of their time and place. By this I mean that for 200 years Franklin has been a yardstick by which people have measured the worth of popular American ideas concerning success, democracy, freedom, self-reliance, humanitarianism, the benefits deriving from self-education and the essentially secular life, and the practical virtues of hard work and frugality for the common man like Poor Richard or the modest hero who inhabits the pages of the Autobiography.

We can frequently judge what authors thought about American notions of these qualities and ideals by what they have said about Franklin as an economist, moralist, philosopher, humanitarian, or revolutionary. If for one anonymous writer Franklin, though outstanding in many ways, is greatest of all as a human being because of his large sympathy for his fellow man (n.d. 4), others see him as a narrow, vicious person who encouraged the war between England and America, thus destroying a magnificent empire, merely to further his own ambitious and low ends (1774.6; 1860.12).[1] These detractors, one a very resentful, angry Englishman, the other an unyielding American Tory, see Franklin and his causes in light of their own principles, interests and needs, which of course led them to support English policy and oppose American pressures for at first equal treatment and at last for complete independence. Such views are reiterated by a magazine writer and editor who, seeking to express not only his conservatism but his genteel scorn for Franklin's values, particularly his support of vulgarian democracy and opposition to established churches, attacked him on social, political, and religious grounds (1801.3, 4; 1804.4; 1819.1).

Even in France, where Franklin achieved a degree of success, fame, and love beyond that he had ever known or was to know, one's opinion of him has frequently depended on what he thought of the urgings for liberty, popular democracy, revolution, and the values of the basically secular middle class. Those of his French contemporaries who approved of these things, so thoroughly identified Franklin with them that they loved him at times without moderation and treated him with a total lack of critical judgment (1777.4; 1779.2, 4-6; 1783.8; 1784.5). European and American critics of such values, or at least what they judged to be the Franklinian version of them, were free in their criticism, for to them it seemed that Franklin was responsible for helping usher into the world the reign of Chaos and Night (1776.2; 1779.10; 1791.9; 1839.5; 1853.16; 1859.3; 1889.17). Readers of these pages will find evidence enough that judgments of Franklin have, in effect, often been statements about the values he is perceived as having upheld.

Another use of this bibliography concerns Franklin's unique status as the man who created and most fully represents the typical American character (1784.5; 1842.5; 1876.1, 9; 1898.20; 1906.68, 125; n.d. 16, 21). Franklin himself encouraged this image for personal as well as broader reasons,[2] and subsequent generations have made certain that the picture has remained intact. In studying responses to him and his career, we therefore learn a good deal about how America has been perceived by Americans and those from other countries as well. He is thought of as the man who best epitomizes the go-getter spirit of capitalist America both by those who approve of this spirit and those who despise it (1792.1; 1801.3; 1830.4; 1864.3; 1900.18).[3] Whether one finds Franklin's socioeconomic views good or bad depends, of course, on what he thinks of American capitalism and how it has affected life in America and elsewhere.

To be sure, there are writers who have tried to argue that one cannot simply equate Franklin with the history of American capitalism because he was more than a mere advocate of laissez-faire economics (1895.10),[4] or that he would have been wise, compassionate, and pragmatic enough to have modified his views when it was necessary to do so; that, in fact, he would have used even downright socialist techniques to end the economic malaise and the despair caused by the Great Depression until he could get the country back to the rugged individualistic capitalism that had made it great and prosperous.[5] Most writers, though, have found no need to modify their position that Franklin is the archetype of American enterprise and thus of the American way.[6] Given the preponderance of such views on economics and other matters, one need hardly wonder that some recent students of Franklin have bewailed the impoverishment of the man's complexity and the historical inability to do him justice.[7]

Franklin as the representative of the American character has presented problems to those who have insisted that America was a Christian country and that he was necessarily a firm Christian. Such authors have at times sought a way out of their dilemma by asserting that although Franklin is typically American in many ways, in his deism he more nearly expresses his age than customary American values and beliefs (1853.1; 1864.5; 1896.10; 1898.23).

In general, writers who have commented on the philosopher's religious opinions have fallen into one of two groups. The first of these uses him as an example to prove that even the most benevolent of merely secular men is hardly a fit representative of the American character. After all, given the fact that he rejected Christianity, Franklin had to lack the spirituality and sound moral principles that most Americans share (1801.3, 4; 1804.4; 1806.7; 1818.3; 1819.1; 1839.5; 1884.5). One clerical orator apparently caught up in saintly zeal and in a mood to pronounce judgments, took the occasion of an event supposedly paying tribute to Franklin's memory to try and work up some religious sentiment in his audience. He admitted that Franklin had been a valuable man, that he certainly had virtues and abilities which he used for the common good. Yet this was not enough for the Reverend Mr. Hugh M'Neile. No man would be saved by his good works alone, regardless of what quality and number they were. The plain truth for the minister was that Franklin "knew not God" and was consequently "spotted with guilt--and dumb, absolutely dumb, as to the pardon of that guilt" (1841.4). Franklin represented eighteenth-century secularism rather than traditional Anglo-Saxon beliefs. One can perhaps excuse M'Neile's insensitivity and narrow views on the grounds that he was a minister and was hoping to use Franklin as one of God's means to gather up souls. What are we to say, though, when so normally astute a critic of American literature and culture as Brander Matthews charges that Franklin was incapable of faith because he lacked spiritual dimension (1896.22)? What reply can be made to Franklin's detractors who assert that he embodies and, indeed, is responsible for the very worst in the American character, particularly our vulgar materialism?[8] If America has lost intelligent belief and can no longer appreciate spiritual qualities, it can thank its first secular hero, Benjamin Franklin, who taught us how to get ahead in this world, but did not indicate what we would lose in that journey toward success.

It has been Franklin's misfortune to suffer not only from his enemies but at the hands of his friends as well. These are people who either cannot themselves accept a deistic American hero or, in the case of Parson Weems and others, who cannot imagine that American readers will buy books about a national hero blemished by a lack of piety, or at least the appearance of piety. The problem bothered Weems enough so that in his inventive biography he made himself God's instrument of grace and created a Franklin of whom respectable nineteenth-century readers could be proud. In Weems's account, we have a Franklin who, during his last illness, kept constantly before him a picture of the crucified Christ (1818.10). This fiction was echoed two years later by Charles Hulbert, who had the dying Franklin advise a young man to make Bible study the serious work of his life (1820.3). A later apologist, while not quite making Franklin a Christian at last, nevertheless argued that although he was a deist as a young man, his New England background kept him at heart pious, unlike Tom Paine and the French deists (1862.3). In 1880 John Torrey Morse, Jr. asserted that Franklin, though no Christian in doctrine, was essentially Christian in his worship and morality (1880.7). While the twentieth century has felt more comfortable with a deistic hero, we still find Franklin's defenders insisting that he was indeed a solid Christian representative of a solidly Christian country.[9]

The failure to comprehend Franklin adequately and justly has led at times to a depreciation of his mind and accomplishments and a denigration of his character to a far greater degree than any of the other Founding Fathers, with the possible exception of Paine. It is fair to say, in fact, that one would have to search hard to find another even marginally comparable American of later times who has been so widely undervalued and misused as Franklin. It is both amusing and embarrassing to think that the Babbitts of the world have felt that they had a right to make this great man one of them. Surely, their adoption of him calls attention to the present rejection of many of his values. It also indicates in part the degree to which he has been misunderstood by his countrymen who have indeed treated very lightly one of its most remarkable benefactors.

We speak to our own deficiencies as well as to those in a number of images Franklin created of himself when we feel comfortable memorializing him in such verses as the following:

> In leisure time he'd hang around
> Where women, wine and wit abound
> Among the noted seen and water dodgers,
> He'd flip many a merry jest
> With Texas Guinan and Mae West;
> His favorite pal would doubtless be Will Rogers.[10]

And surely this next dubious tribute by another of Franklin's self-styled pals speaks not only to how he and others perceived the philosopher, but also to their perceptions of the American character in

1943. The poem deals with Franklin's supposedly picaresque-like
return to Boston on a donkey. One stanza can represent the entire
effort:

> Poor Richard's ghost ascends here;
> The tale of his ass ends here;
> The dénoument, delayed o'erlong,
> Arrives. They must depart.
> As their brave spirits rise now
> Be this our prayer: May they both share
> A glorious <u>himmelfahrt</u>.[11]

Franklin is obviously not responsible for the misperceptions that
lead to such vulgarity, nor is it his fault he was claimed by the
American Society of Heating and Ventilating Engineers as their Patron
Saint,[12] yet his reputation suffers from these tributes. If we have
ignored the largeness of the mature Franklin's mind and sympathy and
made him at best an Andrew Carnegie or, less pleasantly, a combina-
tion of Poor Richard, Cornelius Vanderbilt, and George Babbitt, then,
as our logic would have it, these images must also be his reality.
Clearly, therefore, the often shallow and generally unfair attacks
on Franklin made by such critics as D. H. Lawrence, William Carlos
Williams, and Charles Angoff[13] must be deserved. While Franklin
often encouraged the image of himself as a commonsensical materialist
who happily accepted the world on its own terms, thus giving cause
for rebuke, his detractors are nonetheless commenting as much on
white America's traditional prosperity and dominant middle-class
culture as on Franklin and his reality. They are also objecting to
what they conceive to be the crudities implicit in Franklinian and
typically American notions of success. "All right," such critics
seem to be saying, "it is necessary to have food, clothing, shelter
and perhaps even some luxuries. But not at the sacrifice of the
expansion of private consciousness, spirituality, and creativity."

Of course, these are middle-class critics speaking, men who can
demean those things on which they enjoy a firm grip. Moreover,
Franklin would have agreed that his system of morals did have obvious
limitations. He himself did not work hard to have money simply to
have money. He retired from business only to strive tirelessly in
behalf of his fellows, and his prudential values have as their object
helping others do the same. Those who belittle these values are
themselves usually testimony to their success, for they can now move
beyond them to what they imagine is the good life. In doing so, such
middle-class descendants of Franklin believe they have adopted values
superior to his. What they have failed to recognize is that Franklin,
as many writers noted here realized, did have in mind moving on to
higher and finer realms of life.

By the middle of the twentieth century, two scholars, recognizing
the injustice done to this remarkable man, tried to encourage modern
readers to look anew at Franklin and reassess his worth.[14] Judging

from the disappointing results, however, it has been generally difficult to overcome the traditional ways, either positive or negative, of seeing Franklin. Even the standard biography of Franklin, that by Carl Van Doren, lacks probity. Van Doren did succeed in showing serious readers that Franklin does not belong to "the dry, prim people," in spite of his widespread Poor-Richard image, and this is no small achievement. Yet Van Doren's biography, though about 300,000 words long, is finally superficial and totally biased in Franklin's favor. There is almost no inner man in the picture Van Doren creates, and so Franklin really does seem to be the bland deist who moves effortlessly from one successful enterprise to another and infuriates Lawrence and others. Moreover, there is far too little sense of the diverse reactions he inspired among his contemporaries and later writers, particularly lesser known ones whose views were often more representative than those expressed by government or university officials and better known men. It seems fair to say that if Van Doren had displayed anything like his wonderful diligence with primary materials in seeking out the commentary on Franklin, his biography would have benefited, and he would certainly have given us a richer and more multi-dimensional Franklin that the one we have from him.

Instead, from Van Doren on, most writers have largely confined their secondary reading to the same articles and books and have therefore also failed to get much beyond Van Doren, at least with regard to probing more deeply into Franklin's mind and character and the perception of him among different people throughout the world at various times.

There is, though, information appearing in these pages that, if less generally known to us, is yet important to a fuller understanding of Franklin the man, the symbol of universal aspirations and the American success story, and the representative of the American character. There is material enough here, for example, to provide scholars the foundation for modern studies of Franklin's changing reputation abroad, studies along the lines of Antonio Pace's <u>Benjamin Franklin and Italy</u>. Then, too, the annotations here should encourage a variety of other endeavors. Those interested can trace the development of Franklin's image as it appeared in juvenile literature. Was the picture of Franklin that irritated Mark Twain as common in the nineteenth century as he thought, or was he generalizing in his wonderfully humorous but typically intrepid manner? To what degree were foreign accounts of Franklin--both adult and juvenile--like those done by Americans? What did Franklin's life and career mean to the millions who left cities, villages and ghettos throughout Europe in the nineteenth and early twentieth centuries for the freedom and uncertainty of the United States? And what of people in Asia, the Middle East, and Spanish-speaking America in times closer to our own? What does Franklin mean to them? Are his life story, maxims, and Revolutionary War writings merely the reading of young captives in school, or does he speak to those who yearn for freedom and some measure of material success? To what extent is Franklin exploited by various groups and governments for their own political, social, religious, or economic ends? The annotations that appear in these volumes may illuminate such important matters. Finally, they should help us to understand better the most remarkable but elusive of early Americans and enable us also to gain additional insight into his country, which has generally taken for granted its superiority and has paid too little attention to what persons of other times and countries have thought of it and its chief archetype.

Notes

1. Citations within the text and in footnotes are intended to be illustrative rather than exhaustive.

2. David Levin, "The Autobiography of Benjamin Franklin: The Puritan Experimenter in Life and Art," Yale Review 53, no. 2 (December 1963):[258]-75; Richard D. Miles, "The American Image of Benjamin Franklin," American Quarterly 9, no. 2, pt. 1 (Summer 1957): 117-43; Melvin H. Buxbaum, Benjamin Franklin and the Zealous Presbyterians (University Park: Pennsylvania State University Press, 1975), pp. [1]-46.

3. Also see the following: R. Kayser, "Benjamin Franklin und der Americanismus," Preusziche Jahrbücher 153 (September 1913): [465]-78; Emma Lillian Dana, "Benjamin Franklin, 'the First Great American,'" Makers of America. . . . (New York: Immigrant Publication Society), pp. 5-38; Daniel G. Hoffman, "The American Hero: His Masquerade," Form and Fable in American Fiction (New York: Oxford University Press, 1961), pp. 37-41; John G. Cawelti, "Natural Aristocracy in the New Republic . . . ," Apostles of the Self-Made Man (Chicago: University of Chicago Press [1965]), pp. 9-24; Paul W. Schmidtchen, "No Mere Dabbler He," Hobbies 72, no. 6 (August 1967): 104.

4. See 1906.134; Erika Seipp, Benjamin Franklins Religion und Ethik (Giessen, 1932), passim; William E. Lingelbach, "American Democracy and European Interpreters," Pennsylvania Magazine of History and Biography 61, no. 1 (1937):21-22; Dixon Wecter, "Poor Richard: The Boy Who Made Good," The Hero in America, a Chronicle of Hero-Worship (New York: Charles Scribner's Sons, 1941), pp. 50-80.

5. Russell Duane, "How Franklin Would Solve Our Two Major Problems," Benjamin Franklin Gazette (May 1933), pp. 3-4, 8-9.

6. Of the great many examples, see the following: "Franklin Thrift Bonds," Benjamin Franklin Gazette 4, no. 1 (February 1943): 10; Frederick B. Tolles, "Benjamin Franklin's Business Mentors: The Philadelphia Quaker Merchants," William and Mary Quarterly, 3d ser.

Introduction

4, no. 1 (July 1947):60-69; William S. Grampp, "The Political Economy of Poor Richard," Journal of Political Economy 55, no. 2 (April 1947): 132-41; Seiichiro Minabe, "Benjamin Franklin and Modern Capitalism," Socio-Economic History 18, no. 6 (1953):47-60; Irvin G. Wyllie, The Self-Made Man in America. The Myth of Rags to Riches. (New Brunswick: Rutgers University Press, 1954), passim.

7. Also see William B. Cairns, "The Colonial Time," A History of American Literature (New York: Oxford University Press, 1912), pp. 91-99; Percy H[olmes] Boynton, "Jonathan Edwards and Benjamin Franklin," A History of American Literature (Boston: Ginn & Co., c. 1919), pp. 44-58.

8. Charles Angoff, "Benjamin Franklin," A Literary History of the American People, 2 vols in 1 (New York: Alfred Knopf, 1931), 2:295-310.

9. See, for example, Louis C. Washburn, Benjamin Franklin's Religion (Philadelphia: Patriot's Sanctuary [1928]); Albert Hyma, The Religious Views of Benjamin Franklin (Ann Arbor: George Wahr Publishing Co., 1958). Among writers who have accepted Franklin's deism, see the following: 1849.4; 1850.5; 1892.9; 1900.10, 11; James Madison Stifler, The Religion of Benjamin Franklin (New York: D. Appleton & Co., 1925); John William Ward, "'Who Was Benjamin Franklin?'" American Scholar 32, no. 4 (August 1963):541-53; Alfred Owen Aldridge, Benjamin Franklin and Nature's God (Durham: Duke University Press, 1967).

10. Earl H. Emmons, Odeography of B. Franklin (New York: Ayerdale Press, 1929).

11. James B. Loughry, Ben Franklin and His Ass Return to Boston (Manomet, Mass., [Manomet Publishing Co., c. 1943]).

12. Paul F. Anderson, "Franklin, Our Patron Saint," The Amazing Benjamin Franklin, ed. and comp. Henry J. Smythe, Jr. (New York: Frederick A. Stokes Co., 1929), pp. 84-88.

13. D[avid] H[erbert] Lawrence, "Benjamin Franklin," Studies in Classic American Literature (New York: Thomas Seltzer, 1923), pp. 13-31; William Carlos Williams, "Poor Richard," In the American Grain (New York: Bone, 1925), pp. 144-57; Angoff, 2:295-310.

14. Miles, pp. 117-43; Perry Miller, "The Place of Franklin in American Thought," United States Information Service, Benjamin Franklin Anniversary [Washington: United States Government Printing Office, 1956], unpaginated.

Abbreviations

Aldridge--Alfred Owen Aldridge. Franklin and His French Contemporaries. New York: New York University Press, 1957.

BM--British Museum. Department of Printed Books. Catalogue of Printed Books. London: Trustees of the British Museum, 1955--.

DAB--Dictionary of American Biography. Edited by Allen Johnson and Dumas Malone. New York: Charles Scribner's Sons, 1928-1937.

FCL--Franklin Collection. Yale University.

NUC--National Union Catalogue.

NYPL--New York Public Library.

Pace--Antonio Pace. Benjamin Franklin and Italy. Philadelphia: American Philosophical Society, 1958.

Writings about
Benjamin Franklin, 1721-1906

1721

1 WALTER, THOMAS [Zacharia Touchstone]. The Little-Compton
   Scourge; or, the Anti-Courant. Boston: James Franklin,
   broadside.
       Attacks Silence Dogood as incompetent to write satires
   or anything else.

1748

1 [SMITH, SAMUEL.] Necessary Truth: or Seasonable Considera-
   tions for the Inhabitants of the City of Philadelphia, and
   the Province of Pennsylvania, in Relation to the Pamphlet
   Call'd Plain Truth: and Two Other Writers in the News-
   Paper. Philadelphia, 16 pp.
       Attempts to refute Franklin's arguments in Plain Truth,
   which calls for effective defense of Pennsylvania and its
   trade, and reasserts Quaker pacifist principles.

1751

1 WATSON, W[ILLIA]M. "An Account of Benjamin Franklin's
   Treatise, Lately Published, Intitled, Experiments and
   Observations in Electricity, Made at Philadelphia in
   America," Royal Society of London, Philosophical Transac-
   tions 47:202-11.
       Describes Franklin's experiments and generally lauds
   his work.

1752

1 Le CAT, CLAUDE-NICOLAS. "Remarques sur les principales
   expériences, & sur la doctrine du livre de M. Benjamin
   Franklin de Philadelphie en Amérique, concernant
   l'électricité." Journal Oeconomique (November), pp. 89-112.

1752

Writes to Phineas Bond praising Franklin for the nobility of his efforts in electrical science. Le Cat, though,
disagrees in some instances with Franklin's conclusions,
having worked out the experiments for himself. He does
point out to Bond that because of his dramatic work in
electricity, Franklin has become very famous and popular
in France.

1753

1 ANON. "Historical Chronicle, Dec. 1753." Gentleman's
   Magazine 23 (December):[587].
       Report of Franklin being awarded the Copley medal of the
   Royal Society for his work in electricity.

2 BECCARIA, G[IOVANNI] B[ATTISTA]. Dell'elettricismo artificiale
   e naturale libri due. . . . Turin: F. A. Campana,
   pp. 144-58.
       Contains Beccaria's defense of Franklin, whose work in
   electricity had been attacked by Nollet.

*3 NOLLET, JEAN ANTOINE. Lettres sur l'électricité. Dans
   lesquelles on examine les dernières découvertes qui ont
   été faites sur cette matière, & les consequences que l'on
   en peut tirer. Paris: H.L. Guerin, & L.F. Delatour.
   Source: NUC. See 1774.4.

1754

*1 COLDEN, DAVID. "Remarques sur les lettres de l'Abbé Nollet
   sur l'électricité, à B. Franklin ecuyer à Philadelphie. . . ."
   In Expériences et observations sur l'électricité faites à
   Philadelphie en Amérique par M. Benjamin Franklin; &
   communiques dans plusieurs lettres à M. P. Collinson, de
   la Société Royale de Londres. 2d ed. Paris: Gordon D.
   Henry & R. Cave, pt. 3.
       Source: NUC. This is the first printing of Colden's
   "Remarques." See 1756.2.

2 W[OODMASON], C[HARLES]. "To Benjamin Franklin Esq.; of
   Philadelphia, on His Experiments and Discoveries in Electricity." Gentleman's Magazine 24 (February):88.
       Franklin is praised for his scientific work, which took
   us from superstition and brought us to knowledge. As
   Woodmason says,

To gull an ign'rant crowd, the jugglers trade;
Within the line no blue internal fire,
Could pierce, but hence, malignant powers, retire;
What these pretended, Franklin, thou has wrought,
And truth is own'd what once was fiction thought;
Within thy magic circle calm I sit,
Nor friends nor business in confusion quit;
Whate'er explosions dreadful break around,
Or fiery meteors sweep the crackling ground.

1755

STILES, EZRA. Oration Addressed to Benjamin Franklin in the
Hall of Yale Academy, February 5, 1755. N.p. Van Pelt
Library, University of Pennsylvania, no. 973.3D F85st.
Praises Franklin for his work in electrical science
and notes that his fame is deservedly spreading as far as
the Indies and Europe. It is only fitting that Yale join
Harvard in paying such tribute as America can make to so
great a human benefactor as Franklin. (It is uncertain
that the Oration was published.)

1756

1 CANTON, JEAN. "Expériences électriques avec un essai pour
revene raison de leurs différens phénomènes, & ques-que
observations sur les nuages de tonnerre, pour confirmer
encore les remarques de M. Benjamin Franklin sur l'état
électrique positiv & négatif des nuages." In Expériences
et observations sur l'électricité faites à Philadelphie en
Amérique par M. Benjamin Franklin; & communiques dans
plusieurs lettres à M. P. Collinson, de la Société Royale
de Londres. 2d ed. Vol. 2. Paris: Durand, pp. 280-302.
Experiments conducted in London at the time Franklin was
performing his experiments in Philadelphia confirm his findings generally about the positive and negative conditions of
clouds. (Apparently the earliest printing of Canton's essay.)

2 COLDEN, DAVID. "Remarques sur les lettres de l'Abbé Nollet
sur l'électricité, à B. Franklin ecuyer à Philadelphie. . . ."
In Expériences et observations sur l'électricité faites à
Philadelphie en Amérique par M. Benjamin Franklin; &
communiques dans plusieurs lettres à M. P. Collinson, de
la Société Royale de Londres. 2d ed. Vol. 2. Paris:
Durand, pp. 247-79.
Considers in detail Nollet's objections to Franklin's
theory of electricity and refutes them. See 1754.1.

1756

3   DALIBARD, [THOMAS FRANÇOIS]. "Memoire lû à l'Académie Royale
     des Sciences, le 13 Mai 1752." In Expériences et
     observations sur l'électricité faites à Philadelphie en
     Amérique par M. Benjamin Franklin; & communiques dans
     plusieurs lettres à M. P. Collinson, de la Société Royale
     de Londres. 2d. ed. Vol. 2. Paris: Durand, pp. 67-133.
     Tells the story of the acceptance of the Franklinian
     theory of electricity. (Apparently the earliest printing
     of Dalibard's essay.)

                              1758

1   EULER, JOHANN ALBRECHT. "Recherches sur la cause physique de
     l'électricité." Histoire de l'Académie Royale des Sciences
     et Belles Lettres 13:125-59.
     Lengthy discussion of Franklin's studies in electricity.

2   [WILCKE, JOHAN CARL.] "Anmerkungen zu den Briefen des Hrn.
     Benjamin Franklins von der Electricität." In Des Herrn
     Benjamin Franklins, Esq.[:] Briefe von den Electricität.
     Leipzig: Gottfried Kiesewetter, pp. 217-354.
     Explains Franklin's work, praises and recommends the
     work and the author to Germans.

                              1764

1   ANON. An die Freyhalter und Einwoheb der Stadt und County
     Philadelphia, Deutscher Nation. [Philadelphia], 4 pp.
     Attacks Franklin for anti-German bias in an effort to
     defeat him in the election for Assembly and thereby foil
     his plans to make Pennsylvania a Crown colony.

2   ANON. An Answer to the Plot. [Philadelphia: Anthony
     Armbruster], broadside.
     Charges that Franklin is a womanizer and troublemaker.
     (The plot, led by Franklin, is the effort to bring Pennsyl-
     vania under the control of the Crown. Franklin himself,
     according to this scenario, would likely very soon become
     the royal governor of Pennsylvania, and the people would
     lose their religious liberties.) See also 1764.7.

3   ANON. The Authentic One. The Addition to the Epitaph, With-
     out the Copper-Plate. [Philadelphia: Anthony Armbruster],
     broadside.
     Favors the political policies of Franklin and Joseph
     Galloway. This piece has been attributed to David James

Dove, but such an attribution seems inaccurate, for Dove
was opposed to the efforts of Franklin and Galloway to
make Pennsylvania a Crown colony.

4   ANON. A Broadside Directed Against Benjamin Franklin, Candi-
date for the Assembly, by German Freeholders of Philadelphia County in 1764. [Philadelphia.]
        Franklin is attacked for anti-German prejudice.

5   ANON. Eine Anrede au die Deutschen Freyhalter der Stadt und
County Philadelphia. Philadelphia: [Anthony Armbruster?],
8 pp.
        Defends Franklin by declaring that he is not at all
hostile to the Germans of Pennsylvania. His earlier reference to them as "boors" had been misrepresented by the
Proprietary Party. The word actually means "peasants,"
and it was in this sense that Franklin, who has always
been a friend to the Germans, used it.

6   ANON. Observations on a Late Epitaph, in a Letter From a
Gentleman in the Country to His Friend in Philadelphia.
Philadelphia: Anthony Armbruster, 8 pp.
        Defends Franklin as a man and supports his policies.

7   ANON. The Plot. By Way of a Burlesk, to Turn F------n out
of the Assembly; Between H. and P[.]; Proprietary Officers,
Being Two of the WISER Sort. [Philadelphia], broadside.
        Tries to defend Franklin from the charge of being hos-
tile to Pennsylvania Germans. The author asserts that
Franklin's reference to the Germans as "Boors" was no
insult, since the word means "Peasant."

8   ANON. Protestation gegen die Bestellung Herrn Benjamin
Franklins zu einem Agenten für diese Provinz. Philadelphia:
Heinrich Miller, broadside.
        Franklin should not be allowed to be sent to England as
agent for Pennsylvania, nor should he be permitted to work
to change the government. The majority of people in the
province support these positions against Franklin. (The
arguments presented are those of the Proprietary Party,
and only one of the men who signed the Protestation had a
German name.)

9   ANON. The Scribbler: Being a Letter From a Gentleman.
[Philadelphia: Anthony Armbruster], 24 pp.
        Defends Franklin and his policies. Franklin is depicted
as a selfless patriot who is unfairly being attacked by the
Presbyterian supporters and friends of the proprietor,
Thomas Penn.

1764

10   ANON. <u>To the Freeholders and Electors of the City and County</u>
     <u>of Philadelphia.</u> [Philadelphia: Bradford?], 2 pp.
        Franklin is the chief architect of the plan to bring
     Pennsylvania under the control of the Crown and thereby
     "to deliver up your Charter Rights." Throughout the
     years, Franklin has abused the public, spending huge sums
     of money in England "to promote his Schemes." Yet these
     schemes, though they serve his desire for power, have set
     the province on fire. It is his present intention to be-
     come the Royal Governor of Pennsylvania. He and his allies
     must be defeated in the coming Assembly election.

11   [BARTON, THOMAS.] <u>The Conduct of the Paxton-Men, Impartially</u>
     <u>Represented: With Some Remarks on the Narrative.</u>
     Philadelphia: Andrew Steuart, 34 pp.
        Scores Franklin and charges that his <u>Narrative of the</u>
     <u>Late Massacres</u> is unfair and intended to vilify rather than
     to explore fairly the explosive and tragic situation on the
     frontier of Pennsylvania.

*12 DICKINSON, JOHN, et al. "The Reasons on Which Were Founded the
     Protest Offered by Certain Members of the Assembly to That
     Body Concerning the Sending of Mr. Franklin to England As
     Assistant to Our Agent There." <u>Pennsylvania Journal,</u>
     1 November.
        Source: <u>NUC</u>. See 1878.1.

13   [SAUER, CHRISTOPHER?] <u>Anmerkungen über ein noch nie</u>
     <u>erhoert. . . .</u> Germantown, Pa.: [Christopher Sauer],
     16 pp.
        Attacks Franklin and the plan to bring Pennsylvania
     under the Crown as being adverse to German interests.

14   [SMITH, WILLIAM.] <u>An Answer to Mr. Franklin's Remarks, on a</u>
     <u>Late Protest.</u> Philadelphia: William Bradford, 22 pp.
        An attack on Franklin's character, accusing him of dis-
     honesty and deceit. His chief aim is to promote his own
     interests, and he uses all people toward this end. He is
     not even loyal to the king, though he pretends to be, and
     in short has proved himself to be a villain.

15   [WEISS, LUDWIG?] <u>Getreue Warnung gegen die Löckvogel, samt</u>
     <u>einer Antwort auf die andere Anrede an die deutsche</u>
     <u>Freihalter der Stadt und County von Philadelphia.</u>
     Philadelphia: [Heinrich Miller], 15 pp.
        Opposes Franklin's plan to go to England in order to
     bring the province of Pennsylvania under the control of
     the Crown.

1765

16 WILLIAMSON, HUGH [X.Y.Z. Gentleman]. The Plain Dealer:
    Numb. II, Being a Tickler; for the Leisure Hour's Amuse-
    ment of the Author of Cool Thoughts. Philadelphia:
    [Andrew Steuart], 16 pp.
        Attacks Franklin's Cool Thoughts, which Williamson
    charges is designed "to kindle, rather than to extinguish"
    the flames of contention. Moreover, that author's plan to
    change the government of Pennsylvania is completely unnec-
    essary and intended to be contentious.

17 WILLIAMSON, HUGH [D.W., pseud.]. The Plain Dealer: or,
    Remarks on Quaker Politicks in Pennsylvania. Numb. III.
    Philadelphia: [William Dunlap], 24 pp.
        Attacks Franklin's competence and honesty and, further-
    more, accuses him of being a mere tool of Quaker politics.

18 [WILLIAMSON, HUGH.] What Is Sauce for the Goose Is Also Sauce
    for the Gander. Being a Small Touch in the Lapidary Way.
    Or Tit for Tat, in Your Own Way. Philadelphia: [Anthony
    Armbruster], 8 pp.
        Vilifies Franklin for his "Badness of Heart" and great
    vice. He has betrayed the Quakers, who first brought him
    to power, stolen electrical experiments and passed them off
    as his own, bought his honorary degrees, has tried to become
    a tyrant, defamed the Quakers and Germans alike, endeavored
    to take away the rights of the people through forcing royal
    government on the province, attempted to create a society
    without necessary social distinctions, treated the mother
    of his bastard son shamelessly and, in brief, is completely
    evil.

1765

1   ANON. The Counter-Medley, Being a Proper Answer to All the
    Dunces of the Medley and Their Abettors. Philadelphia:
    [Anthony Armbruster], broadside.
        Attacks Franklin and his supporters on political and
    moral grounds.

2   ANON. "To All True and Faithful Brethren." In Lucifer's
    Decree, After a Fray. Or, a Friendly Warning to All Per-
    sons of Whatsoever Station, Nation, or Qualification, in
    the City of Deceit, and Province of Transylvania.
    [Philadelphia,] 7 pp.
        A poem that, coming at the end of the Decree, attacks
    Franklin for being a rebel and a Mason. Lucifer says in
    one stanza:

7

1765

> But FRANKLIN is true,
> He can put on my shoe
> And buckle it on occasion:
> Then thus tight and trim,
> He can shew you the limb
> Of a free and accepted mason.

3   ANON. To the Freeholders and Others Electors of Assembly-Men,
     for Pennsylvania. [Philadelphia:] Anthony Armbruster,
     2 pp.
        Defends Franklin's efforts to change the government of
     Pennsylvania and denies the charge that he promoted the
     passage of the Stamp Act in Parliament.

*4   BIDDLE, JAMES. Address Read . . . Sept. 26, 1765, Charging
     B. Franklin and Gov. Franklin With Having Promoted Passage
     of the Stamp Act, &c. [Philadelphia.]
        Source: NUC, volume 52, page 667 and is said to be
     Evans no. 9915; however, the information does not appear
     to be accurate. Correspondents at the National Union
     Catalog Service have been unable to locate the Address.
     Biddle's 1765 piece is 1765.5.

5   [BIDDLE, JAMES.] To the Freeholders and Electors of the
     Province of Pennsylvania. [Philadelphia], broadside.
        Calls for keeping Franklin, a most "ambitious" man, out
     of the Assembly. He and his political colleagues have en-
     riched themselves at the expense of the public and are en-
     deavoring to become the "perpetual masters" of the citizens
     of Pennsylvania. Moreover, Franklin has promoted himself
     and his design to change the government by supporting the
     Stamp Act.

6   FRANKLIN, WILLIAM. The Answer of His Excellency William
     Franklin, Esq., Governor, of His Majesty's Province of
     New-Jersey, to the Invidious Charges of the Proprietary
     Party, Contained in a Libel, Read by Mr. James Biddle,
     Clerk of the Common Pleas for the County of Philadelphia,
     on Saturday Last, and Afterwards Published and Industri-
     ously Dispersed Through the Province. [Philadelphia],
     broadside.
        William Franklin defends himself and his father from
     the accusation that they were secretly supporting the
     Stamp Act.

7   A FRIEND of PENNSYLVANIA [pseud.]. To the Freeholders and
     Other Electors of Assembly-Men, for Pennsylvania.
     [Philadelphia], 2 pp.

Opposes especially the election of Franklin, rebuking him for his bigoted comment on Pennsylvania Germans and his effort to bring Royal Government to the colony and thereby threaten the religious liberty previously enjoyed by the people.

8 HUNT, ISAAC [Jack Retort]. A Humble Attempt at Scurrility in Imitation of Those Great Masters of the Art, the Rev. Dr. S---h; the Rev. Dr. Al--n; the Rev. Mr. Ew-n; the Irreverend D. J. Dove, and the Heroic J--n D------n, Esq.; Being a Full Answer to the Observations on Mr. H----s's Advertisement. Quilsylvania [Pennsylvania], 42 pp.
    Defends Franklin's character and policies from attacks by the Proprietary Party.

9 [SMITH, WILLIAM?] Antwort auf Hrn. Franklins Anmerkungen. . . . [Germantown, Pa.: Christopher Sauer], 27 pp.
    Attack on Franklin which charges that he would betray the inhabitants of Pennsylvania to gain his political ends. He is a man of grossly unethical character who should not be permitted to exercise authority in the province of Pennsylvania. Should Franklin gain power again, he would cause Pennsylvanians to lose their freedom.

1767

1 ANON. "Beschreibung der Armonica des Hrn. Franklins." Neue Bibliothek der schoenen Wissenschaften und der freyen Kuenste 4:116-27.
    The author describes Franklin's armonica and praises Franklin as a scientist, political force, and patriot.

2 BECCARIA, GIOVANNI BATTISTA. De electricitate vindice. Turin: Typis Jannis Baptistae Fontana, 4 pp.
    Ostensibly a letter to Franklin in which Beccaria defends the American's single fluid theory of electricity against supporters of Nollet's double fluid theory.

3 FERGUSON, JAMES. [On Franklin's Magic Square.] In Tables and Tracts. London: printed for A. Millar & T. Cadell, pp. 309-17.
    Discusses the square and says it is extraordinary, going "far beyond any thing of the kind I ever saw before" and that Franklin's "magic circle of circles" is even more surprising.

1767

*4   MAZZOLARI, GIUSEPPE MARIA. Electricorum libri VI. Rome:
     Salomoni.
        Source: Pace, pp. 350-51, no.32,34,35. A poetic
     account of electricity. The fourth and fifth books deal
     with Franklin's work in the field and exalt him as a hero
     among philosophers. Franklin's accomplishments are all the
     more remarkable because he came from uncultivated America
     rather than from Europe.

                              1768

1   [ACHENWALL, GOTTFRIED.] "Einige Anmerkungen über Nordamerika
       und über dasige Grossbritannische Colonien. (Aus müdlichen
       Nachrichten des Herrn Franklins)." Hannoverisches Magazin
       19 (27 February):257-96; (17 April):481-508.
          Asserts that he was privileged to discuss American
       affairs at great length with Franklin; however, his inac-
       curacies on matters thoroughly familiar to Franklin cast
       considerable doubt on this declaration.

2   A SOCIETY of GENTLEMEN [pseud.]. "Poor Richard's Maxims."
       Oxford Magazine: or, University Museum 1 (July):218-20.
          In presenting a list of Poor Richard's sayings, the
       author apparently believes his readers will not recognize
       that Franklin was the creator, for we are told: "Who the
       writer was, where he resided, or in what area he existed,
       is immaterial. . . ."

                              1770

1   [REIMARUS, JOHANN ALBERT HEINRICH.] [Electricität.]
       Columbia University, Rare Books Room, no. B621,328 E125.
          This work derives from the author's 1768 piece, Die
       Ursachen des Einschlagens vom Blitz. Deals with Franklin's
       discoveries in electrical science and especially with his
       lightning rod.

                              1771

1   BARLETTI, CARLO. Nuove sperienze elettriche seconda la teoria
       del sig. Franklin e le produzioni de P. Beccaria. Milan:
       Giuseppe Galeazzi, 134 pp.
          Barletti, a formidable opponent of the Franklinian theory,
       discusses it in detail. Barletti supports the double fluid
       theory of electricity advocated by Robert Symmer and openly
       argues against Franklin and Beccaria.

2 BRUGMANS, ANTONIUS. Dissertatio physicia De theoria
   electricitatis Franklini in Explicando Experimento
   Leidensi Cum Dubiis Eandem Non Mediocriter Infirmantibus.
   Gronigae: Hajonem Spandaw.
       A detailed analysis of Franklin's scientific hypotheses
   and experiments. It is clear to the author that Franklin
   was no backwoodsman genius or happy accident, but a learned
   and sophisticated man.

3 EELES, HENRY. Preface to Philosophical Essays. Dublin:
   printed for L. Flin, pp. [iii]-xlix.
       Nearly the entire preface is a discussion of Franklin's
   theories of electricity, especially that concerning thunder.
   Eeles rejects much of Franklin's thinking and puts forth
   his own theories.

4 TODERINI, GIAMBATTISTA. Filosofia frankliniana delle punte
   preservatrici dal fulmine particolarmente applicata alle
   polveriere, alle navi, e a Santa Barbara in mare:
   dissertazione . . . letta in una adunanza accademica
   degli Icneutici nel palazzo del sig. conte Piàzzo in Forlì
   l'anno 1770. Modena: Eredi Soliani, 65 pp.
       Lightning rods after Franklin's description were applied
   to military use in Italy. Specifically, the rods were used
   to protect Venetian powder magazines, ships, and the ship-
   yard at Santa Barbara.

1772

1 EVANS, NATHANIEL. "To Benjamin Franklin, Esq., L.L.D.
   Occasioned by Hearing Him Play on the Harmonica." In
   Poems on Several Occasions, With Some Other Compositions.
   Philadelphia: John Dunlap, pp. 108-9.
       Poetic tribute to Franklin's abilities, achievements
   and intense desire "to serve mankind,/The noble province
   of the sapient mind!"

2 POLI, G[IUSEPPE] S[AVERIO]. La formazione del tuono, della
   folgore, e di varie altre meteore giusta le idee del
   signor Franklin . . . diretta Daniello Avelloni. Naples:
   Campo, 24 pp.
       Explains the Franklinian theory and popularizes it but
   concentrates on its flaws, perhaps responding to critics of
   Franklin who upheld the dual fluid theory.

1773

1 ANON. "Extrait de la doctrine de M. Franklin, sur
l'électricité." Journal de physique. (Observations sur
la physique, sur l'histoire naturelle et sur les
arts. . . .) n.s. 2 (September):204-9.
Describes and supports the Franklinian theory of
electricity.

*2 ANON. Gionrale de letterati (Pisa) 9:307-8.
Source: Pace, p. 336, n. 14. In commenting on the
Transactions of the American Philosophical Society, published in 1771, the writer praised Franklin, the Society,
and the New World, which was already beginning to prove
that the arts move westward. (Pace points out that the
view toward America expressed in the Gionrale was typical
in Italy and current also in other European countries.
While Europe was thought to be in its decline, Franklin,
as New World representative, symbolized its genius and
inevitable future superiority.)

1774

1 ANON. "Benjamin Franklin, Esq. L.L.D. and F.R.S."
Westminster Magazine (July):[p. 331].
Praises Franklin as a scientist and as a defender of
America on the issue of taxation without representation.

2 ANON. A Faithful Account of the Whole Transaction Relating
to a Late Affair of Honour Between J. Temple, and
W. Whatley, Esqrs., Containing a Particular History of
That Unhappy Quarrel. Likewise, the Whole of Their Letters That Passed on That Occasion, With Those Signed
Antenor, an Enemy to Villains of Every Denomination, &c.
&c. London: printed for R. Snagg & T. Axtell, 38 pp.
In part this piece deals with Franklin's procurement of
the Hutchinson-Oliver letters and the consequences of their
having been sent to America and become known. (Late in
1772, Franklin, who was London agent for the Massachusetts
House of Representatives, sent to its speaker, Thomas
Cushing, ten letters written to the British government.
Six of the letters had been written between 1767 and 1769
by Chief Justice Thomas Hutchinson; the other four letters
were from Andrew Oliver, the provincial secretary. All the
letters had been addressed to Thomas Whatley, who had been
a member of the ministries of Grenville and North. After
Whatley's death, Franklin received the letters and saw that

a good deal of the British government's hostility toward Massachusetts had been initiated and encouraged by Hutchinson and Oliver. When Franklin received the letters, he agreed that the giver's identity would remain secret and, further, that the letters would be neither copied nor printed. As he told Cushing when he sent the letters to Boston, Franklin had agreed to the stipulations and asked that they be respected. Nevertheless, in June 1773 the letters were read by Samuel Adams to a secret session of the Massachusetts House of Representatives. Moreover, he later had the letters copied and printed. The publication of the letters created a scandal in London and provoked a duel between two innocent men, William Whatley, brother of the deceased, and John Temple. When Franklin learned of the duel, he publicly exonerated both men of any role in giving him the letters and also admitted that it was he who had sent them to Massachusetts. Eventually, the political enemies of America and Franklin used the incident to have Alexander Wedderburn excoriate Franklin publicly at the cockpit.)

3   Del MUSICO, G[IAN] G[AETANO]. Dissertazione . . . con cui si risponde a varj dubbj promossi contro la teoria dell'elettricismo del Franklin dal dottor Giuseppe Saverio Poli nelle sue riflessioni intorno agli effeti di alcuni fulmini. Naples.
       Defends Franklin's reputation as an electrician against what del Musico considered inaccurate criticism by Poli. See 1772.2.

4   NOLLET, [JEAN ANTOINE]. Lettres sur l'électricité dans lesquelles on examine les découvertes qui ont été faites sur cette matière depuis l'anée 1752, & les conséquences que l'on en peut tirer. New ed. Vols. 1-2, Paris: Durand.
       Nollet attacks Franklin's electrical theories and work in a series of letters to the American scientist. See 1753.3.

*5   WEDDERBURN, ALEXANDER. "Speech at the Council Chamber, Saturday, Jan. 29, 1774." In The Letters of Governor Hutchinson, and Lieutenant Governor Oliver, &c., Printed at Boston. And Remarks Thereon. With the Assembly's Address, and the Proceedings of the Lord's Committee of Council. Together With the Substance of Mr. Wedderburn's Speech Relating to Those Letters. Dublin: W. Gilbert, 97 pp.
       Source: BM. See 1774.6.

1774

6   WEDDERBURN, [ALEXANDER]. [Speech] "At the Council Chamber,
    Saturday, Jan. 29, 1774." In The Letters of Governor
    Hutchinson and Lieut. Governor Oliver, &c., Printed at
    Boston. [Edited by Israel Mauduit.] 2d. ed. London:
    printed for J. Wilkie, pp. 83-121.
        Franklin is vilified because the letters of Hutchinson
    and Oliver were sent to America, according to Wedderburn,
    as a malicious, dishonest, incendiary, and traitorous
    attempt to foment war between Britain and America. See
    1774.5.

1776

1   BOSSI, LUIGI. I parafulmini: poemetto. Milan.
        In this brief poetic account of lightning rods, the
    Italian poet praises the American inventor and scientist.

2   [TUCKER, JOSIAH.] Preface to A Series of Answers to Certain
    Popular Objections, Against Separating From the Rebellious
    Colonies, and Discarding Them Entirely: Being the Conclud-
    ing Tract of the Dean of Glocester on the Subject of Amer-
    ican Affairs. Glocester, Eng.: R. Raikes,
    pp. [iii]-xv.
        Franklin is treated as the leader of "the whole Band of
    Mock-Patriots, and Republican Zealots" who have worked up
    the Americans against any taxation imposed on them by the
    Mother country. Franklin is worse than the other American
    leaders, for he held a lucrative Crown position while oppos-
    ing the just measures of the king and Parliament to make
    America pay a fair tax.

1777

1   ANON. A Letter to Benjamin Franklin, LL. D., Fellow of the
    Royal Society. In Which His Pretensions to the Title of
    Natural Philosopher Are Considered. London: printed for
    J. Bew, 24 pp.
        A politically inspired piece in which Franklin is de-
    clared to lack the formal education, method, and acuity of
    a natural philosopher. His experiments are few and do not
    lead to some "general principle, the effects of which can
    be accurately computed." He is therefore one of those
    group of men who, feverish to make experiments, discover
    minor things and, elated, think themselves better than they
    are, and even Newtons. Moreover, Franklin's lack of mathe-
    matics makes it impossible for him to be taken seriously by

people who have studied natural philosophy. He and those of his ilk call to mind not the great Newton, but "the virtuosos in Gulliver's Travels."

2   ANON. [On Franklin.] Town and Country Magazine (January), p. 49.
       Announces arrival of Franklin in France.

3   ANON. "Sketch of the Character of Dr. Franklin." Town and Country Magazine (September), pp. 451-53.
       Extols Franklin for his accomplishments and remarkable rise in life as well as for his loyalty to America. Asserts, however, that Franklin, who is deeply involved in negotiations with France, may fail to win French support for the American Revolution. Outstanding as he is, Franklin is "a man of austere manners, little suited to the pliability of courts, or the genius of the French nation."

*4   [BARBEU-DUBOURG, JACQUES.] Calendrier de Philadelphie par l'année M DCC LXXVII. London [printed in Paris]: 118 pp.
       Source: NUC. See 1778.1.

5   [BETTI, LUIGI.] L'origine del fulmine: poemetto. Pisa: Pizzorni, 16 pp.
       In the dedication and the poem, Betti sees Franklin as a humanitarian and as the embodiment of physics.

6   HENLY, WILLIAM. "Observations on Some New and Singular Phenomena in Excited and Charged Glass; With Experiments Made in Consequence of These Phenomena, Further Illustrating the Franklinian Theory of the Leyden Bottle; and a Description of the Apparatus Conducted for That Purpose. . . ." Royal Society of London, Philosophical Transactions 67, pt. 1:98-116.
       It was necessary to prove Franklin's theory correct because "a number of gentlemen . . . not only doubted, but seemed absolutely to deny it."

1778

1   BARBEU-DUBOURG, JACQUES. Introduction to Calendrier de Philadelphie, ou constitutions de Sancho-Panca et du Bon-homme Richard, en Pensylvanie, 118 pp.
       The Poor Richard virtues of typical Americans are contrasted with the manners of Europeans and found far superior. See 1777.4.

1778

2   GRAY, EDWARD WHITAKER. "Observations on the Manner in Which
    Glass Is Charged With the Electric Fluid and Discharged."
    Royal Society of London, Philosophical Transactions 78,
    pt. 1:121-24.
        Franklin and his followers are wrong in asserting that
    one cannot add to or subtract from "the natural quantity
    of electric fluid in a glass," or add fluid to the surface
    of a jar or plate without taking some of the quantity from
    the other surface.

1779

1   ANON. [Notice of a poem on America and Franklin.] Almanach
    des muses 1779. Paris: [Delalain], p. 281.
        The author calls attention to the poem. See 1779.3.)

2   ALEMBERT, [JEAN Le ROND] d'. "Vers sur M. Franklin." In
    Almanach littéraire. N.p., p. 110.
        Inspired by Turgot's epigram on Franklin, d'Alembert
    wrote this poetic tribute praising Franklin for his human-
    ity, simplicity, and courage, qualities that have won him
    the admiration of Europeans and Americans alike.

3   D., M.L.C.D.B. "Épitre aux Etats-Unis & à M. Franklin."
    In Almanach des muses 1779. Paris: [Delalain], p. 281.
        Takes notice of an unidentified eight-page verse tribute
    to America and Franklin. The poem was published in Paris
    by Onfroy.

4   FEUTRY, AIMÉ AMBROISE JOSEPH. "In-Promptu à M. Benjamin
    Franklin. 22 mars 1778." In Nouveaux opuscules. . . .
    Paris: Chez les libraires qui vendent des nouveautés,
    p. 94.
        Franklin's name creates terror in the hearts of tyrants,
    but he is loved by all virtuous people.

5   _____. "Inscription que Madame Greuze a mise sur une urne de
    porcelaine, où elle garde les restes d'un bouquet des roses,
    que M. Franklin lui a donné, en juin 1777." In Nouveaux
    opuscules. . . . Paris: Chez les libraires qui vendent
    des nouveautés, p. 59.
        Franklin honored as "le Solon du nouvel hémisphere."

6   _____. "Pour le portrait du Docteur Benjamin Franklin." In
    Nouveaux opuscules. . . . Paris: Chez les libraires qui
    vendent des nouveautés, p. 59.
        Franklin is honored by mankind as a guide and inspiration.

7   INGENHOUSZ, JOHN [ie. JAN]. "Electrical Experiments, to Ex-
    plain How Far the Phenomena of the Electrophorus May Be
    Accounted for by Dr. Franklin's Theory of Positive and
    Negative Electricity; Being the Annual Lecture Instituted
    by the Will of Henry Baker, Esq.[,] F.R.S." Royal Society
    of London, Philosophical Transactions For the Year 1778 68,
    pt. 2:[1027]-48.
        Ingenhousz argues that Franklin's theory of positive and
    negative charges does account for the phenomenon of elec-
    trophore. Those scientists who assert that another theory
    is needed to account for the mechanically induced charges
    are incorrect.

8   Le BRUN [PONCE DENIS ÉCOUCHARD?]. "Vers Pour le Portrait du
    Docteur Franklin." In Almanach des muses, 1779. Paris:
    [Delalain], p. 170.
        Franklin praised as a liberator.

9   LEROUX des TILLETS, JEAN JACQUES. Dialogue entre Pasquin et
    Marphorio. N.p., 16 pp.
        Franklin seems to have been forced by the author into a
    battle between opposing French medical groups, the Faculté
    de Médecine and the Société Royale de Médecine. Franklin
    is at once a magician and sage whose loyalty is to truth
    and science, and so he destroys the idol that is intended
    to represent the Société Royale de Médecine. (The conjec-
    ture of the date is based on a penned-in note on the copy
    of this work at the University of California, Berkeley.
    The note reads: "distribué le 18 janvr. 1779." The full-
    est account of the Dialogue appears in Aldridge, pp. 106-8.

10 [TICKELL, RICHARD. La casette verte de Monsieur de Sartine,
    trouvée chez Mademoiselle du Thé. 5th ed. The Hague:
    Wisherfield, 71 pp.
        The object of Tickell's political satire, Franklin, is
    made to seem a complete failure in France. This fiction
    depicts the American minister as a pseudo-patriot, who
    actually seeks gain for himself through the War of Inde-
    pendence. (Aldridge, p. 112, cites a possible 1777 edition.
    I have been unable to locate an earlier edition, and Aldridge
    doubts any were published before 1779.)

1780

1   ANON. "Life & Character of Dr. Franklin." Political Magazine
    and Parliamentary Naval, Military, and Literary Journal 4
    (October):[631]-33.

1780

All of Franklin's earlier life has been devoted to
bringing about "the American rebellion," says the author
of this inaccurate and abusive account of Franklin.

2   Le BRUN [PONCE DENIS ECOUCHARD?]. "Traduction du vers latin
mis au bas du Portrait de M. Francklin." In Almanach des
muses, 1780. Paris: [Delalain], p. 180.
The translation is as follows: "Le sage que tu vois,
sublime en tous les tems, ravit la foudre aux Dieux & le
sceptre aux tyrans."

3   LEE, ARTHUR. Observations on Certain Commercial Transactions
in France, Laid Before Congress. Philadelphia: F. Bailey,
51 pp.
A lengthy argument charging that Franklin, his nephew,
Jonathan Williams, Beaumarchais, and Silas Deane, not being
accountable for their use of public funds, were profiting
from the war by misusing the funds.

1781

1   S., H. "A Plagiarism of Dr. Franklin." Gentleman's Magazine
51 (November):514-15.
Franklin's Parable Against Persecution was taken without
acknowledgement from the Liberty of Prophesying by Bishop
Jeremy Taylor.

1782

1   ALLEN, BENNET. "Characters of Some of the Leading Men in the
Present American Rebellion: Benjamin Franklin." Political
Magazine and Parliamentary, Naval, Military, and Literary
Journal 3 (July):446.
Attacks Franklin's morals and calls him a "hoary
traitor."

2   ANON. "Dr. Franklin's Representations to the Court of France."
Political Magazine and Parliamentary, Naval, Military, and
Literary Journal 3 (April):269-70.
Quotes the substance of the Representations to show that
Franklin's task of satisfying the demands and desires of
Congress and those of the French made negotiating the peace
a very difficult matter.

3 ANON. "Songe." Pot-Pourri 1, no. 5:274-81.
In a dream Franklin and the narrator discuss the peace
treaty and its implications for the future of America,
England, and France. A particular focus of attention is
the role of America as a haven for those seeking trade,
healthful growth, abundance, and liberty.

4 GOLITZYN, DIMITRI ALEKSEYEVICH [De Galitizin, Dimitri
Alekseyevich]. "Lettre adressée à l'Académie de Saint-
Petersbourg, sur quelques objets d'electricité." In
Journal de Physique. Observations sur la physique, sur
l'histoire naturelle et sur les arts, avec des planches
en taille-douche. . . . Vol. 21. Paris: Au Bureau du
Journal de Physique, pp. 73-79.
Praises Franklin's work in electrical science, especially
his designation of positive and negative charges.

5 HILLIARD d'AUBERTEUIL, [MICHEL RENÉ]. "Arrivée du docteur
Franklin." In Essais historiques et politiques sur la
revolution de l'Amerique septentrionale. Vol. 2.
Brussels and Paris: Chez l'auteur, pp. 60-65.
Summary of Franklin's very promising arrival in France.
His mission was made easier because his great reputation
preceded him.

1783

1 ANON. A Mr. Franklin, en lui présentant, de la part de
Madame la Comtesse Douauiere de Deux Ponts, un bâton
d'épine surmonté d'une pomme d'or, figurant la chapeau
de la liberté. [Paris]: Didot l'Aîné.
A symbolic verse entertainment extolling the virtues
and achievements of Franklin, Washington, and their new
nation.

2 ANON. [Benjamin Franklin.] In Historisch-genealogischer
Kalender, oder Jahrbuch der merkwürdigsten neuen Welt-
Begebenheiten für 1784. Leipzig: Haude & Spener,
pp. 172-75.
Biographical sketch of Franklin.

3 ANON. "Extract From a Comparative View of the American and
the Mother Country." English Review (January), pp. 27-28.
Franklin owed much of his success to his American background, which encouraged people of all stations to develop
their talents. He could not have become more than a great
printer in the more populous and settled city of London.

1783

4 ANON. Memoir of the Celebrated Dr. Benjamin Franklin."
Gentleman's and London Magazine 53:359-61.
    A survey of Franklin's career pointing out that the
wisdom of his actions shows him to have studied man as
well as electricity.

5 ANON. "Some Account of Benjamin Franklin, L.L.D. and F.R.S.[,]
Member of the Royal Academy of Sciences . . . ., and
Now Minister Pleniopotentiary From the United States of
America to the Court of France." European Magazine and
London Review 3 (March):[163]-66.
    Franklin is a self-made man. Doubtless he has been an
outstanding American patriot. In fact, it is possible that
even while he was supposedly a loyal British subject, he
had in mind helping America become independent. "However
we may respect Doctor Franklin's talents, however we may
execrate the instruments which forced him to exert those
talents against the kingdom, we should feel for the abase-
ment of Great-Britain, even more than we do at present,
should the destroyer of the empire be admitted as the spectator of so despicable a scene of humiliation" while serving as ambassador from the United States of America to
Great Britain.

6 BIESTER, J.E. "Etwas über Benjamin Franklin." Berlinische
Monatschrift 2, no. 7 (July):11-38.
    Points out that while Franklin was born in America, he
has been in Europe long and is a man of international significance in the realms of philosophy and diplomacy. Even
while Franklin remained in America, before 1757, his scientific and political work and his correspondence with prominent Europeans prepared him for the international phase of
his long and most useful life. As the memoirs point out,
a major link in the American and European years is that
Franklin dedicated himself to the welfare of his fellow man.

7 [BRIZZARD, GABRIEL.] Fragment de Xénophon, nouvellement
trouvé dans les ruines de Palmyres, par un Anglois; &
déposé au Museum Britannicum, à Londres. Traduit du grec,
par un François; et lu à l'assemblée publique de Musée de
Paris, du jeudi 6 mars 1783. Paris: P.D. Pierres, 52 pp.
    An allegory which describes the War of Independence and
the peace treaty. France and the United States are praised,
but it is Franklin who is most celebrated as the scourge of
tyrants and the embodiment of the good, simple life of the
free man. In the back of the work there is a key in which
the characters in the allegory are identified.

8 An ENGLISHMAN, pseud. "On Seeing a Small Mezzotint Print of Doctor Franklin in the Case of a Watch, 1778." European Magazine and London Review 3 (March):166.
   Had England paid attention to Franklin, it could have avoided the war with America. But England, the poet complains, did not heed the great man's warning and now its liberty is "sunk in shade," whereas in America "there blooms sweetly the celestial maid."

9 [MAIROBERT, MATHIEU FRANÇOIS PIDANZAT de.] "Lettre I. Sur M. Franklin. Dialogue avec lui. Faits qui annoncent la continuation des irrésolutions du Ministre de France, & de la Paix consequement." In L'Espion Anglois, ou correspondance secret entre Milord All'eye et Milord All'ear. Rev., enl. ed. Vol. 5. London [Amsterdam?]: John Adamson, pp. [1]-31.
   This piece was ostensibly written by an English spy and deals with the joyous welcome Franklin received in France, in contrast to the relative indifference with which Silas Deane was met. The author also considers the speculations concerning Franklin's reasons for coming to France and reports on an alleged interview with the American statesman. (The first edition was published over the period 1777-1786.)

10 MEISSNER, [AUGUST GOTTLIEB?]. "Erinnerung gegen eine Stelle in Franklins Leben." Berlinische Monatschrift 2, no. 10 (October):307-8.
   Franklin's "Parable Against Persecution" is actually a retelling of the anecdote as related by Saadi.

*11 SPRENGEL, M[ATTHIAS] C[HRISTIAN]. "Benjamin Franklin." In Historisch genealogischer Calender; oder Jahrbuch der merkwürdigsten neuen Welt--Begebenheiten. Leipzig: Haude & Spener.
   Source: NUC. See 1785.4.

1784

1 ADAMS, GEORGE. An Essay on Electricity, Explaining the Theory and Practice of That Useful Science; and the Mode of Applying It to Medical Purposes. With an Essay on Magnetism. London: printed for the author, pp. 86-110.
   These pages, which constitute the seventh chapter of the book, deal with "Dr. Franklin's Theory of the Leyden Bottle" as well as with a view that opposes his. After presenting a theoretical discussion and the descriptions of various experiments, Adams determines that Franklin's theory of

1784

positive and negative charges cannot be proved and that,
therefore, one can draw no conclusions from it.

2 ANON. "Anecdotal Notices of Dr. Franklin." <u>Boston Magazine</u>
 1 (May):294.
  Franklin is called the "first fruits of American
 genius." Nevertheless, "perhaps no other man ever owed
 more to the time and place of his birth," for had be been
 born and raised in London as the son of a modest working
 family, he would never have achieved eminence in philosophy
 or politics. The anonymous author clearly wishes that such
 had been the case, since he believes Franklin to be the primary force in dismembering the British Empire and erecting
 "a congeries of Republics." He is therefore a "greater
 enemy to England than even Philip II or Louis XIV." While
 it is true that Franklin is a humanitarian and as a result
 has won popular acclaim, such admiration "is no proof of
 merit." (This piece is said to have appeared first in the
 <u>Westminster Magazine</u>, but I have been unable to locate it
 there.) <u>See</u> 1784.3.)

*3 ANON. "Anecdotal Notices of Dr. Franklin." <u>Westminster</u>
 <u>Magazine</u>.
  1784.2.

4 ANON. "Benjamin Franklin." In <u>Historisch genealogischer</u>
 <u>Calender oder Jahrbuch der merkwürdigsten neuen Welt</u>
 <u>Begebenheiten für 1784</u>. Berlin: Haude & Spener,
 pp. 172-75.
  Biographical account leading up to Franklin's key role
 in the Treaty of Paris.

5 ANON. "Remarques historiques sur le Docteur Franklin." In
 <u>Anecdotes historiques sur les principaux personnages qui</u>
 <u>jouent maintenant en Angleterre</u>. N.p.
  Franklin is the most brilliant representative of the
 genius of America and a principal guiding light of the
 American Revolution. Praises his simple, unaffected manners and precision of thought as well as his versatility.

6 BOURDIC [-VIOT, MARIE-ANNE-HENRIETTE PAYAN de L'ESTANG].
 "In-promptu pour le portrait de M. Franklin, fait au
 crayon, par Mademoiselle de Givonne, âgée de 12 ans."
 In <u>Almanach des muses</u>, 1784. Paris: Delalain, p. 70.
  Largely a verse tribute to Franklin for his role in
 liberating America. The young artist is also acclaimed.

7 [LUCHET, JEAN PIERRE.] Vicomte de Barjac, ou Mémoires pour servir a l'histoire de ce siècle. London: pp. 78, 120.
　　Franklin is belittled as a statesman, scientist, and man. (The attribution of the author is by Aldridge, p. 107.)

1785

1 ANON. Review of "A Poem Addressed to the Armies of the United States of America. By David Humphries [Humphreys] Esq.[,] Colonel in the Service of the United States, and Aid-de-Camp to His Excellency[,] the Commander in Chief." English Review (April), pp. 312-14.
　　The author, in addition to reviewing the Poem, launches an attack on Franklin, whom he clearly hates. We are told that while it is understandable that Humphries might be rash in his judgments, it is inexcusable that Franklin, an ambassador, should have the Poem reprinted in France. And English readers must keep in mind that this "veteran in politics does nothing in vain." In the present case, Franklin intends to encourage American hostility toward Great Britain as well as "to flatter the king of France and the Irish," to defame the character and hurt the interests of the former mother country. (The Poem does not treat Franklin.)

2 De P. "Epître a madame la Bāronne de Bourdic sur ses relations avec le Docteur Franklin." In Almanach des muses. Paris: Delalain, pp. 222-25.
　　Madame de Bourdic was pleasantly chided for devoting herself to Franklin instead of to the gala life of Paris. While, to be sure, Franklin is the Nestor of Philadelphia, the man who tamed lightning and tyrants, he has already had admirers enough. It was therefore unnecessary for him to conquer Madame de Bourdic too.

3 NEVIN, DAVID R.B. "Benjamin Franklin." In Continental Sketches of Distinguished Pennsylvanians. Philadelphia: Porter & Coates, pp. 26-38.
　　Franklin "was always at his post of duty, calm and serene, but firm and immovable as the cliffs of Gibraltar."

4 SPRENGEL, M[ATTHIAS] C[HRISTIAN]. "Benjamin Franklin." In Geschichte der Revolution von Nord-Amerika. Frankenthal: Gegel, pp. 262-66.
　　Franklin's achievements in diplomacy were just as great as those of his in science. See 1783.11.

1785

5   SUTHERLAND, JAMES. <u>Copy of Mr. Sutherland's Petition, Which</u>
    <u>Is Intended to Be Presented to the Honourable House of</u>
    <u>Commons</u>. N.p., 11 pp. Franklin Collection, Sterling
    Library, Yale University, no. F.785 Su8.
         Sutherland, "late His Majesty's Commissary, and Judge
    of the Vice Admirality Court in the Island of Minorca,"
    had been accused by General James Murray of having had
    secret correspondence with Franklin in November 1782. As
    a result, Sutherland was suspended from his office.
    Sutherland denies the charge, saying that the only letter
    he ever wrote Franklin was while a prisoner in France as a
    consequence of his having rendered valuable services to
    England during the war.

                            1786

1   [BOURDON, LOUIS-GABRIEL.] <u>Voyage d'Amerique dialogue en vers,</u>
    <u>entre l'auteur et l'Abbé+++</u>. London: Chez Pichard,
    156 pp.
         Franklin is more than a political and philosophical
    sage. He is a benefactor to mankind, and his life is an
    expression of the triumph of sound morality.

2   FOSSÉ, CHARLES LOUIS FRANÇOIS de. <u>Cheminée économique, a</u>
    <u>laquelle on a adapté la mécanique de M. Franklin</u>. Paris:
    Jombert, jeune, Dessine, 50 pp.
         A detailed explanation of Franklin's scientific work
    and what it means theoretically and practically.

3   [SOUCI, ANTOINE?] "Sur l'origine du grand Docteur Franklin."
    In <u>Almanac historique, nomé le messager boiteux, contenant</u>
    <u>des observations astrologiques sur chaque, le cours du</u>
    <u>soleil & de la luna, 7 le changement de jour en jour,</u>
    <u>exactement calculé pour l'an de grace MDCCLXXXVII. . . .</u>
    Basle: Jean Henri Decker, pp. [50-51].
         Seeks to correct widespread, foolish misconceptions
    about Franklin's life.

                            1787

1   ANON. "On Dr. Franklin's Making a Present of His Bust to Sir
    Edward Newenham." <u>Columbian Magazine</u> 1, no. 11 (July):
    560.
         Franklin is lauded for his sagacity, patriotism, honesty,
    and love of freedom, and Newenham of Ireland is like him.
    The poet, thinking of American independence, asks when

1787

> Will Irish natives act like men;
> Increasing tyranny withstand,
> The guardians of their native land,
> From wond'ring nations win applause,
> A Franklin each, in Ireland's cause?

2   CRÈVECOEUR, MICHEL GUILLAUME St. JEAN de. "Arrive du Docteur
    Benjamin Franklin à Philadelphie." In Lettres d'un
    cultivateur américain. Vol. 2. Paris: Cuchet, pp. 416-37.
       Franklin was warmly welcomed from France by his fellow
    Pennsylvanians. They recognized his invaluable contribu-
    tions to American successes in the war and in the negotia-
    tions that brought peace.

3   _____. "XLIXe anecdote." In Lettres d'un cultivateur
    américain. Vol. 3. Paris: Cuchet, pp. 150-51.
       Franklin is revered and honored on his eightieth birth-
    day by the printers of Philadelphia.

4   [Le MANNISSIER.] Le Docteur Franklin. Poëme. Caen:
    L.J. Poisson, 31 pp.
       Divided into four chants, the poem praises Franklin as a
    sage and liberator. Louis XVI, of course, is depicted as
    America's benefactor. If Franklin persuades the monarch to
    help the new, struggling nation, it is also true that Louis
    is disposed to provide aid. On the philosopher's return to
    America, he is made to stop off in Cuba and Santo Domingo
    and bemoan the cruelty of the Spaniards toward the natives,
    whose lot is contrasted with that of the happy residents of
    Philadelphia. In the fourth chant, Le Mannissier proclaims
    the virtues of Franklin, Washington, and Louis and calls
    for liberty for Negroes and Indians. (See also Aldridge,
    pp. 139-42, for a complete discussion of the poem.)

5   MEYEN, JOHANN JACOB. Franklin der Philosoph und Staatsmann.
    In fünf Gesängen. Alt Stettin: J.F. Witwe, 130 pp.
       These five poems are a fanciful tribute to Franklin for
    his achievements in science, philosophy, and diplomacy. He
    is especially praised for his steadfast patriotism during
    the difficult years in England prior to the Revolution.
    Franklin's calm wisdom enabled him to withstand the strain
    imposed even by Wedderburn and to work for the benefit of
    his fellow Americans. He is an example to old and young
    alike throughout the world and truly deserves the praise
    of Turgot.

1787

6   [PLAYFAIR, WILLIAM.] <u>Joseph and Benjamin, a Conversation.</u>
     <u>Translated From a French Manuscript.</u> London: printed at
     the Logographic Press for J. Murray, 238 pp.
         It is a wise and sad Franklin who expresses skepticism
     about the ability of men to live virtuously. He also doubts
     the value of education for mature people who already know
     their minds. Joseph II is told, in this fiction, that he
     might be a better and more compassionate ruler if he did
     not know mankind well, for to know men is to see how wicked
     they can be. Franklin is also made to express greater lik-
     ing of England than of France. Yet England relies too much
     on credit and will almost certainly be ruined by its debts.
     As for America, Franklin is "not very sanguine in my expec-
     tations" and believes "it will be many centuries before"
     his country "will appear great in the eyes of European
     nations."

1788

1   ANON. "Cheminee economique, a laquelle on a adapte le
     Mechanique de M. Franklin." In <u>Bibliothèque physico-</u>
     <u>economique, instructive et amusante. . . .</u> Vol. 1.
     Paris: Chez Buisson, pp. 235-37.
         On economical modifications of the Franklin stove.

2   ANON. "Description y usage du Poêle de M. Franklin, pour
     brûler de la braise de Charbon de terre." In <u>Bibliothèque</u>
     <u>physico-economiqe, instructive et amusante. . . .</u> Vol. 1
     Paris: Chez Buisson, pp. 137-56.
         A detailed discussion of the Franklin stove. Also deals
     generally with Franklin as an inventor.

3   ANON. "Projet d'un nouvel Hygromette, par M. Franklin." In
     <u>Bibliothèque physico-economique, instructive et</u>
     <u>amusante. . . .</u> Vol. 2. Paris: Chez Buisson, pp. 340-41.
         Describes and explains the advantages of the hygrometer
     recommended by Franklin.

4   ANON. "To the Editor of the Columbian Magazine." <u>Columbian</u>
     <u>Magazine</u> 2 (March):144-45.
         M. Lavater, in his studies of physiognomy (1789.4),
     offered a sketch that clearly resembles Franklin. Lavater
     claimed not to have known the subject of the sketch and yet
     concluded that the subject was one whose mind did not become
     troubled easily and, furthermore, that he was a very intel-
     ligent man of business.

5 ANON. "To the Editor of the Repository." Repository Containing Various Political, Philosophical, Literary and Miscellaneous Articles 2, pt. 2, no. 9 (1 May):41-42.
      While Franklin never said he was the author of the
   Parable Against Persecution, the piece has been generally
   ascribed to him. The story actually appears "in G. Tentius's
   dedication of a book, entitled Tribus Judae Salamanis &c.
   (printed by Westein, A.D. 1680), as quoted from a more
   ancient writer."

6 DESARNOD, [JOSEPH-FRANÇOIS]. Mémoire sur les foyers
   économiques et salubres. Paris: Desenne & Gattey, 58 pp.
      Much of the book deals with Franklin's stove, showing
   why it was an improvement over earlier heating devices and
   calling attention to subsequent modifications of the design.

7 LINDSAY, J. "Dr. Lindsay on Dr. Franklin's Doctrine of
   Water-Spouts." Gentleman's Magazine 58, pt. 1 (February):
   106-8.
      In presenting his own theory of waterspouts, Lindsay
   modifies Franklin's.

8 VAUGHAN, BENJAMIN [O.P., pseud.]. "To The Editor of the
   Repository." Repository Containing Various Political,
   Philosophical, Literary and Miscellaneous Articles 2, pt. 2,
   no. 10 (1 June):71-72.
      While the correspondent who noted that the basic idea of
   the "Parable Against Persecution" was not Franklin's is
   correct (see 1788.5), he overlooks some important facts.
   Franklin's "free version" of the piece shows that he did
   not merely imitate any source, but made the "Parable" his
   own. Second, the imitation of scriptural style is his contribution to the story and is very effective. In no way,
   then, can he be considered a plagiarist.

                              1789

1 ANON. [Anecdote about Franklin at the Federal Convention.]
   In The American Jest Book: Containing a Curious Variety of
   Jests, Anecdotes, Bon Mots, Stories, &c. Part 1.
   Philadelphia: printed for M. Carey, & W. Spotswood, p. 18.
      Anecdote about Franklin, who, after the Constitution had
   been agreed to, suggested that the picture of the sun on the
   back of the president's chair symbolized a rising sun.

2 ANON. [Anecdote about Franklin in Paris.] In The American
   Jest Book: Containing a Curious Variety of Jests, Anecdotes,

1789

Bon Mots, Stories, &c. Part 1. Philadelphia: printed for
M. Carey, & W. Spotswood, pp. 11-12.
A Frenchman gave Franklin some wine from his private
stock. When the American minister became ill, the Frenchman was imprisoned until he could clear up the difficulty
by drinking some of the wine himself.

3 BROWN, CHARLES BROCKDEN. "An Inscription for General
Washington's Tomb." State Gazette of North Carolina,
26 February.
The poem appeared in the State Gazette of North Carolina,
a newspaper whose printer had made a mistake in attributing
Washington's name for what clearly was intended to be that
of Franklin, as the first stanza shows:

> The Shade of great Newton shall mourn,
> And yield him Philosophy's throne,
> The palm from her brow shall be torn,
> And given to Washington alone.

(This poem is also available in David Lee Clark, Charles
Brockden Brown: Pioneer Voice of America (Durham: Duke
University Press, 1952), p. 46.)

4 LAVATER, JOHN CASPAR. [Portrait of Benjamin Franklin Exam-
ined.] In Essays on Physiognomy, Designed to Promote the
Knowledge and Love of Mankind. Translated by Henry Hunter.
Vol. 2. London: printed for John Murray, H. Hunter &
T. Holloway, p. 318.
While the portrait is identified in the contents as
being of Franklin, Lavater does not mention the American's
name in commenting on him. He therefore implies that he
does not know the subject of the portrait and is able to
arrive at his characteristics only by physiognomical analy-
sis. Lavater says of his subject: "As to the portrait
under review, it may be adduced as the model of a Thinker
of singular sagacity and penetration. This happy psysionomy
[sic] is wonderfully characteristic of a mind capable of
rising without effort; he is a man who pursues his object
with reflecting firmness, but wholly exempted from obsti-
nacy." (The Essays were published first in Germany in
1775-1778, and that edition, which I have not seen, may
include the piece on Franklin.)

5 WEBSTER, NOAH. "To His Excellency, Benjamin Franklin, Esq.,
LL.D., FRS, Late President of the Commonwealth of Pennsyl-
vania, the Following Dissertations Are Most Respectfully
Inscribed. . . ." In Dissertations on the English Language.
Boston: printed for the author by Isaiah Thomas & Co.,
pp. [iii]-vi.

Franklin is "great in common things" that are useful to
mankind. His wisdom, moderation, research, and practicality have made him respected and beloved throughout the
world.

179-

1 ADAMS, MICHAEL. "Benjamin Franklin." The New, Complete, and
General Biographical Dictionary; or, Universal, Historical,
and Literary Repository of Human Knowledge. A Work Consist-
ing Entirely of Historical, Critical and Impartial Lives of
the Most Eminent Persons of Every Nation in the World.
Vol. 5, London: [printed for the author], pp. 248-51.
   Sketch emphasizing Franklin's desire to lead a useful
life.

2 ANON. "Character of Dr. Franklin, by One of His Intimate
Friends." Annual Register, or a View of the History, Politics, and Literature for the Year 1793. Vol. 35. London:
printed by assignment from the execution of the late
Mr. James Dodsley, pp. 254-55.
   Acclaims Franklin as a useful and good man of unusual
ability.

*3 PLANCHER-VALCOUR, PHILIPPE ALEXANDRE LOUIS PIERRE. [A Hymn
on Franklin.] In Le Chansonnier de la Montagne. Vol. 3.
Paris.
   Source: FCL. The hymn supposedly develops Turgot's
epitaph to show that Franklin was a benefactor to mankind.
(The piece on Franklin most likely appeared first in the
poet's Hymn aux Bienfaiteurs de l'Humanité.)

1790

1 ANON. "Anecdote of Dr. Franklin." American Museum, or
Universal Magazine 7, no. 6 (June):284.
   British practice of sending convicts to America angered
Franklin. In retaliation, he proposed introducing rattlesnakes into the king's gardens at Kew, assuring him that
they would be just as beneficial to England as the felons
were to America.

2 ANON. B. Franklin: Vir vixit integer, liber obit, Regeneratur
immortalis: Pril. Gall. Lib. An. M. DCC. XC. [New York]:
broadside. American Antiquarian Society's Early American
Imprint Series, no. 45827.

1790

> A curious broadside in which one Major General Eustace
> "Imitated" and applied to Franklin verses by the Abbé
> François, who wrote:
>
>> Rien n'est plus vrai; les Hommes sont égaux;
>> Ce n'est ni l'Or ni la haute Naissance,
>> Mais les Talens (effet de leur travaux)
>> Et la Vertu seule qui sont la difference.
>
> Eustace wrote from this "An Impromptu" entitled "SACRED TO
> THE MEMORY OF FRANKLIN," which reads:
>
>> A Life of spotless Fame, in Freedom clos'd,
>> The PATRIOT soar'd to Immortality:
>> Anno Domini M. DCC. XC.
>> The auspicious Dawn of Gallic Liberty.
>
> Eustace then translated the French of François.

3   ANON. "Character of Dr. Franklin." American Museum, or
      Universal Magazine 8 (November):212–14.
         An uncritical appreciation allegedly written by one of
      Franklin's "intimate friends." (The anonymous author may
      be the editor of the American Museum, Matthew Carey, al-
      though Francis Hopkinson and Benjamin Rush, both friends of
      Franklin, also contributed to the magazine.)

4   ANON. "Death and Burial of Dr. Franklin." Universal Asylum
      and Columbian Magazine 4 (April):261–62.
         Tells of Franklin's courageous and peaceful death and
      of the funeral and other affairs honoring his memory.

5   ANON. "Death of Dr. Franklin." Universal Magazine and Review,
      or Repository of Literature 3 (June):557.
         On Franklin's last days and the great respect shown his
      memory. "Perhaps no literary man ever filled a greater
      space in our world with his name, or deserved more from
      his fellow creatures."

6   ANON. "Dr. Franklin." Massachusetts Magazine 2, no. 8
      (August):509.
         On the regard for Franklin by Jacques Barbeu Dubourg
      and the National Assembly of France.

7   ANON. "Dr. Franklin." Massachusetts Magazine 2, no. 9
      (September):575.
         "It will be a monument of the victory of Philosophy over
      prejudice that Benjamin Franklin," who once worked as a

printer in London, should have become "the author of a
Revolution that emancipated a Continent; and that a solemn
publick mourning should be decreed to his memory by the
greatest nation in Europe." The nation, of course, is
France.

8   ANON. [Life and Death of Benjamin Franklin.] Gentleman's
     Magazine 61, pt. 1, no. 6 (June):571-74.
          Summary of Franklin's career, praise for his achievements
     and a defense of him against his political antagonists in
     England.

9   ANON. "Ode, Sacred to the Memory of Our Great Franklin."
     New York Magazine 1, no. 9 (September):545.
          Franklin is praised for his patriotism, vision, and
     achievements in science. The last of three stanzas reads
     as follows:

          The Earth wrapt in fire, from her orbit shall roll,
             The Heav'ns folded up, shall depart as a scroll,
          But he who the lightning controul'd with his rod,
             Unhurt thru' the flames, shall ascend to his God.

10   ANON. "Of Dr. Franklin." Massachusetts Magazine 5, no. 2
     (May):[259]-62.
          Franklin is commended for his ability, perseverance, and
     especially for his humanitarianism.

11   ANON. "Short Account of Dr. Franklin's Last Illness: by His
     Attending Physician." American Museum, or Universal Maga-
     zine 7, no. 5 (May):266.
          The author quotes the account by Dr. Jones of the peace-
     ful manner in which Franklin died. This account was pub-
     lished very widely, particularly in newspapers.

12   ANON. "Sketch of the Character of Dr. Franklin." Christian's,
     Scholar's, and Farmer's Magazine 1, no. 2 (April-May):
     109-10.
          Franklin was a great philosopher and statesman, but he
     was most outstanding as a human being and citizen. (This
     piece appeared first in a newspaper, the Gazette of the
     United States.)

13   ANON. "Sketch of the Life of Dr. Franklin." American Museum,
     or Universal Magazine 8 (July):12-20; (November):210-12.
          An appreciative survey of Franklin's life, focusing
     especially on his services to America.

1790

14 ANON. "Sur Franklin." <u>Revolutions de Paris, dediees a la
    nation etau district des Petits-Augustins</u> 2, no. 49
    (12 June):565-68.
        A tribute to Franklin which asserts that his examination
    before the House, so helpful in gaining the repeal of the
    Stamp Act, is an example of his forceful mind.

15 ANON. "Verses Sacred to the Memory of Benjamin Franklin,
    L.L.D., &c &c." <u>American Museum, or Universal Magazine</u> 7,
    no. 6 (June):35-37.
        Poetic tribute, part of which reads:

        Say, how shall I begin his various praise?
        Truth led him through all Nature's wond'rous maze.
        Earth! to the sage thy greatest wreaths allow,
        Whose wisdom taught the swain to guide the plow
        By Reason's laws--to turn the fruitful soil
        By useful rules, and scientific toil;
        Thy cultivated bosom to adorn
        With cooling fruits, and life-sustaining corn;
        And prov'd philosophy! to thy true friends,
        The man, who pants for heav'n, to earth attends.

16 AQUIN de, [CHÂTEAU-LYON, PIERRE LOUIS d']. "Franckliniana,"
    <u>Almanach littéraire, ou étrennes d'apollon, pour l'année
    1791</u>. Paris: Mme. la Veuve Duchesne, pp. 78-85.
        Anecdotes by and about Franklin, which show him to be
    versatile and benevolent.

17 CALOC [pseud.]. "Sacred to Heaven! and Franklin!"
    <u>Massachusetts Magazine</u> 5, no. 2 (May):[309].
        Poetic tribute honoring Franklin for his scientific work
    which clearly shows that thunder and lightning are to him
    "servants."

18 CEREMONY [pseud.]. "Of Dr. Franklin." <u>Massachusetts Magazine</u>
    2, no. 5 (May):[259]-62.
        Biographical account praising Franklin's abilities,
    services and humanitarianism.

19 [CONDORCET, MARIE JEAN ANTOINE NICOLAS.] <u>Éloge de M.
    Franklin. Lu a la séance publique de l'Académie des
    Sciences, le 13 Nov. 1790</u>. Paris: Pyre [&] Petit, 42 pp.
        While one would reasonably expect Condorcet to acclaim
    Franklin's scientific accomplishments, there is almost
    nothing said on this subject. Instead, the Frenchman
    celebrates Franklin as a moralist, philosopher, liberal
    humanitarian, and statesman. Condorcet especially lauds
    Franklin as a consistently advanced thinker, a quality

32

readily apparent during his remarkably successful years in France.

20 EUGENIO [pseud.]. "On the Death of Dr. Franklin, a Fragment." Massachusetts Magazine 2, no. 5 (May):[309].
    Franklin praised as a scientist, patriot, and liberator. Columbia hears "Warren's voice" announce that he is coming to bear "my Franklin to the skies!" She pleads:

    > O save my friend!...let Franklin stay,
    > Him whom the raging elements obey,
    > Whose hand, my head with deathless honors crown'd
    > And dash'd a tyrant's sceptre to the ground!

21 FAUCHET, [Claude]. Éloge Civique de Benjamin Franklin, prononcé le 21 Juillet 1790 dans la Rotonde, au nom de la Commune de Paris . . . , an présence de MM. les Députés de l'Assemblée Nationale, de MM. les Députés de tous les Départemens du Royaume à la confédération, de le Marie, de M. de Commandant-Général, de MM. les Représentans de la Commune, de MM. les Presidens des Districts, & de MM. les Electeurs de Paris. Paris: J.R. Lottin, G.L. Bailly, Vict. Desenne & J. Cussac, 50 pp.
    An elaborate tribute to Franklin the enlightened and therefore tolerant moralist and legislator. Fauchet's regard for Franklin is clear; however, his eulogy suffers from factual errors.

22 FREMERY, NICOLAUS CORNELIUS de. "De identitate phaenomenorum fulminis et electricitatis." In Dissertatio philosophica inauguralis de fulmine quam annuente summo numine. . . . Leyden: Samuel & Joann Luchtmans, pp. 4-17.
    Explains Franklin's theory that lightning and electricity are identical.

23 GERBER, ERNST LUDWIG. "Francklin (Dr. Benjamin)." In Historisch biographisches Lexicon der Tonkünstler, welches Nachrichten von dem Leben und Werken musikalischer Schriftsteller. . . . Vol. 1. Leipzig: Johann Gottlob Immanuel Breitkopf, pp. 435-36.
    Franklin is accorded a place in music history because of his glass armonica.

*24 L., M. Discours prononcé le 10 août 1790, à la fête célébrée en l'honneur de Benjamin Franklin par la société des Ouvriers Imprimeurs de Paris. . . . [Paris?]
    Source: NUC. Aldridge, pp. 232-33, discusses this piece. He says that the speaker acclaimed Franklin as a

1790

printer, reader, lover of liberty and excellent citizen
whose achievements should inspire his fellow printers.
(The National Union Catalogue, Vol. 144, p. 475, indicates
that this work is in the New York Public Library. As of
this writing, it is missing.)

25   LAMONT. "Lines on the Death of Doctor Franklin." Universal
Magazine and Review or, Repository of Literature 3 (June):
582.
Lamont, apparently a citizen of Belfast, Ireland, pays
tribute in verse to Franklin, praising him for his personal
qualities and liberal, humane nature. The following extract
suggests the tone and quality of the whole:

Cold lies that heart which beat for all mankind,
Now lost to all that comprehensive mind;
No more shall age admire, no more the young,
Imbibe the virtuous lesson from his tongue;
No more Poor Richard's annual tale afford,
Instructive converse round the rustic board;
No more correct the proud, inform the gay,
No more the world's calm censor now display;
No more industry, studious to be great,
The high reward he freely gave await.

All good people should express their gratitude to Franklin
by shedding tears and by imitating the life of the man.

*26   La ROCHEFOUCAULD d'ENVILLE, LOUIS ALEXANDRE. "Hommage rendu
par le voeu unanime de la société de 1789 à Benjamin
Franklin, objet de l'admiration et des regrets des amis de
la amis de la liberté." Journal de la Société de 1789
(19 June).
Source: Aldridge, pp. 157-58. Franklin is not only a
genius but a benefactor to mankind and one who was personally charming and always interesting.

27   Le ROY, [JEAN BAPTISTE]. "Biographical Anecdotes of Dr.
Franklin." English Review 16 (August):130-36.
Le Roy's account was abridged by the Review because it
seemed "superfluous, or to favour too much of national
prejudice." Franklin's life and character are presented
in a very positive light. Readers learn that the American
philosopher-statesman was a man of perfect composure and
balance. He had the boldness to undertake great projects
and the discretion to see them through to successful com-
pletion. Finally, Franklin had the ability to find the
"plainest side" of problems and to achieve at once the
simplest and most effective means of solving them.

28 _____. "Note . . . sur Franklin." In Éloge Civique de
Benjamin Franklin, prononcé le 21 Juillet 1790 dans la
Rotonde, au non de la Commune de Paris. . . ., by Claude
Fauchet. Paris: J.R. Lottin, G.L. Bailly, Vict. Desenne
& J. Cussac, 50 pp.
A tribute by Franklin's fellow scientist.

*29 MICHAUD, JOSEPH FRANÇOIS. Franklin législateur du nouveau
monde. [Signe: Michaud.]
Source: Aldridge, pp. 138-39. See 1791.15.

30 MIRABEAU, [HONORÉ GABRIEL RIQUETTI]. Discours du comte de
Mirabeau dans la séance du 11 juin, sur la mort de
Benjamin Francklin. . . . Paris: Baudouin, 3 pp.
Franklin deserves to be mourned in Europe and in America,
for he was not only great in physical and political sciences, but he was preeminent in championing human rights
and will remain one of humanity's heroes.

31 MUSSI, ANTONIO. "In virgam Franklinianam, ode Alcaica."
American Museum, or Universal Magazine 7, no. 6 (June):
appendix 1, 41.
Tribute to Franklin for his achievements in science,
especially the lightning rod, and for his accomplishments
as a philosopher, patriot, and man. (Written in 1784 but
first published in 1790. See Pace, pp. 242 and 350n, and
the correction of Pace's assertion on the first publication
of the piece by Leo Max Kaiser in the April 1967 William
and Mary Quarterly, pp. 288-91.

32 PARIS, COMMONALITY of. "Translation of a Letter Addressed to
the President of the United States of America . . . and
Which Was Accompanied with 25 Copies of the Abbé Fauchet's
Eulogy on Dr. Franklin." Massachusetts Magazine 2, no. 12
(December):768.
Tribute to Franklin.

33 PENNSYLVANIA, UNIVERSITY of. An Exercise, Performed at the
Public Commencement, in the College of Philadelphia, July 17,
1790. Containing an Ode, Set to Music, Sacred to the Memory
of Dr. Franklin. Philadelphia: William Young, 11 pp.
Special Collections, University of Pennsylvania.
The audience was told that "fair SCIENCE"

> Reserv'd for FRANKLIN'S hand, the golden key
> That opes her inmost doors--O last and best
> Of Patriots and Philosophers confess'd,
> Whose ever-waking comprehensive mind

1790

Labour'd alone to benefit mankind!
All-hail, COLUMBIA, to your favourite son!
All-hail, these happy walls! your FOUNDER own!
While grateful strains, ye sons of Science, come,
While trembles with his DIRGE this hallow'd dome!

There follows the "Ode," which calls on "Sages" and
"Patriots" to "Suspend for a moment your la--bours and
care; / And to the green grave of Franklin re--pair."
There they will "deck the green grave where your FRANKLIN
is laid" and pay homage to this great man who worked in
behalf of peace and science for the benefit of his fellows.

34 [PRICE, RICHARD.] [Extract of a Letter Dated 19 June.]
    Massachusetts Magazine 2, no. 12 (December):770.
        Franklin's memoirs show strikingly "how a man, by
    talents, industry, and integrity, may rise from obscurity
    to the first eminence and consequence in the world."
    Franklin deserves all honors accorded to him, and those
    by the French are without parallel in the history of the
    world.

35 S[TEVENSON], M[ARGARET]. "Verses by a Lady. Addressed to
    Dr. Franklin, With a Pair of Worked Ruffles, Dec. 1769."
    American Museum, or Universal Magazine 7, no. 6 (June):
    appendix 1, 43-44.
        Franklin's younger and dear friend praises him in lines
    that accompany her gift. The following is a sample:

        My noble friend! this artless line excuse,
        Nor blame the weakness of your Polly's muse;
        The humble gift with kind complacence take,
        And wear it for the grateful giver's sake.

36 STUBER, HENRY. "History of the Life and Character of
    Benjamin Franklin, L.L.D. &c &c. &c." Universal Asylum
    and Columbian Magazine 4 (June):332-39; 5 (July):4-9;
    5 (September):139-45; 5 (October):211-16; 5 (November):
    283-87; 6 (February 1791):68-70; 6 (March 1791):[131]-34;
    6 (May 1791): 297-300; 6 (June 1791):[363]-66.
        These pages constitute Stuber's continuation of
    Franklin's Autobiography and is a generally straightforward
    account of the philosopher's later years. (The June 1791
    issue indicates that Stuber's narrative was "to be con-
    tinued"; however, it was not. NUC)

37 [WILMER, JAMES JONES.] Memoirs of the late Dr. Benjamin
    Franklin: With a Review of His Pamphlet Entitled "Informa-
    tion to Those Who Would Wish to Remove to America." London:
    printed and sold for the author, by A. Grant, 94 pp.

Surveys Franklin's career, noting that he was a genius
and a very complex man whose abilities and goodness enabled
him to rise above common prejudices. (Yet Wilmer is clearly
negative toward Franklin for political reasons. As P.L.
Ford, in his Bibliography, no. 997, p. 393, notes, Wilmer
was "caustically handled in the Monthly Review, 4, 83,"
because of his hostility toward Franklin.)

1791

1   A., S. [Franklin's Thoughts on Catching Cold.] Gentleman's
    Magazine 61, pt. 1, no. 3 (March):200.
        Franklin recognized a number of the causes of colds and
    developed what have been subsequently accepted as sound
    theories on the relationship between colds and diet.

2   ANON. [Anecdote about Franklin.] Massachusetts Magazine 3,
    no. 5 (May):306.
        When Franklin was President of Pennsylvania, some people
    came to him and asserted that he was being commanded by God
    to reprieve two prisoners. Franklin, it is said, called
    his visitors obvious imposters, since the prisoners had
    already been hanged.

3   ANON. "Benjamin Franklin." In Nekrolog auf das Jahr 1790.
    Compiled by Friedrich Schlictergoll. Vol. 1. Gotha:
    J. Perthes, pp. 262-311.
        Biographical sketch focusing attention on Franklin's
    early life but also commending him for his numerous contri-
    butions to American independence.

4   ANON. "Elogio de Benjamino Franklin." Almanacco ed
    effemeridi per l'anno MDCCXCII. Venice: Nella Stamperia
    Grazoisi, pp. 65-66.
        Tribute to Franklin for his many achievements and
    patriotism.

5   ANON. "Life of Dr. Franklin. With an Elegant Head."
    Literary and Biographical Magazine, and British Review
    6 (January):[1]-5.
        A summary of Franklin's career and a staunch defense of
    it.

6   ANON. "Memories of the Life and Writings of the Late
    Benjamin Franklin, LL.D." Weekly Entertainer 18, no. 462
    (12 December):571-78.
        Biographical account praising Franklin's career and
    character.

1791

7   ANON. "Ode. On the Death of Dr. Franklin." Massachusetts
    Magazine 3, no. 11 (November):706.
        Praise for the immortal Franklin.

            To him be devoted the lay,
            Whom Science and Liberty crown;
            For him let the Muses display,
            The garland of tuneful renown.
        and
            Let Justice inscribe on the stone,
            Where Newton, neglected decays,
            To Franklin be sacred alone,
            The Laurel, the symbol of peace.

8   ANON. [On the Smith Eulogy.] Massachusetts Magazine 3, no. 3
    (March):199.
        Announces that the Reverend Dr. William Smith eulogized
    Franklin at the service conducted by the American Philo-
    sophical Society.

9   ANON. "Vindication of Dr. Franklin. Extract from the Monthly
    Review of the Second Part of the 'Collection of Papers on
    Naval Architecture.'" In Supplement. Naval Communications.
    No. XIII. [London]:pp. 147-48.
        A French naval officer who had served in the American
    Revolution, a Monsieur de Landais, charged that Franklin
    was vain and, in his desire to win "popular applause,"
    had betrayed his public trust in France. Specifically,
    the officer charged that Franklin misused funds "entrusted
    to him from the United States, and had evaded giving any
    account" of the money. These unsupported assertions are
    challenged, and the anonymous author says that Captain
    Landais did not know Franklin and was motivated only by
    "unprovoked malevolence" to publish such a "groundless
    calumny." Franklin's reputation in France testifies to his
    outstanding conduct and integrity. (The first part of the
    Collection appears in volume six, pp. 191-92, but the Sup-
    plement with the "Vindication of Dr. Franklin" is not on
    these pages or anywhere else in the volume.)

10 BRISSOT de WARVILLE, JACQUES PIERRE. "Sur Benjamin Franklin."
    In Nouveau voyage dans les Etats-Unis. Vol. 1. Paris:
    Buisson, pp. 311-37.
        A piece on Franklin constituting the fifteenth letter in
    the book. The chief point is that Franklin, a genuine phi-
    losopher and great genius, descended from his elevated
    sphere of existence to teach mortals about living a worth-
    while life. Franklin's success, outstanding by any criteria,

is even more remarkable in light of his inauspicious beginning.

11 An ENGLISHMAN WHO LOVES HIS COUNTRY, pseud. "Thoughts on the Character of Dr. Franklin." Gentleman's Magazine 61, pt. 1, no. 5 (May):413-14.
    Attacks Franklin for his role in the Revolution and in the peace negotiations; however, the criticism also extends to Franklin's private character.

12 FRANCE, Assemblée nationale constituante, 1789-1791. Suite du procès-verbal de l'Assemblée Nationale. No. 669. Paris: Baudouin, Imprimeur de l'Assemblée Nationale, 15 pp.
    On the eulogies and other honors accorded Franklin by the French government and various groups in France.

13 FRANCE, Laws, Statutes, etc. Loi relative à deux lettres écrites, l'une par le Ministre des Etats-Unis de l'Amérique, l'autre par les représentans de l'Etat de Pensilvanie . . . 2 juin 1791. Paris: Imprimerie royale, 2 pp.
    Responses to French eulogies on Franklin.

14 LYON, JOHN. Remarks on the Leading Proofs Offered in Favour of the Franklinian System of Electricity; With Experiments to Shew the Direction of the Electric Effluvia Visibly Passing From What Has Been Termed Negatively Electrified Bodies. London: J. Phillips, 47 pp.
    Franklin's theory of positive and negative charges and, indeed, most of what he has to say about electricity, is wrong. He has been supported by "Franklinists" almost blindly.

*15 [MICHAUD, JOSEPH FRANÇOIS.] "Franklin législateur du nouveau monde." In Le tribut de la société nationale des neuf soeurs, ou recueil de mémoires sur les sciences, belles lettres et arts, et d'autres pièces lues dans les séances de cette societe. Paris: pp. 51-57.
    Source: Aldridge, pp. 138-39. An idealized Franklin, the sage-patriot, helps win freedom for an even more idealized America. His mission accomplished, Franklin dies peacefully and happily. His memory is praised by John Adams and then Franklin descends to earth again for a time to express the happiness he has found in heaven. Finally, he announces the Golden Age of man who, having been freed, is able to live virtuously. See 1790.29.

16 N., R. "Dr. Franklin's Parable Traced to Its Source." Gentleman's Magazine 61, pt. 1, no. 4 (April):313-14.

1791

> This part of a somewhat longer piece says that the
> source of Franklin's <u>Parable Against Persecution</u> is Bishop
> Jeremy Taylor's "Liberty of Prophesying."

17   TRESSAN, LOUIS ELISABETH de la VERGNE de BROUSSIN. "Vers
     adressés à M. Francklin, au moment où il plantoit, de sa
     main, un acacia de Virginie, dans un bosquet des jardins
     de Sanois, chez Madame la Comtesse d'Houdettot." In
     <u>Oeuvres posthumes du comte de Tressan</u>. [Paris: Desray],
     pp. 140-41.
       Tribute to an idealized Franklin, the symbol of hope
     for lovers of wisdom and liberty.

18   U.S. Laws, Statutes, etc., 1790-1791 (1st Congress, 3rd
     Session). <u>Resolved by the Senate and the House of Repre-</u>
     <u>sentatives of the United States of America in Congress</u>
     <u>Assembled, That the President of the United States of</u>
     <u>America Be Requested to Cause to Be Communicated to the</u>
     <u>National Assembly of France the Peculiar Sensibility of</u>
     <u>Congress to the Tribute Paid to the Memory of Benjamin</u>
     <u>Franklin, by the Enlightened and Free Representatives of a</u>
     <u>Great Nation, in Their Decree of the Eleventh of June, One</u>
     <u>Thousand Seven Hundred and Ninety</u>. [Philadelphia]:
     broadside.
       Self-explanatory.

19   WEHRS, G[EORGE] F[RIEDRICH]. "Doctor Franklin."
     <u>Hannoverisches Magazin. . .</u> , vom Jahre 1790 28:1035-38.
       Story of Franklin's last illness.

                              1792

1   ANON. "Biographia Addenda. [No. 3] Benjamin Franklin." In
     <u>An Interesting Collection of Modern Lives; With Observations</u>
     <u>of the Characters and Writings, of the Following Eminent</u>
     <u>Men, Jeffrey Lord Amherst, Mr. John Howard, Dr. Benjamin</u>
     <u>Franklin, Barnard Gates, Esq., Dr. Arne, John Horne Tooke,</u>
     <u>Esq. and Mr. Thomas Paine, Author of the Rights of Man, &c.</u>
     <u>&c</u>. London: printed for G. Riebau, pp. [36]-40.
       Franklin's virtues of "frugality and industry" were im-
     portant factors in his eventual rise to independence. His
     newspaper, the <u>Pennsylvania Gazette</u>, and his <u>Poor Richard's</u>
     <u>Almanacks</u> were also important to him because they were very
     profitable and, more significantly, because they "were the
     first vehicles which made his talents known to the world."
     Also discusses Franklin's contributions as a public-spirited
     citizen, scientist, and diplomat.

2   ANON. "Discours de Franklin au parlement d'Angleterre." In
<u>Le panthéon des philantropes, ou l'école de la
révolution.</u> . . . Paris: [Janet], pp. 20-22.
    Franklin speaks for and represents liberty and the virtue
of free, independent men.

3   ANON. "Precis historique de la vie de Benjamin Franklin."
In <u>Le panthéon des philantropes, ou l'école de la
révolution.</u> . . . Paris: [Janet], pp. 15-19.
    A brief account of Franklin's life and career.

*4   GEDIKE, FRIEDRICH. "Sur Benjamin Franklin." In <u>Franzoesische
Chrestomathie zum Gebrauch des hoehern Klassen, aus den
vorzueglichsten neuren Schriftstellen gestammlet.</u> . . .
Berlin.
    Source: <u>NUC.</u> See 1803.3.

5   LOUSTALOT, [ELYSÉE?]. "Mort de Franklin." <u>Le panthéon des
philantropes, ou l'école de la révolution.</u> . . . Paris:
[Janet], p. 15.
    On the Assemblée's tribute to Franklin. (Elysée
Loustalot died in 1790.)

6   SMITH, WILLIAM. <u>Eulogium on Benjamin Franklin, L.L.D.</u>
Philadelphia: Benjamin Franklin Bache for the American
Philosophical Society, 40 pp.
    Smith pays tribute, in the grand oratorical manner of
the time, to Franklin as a citizen of Pennsylvania, of
America, and of the world. Since Smith was a long-time
political enemy to Franklin, his sincerity has been ques-
tioned, and students have wondered why the Society chose
him to deliver the eulogy. He read carefully through some
of Franklin's papers and performed his task gracefully and
well. Yet Smith used Jonathan Odell's satirical "Inscription" as a parting attack on Franklin.

1793

1   ANON. [Benjamin Franklin.] In <u>The Annual Register, or a
View of the History, Politics, and Literature. For the
Year 1790.</u> Vol. 35. London: J. Dodsley, pp. 201-4.
    An obituary that calls attention to Franklin's lifelong
love of science, his significance as a political figure and
diplomat, his concern with common events that could make
people happier and better, and his importance as a writer
on a variety of useful topics.

1793

2   ANON. "Character of Dr. Franklin." European Magazine and
    London Review 23 (June):404-5.
        The death of Franklin means that "one of the lights of
    the world" is extinguished. He was a peculiarly original
    genius, witness the astonishing range and depth of his ob-
    servations on nature. Moreover, his accomplishments in
    politics were as great as those in science. Yet he was
    greatest as a citizen, for he was perhaps the most "useful"
    man of all time. His whole life "was a perpetual lecture
    against the idle, the extravagant, and the proud."

3   ANON. "Life of Dr. Franklin." Lady's Magazine, or, Enter-
    taining Companion for the Fair Sex, Appropriated Solely to
    Their Use and Amusement 24 (December):681-85; 25 (January
    1794):20-23; 25 (February 1794):76-81; 25 (March 1794):
    128-33; 25 (April 1794):178-83; 25 (May 1794):242-45.
        Franklin's memoirs began in the January 1793 issue and
    ran through November of that year. Beginning in December
    1793 and continuing through May 1794 the anonymous author
    provided a relatively objective continuation of Franklin's
    life.

4   FORSTER, GEORG. "Der Philosoph von Ferney segnet den jungen
    Gross-Sohn Franklins." In Erinnerungen aus dem Jahr 1790.
    Berlin: Vossischen Buchhandlung, pp. 30-35.
        Franklin took his grandson Temple to see Voltaire, and
    the Frenchman, who had only a short time to live, performed
    a benediction over the boy, pronouncing the words: "God,
    freedom, peace." (Forster uses "Friede," though others
    report that Voltaire said only "God and liberty," or "God,
    liberty and tolerance.")

5   [MARMONTEL, JEAN FRANÇOIS?]. "Les Souvenirs du Coin du Feu."
    Mercure de France, Supplément au no. 1 (January).
        An elderly, sage Franklin calls for the respect of the
    aged and for the recognition that they still have contribu-
    tions to make.

6   MILON, C. Denkwürdigkeiten zur Geschichte Benjamin Franklins.
    St. Petersburg: J. Z. Logan, 110 pp.
        About one-third of this book is made up of correspondence,
    but Milon does provide a detailed account of Franklin as a
    political leader. His assessment of Franklin's achievement
    is very favorable. The American statesman prepared his
    country for independence when he knew that it could not re-
    main part of Great Britain. Franklin's well deserved repu-
    tation for brilliance and humanitarianism helped him lead
    his fellow Americans to see the unfortunate necessity of

1793

separation and aided also in his remarkable success in
making an open ally of France.

7   PATTERSON, ROBERT. "Explorations of a Singular Phenomenon,
First Observed by Dr. Franklin, and Not Hitherto Satis-
factorily Accounted For." Transactions of the American
Philosophical Society 3:13-16.
Franklin observed that oil calmed water, but neither he
nor anyone else had provided a sound explanation of the
phenomenon. Patterson offers his own theory.

1794

1   ALGAROTTI, FRANCESCO. Opere. Vol. 9. Venice: Palese,
p. 286.
Algarotti, an Italian philosopher, noted in 1755 that
the electricians of Europe would have to show genuine
respect to Franklin.

2   ANON. "Geologische Phantasien (Franklin's Geogenie)." In
Göttinger Taschen Kalender für das Jahr 1795. [Göttingen]:
U.C. Dieterich, pp. [79]-108.
A commentary on speculations about the earth's structure
made by Franklin in a letter written to the Abbé Soulavie
on 22 September 1782.

3   ANON. "Poor Richard's Parody." In The Farmer's Useful and
Entertaining Companion: or, New Hampshire, Massachusetts,
and Vermont Almanack for the Year of Our Lord 1795. . . .
Exeter, N.H.: Stearns & Winslow, p. [24].
Poor Richard-like maxims used to attack both spendthrifts
and misers, people who have not achieved the kind of balance
about money Franklin had.

4   SPRENGEL, KURT [POLYCARP JOACHIM]. "Franklin's Geogenie im
frühesten Alterthum." In Beiträge zur Geschichte der
Medicin. Vol. 1. Halle: Regenschen Buchhandlung,
pp. 237-43.
Acclaims Franklin as one of those scientists who under-
stood and revealed basic truths about natural phenomena.
The genesis of a number of his ideas goes back to antiquity.

1795

1   ANON. "Anecdote of Franklin and Voltaire." European Magazine
and London Review 28 (September):156-57.

1795

> Franklin took Temple Franklin to see Voltaire and asked the dying Frenchman to bless the boy. Voltaire did so, and those who were present at the occasion were horrified, believing that Franklin was using Voltaire to ridicule religion.

2   ANON. Dr. Benjamin Franklin's Leben. Biographien für die
    Jugend. Tübingen: J.G. Cottaische Buchhandlung.
    Heavy reliance on Franklin's own writings, which are
    quoted at length, to show his patriotism. NUC considers
    this work Franklin's Autobiography; however, it is rewritten
    in the third person. Moreover, some incidents are rear-
    ranged, and the whole sounds very little like the Autobiog-
    raphy. German bibliographers consider this a secondary
    account.

3   ANON. "Dr. Franklin." European Magazine and London Review 28
    (November):304.
    "Had our idiotic Ministry" listened to the wise Franklin
    instead of abusing him, there would have been no war with
    America.

4   ANON. Introduction to La science du Bonhomme Richard, ou moyen
    facile de prayer les impôts opuscules de Franklin. Paris:
    Chez Ant. Aug. Renouard, pp. [35-42].
    An interesting early account of the effectiveness of
    the mask of Poor Richard and of the popularity of the
    almanacs.

5   ANON. "Lebensgeschichte des Benjamin Franklin." Allgemeines
    europäisches Journal 8 (July-August):86-102; 9 (September-
    October):135-46.
    A marginally accurate account of Franklin's life and
    career, stressing the rags-to-riches success story.

*6 [COBBETT, WILLIAM.] "A Little Plain English." In Porcupine's
    Works. 6 vols. Philadelphia: T. Bradford.
    Source: NUC. See 1801.1.

7   FRENEAU, PHILIP [MORIN]. "Epistle From Dr. Franklin [Deceased]
    to His Poetical Panegyrists." In Poems Written Between the
    Years 1768 & 1794. Monmouth, N.J.: printed at the press
    of the author, pp. 417-18.
    In a poem Freneau wrote in 1790, Franklin is made to
    ridicule the excessive praise of poets who wax too
    enthusiastic:

> "'Good Poets, why so full of pain,
> Are you sincere--or do you feign?'"

It is contrary to nature and to sense to write that nature wept and the ocean sighed when he died. (The poem is readily available in a photoprint of the above cited work: Poems Written Between the Years 1768 & 1794, a facsimile reproduction, Delmar, N.Y.: Scholars' Facsimiles & Reprints, 1976.)

8   _____. "An Ode on the Death of Dr. Benjamin Franklin." In Poems Written Between the Years 1768 & 1794. Monmouth, N.J.: printed at the press of the author, p. 417.
Of Franklin, Freneau writes, in 1790:

> When monarchs tumble to the ground,
> Successors easily are found:
> But matchless Franklin! what a few
> Can hope to rival such as you
> Who seized from kings their sceptred pride,
> And turned the lightnings darts aside!

(The poem is readily available in a photoprint of the above cited work: Poems Written Between the Years 1768 & 1794, a facsimile reproduction. Delmar, N.Y.: Scholars' Facsimiles & Reprints, 1976.)

9   [MOUNTMORRES, HERVEY REDMOND MORRES.] "The Character of Dr. Franklin." In The Letters of Themistocles. London: printed for Hokham & Carpenter, appendix, pp. 1-8. (The appendix follows p. 244.)
Franklin is praised for his successful rise in fortune, his extraordinary intellectual powers even into old age, and for his sincere attempt to prevent the Revolutionary War.

1796

1   ANON. [Anecdote about Franklin.] In Weatherwise Almanack for the Year of Our Lord 1797. . . . Boston: J. Boyle, C. Bingham, B. Larkin, pp. [19-20].
How Franklin rids himself of pesty inquisitors at inns and enjoys a peaceful supper.

2   IDELER, [CHRISTIAN] LUDWIG, and NOLTE, [JOHANN WILHELM] H[EINRICH]. "Franklin." In Handbuch der englischen Sprache und Litteratur. 6th ed. Vol. 1. [Eben]: Ideler & Nolte, pp. 334-44.
A biographical and bibliographical survey noting the importance of printing, study, and diligence in the

1796

successful life of this self-made man. (The Handbuch is
often listed under Nolte. Ideler wrote the essay on
Franklin and parts of the Handbuch. The publication history of this book is complex. Evidently the 1796 printing
is the first, and the 6th Auflage denomination was retained
until at least 1853.)

1797

1 [ALMON, JOHN.] "Dr. Benjamin Franklin." In Biographical,
   Literary, and Political Anecdotes, of Several of the Most
   Eminent Persons of the Present Age. Vol. 2. London:
   printed for T.N. Longman & L.B. Seeley, pp. 175-344.
      Nearly the whole of this lengthy account is comprised of
   quotes from Franklin's letters and documents concerning his
   political career in England. Summarizes Franklin's earlier
   years very briefly and offers only ten pages on his career
   after 1776. Expresses his feelings toward Franklin at the
   outset, saying that "he was the projector and founder of
   his country's greatness and power," a man who tried to keep
   the British Empire intact until England threatened to en-
   slave America.

2 ANON. "Franklin (Dr. Benjamin)." In Encyclopaedia Britannica;
   or, a Dictionary of Arts, Sciences, and Miscellaneous
   Literature. . . . 3d ed. Vol. 7. Edinburgh: printed
   for A. Bell & C. Macfarquhar, pp. 449-51.
      Summarizes Franklin's life but is guilty of errors. The
   author asserts, for example, that the English did not even
   realize Franklin was leaving in 1775 until, presumably, it
   was too late to detain him. We are also told that Franklin
   "was a firm believer in the Scriptures." (The piece on
   Franklin appears for the first time in the third edition.)

3 BOUCHER, JONATHAN. "On the Character of Ahitophel" and
   "Appendix to the Two Sermons on Absalom and Ahitophel."
   In A View of the Causes and Consequences of the American
   Revolution; In Thirteen Discourses, Preached in North
   America Between the Years 1763 and 1775; With an Historical
   Preface. . . . London: printed for G.G. & J. Robinson,
   pp. 407-34, 435-49.
      Franklin is likened to Ahitophel, who "acted a busy and
   important part" in the revolt of Absalom and thus is a
   major cause of the American Revolution, according to Boucher
   in the first part of his discussion. The "Appendix" had
   been delivered in 1774, and caused Boucher to be rebuked
   for his comparison of Franklin with Ahitophel. Yet in 1797

the minister defended the comparison, charging that
Franklin and the other American leaders were demagogues.
It is, of course, difficult, Boucher says, to appraise
Franklin's full character, for he was controversial even
in America. Actually, it would seem that he was neither so
great nor so bad as he has been portrayed. Still, one must
remember that Franklin may have stolen the theory of lightning from Kinnersley, and that he took the "Parable Against
Persecution" from Jeremy Taylor. Moreover, as a political
person, Franklin proved very inconsistent, at first promoting Royal Government but later becoming an ardent republican
and revolutionary. Further, it was likely Franklin himself
who "originated" the idea of the stamp tax; however, he
eventually worked against it. One should not look for
political idealism from him. Indeed, he became a rebel
only because he was personally insulted by Wedderburn in
the cockpit. Finally, Franklin was a deist and so was
really no better than such a pre-Christian as Socrates.

4   EINEM, [JOHANN KONRAD von]. "Auf Franklin. Nach dem
    Französisischen des du Bourg." In Musen Almanach[:] 1797.
    Göttingen: C. Dieterich, p. 62.
       An elegiac tribute.

1798

1   ANON. Vida del Dr. Benjamin Franklin sacada de documentos
    authenticos. Madrid: Pantaleon Aznar, 216 pp.
       Nearly eighty percent of this book deals with Franklin's
    life during the period covered by the Autobiography. The
    entire account is dedicated to praising Franklin for his
    many well known virtues and for his humanity.

1799

1   ANON. "Merkwürdiger Scheintod." Athenaeum. Eine Zeitschrift
    von August Wilhelm Schlegel und Friedrich Schlegel 2:336.
       Franklin's morality is essentially of a materialistic
    nature.

18--

1   ANON. Benjamin Franklin. Madras: C.L.S. Press, 24 pp.
       A brief biography.

18--

2 ANON. Benjamin Franklin. Temperance Tracts for Children.
   N.p., 4 pp. FCL.
   Franklin's Poor Richard qualities made him "prosperous
   and wealthy" and he was a believer in temperance all his
   life.

3 ANON. Leben Benjamin Franklins, beschrieben für das Volk
   eigenthum des württembergischen volkschriften-vereins.
   Ulm: Hearbrandt & Thamel, 111 pp.
   Biography praising Franklin's humanity, wisdom, and
   patriotism.

4 ANON. "Remarks on the Life of Benjamin Franklin." In Famous
   Men. N.p., pp. 1-10.
   Franklin overcame numerous obstacles and became truly
   great in many areas. For youngsters he is a model of the
   self-made man and of one who gained success for himself
   while serving others. This piece was also published in
   Dutch at about the same time.

*5 CARR, ROBERT. "Reminiscences of Dr. Franklin." In Contribu-
   tion to the Great Sanitary Fair.
   Source: NYPL. This may be the same as his 1868
   "Personal Recollections of Benjamin Franklin." See 1868.4.

6 Du CHATENET, E. Benjamin Franklin; sa vie, ses succés dans
   l'art de faire le bien. Limoges: Eugene Ardant, 180 pp.
   Extensive quotes from the Autobiography are interspersed
   with the author's idealized account of Franklin's life to
   show that Franklin was justly loved by the French as well
   as by his countrymen.

7 EYMA, XAVIER. "Franklin." N.p., pp. [337]-58. "Le livre
   d'or" at the top of the verso pages. Huntington Collection
   of Frankliniana, American Philosophical Society, vol. 1,
   no. 7. HM BF 85xh.
   Franklin was a remarkable man and patriot. He loved the
   French people and they, recognizing not only his outstanding abilities but his simple goodness, returned his love
   completely. It is accurate to say that Franklin captivated
   France.

8 [MANGIN, ALBERT. Begins: "Benjamin Franklin naquit à
   Boston," and the headnote reads: "Les Savants Illustre,"]
   pp. 501-5. FCL.
   A brief sketch of Franklin's earlier career leading up
   to his accomplishments as a scientist.

9   NAQUET, GUSTAVE. "Benjamin Franklin." In Le livre d'or de
     la république[.] Premiere livraison[:] Franklin[.]
     Sommaire: biographie avec portrait--histoire des
     republiques. 1st ser. [Paris: Robert & Buhl], pp. [1]-4.
         This piece is the second in the book, each of which is
     separately paginated; a summary of Franklin's career that
     remarks on how much he loved France and the French people
     who supported the American Revolution.

10   RENOUARD, AUGUSTIN CHARLES. Franklin[:] 1706-1790. N.p.,
     61 pp.
         Franklin is shown to be a great and humane friend to his
     fellow men throughout the world. Indeed, he is a symbol of
     hope for mankind.

11   SULC, PAVEL JOSEF. Benjamin Franklin. . . . Prague:
     Nákladem A. Hynka, 48 pp.
         Brief biography of Franklin highlighting his achievements
     as a scientist, moralist, and patriot.

1800

1   ANON. Child's Life of Franklin. Philadelphia: Fisher &
     Brothers, 192 pp.
         Narrative supplemented by extensive quotations from
     Franklin is intended to emphasize his patriotism and his
     general benevolence.

2   ANON. Frankliniana; ou recueil d'anecdotes, bon mots,
     reflexions, maximes et observations de Benjamin Franklin.
     Paris: Tiger, 108 pp.
         The first twenty-seven pages sketch Franklin's life and
     comment favorably on his reputation in France. The next
     eighty-eight pages are made up largely of primary materials
     with commentary interspersed. There is also a poem
     (pp. 105-6), "Couplets chantés à un repas où se trouvait
     le docteur Franklin," in which Franklin is lauded as a
     patriot, liberator, and humanitarian.

1801

1   COBBETT, WILLIAM. "A Little Plain English." In Porcupine's
     Works; Containing Various Writings and Selections, Exhibit-
     ing a Faithful Picture of the United States of America . . .
     From the End of the War in 1783, to the Election of the
     President, in March, 1801. Vol. 2. London: printed for
     Cobbett & Morgan, pp. [281]-366.

1801

Attacks Franklin for his hostility to England, which was manifested in his very inflexible negotiating stance with the English commissioners in France. See 1795.6.

2 CRÈVECOEUR, [MICHEL GUILLAUME] St. JEAN de. Voyage dans la Haute Pennsylvanie et dans l'etat de New-York, par un membre adoptif de la nation Oneida. Vol. 1. Paris: Maradan, pp. 26-34.
Discusses Franklin's opinions concerning "the origin of the American Indians," and pages 353-56 contain a brief account of Franklin.

3 DENNIE, JOSEPH [Oliver Oldschool]. "An Author's Evenings. From the Shop of Messers. Colon and Spondee." Port Folio, ser. 1, 1, no. 7 (14 February):53-54.
Attacks Franklin as miserly, a mere hack who lifted bits from other men's writings and passed them off as his own, an immoral deist, and "one of our first jacobins." Worse yet, "he was the author of that pitiful system of Economics, the adoption of which has degraded our national character."

4 _____. "Epistolary. For the Port Folio." Port Folio, ser. 1, 1, no. 21 (23 May):165.
In a preface to a Franklin letter, Dennie attacks him as immoral, deistic, and republican.

5 SOULAVIE, JEAN-LOUIS. "Suite des influences des puissances étrangères sur les affaires de l'intérieur de la France. Conférence à cet égard entre B. Franklin et l'auteur de ces mémoires." In Mémoires historiques et politiques du règne de Louis XVI depuis son mariage jusqu'a sa mort. Vol. 5. Paris: Treuttel & Würtz, pp. 174-99.
Soulavie reports a conference held with Franklin in which the American states the historical and political grounds of his treaty demands on the British. Soulavie, in his discussion with Franklin, reveals the serious concern of Louis XVI with having supported a revolution, even against Britain, and also Franklin's efforts to calm the monarch's fears.

1802

1 ANON. "Benjamin Franklin." In Almanac américain pour l'année 1803. Paris: pp. [1]-50.
Outline of Franklin's beliefs and later political career. The author deals with the industriousness, frugality, honesty, good will, sagacity, and other virtues that made up

Franklin's character and enabled him to succeed in so great a variety of endeavors. Franklin's reputation and his personal qualities, as well as the cause he represented, gained for him the affection and support of the French people.

2   BURDICK, WILLIAM. An Oration on the Nature and Effects of the Art of Printing. Delivered in Franklin Hall, July 5, 1802, before the Boston Franklin Associates. Boston: Munroe & Francis, 31 pp.
    Franklin is mentioned throughout; nearly the entire last half of the book is an extremely favorable discussion of his life and achievements.

1803

1   ANON. "Papers Owned by the American Philosophical Society." Popular Science Monthly 63 (August):382-83.
    The collection of Franklin's papers owned by the American Philosophical Society is both of great interest and value.

2   DAVIS, JOHN. Travels of Four Years and a Half in the United States of America; During 1798, 1799, 1800, 1801, and 1802. London: pp. 209-18.
    A New Englander and a Virginian argue whether Franklin was original as a writer. The New England man loses badly, as his opponent proves that Franklin plagiarized extensively.

3   GEDIKE, FRIEDRICH. "Sur Benjamin Franklin." In Franzoesische Chrestomathie zum Gebrauch des hoehern Klassen. Aus den vorzueglichsten neuren Schriftstellen gestammlet. . . . 3d ed. No. 25, Berlin: pp. 187-205.
    Franklin's life is proof that if one is good, industrious, honest, and frugal, he can overcome obstacles and succeed. See 1792.4.

4   PRIESTLY, JOSEPH. "To the Editor of the Monthly Magazine." Monthly Magazine 15, no. 1 (February):[1]-2.
    Defends Franklin from the charge of secretly planning the Revolution. The truth of the matter, Priestly writes, is that Franklin so steadfastly counseled his fellow Americans to be patient, he lost much of his popularity in America. No one worked harder to prevent war and separation than the philosopher who, for the sake of peace and unity, bore suspicion and insults from his countrymen and from persons in England. He knew the truth about his efforts better than his detractors and so was even able to bear the assault of Wedderburn in the Privy Council.

1804

1   ANON. "Benjamin Franklin. With a Portrait." Literary Maga-
     zine and American Register 2, no. 14 (November):[571].
          Criticizes the attempt by Stuber--or future attempts by
     anyone else--to bring Franklin's account of his life to
     1790. One should not tamper with so great and inimitable
     a story.

2   ANON. The Life of Dr. Franklin, L.L.D.   Poughnill: George
     Nicholson, 56 pp.
          Franklin was outstanding in many areas and in many ways;
     however, the sources of his success were his greatness "in
     common things" and his usefulness.

3   BAUR, SAMUEL. "Benjamin Franklin. Präsident der gelehrten
     Gesellschaft zu Philadelphia." In Gallerie historischer
     Gemählde aus dem Achtzehnten Jahrhundert. Vol. 2.   Hof:
     Gottfried Adolph Grau, pp. 174-80.
          Biographical sketch of Franklin which calls attention
     to his diligence, a quality to be found throughout his
     long and useful life and one that was important in his
     success.

4   DENNIE, JOSEPH [Oliver Oldschool]. "General Letter From
     Dr. Franklin." Port Folio 4, no. 24 (16 June):187.
          The preface to the letter attacks Franklin for his deism
     and hostility toward established churches.

1805

1   ANON. "Franklin's Birthday in 1805." University of Pennsyl-
     vania Library Chronicle 9, no. 3 (December):74-77.
          Notes that the Boston Franklin Association celebrated
     Franklin's birthday with somewhat less moderation than
     advocated by the young Franklin and by Poor Richard, as
     it drank eighteen toasts on the occasion. The Columbian
     Centinel 42, no. 42 (19 January):[4] announced that in
     addition to the toast there was an "Ode," part of the last
     stanza and the refrain of which are as follows:

               And while libations pass around,
               And ev'ry heart with Joy is found,
               And while we chaunt the festive day,
               With Gratitude repeat, and say,
               Franklin!--thy memory's in our breast,
               It warms, invig'rates--and we're blest!

> Hence dull care! and toil away!
> 'Tis Great FRANKLIN'S natal day!--
> As a band of brothers, we
> Hail the day!--our Jubilee!

2 HOEUFFT, JACOB HENDRIK. "Carmina ad Benjaminum Franklin."
   In Carmina. Bredae: G. van Bergen, pp. 233-34.
      Hoeufft writes: "You, the great honor of our time,
   just as you are a Nestor in age, you are the Nestor in
   counsel and in speech." In another song, Hoeufft wants
   to imitate Franklin's "pleasant wit" and pay tribute to
   the philosopher in poetry "worthy" of him.

3 _____. "Carmina in Franklini mortem falso nuntiatam." In
   Carmina. Bredae: G. van Bergen, p. 130.
      On the inaccurately announced death of Franklin, Hoeufft
   writes:

Him whom America worships and pits against all of Europe, him whom
Albion herself honors although he is her enemy;
And him whom Enceladus' lying sister, after crossing the ocean,
had announced as having mixed with the Elysian shades;
Hurra, as before, Franklin lives (and may he live long!), and
he gives the fatherland changing fates.
Has he not, therefore, conquered Styx who had wrenched the
three-lightning weapons from the father of the gods, and conquered Jove?

4 _____. "Epitaphium Benjamini Franklin." In Carmina. Bredae:
   G. van Bergen, pp. 129-30.
      The epitaph in part reads:

Here lies Franklin. Are you looking for monuments, traveler?
Marble and bronze will not suffice for the man.
All of America, free of the yoke, shall look; she deserves to
decide if you want monuments of Franklin.
Look, even before the day the widow mourns the husband, and both
sons with the sister mourn the father.
The faithful flock of friends mourns the faithful friend, among
whose number there is a certain part of himself. And my muse,
so often praised by you, would be silent!

5 LANDON, C[HARLES] P[AUL]. "Francklin." In Galerie historique
   des hommes les plus célèbres. Vol. 3. Paris: C.P.
   Landon, unpaginated.
      Each volume is divided into two series of sketches; the
   one on Franklin is the thirty-fifth of the first section.

1805

Most of the sketch deals with Franklin's triumphs in France
and his many virtues. Landon believes that Franklin's personal qualities helped him succeed in his diplomatic
mission.

6   MAGAROTTO, ANTONIO. Franklini Theoria de Electricitatis
     Principio in compendium redacta. . . . Padua: Typis
     Seminarii, 158 pp.
        This book is a very detailed account of Franklin's theory
     of electricity set against the historical background of
     electrical work before and after his chief experiments.
     The book was evidently based on a series of laboriously
     organized lectures Magarotto gave to university students.

7   PHILADELPHIA, COMMITTEE of ACCOUNTS. Report of the Committee
     of Accounts, on the Accounts of the Fourth Quarter of the
     City Treasurer; and on the Account of the Debts Due to, and
     Owing by the Corporation; and on the Accounts of the Several
     Legacies of Dr. Benjamin Franklin, John Bleakley, &
     Elizabeth Kirkpatrick, Deceased. Philadelphia: William
     D[?], 8 pp.
        The Franklin account was nearly $3,000.

1806

1   ANON. "Dr. Franklin." In Science in Sport, or the Pleasures
     of Natural Philosophy. A New Game. London: printed for
     John Wallis, p. 8.
        Franklin discovered the identity of lightning and
     electricity.

2   ANON. "On the Literary Character of Dr. Franklin." Monthly
     Anthology 3, no. 12 (December):661-69.
        The editor claims that this piece appeared first in "A
     Celebrated English Publication." Franklin was perhaps the
     soundest, most sensible, and most just of all philosophers.
     The lack of formal education and a cultural environment
     generally proves disadvantageous to people, but to so
     forceful a mind as Franklin's, it proved "propitious."
     His self-education did more for him than formal education
     could have done. He is at his best in his moral writings
     which are well calculated to promote diligence and thrift.
     His memoirs are also written with "liveliness"; however, it
     is weighted down with trivialities which, while they may
     detract from its literary merits to a degree, do not lessen
     its example of a rise in life from obscurity to prominence.
     America is embarrassed by not yet bringing out an edition
     of Franklin's works.

54

3   BAUER, JOHANN CHRISTIAN AUGUST. "Franklin." In Franklin und
    Washington[:] oder[,] Sammlung der merkwürdigsten bekannten
    Züge aus dem Leben dieser um Amerika verdienten Männer.
    Berlin: Frölich'schen Buchhandlung, pp. [1]-166.
        These pages, which constitute about half the book, are
    a sketch of Franklin's life and career based on published
    writings and familiar anecdotes.

4   BEERS, ANDREW. "Anecdote of Dr. Franklin." In Franklin's
    Legacy; or, the New-York & Vermont Almanac, for the Year
    of Our Lord 1807. . . . Troy, N.Y.: [Moffitt & Lyon,
    p. 28].
        Franklin's "peculiar talent was that of illustrating sub-
    jects by apposite anecdotes."

5   BLANCHARD, PIERRE. "Benjamin Franklin, ein philosophischen
    Gesetzgeben." In Neuer Plutarch, oder kurze
    Lebensbeschreibungen der berühmtesten Männer und Frauen
    aller Nationen von den ältesten bis auf unsere Zeiten.
    Vol. 2. Vienna: Anton Doll, pp. 167-74.
        An inaccurate and thoroughly idealized account of
    Franklin's life. He is made the epitome of the philosopher-
    king, and Blanchard's young readers are obviously expected
    to follow in the righteous paths of the perfected hero who
    appears in these pages.

6   BROWN, CHARLES BROCKDEN. "Character of Dr. Franklin."
    Literary Magazine and Register 6, no. 38 (November):367-74.
        "A just view of the character of Dr. Franklin has prob-
    ably never been given by his countrymen." During his life,
    he was too controversial to make fair treatment possible,
    and since his death political sympathies have turned many
    of his fellow Americans against him. It was therefore
    necessary that this account of Franklin be taken
    from a "foreign publication." America is shamed in that
    the great patriot's works have not yet been published in a
    full collection, for his life was filled with deeds of true
    significance. He overcame the disadvantages of being born
    in a provincial city and, indeed, profited from having to
    educate himself by becoming more original than if he had
    received a traditional education. Yet one must realize
    that Franklin, for all his abilities, was not a scholar,
    nor did he ever pretend that he was. His philosophical and
    scientific conclusions are often hasty, and his pre-
    Revolution political writings, once quite valuable, have
    no continuing interest. Unfortunately, even in some of his
    best writings there is "a good deal of vulgarity," and his
    pleasant wit is often mere childishness. In sum, Franklin

1806

had "a sound and well directed understanding" and accomplished much through his labors and native talents.

7   DENNIE, JOSEPH [Oliver Oldschool]. "Plagiarism of
    Dr. Franklin." Port Folio, 1st ser. 2, no. 28
    (19 July):29-30.
        Suggests strongly that Franklin plagiarized his
    "Parable Against Persecution."

8   EBORACENSIS, pseud. "Miscellany." Port Folio, n.s. 2,
    no. 27 (12 July):29-30.
        Franklin improved but nonetheless plagiarized his
    "Parable Against Persecution" from "G. Gentius's dedication of a book entitled Isribu Judae Salomonis, &c. and
    printed in 1688."

9   [JEFFREY, FRANCIS.] [Review of the 1806 edition of Franklin's
    Works and Memoirs.] Edinburgh Review 8, no. 16 (July):
    327-44.
        In general a very intelligent and perceptive commentary
    on Franklin's strengths and weaknesses and their relationship to the American environment in which he grew. Points
    out that while the colonial landscape offered opportunities
    for nonprofessionals to become splended amateurs free of
    academic restraints, it nevertheless created a restlessness
    that was at odds with laborious scholarly method; thus,
    when Franklin deals on the levels of common sense, experiments, and insight, he does brilliantly, but in finding it
    necessary to master vast amounts of material (when it was
    available to him), he lacks the steady purpose and desire
    for such work and, settling for incompleteness, moves on
    to something else interesting. When writing about what he
    observes, about human nature in particular, he excels.

1807

1   ANON. "Franklin." In Historic Gallery of Portraits and
    Paintings. London: Vernor, Hood & Sharpe, pp. 105-8.
        A sketch of Franklin as the wise, public-spirited citizen of the world.

2   ANON. "Life of Dr. Franklin--With a Portrait." Britannic
    Magazine 12, no. 182:433-40.
        "In whatever other virtues Franklin might be defective,"
    and the author clearly has in mind spiritual and moral virtues, "he retained in a high degree, those of industry and
    temperance, which were eventually the means of securing his

morals, as well as of raising his fortune." While still a young man, Franklin turned to developing himself as a philosopher and politician, and his rise in these areas was aided significantly by his ability to write. Also very useful to his advancement was his important scientific work, for it increased even further the regard in which he was held by his fellow citizens. In judging his whole life, it may be said that Franklin was unsurpassed "in that solid practical wisdom, which consists in pursuing valuable ends by the most appropriate means," by good judgment and by benevolence.

<u>1809</u>

1 ALLEN, WILLIAM. "Franklin (B.[,] LL.D.)." In <u>An American Biographical and Historical Dictionary, Containing an Account of the Lives, Character and Writings of the Most Eminent Persons in North America From Its First Discovery to the Present Time, and a Summary of the History of the Several Colonies.</u> Cambridge, Mass.: Hillard & Metcalf, Printers, pp. 293-99.
    A brief biography of Franklin's life that calls attention to his achievements and accepts his deism.

2 ANON. "Doktor Benjamin Franklins Lefverne." In <u>Valda stycken. . . .</u> [Doctor Benjamin Franklin's life. Selected pieces.] Edited by J[ohan Fredrik] Bagge. Orebro: pp. 278-302.
    A sketch of Franklin's life that focuses attention on his political activities.

3 [GREEN, JACOB.] "The Franklinian Theory of Electricity." In <u>An Epitome of Electricity and Galvanism.</u> Philadelphia: Jane Aitken, pp. 116-23.
    Describes Franklin's theory and quotes extensively from his account of his investigations.

4 _____. "The Identity of Electricity With Lightning." In <u>An Epitome of Electricity and Galvanism.</u> Philadelphia: Jane Aitken, pp. 40-41.
    Tells the story of Franklin's kite experiment which proved lightning and electricity are the same.

181-

1   HULBERT, C[HARLES].   The Life of Doctor Franklin, and the Way
    to Wealth, to Which is Added a Collection of Sacred Poems.
    Shrewsbury, Eng.:   C. Hulbert, pp. [3]-10.
        A sketch of Franklin's career, highlighting his patience
    and industry, which helped him succeed in life. (This work
    is far more readily available in Hulbert's Biographical
    Sketches of Dr. Benjamin Franklin, General Washington, and
    Thomas Paine; With an Essay on Atheism and Infidelity
    (London: G. & W.B. Whittaker, for C. Hulbert, 1820),
    pp. 1-7. The problem with the later edition is that the
    pagination is inaccurate. Actually the life of Franklin
    is irregularly paginated A-6.)

1810

1   ANON. "Anecdote of Dr. Franklin." Weekly Visitor 2, no. 7
    (22 December):109.
        Having learned that he could sleep on the floor and live
    well enough on bread and water, the young Franklin deter-
    mined in 1728 that he would never use the Pennsylvania
    Gazette, over which he had recently assumed control, to
    publish "scurrilous and defamatory" pieces.

2   CHAUDON, LOUIS MAYEUL. "Franklin." In Dictionnaire universel,
    historique, critique et bibliographique. 9th rev. ed.
    Vol. 7. Paris: [Mame frères], pp. [157]-61.
        Sketch of Franklin's life which notes a number of his
    accomplishments. (Apparently the first publication of the
    piece on Franklin. NUC.)

3   [GALIGNANI, GIOVANNI ANTONIO.] "Dr. Franklin." In A Collec-
    tion of Historical and Literary Anecdotes, Memoirs, Polit-
    ical Fragments, Bon-Mots, etc. 2d ed. Paris: Galignani,
    pp. 124-26.
        Anecdote telling of how a weary and frustrated Franklin
    rid himself of persistent questioners at public inns by
    gathering them together, providing basic information about
    himself and then asking not to be disturbed further. (I
    found no earlier edition.)

4   ROGGE, C[HRISTIAN]. Het leven van Benjamin Franklin. . . .
    [The life of Benjamin Franklin]. Leyden: D. Du Mortier en
    zoon, 192 pp.
        Mostly on Franklin's early years, showing that his well
    publicized virtues of diligence, thrift, and other Poor

1813

Richard qualities were not only instrumental in his success but in his greatness.

5   THOMAS, ISAIAH. "Benjamin Franklin." In History of Printing in America. With a Biography of Printers, and an Account of Newspapers. To Which Is Prefixed a Concise View of the Discovery and Progress of the Art in Other Parts of the World. Vol. 1. Worcester, Mass.: Isaiah Thomas, Jr., pp. 312-20.
     Franklin becomes apprentice to his brother, is unhappy and eventually makes his way to Keimer's shop in Philadelphia.

6   ____. "Benjamin Franklin." In History of Printing in America. With a Biography of Printers, and an Account of Newspapers. To Which Is Prefixed a Concise View of the Discovery and Progress of the Art in Other Parts of the World. Vol. 2. Worcester, Mass.: Isaiah Thomas, Jr., pp. 39-45.
     Tells the story of how Franklin and Meredith became partners. Later, both realized that the partnership was a mistake, at which time Meredith sold out his share of the business to Franklin, who ran it alone until he took in David Hall as a partner in 1748.

1812

1   GERBER, ERNST LUDWIG. "Franklin (Benjamin)." In Neues historisch-biographisches Lexikon der Tonkünstler welches Nachrichten von dem Leben und Werken musikalischer Schriftsteller berühmter Komponisten Sänger. Vol. 2. Leipzig: A. Kühnel, pp. 185-86.
     Discusses the armonica, Franklin's interest in music generally, and the lightning rod.

2   THOMPSON, THOMAS. "Franklin." In History of the Royal Society From Its Institution to the End of the Eighteenth Century. London: printed for R. Baldwin, pp. 435-41.
     Describes Franklin's various scientific discoveries and says that his greatest one is the famous identification of lightning with electricity.

1813

1   De LÉVIS, [François-Gaston]. "Franklin." In Souvenirs et portraits, 1780-1789. Paris: François Buisson, pp. 51-52.
     An uncritical tribute to Franklin.

1813

2   ROGERS, THOMAS J. "Franklin." In A New American Biographical
    Dictionary; or Remembrancer of the Departed Heroes & States-
    men of America. Confined Exclusively to Those Who Have
    Signalized Themselves in Either Capacity, in the Revolu-
    tionary War Which Obtained the Independence of Their Country.
    Easton, Pa.: T.J. Rogers, pp. 112-22.
        Summarizes Franklin's career and says that all his
    "meditations and his labours" were "directed to public
    utility," though he did not sacrifice personal friendships.

3   WOODS, SAM[UEL]. "Essay on the Franklinian Theory of Elec-
    tricity." Philosophical Magazine, 1st ser. 17:97-113.
        Woods discusses the "advantages and defects of the
    Franklinian theory" in an objective essay.

                              1814

1   DONOVAN, M[ICHAEL]. "Reflection on the Inadequcy of the
    Principal Hypotheses to Account for the Phoenomena of
    Electricity." Philosophical Magazine and Journal: Com-
    prehending the Various Branches of Science, the Liberal
    and Fine Arts, Geology, Agriculture, Manufactures and
    Commerce 44, no. 199 (November):334-50.
        Argues against the hypothesis of electricity put forward
    by Franklin and upheld by his followers. The article con-
    tinues on pp. 401-8, but these pages deal essentially with
    scientists other than Franklin.

2   MILLS, ALFRED. "Dr. Franklin." In Biography of Eminent Per-
    sons, Alphabetically Arranged. London: printed for Darton,
    Harvey & Darton, pp. 33-34.
        Franklin was a self-made man.

                              1815

1   Un AMERICAIN, pseud. "Vie de Franklin." In Frankliniana, ou
    recueil d'anecdotes, bons mots, reflexions, maximes et
    observations de Benjamin Franklin. . . . Paris: Tiger,
    pp. [5]-14.
        Another of the idealized French treatments of Franklin's
    life and character. Franklin is depicted as being almost
    instinctively humanitarian and selfless.

2   ANON. [Anecdote about Franklin.] In The Rational Humorist;
    Being a Choice Collection of Bon Mots & Pleasing Witticisms,
    the Whole Purged From Every Thing Obscene or Indelicate and

Forming a Choice Repository of Chaste Wit and Rational
Humor. Beverley, Eng.: printed by M. Turner, for
Baldwin & Co., p. 15.
 Franklin is saved from a fight because he is wearing
his glasses.

3   ANON. The Celebrated Dr. Benjamin Franklin Was Born Jan. 17,
 1706. N.p. FCL.
 Sketch of Franklin's career.

4   ARICI, CESARE. "Vita di Benjamino Franklin." In Vite e
 ritratti di cento uomini illustri. Padua: Bettoni,
 unpaginated.
 A brief study of Franklin's career in which he is praised
as a wise, benevolent, and enlightened patriot who liber-
ated his countrymen from English oppression. Arici sees
Franklin's simple and modest manner as a true expression
of the man.

5   [DELAPLAINE, JOSEPH.] "Life of Benjamin Franklin." In
 Delaplaine's Repository of the Lives and Portraits of
 Distinguished Americans. Vol. 2. Philadelphia:
 [privately printed], pp. [41]-124.
 A rather idealized account of Franklin, concentrating
on his political career but also showing that in his democratic sentiments, benevolence, and diversity, he was the
"model of an American citizen,--which, indeed, may be said
to include the general archetype."

6   HOWLDY, THOMAS. "On the Franklinian Theory of the Leyden Jar;
 With Remarks on Mr. Donovan's Experiments." Philosophical
 Magazine and Journal: Comprehending the Various Branches
 of Science, the Liberal and Fine Arts, Geology, Agriculture,
 Manufactures and Commerce 46, no. 212 (December):401-8.
 Donovan (see 1814.1) had tried to refute the Franklinian
theory. Howldy defends Franklin's theory of positive and
negative charges and calls Donovan's experiments deficient
and fallacious.

7   REDDINGIUS, W[IBRANDUS] G[ERARD]. Het Leven van Benjamin
 Franklin een Leesboek voor Kinderen. . . . [The life of
 Benjamin Franklin in a reader for children.] Groningen:
 W. Zuidema, 77 pp.
 Deals almost entirely with Franklin's youth and young
manhood. Somewhat sanitized, he is made to represent the
prudential virtues he popularized as Poor Richard. These
are the qualities Reddingius encourages the young to adopt.
(According to Paul L. Ford's Franklin Bibliography, there
was an 1807 edition.)

1815

8   SANTON, J. Denkwürdiges Gesprach zwischen Franklin und
     Washington. Leipzig: J.G. Neubert, 47 pp.
          Franklin and Washington discuss the problems and foibles
     that make men and nations unhappy and the way to achieve
     happiness for peoples and states. The conversation is un-
     derstandably directed at European audiences, as the two
     Americans converse about money and culture as means to
     fulfillment.

1816

1   BIOT, JEAN BAPTISTE. "Franklin." In Biographie universelle
     (Michaud) ancienne et moderne. New ed. Vol. 15. Paris:
     [G. Michaud], pp. 512-29.
          Biographical sketch of Franklin's life emphasizing his
     calm, philosophical temperament that enabled him to rise
     above serious difficulties and frustrations. His love of
     mankind and his achievements make the extraordinary compli-
     ment paid him by Turgot fully deserved.

1817

1   ANON. "Life and Writings of Dr. Franklin." Analectic Maga-
     zine 9 (May):[353]-94.
          In addition to providing a review of the William Temple
     Franklin editions of Franklin's Works and Private Correspon-
     dence and a new edition of Weems's Life of Franklin, the
     critic surveys Franklin's life and career and finds him
     far superior to his editor and biographer. Yet it is cer-
     tainly true that the philosopher's astonishing versatility
     creates many problems for an editor.

*2   ANON. Merkwürdige Gesprache zwischen Franklin und Washington.
     Konigsberg.
          Source: Beatrice M. Victory, Benjamin Franklin and
     Germany, Americana Germanica, no. 21, ed. Marion Dexter
     Learned (Philadelphia: University of Pennsylvania Press,
     1915). This may be the same as J. Santon's Denkwürdiges
     Gesprach. . . . See 1815.8.

3   DENNIE, JOSEPH [Oliver Oldschool]. "Dr. Franklin." Port Folio,
     4th ser. [sic 5th ser.] 4, no. 6 (December):504.
          Lord Chatham defended Franklin from an attack by a member
     of the House of Lords in 1775.

4   DEWAILLEY, M. [Poem on the invention of the lightning con-
    ductor by Franklin.] In Barberri Hermes romanus; ou,
    Mercure latin. Edited by Joseph Nicholas Barbier-Vémars.
    2d ed. Vol. 1. Paris: Hermes, pp. 10-12.
        Franklin is praised for his invention of the lightning
    rod, which is both a theoretical and practical achievement
    of genius. (Originally published as a monthly periodical,
    according to the National Union Catalog Pre-1956 Imprints,
    Vol. 34, p. 670. I have been unable, however, to locate
    any earlier edition or printing.)

5   [JEFFREY, FRANCIS.] [Review of The Private Correspondence of
    Benjamin Franklin.] Edinburgh Review 28, no. 56 (August):
    [275]-302.
        An intelligent and sensitive commentary on Franklin's
    character, changing politics, religious and social "senti-
    ments," and on his style. Excerpts from Franklin's letters
    are used to illustrate his wisdom, compassion, and
    forcefulness.

1818

1   ANON. [On Franklin.] In Time's Telescope for 1818; or, a
    Complete Guide to the Almanack: Containing an Explanation
    of Saints' Days and Holidays. . . . London: printed for
    Sherwood, Neely, & Jones, pp. 79-80.
        Franklin is unsurpassed in "practical wisdom."

2   ANON. Review of "Memoirs of the Life and Writings of Benjamin
    Franklin, &c. Written by Himself to a Late Period, and
    Continued to His Death by His Grandson, William Temple
    Franklin. Now First Published from the Original MSS.
    Quarto. London, 1818." Analectic Magazine 11 (June):
    [449]-84.
        In addition to being a full review, this piece is also
    an extensive commentary on Franklin's virtues of mind and
    character. It particularly pays tribute to him for his
    tireless opposition to "oppression and tyranny, in whatever
    guise." The reviewer also castigates William Temple
    Franklin for delaying publication of his grandfather's
    papers.

3   ANON. [Review of the William Temple Franklin edition of the
    Memoirs of the Life and Writings of Benjamin Franklin. . . .]
    North American Review 7, no. 3 (September):[289]-323.
        Less of a review than an attack on Franklin for his
    deficiency of religious sentiment and, especially in his

1818

youth, his lack of morals. The reviewer also asserts that
Franklin's Autobiography is overrated as literature and is
anything but the guide for the young it is often claimed to
be. At his best, Franklin is generally little more than a
shrewd, energetic, and talented man. Too often, he is
merely cunning. In England, though in the midst of major
political events and turmoil, he always kept his own interest in view. He was most honorable in France, but here too
he is found lacking by the reviewer, who charges that
Franklin was too pro-French and had to be brought around
to the more reasonable and nationalist position of the other
Commissioners. In sum, then, Franklin was a man of energy,
talent, and "sharp-sightedness"; however, his "defects" of
character and sensibility are very considerable. America
needs men of literature and science who can achieve more
than Franklin and who are not tainted by serious faults.

4   BLOOMFIELD, OBADIAH BENJAMIN FRANKLIN, pseud. Life and Adven-
    tures of Obadiah Benjamin Franklin Bloomfield, M.D.   A
    Native of the United States of America, Now on Tour of
    Europe.   Interspersed With Episodes, and Remarks, Religious,
    Moral, Public Spirited, and Humorous.   Philadelphia: pub-
    lished for the proprietor, 210 pp.
        A parody on the moralisms of Poor Richard and on the
    success story in the Autobiography; other works of Franklin's
    are also spoofed.

5   [BROUGHAM, HENRY PETER.]   "Franklin's Correspondence."
    Edinburgh Review 28, no. 56 (August):[275]-302.
        In addition to reviewing the William Temple Franklin
    edition of his grandfather's works, the critic praises
    Franklin as one of those rare men who combine the virtues
    of the diplomat and the philosopher, since his chief dis-
    tinguishing quality is sagacity.

6   EITH, GABRIEL.   Seelengrösse in Gemälden aus der Geschichte.
    2 vols. Augsburg: Jenisch & Stagesche Buchhandlung,
    2:249-66.
        As a politician and diplomat Franklin typically worked
    for the good of his fellow Americans.

7   [FOSTER, J.]   "Franklin's Correspondence."   Eclectic Review
    27, 2d ser. 9 (May):433-50.
        In addition to reviewing the second edition of William
    Temple Franklin's The Private Correspondence of Benjamin
    Franklin, LL.D., the critic asserts that Franklin was supe-
    rior to his colleagues and rivals in diplomacy and other
    fields, that he was the completely honest politician and,

1818

contrary to charges made in some quarters, perfectly independent of French or other improper influence in making
judgments about the well being of his country.

8   FRANKLIN, WILLIAM TEMPLE. Memoirs of the Life and Writings of
     Benjamin Franklin, L.L.D. F. R. S. &c. Minister Plenipoten-
     tiary From the United States of America at the Court of
     France, and for the Treaty of Peace and Independence With
     Great Britain, &c. &c. Written by Himself to a Late Period,
     and Continued to the Time of His Death by His Grandson,
     William Temple Franklin. . . . 3d ed. London: printed
     for Henry Colburn, 1:259-541, 2:[2]-244.
        Temple Franklin's continuation of his grandfather's life
     is generally more thorough and objective than other early
     biographies. Nevertheless, it is clear Temple Franklin
     intends to show that Franklin was no radical or visionary
     and cannot be held responsible in any way for the revolu-
     tionary fervor and schemes undertaken by men who invoke his
     name. Franklin emerges here as a moderate, philosophic man
     whose plans and efforts were always carefully considered and
     directed toward the public good. (The first edition of
     Temple Franklin's three-volume edition of his grandfather's
     Life and Writings was also published in 1818.)

9   von KLEIN, ANTON. "Empfindungen des Doctor Franklin bei einem
     Blicke in die Natur." In Litterärisches Leben des
     königlich-baierischen geheimen Rathes und Ritters Anton
     von Klein, mit Rückblicken auf die schönste und wichtigste
     Epoche der deutschen, besonders der pfälzischen Litteratur.
     Wiesbaden: Ludwig Schellinberg, pp. 39-49.
        Poetic tribute to Franklin as a scientist for his pro-
     found understanding and appreciation of nature. He not
     only can control the elements, but he works in harmony
     with them. (This piece is especially difficult to find.
     There was one copy in the United States, at Case Western
     Reserve University, but it is missing. The copy which I
     had duplicated came from the Stadtbibliothek Trier.)

10   WEEMS, MASON LOCKE. Life of Benjamin Franklin. With Many
     Choice Anecdotes and Admirable Sayings of This Great Man,
     Never Before Published by Any of His Biographers. 3d ed.
     Hagerstown, Md.: printed for the author, 337 pp.
        Weems did for Franklin what he did for Washington.
     Franklin is idealized, sanitized, and Christianized and is
     the embodiment of all the Poor Richard virtues. (This edi-
     tion, though little more than a paraphrase of the Autobiog-
     raphy, is Weems's creation. The earlier editions of 1815
     and 1817, on the other hand, are almost entirely by

1818

Franklin and so he rather than Weems must be considered the author of these editions. See NUC, Paul Leicester Ford's Franklin Bibliography (1889.11), and especially Ford's bibliography entitled Mason Locke Weems, His Works and Ways, edited by Emily Ellsworth Ford Skeel, Vol. 1 (New York, 1929), pp. 128-34).

1819

1 DENNIE, JOSEPH [Oliver Oldschool]. "Franklin's Correspondence." Port Folio, 4th ser. [sic 5th ser.] 8, no. 4 (October):313-29.
    In the course of reviewing William Temple Franklin's edition of Franklin's writings, Dennie actually writes an essay on his subject. While Franklin had many virtues, especially wisdom, zeal, and sincerity, he was nevertheless blindly pro-French and sorely deficient in religious principles. With respect to the first fault, his gratitude to the French for their help during the Revolution, while natural and appropriate, should not have caused him to overlook the despotism of the French monarchy. As for his deism, Franklin adopted it because he did not care to inquire into the truth of Christianity, saving his intellectual energy for science.

2 [MACKENZIE, ENEAS.] "Life of Benjamin Franklin." In Select Biography; Containing Instructive and Entertaining Accounts of the Lives, Characters, and Actions of the Most Eminent Persons of All Ages and All Countries. Vol. 2. Newcastle upon Tyne: Mackenzie & Dent, pp. 376-438.
    Much of this biography of Franklin paraphrases the Autobiography; however Mackenzie does assert, interestingly, that Franklin was too large to give himself totally even to the Revolution.

3 NICHOLSON, WILLIAM. "Franklin (Dr. Benjamin)." In British Encyclopedia, or Dictionary of Arts and Sciences, Comprising an Accurate and Popular View of the Present Improved State of Human Knowledge. American ed. Vol. 2. Philadelphia: Mitchell, Ames, & White, unpaginated.
    Subjects are arranged alphabetically. Focus is on Franklin's achievements in electricity and diplomacy.

4 SHARP, JOSHUA. "The Franklin Fund." In Wood's Almanac for the Year 1820. . . . New York: Samuel Wood & Sons, p. 26.
    Reports on the status of the Fund, which is another manifestation of Franklin's goodness.

1820

1 DENNIE, JOSEPH [Oliver Oldschool]. "Anecdotes." Port Folio
   [5th ser.] 10, no. 1 (September):249-50.
   Reports the assertion of Jonathan Boucher that Franklin
   was a plagiarist in his Parable Against Persecution.

2 HOSACK, DAVID. A Biographical Memoir of Hugh Williamson. . . .
   Delivered on the First of November, 1819, at the Request of
   the New-York Historical Society. New York: printed by
   C.S. Winkle, pp. 39-51.
   Recounts Franklin's role in the Hutchinson-Oliver letters.

3 HULBERT, C[HARLES]. "Bible. Doctor Franklin." In Literary
   Beauties and Varieties; or, Interesting Selections, and
   Original Pieces, in Prose and Verse. . . . Shrewsbury,
   Eng.: printed by C. Hulbert, and published for him, by
   G. & W.B. Whittaker, pp. 237-38.
   The dying Franklin advocates devotion to the Bible.

4 _____. "Riches. Doctor Franklin." In Literary Beauties and
   Varieties; or, Interesting Selections, and Original Pieces,
   in Prose and Verse. . . . Shrewsbury, Eng.: printed by
   C. Hulbert, and published for him, by G. & W.B. Whittaker,
   p. 263.
   Franklin points out that one never needs more riches
   than he can enjoy and is foolish for desiring more.

5 VAN MARUM. "On the Theory of Franklin, According to Which
   Electrical Phenomena Are Explained by a Single Fluid."
   Annals of Philosophy 16 (December):440-53.
   Supports Franklin's theory.

6 WILKES, JOHN, comp. "Franklin (Benjamin)." In Encyclopaedia
   Londinensis; or, Universal Dictionary of Arts, Sciences,
   and Literature: Comprehending, Under One General Alpha-
   betical Arrangement, All the Words and Substance of Every
   Kind of Dictionary Extant in the English Language. Vol. 8.
   London: printed for the proprietor by J. Adlard, pp. 10-14.
   Biographical account of Franklin which, pointing out
   many of his accomplishments, says that he epitomizes "practical wisdom, which consists in pursuing valuable ends by
   the most appropriate means." If he desired, as he did, to
   promote his own interests, he always had in view the public
   welfare as well. (Some of this piece is the same as the
   "Life of Dr. Franklin," 1807.2. See, for example, the con-
   cluding paragraph.)

1821

1   ANON. "Dialogue on the Principles of Representative Govern-
    ment Between the President de Montesquieu and Dr. Franklin."
    North American Review 12, no. 31 (April):346-65.
        Franklin convinces Montesquieu that the American form of
    government is superior to that of England because it is a
    democratic republic rather than an aristocratic republic,
    and therefore property is rather equally divided among the
    people.

*2 ANON. "Notizie sulla vita di Beniamino Franklin." In Vite e
    ritratti di uomini celebri di tutti i tempi e di tutte le
    nazioni. Vol. 2. Milan: Bettoni, unpaginated.
        Source: Pace. Biographical sketch noting that Franklin
    was admired in Europe as well as in America. The sketch is
    arranged by alphabetical topics according to important
    events in Franklin's life. (Pace, p. 292, suggests that
    Bettoni may have written this piece.)

3   [DUFRICHE-]DESGENETTES, R[ENÉ NICOLAS]. Franklin. . . .
    [Paris]: C.-L.-F. Panckoucke, 7 pp.
        An extract of seven pages from Biographie médicale in
    which the author recounts Franklin's career.

*4 MORELLET, ANDRÉ. "Francklin." In Mémoires inédits de l'abbé
    Morellet, de l'académie française, sur le dix-huitième
    siècle et sur la révolution; précédés de l'eloge de l'abbé
    Morellet, par M. Lémontey, membre de l'institut, académie
    française. 2 vols. Paris: A la librairie française de
    Ladvocat.
        Source: NUC. See 1822.6.

1822

1   ANON. "Dr. Franklin." In The Percy Anecdotes. Original and
    Select. Vol. 3. London: George Berger, p. 67.
        "Almost all the distinguishing features of Franklin's
    character may be traced to his childhood." He was always
    industrious, diligent, economical, "shrewd and artful."

2   ANON. "Franklin." In The Percy Anecdotes. Original and
    Select. Vol. 10. London: George Berger, p. 164.
        Amusing anecdote which contrasts the foolish assertive-
    ness of a naval captain with Franklin's wisdom and modesty.
    Franklin is a passenger on a ship and is involved in a dis-
    cussion with the captain on the effects of pouring oil on

water. The captain does not recognize his illustrious pas-
senger, but thinks he does understand Franklin's theory.
He therefore cites that theory to prove the philosopher
wrong.

3 ANON. "Franklin." In The Percy Anecdotes. Original and
   Select. Vol. 18. London: George Berger, pp. 48-49.
   Franklin's industry helped him gain a solid reputation
   when he started his printing business in Philadelphia.

4 ANON. "Franklin--Electricity." In The Percy Anecdotes.
   Original and Select. Vol. 6. London: George Berger,
   pp. 141-43.
   Franklin's identification of lightning with electricity
   "is one of the few capital discoveries in science, for
   which we are not at all indebted to chance, but to one of
   those bold and happy sketches of thought, which distinguish
   minds of a superior order." Having made this point, the
   author proceeds to recount Franklin's kite experiment.

5 ARNAULT, A[NTOINE] V[INCENT], et al. "Franklin (Benjamin)."
   In Biographie nouvelle des contemporains, ou dictionnaire
   historique et raisonné de tous les hommes qui, depuis la
   révolution française, ont acquis de la célébrité par leurs
   actions, leurs écrits, leurs erreurs ou leurs crimes, soit
   en france, soit dans les pays étrangers. . . . Vol. 7.
   Paris: Librairie historique, pp. 310-16.
   Much acclaim for Franklin the man, writer, philosopher,
   patriotic leader, and diplomat. Typically, there is also
   praise for France, which loved Franklin and the country he
   so effectively represented.

6 MORELETT, ANDRÉ. "Francklin." In Mémoires inédits de l'abbé
   Morellet, de l'académie française, sur le dix-huitième
   siècle et sur la révolution; précedés de l'eloge de l'abbé
   Morellet, par M. Lémontey, membre de l'institut, académie
   francaise. 2 ed. Vol. 1. Paris: A la librairie de
   Ladvocat, pp. 295-321.
   Relying a good deal on primary material Morellet provides
   evidence to show that Franklin was widely loved in France.
   See 1821.4.

7 PERCY, SHOLTO, and PERCY, RICHARD. "Franklin." In Percy
   Anecdotes. Original and Select. Vol. 10. London:
   George Berger, pp. 92-93.
   A Quaker lawyer complains that uninvited guests drink
   freely at the beer barrel in his backyard and asks Franklin
   how to protect the beer. Franklin replies that the lawyer

1822

should place "a barrel of old Madeira" next to the beer.
The people will then gladly drink the Madeira and leave
the beer for the lawyer.

8   SANDERSON, JOHN.   "Franklin."   In Biography of the Signers of
     of the Declaration of Independence.   Vol. 2.   Philadelphia:
     published by Joseph M. Sanderson for the proprietor, pp.
     [3]-153.
        This life presents an improved Franklin for general
     readers.   While Sanderson deals candidly, if at times
     erroneously with Franklin's youth, he does point out
     Franklin's troubles with the Massachusetts Establishment.
     He says, however, that Franklin's early journalistic "levity"
     and lapse into deism in America and England were the result
     of his youthful ambition to gain a literary reputation, and
     that he outgrew both.   Due notice is paid to Franklin's many
     accomplishments, but it is as a character worthy of emula-
     tion that he is primarily treated.   Franklin's great natural
     abilities and his keen sense of virtue did not permit him to
     lower himself as so many political persons do in times of
     crisis.

                            1823

1   ANON.   [Life of Benjamin Franklin: letters of Poor Richard],
        pp. 7-33.   American Philosophical Society, no. Na814 F 85e.
           Basically a paraphrase in Greek of the early parts of
        the Autobiography.

2   ANON.   "Selection on Electricity."   Monitor 1, no. 9
        (September):307-10.
           Franklin "gave a form and dignity to the science of
        electricity" by virtue of the significance of his discov-
        eries.   Discusses the kite experiment in particular and
        points out that when Professor Richman of St. Petersburg
        tried the same experiment, he was electrocuted.

*3   BARBIERI, GIUSEPPE.   Poemetti descrittivi e didascalici.
        Florence: Chiazi, pp. 145-47.
           Source: Pace, pp. 246, 351n43.   In part of this poem
        Franklin is praised for his achievements in electricity.

4   DENNIE, JOSEPH [Oliver Oldschool].   "Memoirs of Benjamin
        Franklin."   Port Folio, 5th ser. 16, no. 260 (December):
        [441]-55.
           Narration of familiar events in Franklin's life followed
        by praise.

1824

*5   FANTONI, GIOVANNI. "Per il ritorno di Beniamino Franklin a
      Filadelfia dopo la pace del 1783." In Opere di Giovanni
      Fantoni, fra gli Arcadi Labindo. [2d ed.] 3 vols. Lugano.
         Franklin is acclaimed as a scientist and as a benefactor
      to mankind. (This piece has an interesting but complex his-
      tory. It was originally a tribute to the British naval
      figure, Admiral Rodney, and appeared as such through the
      eighteenth century. The poem as a tribute to Franklin
      first appears in the 1823 edition, which was published by
      the poet's nephew, and the dates of composition are given
      at the end of the poem as 1783-1803. See Charles R.D.
      Miller, "American Notes in the Odes of Labindo," Romanic
      Review, 21, no. 3 (July-September 1930):204-5.)

6   TUDOR, WILLIAM. "Dr. Franklin Chosen Agent--Remarks on Certain
      Points of His Character." In The Life of James Otis of
      Massachusetts: Containing Also, Notices of Some Contempo-
      rary Characters and Events From the Year 1760 to 1775.
      Boston: Wells & Lilly, pp. 386-405.
         Although Franklin was appointed agent for Massachusetts
      in England, he did not have the complete trust of all im-
      portant parties, and so Arthur Lee was appointed joint
      agent. There were three reasons for the mistrust of
      Franklin: his deism, his moderate politics, and his repu-
      tation for "worldly shrewdness and thrift." While he was
      a faithful agent, he never gained the full confidence of
      Massachusetts and, in fact, upset many when he seemed will-
      ing to give in to "the insidious designs of the French cabi-
      net" by allowing it to deprive Massachusetts of fisheries
      and thus of maritime strength. Yet he was a true humani-
      tarian and philanthropist.

1824

1   ANON. "Benjamin Franklin." In Practical Wisdom; or the Manual
      of Life. The Counsels of Eminent Men to Their Children.
      Comprising Those of Sir Walter Raleigh, Lord Burleigh, Sir
      Henry Sidney, Earl of Strafford, Francis Osborn, Sir Matthew
      Hale, Earl of Bedford, William Penn, and Benjamin Franklin.
      With Lives of the Authors. London: printed for Henry
      Colburn & Co., pp. [290]-98.
         Franklin's natural abilities and great diligence, pru-
      dence, and integrity enabled him to succeed in life on his
      own and become the chief philosopher and legislator of his
      time.

1824

2 ANON. Brief Memoir of the Life of Dr. Benjamin Franklin, With
 an Appendix. Compiled for the Use of Young Persons. New
 York: Mahlon Day, 90 pp.
 The memoir is followed by "The Way to Wealth" and other
 material thought appropriate and useful to children who want
 to get ahead in the world. Franklin's life, they are told,
 is an illustration of diligence in one's calling and a clear
 indication of how valuable are prudence, honesty, and industry. The author, however, also portrays Franklin as being
 liberal, charitable, and courageous.

3 COURIER de MÉRÉ, PAUL-LOUIS. Pamphlet des pamphlets. Paris:
 Chez les Marchands de nouveautés, pp. 20-25.
 Writing was very important to the heroic Franklin, one
 of mankind's liberators. Among his most important writings
 are those common sensical pieces designed to inculcate
 virtue.

1825

*1 ANON. "Close Chamber and Vase Stoves." In The Theory and
 Practice of Warming and Ventilating Public Buildings,
 Dwelling-Houses and Conservatories. Including a General
 View of the Changes Produced in Atmospheric Air, by Respira-
 tion, Combustion, and Putrefaction, With the Means of Obviat-
 ing Its Deleterious Agency; and a Description of all the
 Known Varieties of Stoves, Grates, and Furnaces; With an
 Examination of Their Comparative Advantages for Economising
 Fuel and Preventing Smoke. London: printed for T. & G.
 Underwood.
 Source: NUC. See 1829.1.

2 ANON. "Dr. Benjamin Franklin." Museum of Foreign Literature
 and Science 6, no. 34 [April]:359-66.
 Franklin was a great and good man and a significant
 moralist and writer; however, he was not a man of genius
 or "brilliancy," his chief asset being his "good sense--
 only plain, good sense--nothing more."

3 CABANIS, [PIERRE] J[EA]N G[EORGE]S. "Notice sur Benjamin
 Franklin." In Oeuvres posthumes de Cabanis. [Paris]:
 Firman Didot, pp. [219]-74.
 Biography that praises Franklin generally but focuses on
 his accomplishments as a scientist and diplomat.

4 [CAREY, GEORGE C.?] "Memoir of Doctor Franklin." Artisan; or
 Mechanic's Instructor. . . . 1 [January]:366-68, 378-80.

1826

A summary of Franklin's life followed by a commentary. As a philosopher, Franklin must be known for his common sense, clear vision and acuity rather than by any ability to penetrate the depths of philosophical speculation.

5   [FRENCH, BENJAMIN FRANKLIN.] "Franklin, Benjamin, LL. D. [,] F.R.S." In Biographia Americana; or, a Historical and Critical Account of the Lives, Actions, and Writings of the Most Distinguished Persons in North America, From the First Settlements to the Present Time. New York: D. Mallory, pp. 113-18.
    A survey of Franklin's career. French himself seems carefully to avoid praising Franklin.

1826

1   ANON. "Dr. Franklin and Thomas Paine." Religious Inquirer 9, no. 2 (19 August):157.
    Incorrectly asserts that Franklin's famous letter in which he argues that men would be even more "wicked" without religion than they were with it was written to Thomas Paine. The author declares that the letter, by which Franklin tried to persuade Paine to stop his plan to ridicule religion, indicates that Franklin was far more religious than Paine and thought him an infidel. (Both the date and recipient of Franklin's letter are matters of uncertainty. The bibliographical debate over the letter is summarized in the Yale-American Philosophical Society edition of The Papers of Benjamin Franklin, ed. Leonard W. Labaree et al. (New Haven: Yale University Press, 1963), 7, 293.)

2   BAILEY, WILLIAM. "Franklin Clubs." In Records of Patriotism and Love of Country. Washington: pp. 72-75.
    Franklin believed in organizations of good men who would give political direction to state affairs. Such clubs, Whig in nature and therefore inherently radical, have been established and are named after their spiritual founder.

3   [WOODS, LEONARD.] The Life of Benjamin Franklin, Including a Sketch of the Rise and Progress of the War of Independence, and of the Various Negotiations at Paris for Peace; With the History of His Political and Other Writings. London: printed for Hunt & Clarke, 407 pp.
    The author contends that it is time for a balanced account of Franklin's life and career. Enough time has passed since the Revolution and his death to make an

73

1826

objective narrative possible, and the significance of
Franklin's life makes one necessary. One must praise
those qualities in the poor, obscure but hardy, industrious,
frugal, and benevolent class of men that enable them to rise
in the world. The chief and most spectacular example of
these qualities and of such rise is Franklin. From being
"an oppressed apprentice" he rose to become one of the
greatest and best men of his time: a philosopher, scientist, philanthropist, and a patriot who was "one of the
most formidable opponents of British cabinet measures, and
of the whole strength of Britain wielded for indefensible
purposes." Franklin had the advantage of coming from good
stock, but it was by his own efforts that he succeeded.
"Let the humblest reader of these pages therefore enter
upon them with the assurance of their being calculated to
give hope to poverty; to brace the sinews of all industrious men with new energy. . . ." In presenting Franklin's
life, it becomes clear that its chief feature was his desire to be useful to his fellowmen. Whatever impeded the
public good or the opportunity for men to achieve self-
fulfillment, such as the base measures of petty Tory poli-
ticians, he opposed with all his great powers. In fact,
Franklin's patriotism was of a piece with his benevolence.
None of this is to say that he did not have faults. It must
be noted that he was rather deficient in "social sympathies,"
and at times he was too prudent about money matters. Also,
one feels uncomfortable by his advocacy of the shrewd manip-
ulation of other people, and many have criticized him for
his religious skepticism. A utilitarian, Franklin found
religious mysteries repugnant and concerned himself instead
with conduct. If this is a fault, it is, like his others,
minor when compared to his virtues. (This life is thought-
ful and quite interesting because of its essential identification of Franklin's character with the American character
and because of the author's attempt to import these qualities to England. The attribution to Woods is by Paul
Leicester Ford.)

1827

1   ANON. "Traek af Benjamin Franklins levnet og skrifter."
    [Selections from Benjamin Franklin's life and writings.]
    <u>Archiv fur histoire og geographie</u> (October):pp. 91-112.
        Sketch of Franklin's life and career, with excerpts from
    his writings illustrating his ideas, character, and
    achievements.

1828

*2 FRANZ, JOHANN FRIEDRICH. "Benjamin Franklin, geb. 1706 zu
    Boston. Erfinder der Gewitterableiter; starb 1790." In
    Neuer Jugendspiegel, oder Anecdoten und Characterzüge. . . .
    Darmstadt: Heyer. FCL.
    See 1830.6.

*3 _____. "Benjamin Franklin." In Neuer Jugendspiegel, oder
    Anecdoten und Characterzüge. . . . Darmstadt: Heyer. FCL.
    See 1830.7.

*4 _____. "Benjamin Franklin." In Neuer Jugendspiegel, oder
    Anecdoten und Characterzüge. . . . Darmstadt: Heyer. FCL.
    See 1830.8.

*5 _____. "Die Feife." In Neuer Jugendspiegel, oder Anecdoten
    und Characterzüge. . . . Darmstadt: Heyer. FCL.
    See 1830.9.

6   [JARRY de MANCY, ADRIEN.] "Franklin (Benjamin)." In
    Iconographie instructive. [Galerie historique, collection
    de portraits des personnages le plus célébres de l'histoire
    modern. . . .] Paris: Rignoux, unpaginated. American
    Philosophical Society, no. HM B F85x.h v. 1.
        A single sheet that lists important dates in Franklin's
    life, reprints his epitaph and provides very brief biblio-
    graphical information. (A note at the bottom of this sheet
    indicates that the piece was extracted from the Atlas
    historiques of Emmanuel Auguste Dieddonné Marius Joseph
    de Las Cases, who wrote under the pseudonym of A. Le Sage.
    The Atlas historiques was first published in Paris in 1804.)

7   MASON, HENRY. A Poem, Delivered at the Fifth Anniversary of
    the Franklin Debating Society, on the Birthday of Benjamin
    Franklin, January 17, 1827. [Boston: Isaac R. Butts & Co.]
        Because of his genius, Franklin rose from "poverty" and
    "obscurity" to international reputation and greatness.
    What is more, he remained free of any vice and became a
    great defender of liberty.

1828

1   ANON. "Benjamin Franklin." Hive 1, no. 10 (26 November):
    [37]-38; no. 11 (3 December):[41]-42; no. 12 (10 December):
    [47]-48; no. 13 (17 December):[49]-50.
        A brief account of Franklin's life.

1828

2   ANON. "Biographical Sketch of Benjamin Franklin." <u>Casket, or</u>
     <u>Flowers of Literature, Wit and Sentiment</u>, n.s. 37, no. 10
     (October):[433]-40.
          Presents an idealized Franklin who desired only to be a
     benefactor to mankind.

3   ANON. "Franklin." <u>Olive Branch</u> 1, no. 1 (26 April):407.
          Franklin was a living testimony to the value of
     industriousness.

4   BOSTON, TRUSTEES of the FRANKLIN FUND. <u>To the Trustees of the</u>
     <u>Franklin Donation Within the Town of Boston.</u> [Boston:
     published by the Trustees], 2 pp.
          The Trustees approved a loan of two hundred dollars from
     the fund to George W. Cram, a young artisan. It was to
     help such people get started in business that Franklin
     created the fund.

1829

1   ANON. "Close Chambers and Vase Stoves." In <u>Practical Observa-</u>
     <u>tions on Ventilating and Warming Public Edifices, Dwelling-</u>
     <u>Houses, Houses, Conservatories, &c. Containing a View of</u>
     <u>the Deleterious Effects of Vitiated Air and a Description</u>
     <u>of All the Varieties of Grates, Stoves, Furnaces, and Steam</u>
     <u>Apparatus. . . .</u> 2d ed. London: printed for Thomas &
     George Underwood, pp. [223]-31.
          Includes a discussion of the Pennsylvania stove. The
     author demeans Franklin's efforts in the field of heating,
     saying that the American does not in the least deserve the
     commendation he has received. Franklin, we are told, made
     no improvements on existing stoves, much less develop any-
     thing original. <u>See</u> 1825.1.

2   ANON. <u>Stories About Dr. Franklin, Designed for the Instruction</u>
     <u>and Amusement of Children.</u> Hartford: D.F. Robinson & Co.,
     70 pp.
          A nationalistic impulse informs this book. The author
     wants the children to know that America, contrary to the
     opinion of at least one French author, has produced great
     men and that Franklin must be numbered among them. Further-
     more, the author sees Franklin as an example for children
     to follow. His life proves that with sincere "exertion" a
     person can rise from poverty to fortune and a position of
     note in the world. The biographical account of Franklin
     contains appropriately moralizing comments on truth, dili-
     gence, sobriety, honesty, and public spirited enterprise.

The author also reprints the fiction that Franklin tricked his mother, who did not recognize him when he returned to Boston as an adult. The last forty or so years of Franklin's life are dealt with in only four of the sixty-nine pages.

3   [BESUCHET, JEAN CLAUDE.] "Franklin." In Précis historique de l'ordre de la Franc-Maçonnerie, depuis son introduction en France jusqu'en 1829, suivi d'une biographie des Membres de l'ordre . . . par J.L.B.   Vol. 2.   Paris: Rapilly, pp. 120-22.
    A brief account of Franklin as a Freemason.

4   GOODRICH, CHARLES A[UGUSTUS]. "Benjamin Franklin." In Lives of the Signers to the Declaration of Independence.   New York: William Reed & Co., pp. 261-82.
    Biography contains errors. Goodrich emphasizes Franklin's good humor, common sense, and decency.

*5   HOFFMAN, FRANÇOIS BENOÎT. "Memoires de Franklin." In Oeuvres. Vol. 3.   Paris: Lefebvre.
    See 1831.7.

6   QUÉARD, J[EAN] M[ARIE]. "Franklin (Benjamin)." In La france littéraire, ou dictionnaire bibliographique. . . . Vol. 3. Paris: Didot Frères, pp. 199-200.
    Bibliographical survey.

1   ANON. "Life of Benjamin Franklin." Chambers Information for the People, no. 23, pp. [177]-84.
    A survey of Franklin's life which says that his chief quality was the "worldly prudence" that is "founded on true wisdom."

2   DRAPER, BOURNE HALL. "Character of Franklin." In The Evergreen; or, a Selection of Religious and Perceptive Pieces in Prose; Being a Companion to the Evergreen in Verse. . . . London: Darton & Clark, pp. 5-13.
    Notes Franklin's widely recognized virtues, his useful life, and his benevolence. These qualities are a testimony to Franklin's position as a true friend to mankind.

<u>1830</u>

1   ANON. "Account of Franklin's Electrical Discoveries." In
<u>The Pursuit of Knowledge Under Difficulties</u>. The Library
of Entertaining Knowledge. London: Charles Knight,
pp. [244]-63.
A very general treatment of Franklin's theories on and
work in electricity.

2   ANON. "Early Life of Franklin" and "Life of Franklin Con-
tinued." In <u>Pursuit of Knowledge Under Difficulties</u>.
The Library of Entertaining Knowledge. London: Charles
Knight, pp. [217]-43.
Franklin's early years and his eventual achievements
show clearly the genuine value of self-education.

3   ANON. <u>Notice sur Benjamin Franklin</u>. N.p., Franklin Collection, Sterling Library, Yale University, no. F412.1.
Franklin was a great servant of humanity and deserved
the praise of Turgot.

4   [CRAIK, GEORGE LILLIE.] "Franklin." In <u>The Pursuit of</u>
<u>Knowledge Under Difficulties</u>. The Library of Entertaining
Knowledge. Vol. 1. [3], Boston: Wells and Lilly,
pp. 217-63.
These pages make up chapters thirteen through fifteen
and deal with Franklin's early life and with his work in
electricity. Craik calls Franklin the greatest of all
self-educated men, one who overcame very unpromising cir-
cumstances as a youth to stand among the chief philosophers
and writers of his time. "The secret of this man's success
in the cultivation of his mental powers was, that he was
ever awake and active in that business; that he suffered
no opportunity of forwarding it to escape him unimproved;
that, however poor, he found at least a few pence, were it
even by diminishing his scanty meals, to pay for the loan
of the books he could not buy; that, however hard-wrought,
he found a few hours in the week, were it by sitting up
half the night after toiling all the day to read and study
them." These qualities, so important to his many successes
as a young and middle age man, were to enable him to excel
as a diplomat.

5   DWIGHT, N[ATHANIEL]. "Benjamin Franklin." In <u>Sketches of the</u>
<u>Lives of the Signers of the Declaration of Independence,</u>
<u>Intended Principally for the Use of Schools</u>. New York:
J. & J. Harper, pp. 171-86.
Much of the information in this biographical account
comes from the <u>Autobiography</u>. Franklin's chief qualities

are shown to be his boundless curiosity, energy, and devotion to the service of his fellow men.

6   FRANZ, JOHANN FRIEDRICH. "Benjamin Franklin, geb. 1706 zu Boston." In Neuer Jugendspiegel, oder Anecdoten und Characterzüge. . . . 2d ed. Chur: Johann Felix Jakob Dalp, pp. 58-61.
    Franklin believed in his thirteen virtues, and following them helped him achieve happiness and lead a useful, good life. See 1827.2.

7   _____. "Benjamin Franklin." In Neuer Jugendspiegel, oder Anecdoten und Characterzüge. . . . 2d ed. Chur: Johann Felix Jakob Dalp, pp. 113-14.
    Anecdote of how the young Franklin, on his way to Philadelphia, was saved by a Quaker matron from falling prey to a couple of designing women. See 1827.3.

8   _____. "Benjamin Franklin." In Neuer Jugendspiegel, oder Anecdoten und Characterzüge. . . . 2d ed. Chur: Johann Felix Jakob Dalp, pp. 127-29.
    Tells of Franklin's youth, including his decision to become a vegetarian. He found valuable the lessons he learned working under Keimer, as Franklin points out in the Autobiography. See 1827.4.

9   _____. "Die Feife." In Neuer Jugendspiegel, oder Anecdoten und Characterzüge. . . . 2d ed. Chur: Johann Felix Jakob Dalp, pp. 114-16.
    Franklin as a child had once suffered the embarrassment of having paid too much for a whistle. In later life he saw others, much older, pay too much for their whistles, but the lesson of his youth was not wasted on him. See 1827.5.

10 [HUNT, FREEMAN.] "The Blue Yarn Stockings." In American Anecdotes. Original and Select. Vol. 2. Boston: Putnam & Hunt, pp. 234-35.
    Franklin teaches the French court about plain, democratic dress.

11 _____. "The Folly of Duelling." In American Anecdotes. Original and Select. Vol. 2. Boston: Putnam & Hunt, pp. 257-58.
    Franklin comes out forcefully against the practice of dueling.

12 _____. "Franklin a Christian." In American Anecdotes. Original and Select. Vol. 2. Boston: Putnam & Hunt, pp. 84-86.

1830

        Repeats the fiction that on his deathbed Franklin de-
lighted in having within view a picture of Christ on the
cross.

13   ____. "Franklin and Gov. Burnet." In <u>American Anecdotes.
Original and Select</u>. Vol. 2. Boston: Putnam & Hunt,
pp. 205-14.
       Franklin impresses Governor Burnet with his range and
the depth of his reading and understanding in this fictional
anecdote.

14   ____. "Franklin and the Barber." In <u>American Anecdotes.
Original and Select</u>. Vol. 2. Boston: Putnam & Hunt,
pp. 257-58.
       Franklin's head proves to be too big for a French wig
and even for "<u>all de French nationg</u>," as the Gallic barber
says in this fictional anecdote.

15   ____. "A Prudent Precaution." In <u>American Anecdotes.
Original and Select</u>. Vol. 2. Boston: Putnam & Hunt,
pp. 214-15.
       How Franklin avoided being assaulted at inns by the
many questions annoying to travelers.

16   WATSON, JOHN F[ANNING]. "Dr. Franklin." In <u>Annals of Philadelphia, Being a Collection of Memoirs, Anecdotes, & Incidents of the City and Its Inhabitants From the Days of the
Pilgrim Founders. Intended to Preserve the Recollections
of Olden Time, and to Exhibit Society in Its Changes of
Manners and Customs, and the City in Its Local Changes and
Improvements</u>. Philadelphia: E.L. Carey & A. Hart,
pp. 513-16.
       Basically anecdotes of Franklin which, as Watson inter-
prets some of them, make Franklin more wary and rather less
ardent a patriot than he was. (By 1857 Watson had "learned
that there are better reasons for believing that Dr. Franklin
had stronger resolutions for the Revolution than I had . . .
supposed." Though he states these reasons, which are now
common knowledge, in all printings of the <u>Annals</u> from 1857,
they are probably most readily available in the three volume
edition enlarged by Willis P. Hazard and published in Philadelphia by Leary, Stuart Co. (1:535-37). The third volume
of this latter edition (437-39) contains various facts about
Franklin and his descendants.)

17   WEBSTER, N[OAH]. "Franklin." In <u>Biography for the Use of
Schools</u>. New Haven: Hezekiah Howe, pp. 126-38.
       Brief survey dealing chiefly with Franklin's life to the
age of thirty.

1831

1 ALZATE y RAMÍREZ, JOSÉ ANTONIO. [Various Brief Pieces on Franklin.] In Gacetas de literatura de Mexico. Vol. 2. Puebla: Reimpresas en la oficina del'hospital de S. Pedro, a cargo del ciudadano M. Buen Abad, pp. 74-83, 204-8.
These pieces, which make extensive use of primary materials, pay tribute to Franklin as a scientist, philosopher, and man. (A reprint of an original presumably printed in 1790.)

2 ANON. "Franklin." Monthly Repository 2, no. 5 (October): 159-62, no. 6 (November):190-94.
Franklin was America's greatest benefactor.

3 ANON. "Life of Dr. Benjamin Franklin." In The Working-Man's Companion: Containing the Results of Machinery, Cottage Evenings, and the Rights of Industry, Addressed to Working-Men. American ed. New York: Leavitt & Allen, pp. 130-47.
Franklin's well known virtues should be emulated by all workingmen, as should his optimism and curiosity.

4 BEAMAN, CHARLES C[OTESWORTH]. A Poem Delivered Before the Franklin Debating Society, at Their Anniversary, January 17, 1831. Being the Birth-day of Franklin. Boston: John H. Eastburn, 12 pp.
To "Keep bright a Boston and a Franklin's name" is the chief end of this celebration of old New England ways, of art, science, and virtue, and of the press, all things very important in Franklin's life.

5 CENTOFANTI, SILVESTRO. Antologia (Florence) 41, no. 2:112-18.
This review of Giunti's anonymously offered edition of Franklin's writings on morality and private economy also praises Franklin as the hope for the common man, who can put Franklin's precepts into practice and improve his lot in life.

6 DURGIN, CLEMENT. An Oration Delivered before The Franklin Debating Society, at Their Anniversary, January 17, 1831, Being the Birth-Day of Franklin. Boston: printed for the Society by John H. Eastburn, 23 pp.
This pamphlet lauds Franklin the sage, philosopher, patriot, and champion of liberty for all. It is especially in this last capacity, as civil libertarian and opponent of slavery, that Franklin speaks to us in America and reminds us of the task before us. Nineteenth-century Americans, particularly in New England, true to our heritage of liberty

1831

and "free institutions," will take up Franklin's work and
ensure liberty for all our countrymen.

7   HOFFMAN, FRANÇOIS BENOÎT. "Mémoires de Franklin." In Oeuvres.
2d ed. Vol. 3. Paris: Lefebvre, pp. 470-510.
Discusses Franklin's role in bringing about the War of
Independence, and then his efforts in behalf of his country
while he was in France. Hoffman also explores the relationship between Franklin and Congress in light of the reaction
of Congress toward him. See 1829.5.

1832

1   [CORNU], FRANCIS et De COURCY [Monsieur Francis]. Franklin à
Passy, ou Le bonhomme Richard, vaudeville anecdotique en un
acte, par MM Francis et Decourcy, representé, pour la
première fois, à Paris, sur le Théatre du Palais-Royal,
le 19 Mai 1832. Paris: Quoy, 34 pp.
Lord "Stermon," the English ambassador to France, is no
diplomatic or political match for the wise, kindly, but
shrewd Franklin. Moreover, the philosopher is also a helpful and gallant friend to James, a young American in
Franklin's service, in his romance with Jeanette, the
servant of M. Doubourg.

2   PARLEY, PETER, pseud. The Life of Benjamin Franklin. Illustrated by Tales, Sketches and Anecdotes. Series of American
School Biographies. New York: Collins & Hannay, 125 pp.
Only a few of the 125 pages of biography deal with the
eventful years after 1756. This narrative, which is intended
for school children, is designed to reveal Franklin's typically Yankee virtues that made him a successful as well as
genuinely good man. Although some parts of the book are
invented, the moralizing is kept to a minimum. The selections from Franklin's shorter pieces illustrate those famous
qualities of his that enabled him to become financially independent and can presumably one day make the young readers
comfortable too. Questions at the bottom of nearly every
page attempt to make certain that the children understand
the importance of the great philosopher-statesman's life.
(This Life of Benjamin Franklin was published at different
times and with different publishers. Samuel Griswold

Goodrich, who wrote under the Parley pseudonym, later in his life denied authorship of the work; however, he did take out the copyright. The 1832 and 1836 editions are difficult to come by, and one of the copies of the 1836 edition in the Franklin Collection at Yale University [No. F 412.164 1836] is incorrectly bound and is missing pages 133-44.)

3   [PHILADELPHIA COUNCILS.] Statement of Devises, Bequests & Grants to the Corporation of the City of Philadelphia. In Trust. Including Girard's Will. Philadelphia: published by order of the Councils, pp. [3]-8.
     On the handling of the Franklin Fund in Philadelphia.

1833

1   ANON. A Brief Memoir of the Life of Dr. Benjamin Franklin. Compiled for the Use of Young Persons. New York: Mahlon Day, 72 pp.
     Franklin's Poor Richard qualities are stressed so that child readers can learn to get ahead as Franklin did.

2   ANON. "Dr. Franklin." In The Rhode-Island Almanack, Enlarged and Improved, for the Year 1833: Being the Latter Part of the 57th and the Beginning of the 58th Year of the Independence of the U. States. . . . Providence: H.H. Brown, p. [14].
     Anecdote of Franklin teaching a young man not to make excuses.

3   BACHE, A[LEXANDER] D[ALLAS]. "Attempt to Fix the Date of the Observation of Doctor Franklin, in Relation to the North-East Storms of the Atlantic Coast of the United States." Journal of the Franklin Institute 12, no. 4 (October): 300-3.
     A question arose whether a 1749 comment by Lewis Evans that northeast storms begin in the Southwest was prior to the same observation made by Franklin. Bache proves that Franklin's observation was made six years earlier, on 21 October 1743.

4   BERANGER, PIERRE JEAN de. FCL, no. F412.1.
     Quotes extensively from Franklin's will and points out his generosity and benevolence. (On the title page the following words have been written: "Sur Franklin." "Pages 65-67 of the 5ᵉ feuille of an unidentified French periodical.")

1834

1834

1 ANON. "Benjamin Franklin." Cultivator 1 (August):83-84;
(September):96-97; (October):108-9.
A survey of Franklin's life showing the diligence,
frugality, and wisdom that made him successful and great.

2 ANON. "Character of Franklin." American Magazine of Useful
and Entertaining Knowledge 1, no. 1 (September):5.
Franklin was a man of perfect common sense, not genius,
who led a remarkably useful life.

3 ANON. [Franklin Anecdote.] American Magazine of Useful and
Entertaining Knowledge 1, no. 7 (March):314.
In 1774 Franklin was asked what might make the colonies
happy. He replied that the answer might be made up "in a
few Res"; and then wrote as follows:

RE
{
--call your troops
--store Castle William
--pair the damage done to Boston
--peal your unconstitutional acts

--nounce your pretensions to taxation; and
--fund the duties you have extorted.
    Afterwards,
--quire and --ceive pay for tea destroyed;
    and then
--joice in a happy reconciliation.
}

4 CLEMSON, TH[OMAS] G[REEN]. "Franklin." In Société Montoyn et
Franklin. Portraits et histoire des hommes utiles, hommes
et femmes des tous pays et de toutes conditions, qui ont
acquis des droits a la reconnaissance publique par des
traits de dévoument, de charité; par des fondations
philantropiques, par des travaux, des tentatives, des
perfectionnemenns des découvertes utiles a l'humanité, etc.
Edited by A[drien] Jarry de Mancy. Vol. 1. Paris: Gayet
et Lebrun, pp. 1-4.
Like Montoyon, Franklin is a benefactor to mankind. His
goodness was one reason for his enormous popularity in
France.

5 MADISON, [JAMES]. "Benjamin Franklin." In Annals of the Congress of the United States. First Congress. Vol. 2.
Washington: Gales & Seaton, p. 1586.
In the brief official eulogy, written in 1790 but published for the first time here, Madison acclaimed Franklin

84

as a scientist, humanitarian, and patriot. Madison offered a resolution to the effect that the House of Representatives honor Franklin by wearing "the customary badge of mourning for one month." The resolution passed.

6   WOOD, GEORGE B[ACON]. "The History of the University of Pennsylvania, From Its Origin to the Year 1827." In Memoirs of the Historical Society of Pennsylvania. Vol. 3. Philadelphia: M'Carty & Davis, pp. 171-225.
    These pages deal with the period of Franklin's involve- ment with the school, but the account continues for another fifty-five pages. Wood does little more than touch upon Franklin's role and pay tribute to his efforts in behalf of the institution.

1835

*1 ANON. "Beniamino Franklin." Cosmorama pittorico (Milan) 1: 188-89.
    Source: Pace, p. 292. One who sees a portrait of Franklin realizes that his features reveal a man of unusual goodness.

2   BERTHOUD, S. HENR[I]. "Miss Keimer." Musée des familles 2 (June):[305]-8.
    Fictional treatment of the young Franklin's efforts to succeed socially with young women and in his craft.

3   ELSNER, HEINRICH. "Franklin." In Befreiungskampt der nordamerikanischen Staaten. Mit der Lebenbeschreibungen der vier berühmtesten Männer desselben: Washington, Franklin, Lafayette und Kosciuszko. Nach den besten Quellen historisch-biographisch bearbeitet. Stuttgart: J. Scheible, pp. 658-91.
    Franklin as a patriot and representative of America's greatness. His accomplishments in diplomacy during his difficult years in France crown his brilliant career.

1835

4   HERRING, JAMES, and LONGACRE, JAMES B. "Benjamin Franklin,
     LL.D., F.R.S." In National Portrait Gallery of Distin-
     guished Americans. Vol. 2. New York: M. Bancroft,
     pp. 1-20.
          Franklin was doubtless a great man, but had he been born
     in "an older and more refined community," he would not have
     achieved as much or gained the recognition he did in America.
     Moreover, his morals were, as a youth, doubtful, and he
     lacked education. He was a naturally able and honest man,
     though, and his faults may be "pardoned."

5   LEDUC, PIERRE ÉTIENNE DENIS. Maitre Pierre; ou, Le savant de
     village. Entretiens sur Franklin. Bibliothèque
     d'instruction populaire, no. 17. Paris: F.G. Levrault,
     174 pp.
          On Franklin's contributions to his own time and to
     posterity. Much use is made of Franklin's writings to
     show him to be humane and wise.

*6   MUZZI, SALVATORE. "Franklin." In Storie e ritratti di uomini
     utili benefattori della umanità. [Vol. 1?] Bologna:
     Tipi Governativi della Volpe al Sassi (Bologna,
     Archiginnasio), unpaginated.
          Source: Pace, pp. 228-30. In her book on practical edu-
     cation for Italians, Mrs. Tommasini offered a Franklinian
     fellow Pennsylvanians.

*7   TOMMASINI, ANTONIETTA. Intorno alla educazione domestica:
     considerazioni. Milan: Stella, 119 pp.
          Source: Pace, p. 228-30. In her book on practical edu-
     cation for Italians, Mrs. Tommasini offered a Franklinian
     approach designed to inculcate virtue and prosperity.

8   VICQ-d'AZYR, [JACQUES] FELIX. "Éloge de Franklin (1791)."
     Revue rétrospective; ou bibliothèque historique, contenant
     des mémoires et documens authentiques, inédits et originaux,
     pour servir a l'histoire proprement dite, à la biographie,
     a l'histoire de la littérature et des arts. 2d ser.
     2:[375]-404.
          The entire tribute is reprinted. Franklin is praised as
     a scientist, statesman, diplomat, and humanitarian. His
     life, which spanned nearly the whole eighteenth century,
     was one filled with achievement, and he lived to become
     the symbol of liberty and the representative of virtue.

1836

1 ANON. "Benjamin Franklin." La Palamede, revue mensuelle
   éches 1:41-44.
       Laudatory biographical account.

2 ANON. "Biographical Sketch of Benjamin Franklin." Casket,
   pp. 112-29.
       Calls particular attention to Franklin's patriotism
   and benevolence.

3 ANON. "Franklin and His (Supposed) Parable on Persecution."
   Literary and Theological Review 3, no. 9 (March):51-56.
       Franklin merely modified the "Parable" which was the
   original work of "Bishop Taylor's Liberty of Prophesying."
   Franklin should not have claimed the work as his own.

4 ANON. "From the MSS. of Franklin." Southern Literary Mes-
   senger 2, no. 7 (June):445.
       Says that Franklin wrote the following poem:

           In vain are musty mortals taught in schools,
           By rigid teachers and as rigid rules,
           Where virtue with a frowning aspect stands,
           And frights the pupil with her rough commands.
           But Woman--
           Charming Woman, can true converts make--
           We love the precepts for the teacher's sake:
           Virtue in them appears so bright and gay,
           We hear with transport, and with pride obey.

5 ANON. Life of Benjamin Franklin. Boston: Russell, Shattuck
   & Co., 208 pp.
       Moralistic biography which emphasizes Franklin's Poor
   Richard qualities.

6 ANON. Life of Benjamin Franklin; Embracing Anecdotes Illustrative of His Character. The Young American's Library.
   Philadelphia: Lindsay & Blakiston, 208 pp.
       A biography which, going beyond the scope of the memoirs,
   stresses Franklin's civil virtues and holds him up as a
   model for the young to emulate.

*7 CANTÙ, CESARE. Benjamin Franklin.
       Source: Pace, p. 427, no. 149 and pp. 231-32; 261-66.
   In this Mc-Guffey-like book for children, Cantù reminds his
   readers that Franklin, far from being born among the elite

1836

of the world, came from humble origins. His life therefore
proves that all people can rise in the world by hard work
and thrift. Of the 1836 publication of this piece, Pace
writes as follows: "An essay first printed in 1836 (so
dated in Cantù's Racconti alla buona, 364, Milan, Agnelli,
1888.)"

*8   GOODRICH, SAMUEL GRISWOLD. "Dr. Franklin's Last Words."   In
      Peter Parley's Book of Anecdotes. . . .   Boston.
           Source: NUC. See 1845.3.

*9   _____. "Eloquence of Whitefield." In Peter Parley's Book of
      Anecdotes. . . .   Boston.
           Source: NUC. See 1845.4.

10   GRIFFITH, WILLIAM. "Franklin Negotiations, 1774-5."   In
      Historical Notes of the American Colonies and Revolution,
      From 1754-1775. Burlington, N.J.: published by his execu-
      tors, pp. 201-5.
           On Franklin's dedicated efforts to work with the British
      ministry to prevent the Revolutionary War.

11   LEAKE, WALTER D. An Oration Delivered Before the Franklinian
      Society of William and Mary College, on the 17th January,
      1836. Richmond: T.W. White, Printer, 16 pp.
           Franklin is beloved and admired because he was a philan-
      thropist, a man of many talents, and a dedicated servant in
      the noble cause of freedom.

12   LINCOLN, ROBERT A. "Benjamin Franklin." In Lives of the
      Presidents of the United States; With Biographical Notices
      of the Signers of the Declaration of Independence; Sketches
      of the Most Remarkable Events in the History of the Country,
      From Its Discovery to the Present Time; and a General View
      of Its Present Condition. New York: N. Watson & Co.,
      pp. 348-52.
           Summary of Franklin's life asserting that he was a
      religious skeptic while a young man but "became in his
      maturer years a believer in divine revelation."

*13   SCHLOSSER, F[RIEDRICH] C[HRISTOPH]. [Franklin.] In Geschichte
      des achtezehnten Jahrhunderts und des neunzehnten bis zum
      Sturz des französischen Kaiserreichs. Mit besonderer
      Rücksicht auf den Gang der Literatur. 8 vols. Heidelberg:
      J.C.B. Mohr.
           Source: NUC. See 1853.17.

14 SPARKS, JARED, ed. The Works of Benjamin Franklin; Containing
    Several Political and Historical Tracts Not Included in Any
    Former Edition, and Many Letters Official and Private Not
    Hitherto Published; With Notes and a Life of the Author.
    Vol. 1. Boston: Hilliard Gray & Co., pp. 229-535.
        Sparks's continuation of Franklin's story. It is a
    readable but superficial affair which avoids unpleasantness
    and even controversy in presenting a very favorable but
    nevertheless incomplete and bland Franklin.

15 WALSH, ROBERT. "Franklin. Retirement: Dissolution:
    Character." In Didactics: Social, Literary, and Political.
    Vol. 2. Philadelphia: Carey, Lea & Blanchard, pp. 262-68.
        Franklin's virtue, wisdom, and dedication to public ser-
    vice make him the true representative of the American char-
    acter. Yet he is the benefactor of all mankind.

                            1837

*1 CANTÙ, CESARE. "Beniamino Franklin, o Lavorare e risparmiare."
    In Il giovinetto drizzato alla bontà, al sapere,
    all'industria. Milan: Truffi.
        Source: Pace. See 1836.7.

2   MARCKMANN, JØRGEN WILHELM. Bogtrykkeren Benjamin Franklins
    liv og levnet . . . Udgivet af Selskabet for trykke-
    frihedens rette brug . . . [Life and career of the printer,
    Benjamin Franklin . . . published by the Society for the
    Proper Use of Freedom of the Press]. Copenhagen: Trykt i
    det Berlingske bogtrykkeri, 159 pp.
        A very simplified account of Franklin's life and career
    to which are appended selections from his works.

3   [RUELLE, CHARLES CLAUDE.] "Sur la vie de Franklin." In La
    science populaire de Claudius[:] Simples discours sur
    toutes choses. Paris: Jules Renouard, 214 pp.
        Franklin is virtually perfected, in the French manner,
    in this study of his character and career.

                            1838

1   B[ACHE], B[ENJAMIN] F[RANKLIN]. "Sonnets on Character:
    Franklin." United States Magazine and Democratic Review 2,
    no. 6 (May):196.
        Franklin was a rich amalgam of such New England traits
    as good sense, inventiveness, an upright but tactful manner,

1838

and nerve. These qualities made him a wise man and great
patriot.

2   BESSIERE, J[ACQUES] F[ÉLIX]. <u>Franklin, comédie historique en
     cinq actes et en prose</u>. Paris: Chez l'Auteur, 6 pp.
          Fanciful, sentimental, and idealized account, often based
     on the <u>Autobiography</u> but radically distorted. In the first
     act, "Josias" is made the sage, eternally patient mediator
     between his sons who agree only in adoring their father. The
     precocious and eminently reasonable young Benjamin is clearly
     the object of sympathy, for James is a rather irascible master
     and brother. James is less than satisfied with his brother's
     performance as an apprentice because of Benjamin's penchant
     for Socratic disputation, particularly on religious matters.
     Moreover, James is irritated because Benjamin is forever
     writing in private, and this irritation turns into hurt
     pride and anger when he discovers that his younger brother
     is the secret illustrious author who has been contributing
     brilliant pieces to the <u>Courant</u>. Things do improve, how-
     ever, in a time of difficulty. Benjamin's brotherly sym-
     pathies are awakened when James is questioned in court about
     pieces in his newspaper. It is John Collins, Benjamin's
     partner in disputation, who suggests the subterfuge of hav-
     ing Benjamin appear as the publisher of the newspaper. The
     second act depicts Franklin as the emerging success and sage
     in Philadelphia, though he is still advised by his father
     who is also in Philadelphia. By this time Franklin and
     James are friends, which is appropriate, since Franklin is
     now the guiding light behind the junto. The third act,
     which is highly fictionalized, deals with the forty-five
     year-old Franklin, father of children the historical
     Franklin would not have known, dabbler in poetry, scientist,
     and prominent member of the Pennsylvania Assembly. In the
     next act Franklin, who is seventy, is a leader in the patri-
     otic cause, works closely with his friend, Washington, and
     is an inspiration to his younger colleagues. In the final
     act, which takes place in 1778, Franklin, aided by Voltaire,
     Madame Helvétius and other French friends of America, wins
     the official support of Louis and France and thus brings
     about what is depicted as the greatest day in Franklin's
     life.

3   BROUGHAM, HENRY PETER. "Character of Franklin." In <u>The Ever-
     green; or a Selection of Religious and Perceptive Pieces</u>.
     London: Darton & Co., pp. 5-13.
          An idealized sketch of Franklin, who is praised as a
     great scientist and philosopher, a self-made man whose
     genius, wit, integrity, and diligence made him universally

known and admired. Moreover, he was a model family man and a true, if "latitudinarian" believer.

*4   RACAGNI, GIUSEPPE MARIA. "Sopra i sistemi di Franklin e di Symmer spettanti all'elettricità . . . Giuseppe Maria Racagni." Memorie dell' I. R. Istituto del Regno Lombardo-Veneto (Milan) 5:187-217.
Source: Pace, p. 48. Argues that it is impossible to judge whether Franklin's single fluid or Symmer's double fluid theory of electricity is correct. (Racagni objectively expresses the gradually increasing detachment with which Franklin's scientific work was held in Italy in the nineteenth century.)

1839

1   A., Ch. Vioi tou V. Phranklinou kai A. Korae, kai, He Episteme tou kalou Richardou, dia tous Hellenikous paidas, hypo Ch. A. [The lives of B. Franklin and A. Korae, and the knowledge of Good Richard for Greek children, by Ch. A.]. Hermopolis: George Polymeres, 68 pp.
This biographical account of Franklin calls the attention of Greek children to the American's practical morality and to its remarkably successful implementation in his own life. Also presents Poor Richard's maxims.

2   ANON. "Benjamin Franklin." In Interesting Biographical Sketches of Distinguished Men. For the Instruction and Amusement of Children and Youth. Vol. 2. Hartford: L. Stebbins, p. 4.
Franklin was a self-made man whose life is "well worthy the perusal of youth."

3   ANON. "Franklin and His Wig." Popular Magazine, or, the 1000 Nights' Entertainments: Containing a Choice Collection of Interesting Tales, Wit and Sentiment, Chemical and Scientific Amusements &c. 4, no. 13:147-50.
Franklin's large head frustrates his French wig maker, who cannot find a wig large enough to fit the American. Franklin is therefore forced to appear at Court in his own hair.

4   ANON. "Franklin's Visit to His Mother." Popular Magazine, or, the 1000 Nights' Entertainments: Containing a Choice Collection of Interesting Tales, Wit and Sentiment, Chemical and Scientific Amusements, &c. 4, no. 13:87-92.

1839

        Familiar anecdote of Franklin returning to Boston to
visit his mother after many years and finding that she does
not recognize him. His visit proved to him that there was
no such thing as natural affection.

5   JULIUS, N[ICHOLAS] H[EINRICH]. Nordamerikas sittliche
      Zustände. 2 vols. Leipzig: Brockhaus, 1:97-100.
         Franklin is here attacked for being the epitome of mate-
rialism, and his entire career and personal life are
criticized.

6   MUZZI, SALVATORE. "Franklin." L'omnibus pittoresco 2,
      no. 38 (28 November):[297]-300, 311-12.
         Praises Franklin as a humane teacher of men and as a
patriot.

7   [SIGURDSSON, JON.] "Aefisaga Benjamīns Franklīns gefin ūt af
      hinu Íslenzka Thjodvinafelag" [Biography of Benjamin
      Franklin, published by the Icelandic Society of Patriots].
      In Tvaer aefisögur útlendra merkismanna [Two biographies
      of famous foreigners].
         Franklin seen as Poor Richard in character and as a
patriot and sage who characteristically saw the truth
quickly and acted accordingly.

184-

1   BEUMER, P[HILIPP] J[ACOB]. Prämien-Büchlein für fleiszige
      Kinder. No. 12, Benjamin Franklin. Mit einer Abbildung.
      Wesel: A. Bagel, pp. [265]-75.
         These pages constitute Beumer's commentary and are fol-
lowed by thirteen pages made up largely of passages from
Franklin's writings. Both parts emphasize Franklin's rise
in life and call upon the young readers to emulate him in
adopting his wise virtues and thereby achieving success and
deserved admiration.

1840

1   [BETTZIECH], H[EINRICH]. "Benjamin Franklin." In Deutscher
      Volks-Kalender[,] 1840. Berlin: Verlag der Vereins-
      Buchhandlung, pp. 135-38.
         A biographical sketch.

2   BROUGHAM, HENRY PETER. "Sketches of American Character:
      Benjamin Franklin." Family Magazine, or Monthly Abstract
      of General Knowledge 7:65-66.

1841

Franklin "stands alone" in being both a great politician
and a great philosopher. He was without "stain" in his private and public lives, and it is to his further credit that
he was truly a self-made man. (This piece is more readily
available as the fifth volume (1856) of Brougham's Works,
entitled Historical Sketches of Statesmen who Flourished
in the Time of George III (London: Richard Griffin &
Co.), pp. 291-95.

*3   HOWE, HENRY. "Benjamin Franklin." In Memoirs of the Most
      Eminent American Mechanics: Also, Lives of Distinguished
      European Mechanics; Together With a Collection of Anecdotes,
      Descriptions, &c. &c. Relating to the Mechanic Arts. New
      York: W.F. Peckham.
          Source: NUC. See 1856.11.

4   PREUSKER, KARL [BENJAMIN]. Gutenberg und Franklin, Eine
      Festgabe zum vierten Jubiläum der Erfindung der
      Buchdruckerkunst. Zugleich mit Antrag zur Gründung von
      Stadt und Dorf-Bibliotheken. Leipzig: Heinrich Weinedel,
      64 pp.
          A tribute to two men whose names are synonymous with
      the printed word.

*5   SCHMALTZ, [JOHANN] CARL [STEPHAN]. Das Leben Benjamin
      Franklins. Leipzig: Carl Schmaltz.
          See 1850.15.

6   TYLER, JOHN, Jr. An Oration on the Life and Character of
      Benjamin Franklin, Delivered Before the Franklin Society
      of William and Mary College, on the 17th January, 1840.
      Norfolk, Va.: printed by W.C. Shields, 27 pp.
          Tyler says that while Franklin was surely a man of out-
      standing and varied abilities, it was his virtue that made
      him great. Moreover, his benevolence and patriotism would
      make him call, if he were alive today, for an end to Amer-
      ican political divisiveness.

1841

1   ANON. "Dr. Franklin's Old Press." Madisonian 5, no. 91
      (December):[4].
          Franklin's old press is being sent for a time to
      Liverpool, England, before it is housed in Philadelphia.

2   CHASLES, PHILARÈTE. "Franklin." Revue des deux mondes 26
      (June):[669]-702.

1841

> Praises Franklin as an extraordinarily gifted diplomat,
> moralist, and sage and credits him with having helped pave
> the way for the liberation of France. His great popularity
> in France was entirely deserved.

3   [A GENTLEMAN of ALABAMA, pseud.] "Benjamin Franklin."
     <u>Southern Literary Messenger</u> 7, no. 9 (September):[593]-605.
     In addition to reviewing the Sparks edition of 1841,
     this piece is a long survey of Franklin's career. The
     author comments extensively on Franklin's personal quali-
     ties and tries to make him not only a good man but a seri-
     ous Christian as well. We are told that Franklin's
     countrymen revere him and that he well deserves reverence.

4   M'NEILE, HUGH. <u>A Lecture on the Life of Dr. Franklin.</u>
     Liverpool: Mitchell, Heaton, & Mitchell, 46 pp.
     The Reverend Mr. M'Neile praises Franklin's moral vir-
     tues and benevolence but considers him religiously ignorant:
     "It would be highly gratifying to be able to speak in terms
     of similar admiration, concerning Franklin's philosophy in
     other and higher respects. But the history of this great
     man supplies no exception to the rule, that 'the world by
     wisdom knew not God.'" Sadly, Franklin's deism only in-
     jures." "I behold in Dr. Franklin, a splendid speciman of
     it in its best estate; and I see him, upon his own showing
     spotted with guilt,--and dumb, absolutely dumb, as to the
     pardon of that guilt." The minister also disagrees with
     Franklin's "political principles." M'Neile ends, after
     implying that he has little hope that Franklin was saved,
     with an appeal to Americans to end the slavery Franklin
     opposed.

5   R., R. "Benjamin Franklin." <u>El apuntador</u> 1, no. 15:225-27.
     A sketch of Franklin's career praising him for his
     kindness as well as for his achievements in diplomacy
     and science.

1842

1   ANON. "Biography: Benjamin Franklin." <u>Practical Mechanic</u>
     <u>and Engineer's Magazine</u> 1, no. 7 (April):256-61.
     Biographical sketch that focuses on Franklin's efforts
     to "enlighten" English public opinion about the effects of
     Tory dealings with America. Franklin wanted to prevent the
     separation between America and England and selflessly con-
     ducted himself as the honorable friend to both sides; how-
     ever, he never once compromised his native land.

1842

2 ANON. "Life and Maxims of Franklin." In Chamber's Information for the People. New and Improved Series, no. 41.
Vol. 1. Edinburgh: William & Robert Chambers, pp. 641-56.
A narrative account of Franklin's life interspersed with
passages (not always quoted) from the Autobiography and with
some of the maxims. The author concludes that Franklin's
life and writings epitomize a high order of "worldly prudence" or virtue that deserves to be a model for all "un-
blessed by birth and fortune." His life "must be considered
as more immediately instructive to the industrious and productive portion of mankind."

3 [BENNER, ENOS.] "Benjamin Franklin." In Lebensbeschreibungen
sämmtlicher unterzeichner der Unabhängigkeits-erklärung der
Vereinigten Staaten von Nord-Amerika. Sunnytown, Pa.:
published by the author, pp. 268-93.
A biography of Franklin that relies on the memoirs to
the year 1757 and then on Benner's imagination for the
remaining thirty-three years of Franklin's life.

4 CASTRO, GIOVANNI de, comp. Operajo e Filosofo (Beniamino
Franklin) ovvero l'arte della virtù[,] accomodata all'
intelligenza di tutti[:] libretto di lettura e di premio
per le scuole primarie, tecniche ed operajo. Milan:
Tipografia Scolastica dell editore Francesco Pagnoni,
158 pp.
The author's comments are interspersed with Franklin's
moralistic works to encourage Italian children to emulate
the virtues of Poor Richard.

5 [CATTANEO, ANTONIO?] "Cenni su la vita di Benjamino
Franklin." In Biblioteca di farmacia, chimica, fisica,
medicina, chirurgia, terapeutica, storia naturale, ecc.
(Milan) 35:v-xlvii.
Franklin credited with being the originator of the
essence of American civilization, its education, public
virtues, and military power. (On page 178 of his book,
Benjamin Franklin and Italy, Pace comments on Antonio
Cattaneo's "biographical sketch of Franklin of the year
1842," but identifies it in his bibliography (p. 426,
no. 146) as another work, S. Muzzi's "Franklin," in Storie
e ritratti di uomini utili benefattori della umanità, Vol.
1, Bologna: Tipi Governativi della Volpe al Sassi (1835).
On page 258, Pace writes of Carlo Cattaneo's "life of
Franklin," written in 1842. In the bibliography (p. 428,
no. 174), he identifies this work as being by A. Cattaneo,
cited above. The piece is on film at the American Philosophical Society and is apparently by Antonio Cattaneo.)

1842

6   DEMPP, KARL WILHELM. "Franklin, der Entdecker der
     Luftelektrizität und der Erfinder der Blitzableiter."
     In <u>Vollständiger Unterricht, in der Technik der
     Blitzableiterstezung nach 66 Modellen, nebst einem
     vorbereitenden Auszüge der Elektrizitätslehre. . . .</u>
     Munich: G. Franz, pp. 20-32.
         A survey of Franklin's work in electrical science and
     of its influence.

7   [GOODRICH, SAMUEL GRISWOLD.] <u>The Life of Benjamin Franklin.</u>
     Philadelphia: Thomas Cowperthwait & Co., 181 pp.
         This account of Franklin's life, intended for school
     children and designed to inculcate in them the virtues of
     Poor Richard even at the expense of accuracy, concentrates
     on Franklin's rise in life before his agencies abroad. A
     brief and cautious sampling of his essays is appended.
     (This book derives from Peter Parley's 1832 <u>Life of
     Benjamin Franklin.</u>)

8   HAWTHORNE, NATHANIEL. "Benjamin Franklin. Born 1706. Died
     1790." In <u>Biographical Stories for Children.</u> Boston:
     Tappan & Dennet, pp. 111-37.
         Fictionalized treatment of Franklin at ten years of age.
     Young Ben, a remarkably precocious leader among the boys of
     Boston, must yet be taught a sound moral lesson. He had
     led his playmates in stealing stones that were being used
     to construct a new house and instead built a wharf, which
     would enable the boys to fish more conveniently. Ben
     pleaded the usefulness of the enterprise, but Josiah
     Franklin, his father, explained to him that nothing dis-
     honest could be good. Hawthorne's attitude toward Franklin
     is ambivalent. He admires Franklin's achievements but says
     that his fame rests upon the maxims of Poor Richard, and
     these are commercial. They have to do with making and keep-
     ing money and were suited chiefly to a new, uncultivated
     country. While the advice of Poor Richard has certainly
     been good, Americans now realize that earning money and
     being frugal constitute only very limited notions of one's
     duty.

1843

1   [ANDREE, KARL THEODOR.] "Benjamin Franklin (Mit Portrait)."
     In <u>Der Volsbote für das Jahr 1844.</u> Stuttgart:
     Hoffmann'sche Verlags Buchhandlung, pp. 24-39.
         Biographical sketch stressing the fact that Franklin
     succeeded by his own diligence and skill.

2 ANON. "Anecdota de Franklin." In El Museo Mexicano. Vol. 1. Mexico: Ignacio Cumplido, p. 543.
Franklin, trying to show that he needs the patronage of no man at the expense of his independence, eats a dish of sawdust pudding. One who can get along on such fare, he explains to an acquaintance, is always in the happy position of being able to follow his conscience rather than the dictates of so-called influential people.

3 FORSTER, GEORG. "Benjamin Franklin und John Howard." In Sämmtliche Schriften. Vol. 6. Leipzig: Brockhaus, pp. 204-20.
Eulogizes Franklin as a great benefactor to mankind in many areas, particularly in science and diplomacy.

4 GRATTAN, THOMAS COLLEY [A British Subject]. The Boundary Question Revised; and Dr. Franklin's Red Line Shown to Be the Right One. New York: printed at the Albion Office, pp. 3-8.
These pages of a longer piece defend the treaty of 1842 between the United States and Great Britain by arguing that the northeastern boundary between the United States and Canada follows the boundary drawn by Franklin, and this is the correct line.

5 S., J. "Franklin." Boys' and Girls' Magazine 2 (May-August): 109-13.
Franklin's industry, "filial obedience" and beneficence helped make him famous and great. Yet, he never lost his republican simplicity and love of his country, even when showered by praise in Europe. Boys and girls should pattern their lives after that of this philosopher and statesman.

6 UNITED STATES CONGRESS. Proceedings in the House of Representatives of the United States on the Presentation of the Sword of Washington and the Staff of Franklin, February 7, 1843. Washington: printed by Gales & Seaton, 15 pp.
This pamphlet records the grateful acceptance by Congress of the gifts made by Samuel T. Washington. The staff is Franklin's "fine crab-tree walking stick, with a gold head, curiously wrought in the form of the cap of Liberty," which he left in his will to Washington.

7 [VAN HARDERWIJK, JAN.] "Levensbeschrijving van Franklin" [Biography of Franklin]. In Beantwoording der Prijsstoffe: Eene leerrijke Keur uit Benjamin Franklin's Zedekundige Schriften, en bekende Levensbeschrijving, grootstendeels

1843

door hem zelven [Answering to the theme: an informative
selection from Benjamin Franklin's ethical writings, and
well known biography, for the most part by himself].
Amsterdam: De Erven H. Van Munster en Zoon en J. Van Der
Hei en Zoon, pp. [12]-18.
   A biographical summary followed by a brief discussion
of Franklin's epitaph. While the author sees Franklin as
a man of great achievement, he is also impressed by the
American as a man of goodness with whom one can identify.

1844

1   [BOWEN, F.] "Sparks' Life and Works of Dr. Franklin." North
    American Review 59, no. 125 (October):446-87.
       Bowen not only reviews the Sparks's edition of
    Franklin's Life and Works, he also surveys Franklin's life
    and achievements and points out that many of the philoso-
    pher's writings must be judged by "ethical" rather than
    literary standards. Franklin was a moralist and a man of
    affairs, not essentially a man of letters.

2   DICKINSON, S.N. "Birth Spot of Franklin." Boston Almanac
    for the Year 1844 2, no. 9:77.
       Notes where Franklin was born in Boston.

3   GOODRICH, SAM[UEL] GRISWOLD. "Franklin." In Lives of Bene-
    factors. New York: J.M. Allen, pp. 113-59.
       All his life Franklin worked to improve the condition of
    his fellow men. His life offers hope to all that we can
    affect our times positively, and his virtues moved us fur-
    ther along the road to civilization. One can see all this
    promise even in Franklin's early years.

4   MAZZONI, MARCELLO. "Dr. Benjamin Franklin." In Fiori e
    glorie della letteratura inglese offerti nelle due lingue
    ed italiano. . . . Milan: Pirotta, pp. 123-24.
       Brief biography.

1845

1   ANON. "Benjamin Franklin." Hogg's Weekly Instructor, no. 16
    (14 June), pp. 242-44.
       Franklin persevered and remained a simple, unspoiled man
    in spite of prosperity and fame.

1846

*2   ANON. "Racconti storici--Le veglie di Maestro Biagio:
     Beniamino Franklin." S'amico de popolo (Lucca) 1:66-67,
     77-79.
         Source: Pace, p. 429n184. Franklin's great and most
     useful career and his writings follow from his commitment
     to mass education.

3   [GOODRICH, SAMUEL GRISWOLD.] "Dr. Franklin's Last Words."
     In Peter Parley's Book of Anecdotes. . . . Philadelphia:
     Thomas Cowperthwait & Co., pp. 127-28.
         According to the author, Franklin's last words were an
     appeal to a young skeptic to study diligently and believe
     in the Bible. See 1836.8.

4   _____. "Eloquence of Whitefield." In Peter Parley's Book of
     Anecdotes. . . . Philadelphia: Thomas Cowperthwait & Co.,
     pp. 135-36.
         The measure of Whitefield's eloquence is that his preach-
     ing inspired Franklin to give all the money he had in his
     pockets for the orphanage Whitefield founded in Georgia.
     See 1836.9.

5   KELL, JULIUS [KARL]. Lebensbeschreibung Benjamin Franklins,
     des thatkräftigen Mannes und freisinnigen Volks-freundes.
     Eine Volkschrift zur Beförderung edler Menschlichkeit,
     tüchtigen Bürgersinnes und uneigennütziger
     Vaterlandsliebe. . . . Leipzig: J. Klinkhardt, 168 pp.
         This full-length biography surveys Franklin's ideas and
     career. Kell is interested in emphasizing Franklin's qual-
     ity of disinterested benevolence toward his fellow Americans
     and, indeed, mankind generally. While Franklin's brilliance
     was certainly a factor in his life of accomplishment, it was
     no more important than his moral qualities and humanity.

6   VAN TENAC, CHARLES. Manuel des jeux de Boston; Boston de
     "Fontainebleau." Boston de Lorient, Boston anglais, Vendome
     et Cassino, par Van Tenac et Delanoue [pseudonym?].
     Bibliothèque de jeux. Paris: Passard, 73 pp.
         Franklin was reported to be the inventor of whist, a
     game that he very much enjoyed playing.

                              1846

1   ANON. Life of Franklin. Embracing Anecdotes Illustrative of
     His Character. Biographical School Series. Philadelphia:
     Lindsay & Blakiston, 208 pp.

1846

Although Franklin's escapades with women are quietly
ignored, the author of this biography does point out his
subject's moral failings with regard to his brother James
and Deborah Read. Yet it becomes clear that by the time
of his return from his first visit to England, Franklin had
determined to correct what few faults he had in his character. In this effort, the school children readers learned,
he was eminently successful. As great as Franklin's scientific, political, and humanitarian achievements were, it is
for his personal qualities that he is best remembered and
most worthy of the admiration of American youth. "Industry,
Frugality, INTEGRITY--such are the leading lessons of
Franklin's life. From them, all other virtues, under
Providence, are derived." In spite of the moralizing, no
attempt is made to Christianize Franklin or even to deal
with his religious beliefs. (This book may have been written by H.H. Weld or John Frost.)

2   DUVEYRIER, ANNE HONORÉ JOSEPH [Mélesville], and CARMOUCHE,
    PIERRE FRIEDRICH ADOLPHE. Le bonhomme Richard[:] Comédie--
    Vaudeville en trois actes. . . . [Paris: Michel Levy],
    75 pp.
       Other than the bonhomme Richard name, this comedy has
    practically nothing to do with Franklin.

3   FARINE, CHARLES. Benjamin Franklin[,] docteur en droit[,]
    membre de la Société Royale de Londres, et de l'Académie
    des Sciences de Paris, Ministère Plénipotentiaire des
    Etats-Unis d'Amérique a la Cour de France, etc. Tours:
    R. Pornim et Cie, 284 pp.
       The sublime Franklin is praised for his heroism, dili-
    gence, patriotism, abilities, accomplishments and, above
    all, for his humanity. He and the French loved each other
    sincerely.

4   LANDOR, WALTER SAVAGE. "Washington and Franklin." In The
    Works of Walter Savage Landor. Vol. 1. London: Edward
    Moxon, pp. 124-35.
       Washington and Franklin defend their new nation's form
    of government, discuss its problems--present and potential--
    and its promise of greatness. They are also made to ex-
    press views antagonistic to Roman Catholicism.

5   ROTH, THEODOR, trans. Leben und Grundsätze Benjamin Franklin.
    Stuttgart: [Scheible, Rieger & Sattler], 48 pp.
       About one-third of this piece is made up of quotes from
    Franklin's writings, and so Roth is considered a translator;
    however, he is essentially an author here and provides a

biography dealing primarily with Franklin's life before
1757, the period dealt with in the Autobiography. The
remaining thirty-three years are summarized very briefly.
Readers are expected to understand that the famous maxims
of Poor Richard are the very practical rules by which
Franklin actually lived. In particular, Roth points out
that the philosopher always worked for the public good and
succeeded in life on his own merit.

6   SPEAR, THOMAS G. "Biographical Sketches. Benjamin Franklin."
     American Journal of Improvement in the Useful Arts, and
     Mirror of the Patent Office 1, no. 4 (April):77-82; no. 5
     (May):110-13.
        A survey of Franklin's life that praises him for his
     character as well as for his achievements. Franklin, "as
     a lover of liberty and servant of his race . . . , secures
     our profoundest gratitude and esteem; but as a man of sci-
     ence and a philosopher it is that he challenges our highest
     admiration." It would be a serious mistake, though, to be-
     lieve that Franklin's success must be unique to him. He
     made his own success, and his path is open to all. "Every
     mechanic has a chance to do the same" by following Franklin's
     example and emulating his virtues.

                              1847

1   [ALLEN, W.H.] "Franklin's Discoveries in Electricity."
     Methodist Quarterly Review, 3d ser. 7 (January):101-20.
        More than a review of Franklin's Philosophical Essays
     and Correspondence, this piece praises him as a philosopher
     and attacks narrow-minded critics who denigrate Franklin's
     philosophical achievements for political and nationalistic
     reasons.

2   ANON. "Anecdote of Dr. Ben Franklin." In Supplements to the
     Connecticut "Courant," for the Year 1847: Containing Tales,
     Travels, History, Biography, Poetry, and a Great Variety of
     Miscellaneous Articles. Vol. 12. Hartford: John L.
     Boswell, p. 24.
        Franklin may have been the first person to conceive of
     spinning more than one thread of cotton at the same time;
     however, he thought that no one would for many years develop
     such a way of spinning.

3   ANON. "Natural Affection." In Supplements to the Connecticut
     "Courant," for the Year 1847: Containing Tales, Travels,
     History, Biography, Poetry, and a Great Variety of

1847

Miscellaneous Articles. Vol. 12. Hartford: John L.
Boswell, pp. 130-31.
Fictional anecdote of Franklin visiting his mother after
years away from Boston and finding that she did not recognize him and even feared him. From this experience, we are
told, Franklin concluded that natural affection does not
exist.

4 ANON. "Plagiarism of Franklin." Democratic Review 20,
no. 104 (February):177-78.
Franklin never intended "A Parable Against Persecution"
to be taken as being his, for it had appeared in earlier
versions. Lord Kames included a copy of the "Parable"
Franklin had given him in Kames's Sketches of the History of
Man and, thinking it Franklin's, presented it as such.
Yet it is important to note that the piece never had
attained any popularity until Franklin put it into biblical
style, and so in a sense Franklin is the author of the piece
that became well known.

5 ANON. "Volksschriftsteller. Zschokee, Seume, Franklin."
Archiv für Natur, Kunst, Wissenschaft und Leben, n.s. 5,
no. 2:16, 18.
These pages of a longer article contain a biographical
sketch of Franklin.

6 [CHAMBERS, WILLIAM, and CHAMBERS, ROBERT.] "Life of Benjamin
Franklin." In Chamber's Information for the People. A
Popular Encyclopedia. First American Edition with Numerous
Additions and More Than Five Hundred Engravings. Vol. 2.
Philadelphia: G.B. Zieber & Co., pp. 223-39.
This biography focuses on Franklin's life before his
career as a Pennsylvania politician and diplomat, though
these years are dealt with briefly. Franklin's life and
thoughts show that he is characterized by a high level of
"worldly prudence," and he is the great proponent of
"practical wisdom."

7 DAIRE, EUGÈNE, and De MOLINARI, G. "Notice sur Franklin."
In Melanges d'economie politique. Vol. 1. Paris:
Guillaumin et Cie, pp. 623-30.
Sketch of Franklin's career, noting particularly those
factors that turned his attention to economics. Following
this discussion are selections of some of Franklin's writings on economics.

8 FOLLETT, FREDERICK. History of the Press of Western New York.
Proceedings of the Printers' Festival Held January 18, 1847.
Rochester: Jerome & Brother, 76 pp.

1847

Tribute to Franklin, whose "name and memory should be
alike enduring and sacred to the members of this Profession
in this Republic."

9   [FROST, JOHN.] "Dr. Franklin in Congress." In Stories of the
     American Revolution; Comprising a Complete Anecdotic History
     of That Great National Event. Philadelphia: Grigg &
     Elliot, pp. 86-88.
        Franklin explains that he never wanted to author public
     papers, since it is likely that they will be revised beyond
     the recognition of the writer.

10   GRISWOLD, RUFUS WILMOT. "Benjamin Franklin." In The Prose
     Writers of America. With a Survey of the History, Condi-
     tion, and Prospects of American Literature. Philadelphia:
     Carey & Hart, pp. 57-62.
        Franklin's writings, which are characterized by "common
     sense," have had a profound impact on the American character.
     Generally this influence has been positive, though one looks
     in vain for the idea in Franklin's writings of doing good
     for other than utilitarian reasons. As a stylist,
     Franklin is superior to Addison.

11   KRIEGE, HERMANN. "Benjamin Franklin." In Die Väter unserer
     Republik in ihrem Leben und Wirken. New York: J. Uhl--
     Helmich u. Co., pp. 7-224.
        Begins with a biography of Franklin somewhat in the
     style of "an example for young readers to follow" (pp. 7-79).
     Next there is a general introduction to Franklin's writings
     which asserts that they reflect development in his life and
     career. Moreover, they reveal the inner Franklin. Kriege
     provides a short introduction before each excerpt from
     Franklin's works (pp. [81]-83). Nearly the entire remain-
     der of the section on Franklin is a collection of his writ-
     ings; however, the author (pp. [129]-31) points out that
     Franklin's literary efforts in behalf of the American cause
     against Britain were intended to enlighten that government
     about the legitimate desires of the Americans. Although
     his works had a great impact on the colonists, they were
     ignored by the English. Only after having tried everything
     in his power to come to a peaceful solution to problems,
     and having seen that England would have recourse to power,
     did Franklin call upon his countrymen to take up arms.
     (This section, as cautious as it is, should be read in
     light of the unstable political situation in Europe at the
     time.)

1847

12   Y., D. "Franklin--the Home of His Boyhood." In Supplements
     to the Connecticut "Courant," for the Year 1847; Containing
     Tales, Travels, History, Biography, Poetry, and a Great
     Variety of Miscellaneous Articles. Vol. 12. Hartford:
     John L. Boswell, pp. 43-44.
         Complains bitterly that the house in which Franklin grew
     up has been desecrated by being altered to suit the com-
     mercial purposes for which the building is used.

1848

1   ANON. "The Little Village and Great America." Howitt's
    Journal 3:322-24.
        Fictionalized account of Madame Helvétius's reasons for
    not marrying Franklin.

2   [CHAMPAGNAC, JEAN BAPTISTE JOSEPH.] "Les ballades du petit
    Benjamin." In Le tour du monde, ou, une fleur de chaque
    pays. . . . Paris: Lehuby, pp. [329]-35.
        Idealized, fictionalized account of the young Franklin
    hawking ballads through the streets of Boston in prepara-
    tion for his career as a printer and publisher. Even at
    this early time one can recognize the qualities that were
    to make him great.

3   FRANKLIN TYPOGRAPHICAL SOCIETY. The Proceedings at the Print-
    ers' Festival, Held by the Franklin Typographical Society,
    at Hancock Hall, January 15, 1848. Boston: published
    by the Society.
        Includes tributes to and addresses on Franklin.

4   HOLLEY, O[RVILLE] L[UTHER]. The Life of Benjamin Franklin.
    New York: George F. Cooledge & Brother, 468 pp.
        Holley intends to present the mental and spiritual life
    of Franklin, especially with regard "to his political ser-
    vices" before the Revolution. He also comments on a number
    of Franklin's writings to show the degree to which they re-
    veal his principles and character. The author concludes
    that while Franklin was not a Christian in any strict sense,
    he was nevertheless filled with a religious spirit that was
    expressed in practical moral virtue. He dedicated his
    great abilities and energy with completely disinterested
    magnanimity to the well being of his fellow man. His wise
    course through life will serve as a model for all succeed-
    ing generations of Americans.

5 LOSSING, B[ENSON] J[OHN] et al. "Benjamin Franklin." In
   Biographical Sketches of the Signers of American Independence: The Declaration Historically Considered: and a
   Sketch of the Leading Events Connected with the Adoption
   of the Articles of Confederation, and of the Federal Constitution. New York: George F. Cooledge & Brother,
   pp. 104-11.
      A sketch of Franklin's life and an assessment of him as
   the greatest person of all time.

6 MIGNET, [FRANÇOIS AUGUSTE MARIE ALEXIS]. Petits traités,
   publiés par l'Académie des Sciences, morales et politiques.
   Vie de Franklin, a l'usage de tout le monde. 2 vols.
   Paris: Pagnerre, 230 pp.
      Franklin had that happy combination of genius, tempera-
   ment, learning, and will that would have enabled him to
   succeed in any endeavor and that led him to become the
   founder of his nation's independence and freedom. Franklin
   is described as a kind of remarkable backwoods philosopher
   who overcame the provinciality of his birth and upbringing
   and formed a number of America's great characteristics.
   Moreover, Franklin epitomizes many of these traits. For-
   tunately, the scope of his curiosity was matched by the
   range of his genius, witness his great scientific achicv-
   ments, and so he belongs to mankind rather than to his
   country alone. (It is frequently easier to locate the
   free German translation by Eduard Burckhardt (Leipzig:
   Carl B. Lorck, 1855) than to find the French original.)

7 MÜLLER, JOHANN. "Franklins Vorschlag." In Der Familienkreis
   zu Marienthal, oder: Unterhaltungen aus dem Gebiete des
   Wissenswürdigen und Belehrenden. Ein Bildungsbuch für die
   Jugend. Leitmeritz: Carl Wilhelm Medau, p. 269.
      Anecdote of the young Franklin asking his father to
   pray over all the meat at once instead of at each meal.

1 HUNT, WILLIAM. "Benjamin Franklin." In American Biographical
   Panorama. [Albany?]: Joel Munsell, pp. 65-74.
      Franklin was a great and good man whose rise in life is
   instructive to all. One reason for his happiness and success is that he lived by his famous thirteen virtues.

2 JEWETT, JOHN L. Franklin--His Genius, Life and Character. An
   Oration Delivered before the N.Y. Typographical Society on
   the Occasion of the Birthday of Franklin, at the Printers'

1849

Festival, Held January 17, 1849. New York: published by
order of the Society by Harper & Brothers, 37 pp.
     Franklin, like Washington, who stands preeminent, repre-
sents the Golden Age of America. Of Franklin, Jewett says:
"All other things might admit of change, modification, or
re-construction; but the great principles of Truth, Justice,
and Integrity could never yield in his mind to further the
success of any cause. . . ." From such conduct we have
"fallen," and we should emulate Franklin to renew ourselves.

3 STANLEY, JOHN. Life of Benjamin Franklin; With Selections
   From His Miscellaneous Work. Boston: Thomas Charlton,
   162 pp.
        Franklin's fame has increased since his death, for he
   embodies the solid virtues of humanitarianism, wit, and
   humor that men love.

4 WELD, H[ORATIO] HASTINGS. [Narrative.] In Benjamin Franklin:
   His Autobiography; With a Narrative of His Public Life and
   Services. New York: Harper & Brothers, pp. 266-549.
        This part of the book is Weld's narrative, which is a
   fairly accurate account of Franklin's greatest years as a
   statesman. The author, however, does gloss over Franklin's
   political intrigues in Pennsylvania and presents a man who
   was always a skilled, selfless patriot-diplomat and moralistic utilitarian. If Franklin was "unsettled" in some
   theological matters, he was basically religious and re-
   sented those who would disturb belief in God. Finally,
   he was no political radical but was certainly as republican
   as any of his peers. He may be called "a conservative
   democrat, in opposition to those who are termed the move-
   ment of the party."

185-

1 ANON. "Benjamin Franklin." In Sketches of Revolutionary
   Worthies. With Fine Portraits. Worcester, Mass.:
   J. Grout, Jr., pp. 12-20.
        Brief biography.

2 ANON. Benjamin Franklin. Temperance Tracts for Children,
   no. 81. New York: American Temperance Union, 4 pp.
        A fictionalized but typical sketch of its kind in which
   children are told that Franklin owed his health, longevity
   and, indeed, much of his success not only to Poor Richard's
   virtues but to temperance. Temperance is made to seem the
   original American Way.

1850

3 ANON. Child's Life of Franklin, With Eight Illustrations.
   Evergreen Miniature Library. Philadelphia: Fisher &
   Brothers, 192 pp.
        More than half the book, which quotes extensively from
   Franklin and others, deals with the philosopher's first
   twenty years. The rest considers briefly and superficially
   Franklin as a scientist and political figure.

                            1850

1 ANON. "Benjamin Franklin." Anecdote Magazine, p. 47.
        Fictional anecdote in which Franklin teaches a Gazette
   subscriber that one need not be ashamed to be plain or
   modest.

*2 ANON. "Biografia e insegnamenti di Beniamino Franklin."
    Museo scientifico, letterario ed artistico (Turin) 12:93-94.
        Sources: NUC and Pace, p. 431, no. 202. Franklin's
    genius and virtue are even more sublime because he cared
    for the poor and ignorant and worked to improve their lives
    and prospects.

3 ANON. "A Century Ago." In Voices From the Press: A Collection of Sketches, Essays, and Poems by Practical Printers.
   Edited by James J. Brenton. New York: Charles B. Norton,
   pp. 308-9.
        Describes the contents of a copy of the Pennsylvania
   Gazette of 22 June 1749, and notes how much has changed in
   the intervening hundred years. The author of this piece
   evidently believes Franklin was still active on the newspaper at this time.

4 ANON. "Franklin As a Printer." In The Illustrated Family
   Christian Almanac for the United States, for the Year of
   Our Lord and Saviour 1850, Being the Second After
   Bissextile, and Until July 4th, the 74th Year of the Inde-
   pendence of the United States. New York: published by
   the American Tract Society, pp. 33-34.
        Printing has advanced significantly since the time of
   Franklin.

5 ANON. "The Lightning King." In Contributions to Herography.
   Rochester: Erastus Darrow, pp. [55]-57.
        Franklin's experiments in electricity reveal his open-
   mindedness, energy, and intelligence. These qualities
   show how inaccurate and unjust a judgment is made by ortho-
   dox Christians who support the doctrines of natural

1850

depravity and the need for conversion. Franklin's life
proves beyond doubt that one must instead work toward
acquiring the habit of virtue, and that this is a reachable
goal.

6   ANON. "Poor Richard's Almanac." In Voices From the Press:
    A Collection of Sketches, Essays, and Poems by Practical
    Printers. Edited by James J. Brenton. New York:
    Charles B. Norton, pp. 310-12.
        Argues that Franklin did the illustrations for the 1749
    edition of Poor Richard's Almanack.

*7 ANON. Vita di Franklin. A spese della Libera Propaganda.
    Turin: Arnaldi, 64 pp.
        Sources: NUC and Pace, p. 431, no. 204. Franklin's
    background as a moralist and educator led to his revolu-
    tionary activities in behalf of his countrymen.

8   BAKER, PETER C[ARPENTER]. "Address." In Proceedings at the
    Printers' Banquet, Held by the N.Y. Typographical Society,
    on the Occasion of Franklin's Birth-Day, Jan. 17, 1850,
    at Niblo's, Broadway. New York: Charles B. Norton,
    pp. [7]-18.
        Franklin's life has encouraged the Society to undertake
    its useful and charitable work. Most of this piece deals
    with the affairs of the Society.

9   BOURNE, W[ILLIA]M OLAND. "Opening Ode." In Proceedings at
    the Printers' Banquet, Held by the N.Y. Typographical Soci-
    ety, on the Occasion of Franklin's Birth-Day, Jan. 17, 1850,
    at Niblo's, Broadway. New York: Charles B. Norton,
    p. [6].
        Praises Franklin as a pioneering intellect and political
    force who, in behalf of mankind, made his way "Up the moun-
    tains of toil, and the stern labor-steeps."

10 BUCKINGHAM, JOSEPH T[INKER]. "Benjamin Franklin." In
    Specimens of Newspaper Literature: With Personal Memoirs,
    Anecdotes, and Reminiscences. Boston: Charles C. Little
    & James Brown, pp. 79-88.
        Relates the story, relying heavily on the Autobiography,
    of the manner in which Franklin became the ostensible pub-
    lisher of the Courant.

11 CORNELIUS, KARL SEBASTIAN. De fluido electrico in rerum
    natura statuendo. Halle: n.p.
        Presents the views of Franklin along with those of
    Symmer and Farraday.

12 EVERETT, EDWARD. "The Boyhood and Youth of Franklin." In
    Orations and Speeches on Various Occasions. Vol. 2.
    Boston: Charles C. Little & James Brown, pp. [1]-46.
       Franklin's early years are clearly the foundation of his
    later greatness. At this time he developed the character
    traits that served him so well as an adult. (Delivered
    first in 1829, as the Orations indicates, but first pub-
    lished in 1850.)

13 HARRISON, W.L.S. "Oration." In Proceedings at the Printers'
    Banquet, Held by the N.Y. Typographical Society, on the
    Occasion of Franklin's Birth-Day, Jan. 17, 1850, at Niblo's,
    Broadway. New York: Charles B. Norton, pp. [19]-36.
       Most of this piece pays tribute to printers, who make
    the world enlightened and free. Harrison does note, how-
    ever, that Franklin is one of those men who "give an im-
    pulse and direction to the character and feelings of their
    countrymen," and who indeed deserve the thanks of all man-
    kind. If Franklin were alive in 1850, he would be at the
    center of the great idealistic debates in America and on
    the side of liberty.

14 NEW YORK TYPOGRAPHICAL SOCIETY. Proceedings at the Printers'
    Banquet, Held by the N.Y. Typographical Society, on the
    Occasion of Franklin's Birth-Day, Jan. 17, 1850, at Niblo's,
    Broadway. New York: Charles B. Norton, 64 pp.
       Opens with an account of the affair and then presents
    the various addresses, orations, and toasts in honor of
    Franklin. (Appropriate parts of the book are cited
    individually.)

15 SCHMALTZ, [JOHANN] CARL [STEPHAN]. Das Leben Benjamin
    Franklins. 2d ed. Leipzig: Carl Schmaltz, 64 pp.
       Schmaltz describes Franklin's youth and early manhood.
    Readers are told that even when he was quite young,
    Franklin knew what qualities were most conducive to a
    successful and useful life. And, great example of self-
    education that he is, Franklin acquired these traits.
    (Information in the New York Public Library indicates that
    this work was first published in 1840. The version I have
    used is, however, the earliest that seems to be available.)
    See 1840.5.

16 SMITH, DANIEL, comp. "The Citizen. Benjamin Franklin." In
    Anecdotes for the Fireside: Or, a Manual for Home. New
    York: Carlton & Porter, p. 191.
       Fictional anecdote illustrating Franklin's ability to
    live on very little and therefore being able to remain

1850

independent and not be forced to publish defamatory pieces in his Gazette.

17 TAYLOR, J. BAYARD. "Franklin." In Voices From the Press: A Collection of Sketches, Essays, and Poems by Practical Printers. Edited by James J. Brenton. New York: Charles B. Norton, p. 119.
Franklin is both "the Printer and the Sage," whose wisdom is eternal.

The power to stay the fleeting Thought,
Unto thy hand was early given,
Till with the mind's quick lightning fraught,
It learned to fetter that of Heaven.

18 WYNNE, JAMES. "Franklin." In Lives of Eminent Literary and Scientific Men of America. New York: D. Appleton & Co., pp. [7]-133.
A rather strangely organized book which surveys Franklin's career well for the time but evaluates him only briefly and only as a scientist. In this capacity Franklin's fame will endure because of his discovery of general principles and because of his versatility.

1851

1 ANON. "Benjamin Franklin." Family Circle and Parlor Annual 9:100-2.
Relates the anecdote that Franklin, as a man, returned to Boston to visit his mother, who did not recognize him and asked him to leave her house.

2 ANON. "Dr. Franklin." Stryker's American Register and Magazine 5 (January):394-96.
Franklin was an original genius, as his versatility shows, and he directed his abilities to making men happier. "The whole tenor of his life was a perpetual lecture against the idle, the extravagant, and the proud." (It has been suggested that Stryker himself wrote this piece.)

3 BREEN, HENRY H. "Latin Verse on Franklin." Notes and Queries 4, no. 110 (6 December):443.
Asks who wrote "Eripuit coelo fulmen, sceptrumque Tyrannis."

1852

4   PIRALA, ANTONIO. "Franklin." <u>Revista Historica</u> 1:295-96.
    Franklin was honored with a medal because of his patri-
    otism, integrity, goodness, useful moral philosophy, and
    achievements as a scientist.

*5 PISTOLESI, ERASMO. "Beniamino Franklin." In <u>Album pittorico</u>
    <u>descritto da Erasmo Pistolesi con note ed osservazioni.</u>
    Vol. 1. Genoa: Co' tipi del R.I. de' Sordo-muti,
    pp. 14-17.
        Source: Pace, pp. 292-93. Franklin's image must command
    our respect and admiration, for it unmistakably reveals his
    virtue and wisdom.

*6 RUSSELL, WILLIAM. "Benjamin Franklin." In <u>Extraordinary Men:</u>
    <u>Their Boyhood and Early Life.</u> National Illustrated Library.
    [London.]
        Source: <u>BM</u>. See 1853.15.

                              1852

1   ABBOTT, JACOB. "Early and Private Life of Benjamin Franklin."
    <u>Harper's New Monthly Magazine</u> 4, no. 20 (January):[145]-65.
        An idealized, moralistic and, at times, fanciful
    Franklin designed to appeal to readers who aspire to suc-
    cess and some measure of gentility. This biographical
    sketch is continued under a separate title in the next
    number of <u>Harper's</u> and is cited separately (1852.2).

2   _____. "Public Life of Benjamin Franklin." <u>Harper's New</u>
    <u>Monthly Magazine</u> 4, no. 21 (February):[289]-309.
        This separately titled piece is actually a continuation
    of Abbott's "Early and Private Life of Benjamin Franklin"
    (1852.1). The idealized, always successful Franklin is
    taken through the Revolutionary War, the peace treaty, and
    brought home to Philadelphia.

3   C. "Line on Franklin." <u>Notes and Queries</u> 5, no. 137
    (12 June):571.
        Responds to J.S. Warden (1852.18) and says that the
    famous Latin verse on Franklin was written by Turgot.

*4 COQUELIN, CH[ARLES], and COQUELIN, GUILLAUMIN. "Franklin (B)."
    In <u>Dictionnaire de l'économie politique contenant</u>
    <u>l'exposition des principes de la science[,] l'opinion des</u>
    <u>écrivains qui ont le plus contribué à sa fondation et ses</u>
    <u>progrès[,] la bibliographie générale de l'économie</u>
    <u>politique par noms d'auteurs et par ordre de matières avec</u>

1852

des notices biographiques et une appréciation raisonnée des principaux ouvrages. Vol. 1. Paris: Guillaumin & Cie.
Source: NUC. See 1854.8.

5   CORNISH, JAMES. "Latin Verse on Franklin." Notes and Queries 5, no. 114 (3 January):17.
Reponds to Henry H. Breen's query (1851.3) and says that the famous Latin epigram on Franklin was written by Mirabeau.

6   CROSSLEY, JA[ME]S. "Dr. Franklin's Tract on Liberty and Necessity." Notes and Queries 5, no. 114 (3 January):6.
Owns a copy of Franklin's Dissertation on Liberty and Necessity, Pleasure and Pain, and, in summarizing Franklin's argument, explains that he later was sorry he had written the piece and rejected its findings.

7   EYMA, XAVIER. "Voyages en Amérique.--Les États-Unis." Musée des familles 19:200-6.
An idealized Franklin is the chief concern of trivia on him, his family, and Philadelphia.

8   H., R.D. "Latin Verse on Franklin." Notes and Queries 5, no. 114 (3 January):17.
The famous Turgot Latin verse on Franklin seems to parody a line of Manilius. Asks if Condorcet, who R.D.H. believes is the author, applied it to Franklin's career. R.D.H. is here responding to a query by Henry H. Breen (1851.3).

9   HARSHMAN, JACOB. Series of Communications Written on Love and Wisdom; by Impressions From the Spirits of James Victor Wilson, Benjamin Franklin, George Washington, and Sir Astley Cooper, M.D. Dayton, Ohio: published by the author, pp. 131-57.
In the preface Harshman writes: "I was formerly sceptical, in what was purported to have come from disembodied spirits, in the state of New York" and "took reason for my compass, and truth and sound philosophy for my polar star." All this changed for him, however, when he moved to Ohio and discovered the truth of "the sublime workings of spirits, that once dwelt upon the earth." Such a transformation apparently also motivated the spiritual Franklin to seize control of Harshman's will and relate the higher truths revealed to him in his improved state. The section on "Progression of the Mineral, Vegetable, Animal, and Spiritual Kingdoms" bears Franklin's name, and Harshman contends that Franklin's spirit actually wrote the piece. Harshman

is merely amanuensis and publisher for a Franklin who rejects materialism and earthly reason in favor of transcendent insights and truths.

10 HUTCHINS, SAMUEL. Benjamin Franklin: A Book for the Young and Old, for All. Cambridge, Mass.: published by the author, 36 pp.
    A moralistic biography for children who are taught to appreciate Franklin's Poor Richard qualities and to strive to learn well the lessons Franklin's life teaches us about virtue and dedication.

11 MONTGOMERY, JAMES. "Franklin, the Printer, Philosopher, and Patriot." In Poetical Works. Philadelphia: Lindsay & Blakiston, p. 387.
    Montgomery applauds Franklin as a scientist who helped mankind get the better of lightning, and as a powerful advocate of a free press. As for Franklin the scientist, he was able "to pierce / The mystery of the universe" and in so doing, perform God's work. Yet, even more significantly:

        A nobler wreath he lived to share,
        He lived a brighter day to see,--
        His country by the PRESS made free.

    The poem was written in 1847 at the request of the Rochester, New York, committee in charge of preparing a national celebration of Franklin's 141st birthday. (This piece is erroneously listed in the National Union Catalog, Pre-1956, Imprints, 392:306, as having possibly been published in London, 1790.)

*12 POLKO, ELISE VOGEL. Musikalische Marchen, Phantasien, und Skizzen. Leipzig: Barth.
     Source: NUC. See 1876.12.

13 R., J. "Latin Verse on Franklin." Notes and Queries 5, no. 119 (7 February):267.
    Addressing himself to queries by Henry H. Breen (1851.3) and to R.D.H. (1852.8), the present author says that Turgot wrote the Latin verse on Franklin.

14 _____. "Lines on Franklin." Notes and Queries 6, no. 143 (24 July):88.
    Points out that in 1847 he had already traced the Latin epigram on Franklin from Turgot back to the Anti-Lucretius of Polignac.

1852

15 [S., J.] Benjamin Franklin. (Ž. Praszského Polsa, sv. 3 a 4)
    Prague: Jarosl[av] Pospíšila, 58 pp.
        A biography which idealizes Franklin, identifies him,
    especially as a young man, with Poor Richard, and stresses
    his patriotism and his astonishing rise in life.

16 S., W. "Epigram on Franklin and Wedderburn." Notes and
    Queries 5, no. 116 (17 January):58.
        Wants to know who wrote the following:

            Sarcastic Sawney, full of spite and hate,
            On modest Franklin pounced his venal prate;
            The calm philosopher without reply
            Withdrew--and gave his country liberty.

17 SMITH, JOHN JAY. Letter to Horace Binney, Esq., Respecting
    the Founder of the Philadelphia Contributorship for the
    Insurance of Houses from Loss by Fire. Philadelphia:
    privately printed, 16 pp.
        Argues that John Smith, and not Franklin, was the
    founder of the Philadelphia Contributorship.

18 WARDEN, J.S. "Line on Franklin." Notes and Queries 5, no.
    136 (5 June):549.
        Responding to Henry H. Breen (1851.3) and R.D.H. (1852.8)
    Warden says that the famous Latin epigram on Franklin was
    taken immediately from the Anti-Lucretius of Polignac, who
    probably borrowed it from Manilius.

1853

1   ALLIBONE, S[AMUEL] AUSTIN. "Franklin, Benjamin." In A Crit-
    ical Dictionary of English Literature, and British and
    American Authors, Living and Deceased, From the Earliest
    Accounts to the Middle of the Nineteenth Century. Contain-
    ing Thirty Thousand Biographies and Literary Notices, With
    Forty Indexes of Subjects. Vol. 1. Philadelphia:
    George W. Child, pp. 629-32.
        Biographical survey of Franklin, who is acclaimed as
    "one of the most distinguished of modern philosophers,"
    a benefactor to mankind, a patriot, and a statesman.
    Allibone condemns Tom Paine and other "Freethinkers" and
    "French deists and atheists" who encouraged Franklin's
    "latitudinarian sentiments"; however, Allibone implies,
    at least, that Franklin was never as radical in his beliefs
    as Paine or the English and French deists.

2 ANON. "Benjamin Franklin." In <u>Illustrated Magazine of Art[,]</u>
<u>Containing Selections From the Various Departments of Paint-</u>
<u>ing, Sculpture, Architecture, History, Biography, Art-</u>
<u>Industry, Manufactures, Scientific Inventions and</u>
<u>Discoveries, Local and Domestic Scenes, Ornamental Works,</u>
<u>etc.[,] etc.</u> Vol. 2. New York: Alexander Montgomery,
pp. 37-39.
A concise account of Franklin's career, particularly in
politics. In an Eastern country, Franklin would be considered a sage. He was not only brilliant and remarkably
versatile, not only a fine politician, a philosopher "of
great accuracy, great penetration, and wonderful originality," but a farsighted statesman and patriot. Franklin was
in fact more than these: he was "a man of such sterling
worth and stainless purity of character, that none of his
enemies, even in the heat of a furious and unnatural con-
flict, ever could allege aught against him that he had need
to be ashamed of."

3 B., G.M. "Dr. Franklin." <u>Notes and Queries</u> 8, no. 200
(27 August):196.
Has in his possession lines of a poem in Franklin's
handwriting and asks the identity of the author. The
poem begins: "When Orpheus went down to the Regions
below. . . ."

4 BETTZIECH, HEINRICH. <u>Benjamin Franklin. Sein Leben, Denken</u>
<u>und Wirken.</u> Leipzig: F.A. Brockhaus, 108 pp.
Franklin is acclaimed as a practical philosopher whose
fertile mind and benevolence led to improvements in the
condition of men.

5 BOSTON CITY COUNCIL. <u>Franklin Fund. City Document, No. 26.</u>
Boston: published by the City Council.
The story and progress of the Franklin Fund for young
married mechanics.

6 BUCKLEY, THEODORE ALOIS. "Benjamin Franklin." In <u>Dawnings of</u>
<u>Genius Exemplified and Exhibited in the Early Lives of Dis-</u>
<u>tinguished Men.</u> London: G. Routledge & Co., pp. [353]-78.
One who judges Franklin by either his intellectual or
social contributions to the world or by his more personal
achievement in reforming himself must conclude that he "has
done much good for society and for all time." Those who
think of Franklin's "practical wisdom" as mere selfish
prudence are seriously mistaken.

7 D., H.G. "Portrait of Franklin." <u>Notes and Queries</u> 7,
no. 182 (23 April):409.

1853

Asks if Franklin left a portrait of himself done by
Benjamin West "to Thurlow." (The Thurlow referred to is
probably Edward Thurlow, the attorney-general of England,
who advised against preventing Franklin from returning to
America in 1775. Thurlow, however, was unfriendly to the
rebelling American colonies and to Franklin.)

8   INGRAHAM, EDWARD D. "Gibbon's Library. . . . West's Portrait
of Franklin. . . ." Notes and Queries 8, no. 200
(27 August):208-9.
Says that H.G.D. (1853.7) was mistaken about the portrait
of Franklin by West. The only portrait of Franklin done by
West was given by Franklin to Edward Duffield, Ingraham's
grandfather. Ingraham owned that painting.

9   JAY, WILLIAM; HEDENBERG, CHARLES J.; and EMERSON, WILLIAM H.
Terms of Subscription to the Elegant Steel Engraving of
Franklin at the Court of France, in 1778. Engraved by
William Overend Geller, From the Original Painting by
Baron Jolly, of Bruxelles. Philadelphia: Jay, Hedenberg &
Emerson, broadside.
The cost of the different impressions ranged from $7.50
for "Plain Impressions" to $25.00 for "Artist Proofs."

*10 JONES, ABNER DUMONT. "Benjamin Franklin." In The Illustrated
American Biography, Containing Correct Portraits and Brief
Notes of the Principal Actors in American History. 3 vols.
New York: J.M. Emerson Co.
Source: NUC. See 1855.3.

11   MERGET, ANTOINE EUGÈNE. "Étude sur les travaux de M. de Romas."
Actes Académie Bordeaux 20:447-518.
Discusses in detail Franklin's experiments on atmospheric
electricity and upholds the view of Jacques de Romas who,
though he supported the single fluid theory of electricity,
doubted that a glass surface could hold an electrical charge.

12   NEW YORK TYPOGRAPHICAL SOCIETY. Celebration of the 147th
Anniversary of the Birth of Benjamin Franklin. New York:
John F. Trow, 3 pp.
Program.

13   NORDEN, Fr. Neue Volksbücher mit holzschnitten. Des
Amerikaners[:] Benjamin Franklin[,] merkwürdiges Leben
und Wirken. Für das Volk erzählt. Vol. 40. Leipzig:
Bernhard Schlicke, pp. 1-21.
A biographical account that delights in the picturesque
qualities of Franklin's early life, but which also goes on

to deal with him as a practical sage whose aim it was to improve the lives of his fellow men.

14   OLDENSHAW, C. "When Orpheus Went Down." Notes and Queries 8, no. 203 (17 September):281.
      Replies to G.M.B. (1853.3) and says that the poem in Franklin's handwriting was written by the Rev. Dr. Lisle, who was probably the Bishop of St. Asaph.

15   RUSSELL, WILLIAM. "Benjamin Franklin." In Extraordinary Men: Their Boyhood and Early Life. London: George Routledge & Sons, pp. [87]-101.
      It is pleasing to think of Franklin's life, for we can much more readily identify with him than with men of genius. Franklin was not a genius, but instead a man who rose to eminence "by the aid alone of a strong, clear common sense, combined with integrity, temperance, and persevering indus-try," qualities which are common enough among mankind. Franklin therefore offers more encouragement to his fellows, who hope to succeed, than do the more dazzling personages of history. See 1851.6.

16   SAINTE-BEUVE, C[HARLES] A[UGUSTIN]. "Franklin." In Causeries du Lundi. [2d ed.] Vol. 7. Paris: Garnier Frères, Libraires, pp. [117]-45.
      Survey of Franklin's career and character which, while paying tribute to his many virtues and achievements, asserts that his chief deficiency was his lack of poetic sensibility and imagination that led him to translate everything into practical terms and uses.

17   SCHLOSSER, F[RIEDRICH] C[HRISTOPH]. "Franklin." In Geschichte des achtezehnten Jahrhunderts und des neunzehnten bis zum Sturz des französischen Kaiserreichs. Mit besonderer Rücksicht auf den Gang der Literatur. Vol. 3. Heidelberg: J.C.B. Mohr, p. 346.
      Franklin's greatness lies chiefly in his political achievements, which comprehended his moral convictions. It is in the realm of politics that he has influenced, through his writings and activities, the largest number of people. He was a model statesman and handled political affairs with the same feeling for practicality that he brought to all his work. See 1836.13.

18   WINTHROP, ROBERT C[HARLES]. Archimedes and Franklin. Boston: printed for the Massachusetts Charitable Mechanic Associa-tion by T.R. Marvin, 47 pp.

1853

Like Archimedes, Franklin used his genius to apply science to art "and in the noblest of all causes, the defence
of one's country." Both men, however, worked for the good
of mankind in general. If Washington is our greatest
American, Franklin is surely the greatest native-born New
Englander and one of the greatest men of the world.

1854

1   ANON. "Anecdotes of Dr. Franklin." In Good Child's Story
    Book. Concord, N.H.: Merriam & Merrill, pp. 7-10.
    (Dated 1855 on cover.)
        There are three anecdotes about Franklin. The second
    is about paying too much for one's whistle and is told in
    the first person; the other two deal with getting money and
    knowing when one has enough.

2   ANON. "Beniamino Franklin." L'album dei fanciulli 1, no. 78
    (6 May):[273]-77.
        Biographical sketch summarizing Franklin's rise to
    international eminence and calling him a founder of the
    United States of America.

3   ANON. "Franklin's Parable." Notes and Queries 10, no. 256
    (23 September):252.
        Points out that the solicitor-general, Alexander
    Wedderburn, had referred to Jeremy Taylor's original of
    Franklin's "Parable Against Persecution" while he was
    attacking the philosopher. This was but one of the methods
    Wedderburn used in the hope of discrediting Franklin.

4   ANON. "Oil Upon the Waves." Household Words 9, no. 5:
    [98]-100.
        Franklin undertook the famous experiment of pouring oil
    on turbulent water because he thought it potentially useful.

5   ANON. "The Philadelphia Printer." Leisure Hour 3, no. 154
    (7 December):772-75; no. 155 (14 December):788-91; no. 156
    (21 December):804-7.
        Franklin unfortunately paid less attention to the state
    of his soul than to even common secular and wordly matters;
    therefore he "may be regarded as a high speciman of a
    merely worldly man."

6   BINGHAM, C.W. "Franklin's Parable." Notes and Queries 10,
    no. 252 (26 August):169.

1854

Franklin's "Parable Against Persecution" has its origins in Jeremy Taylor's Liberty of Prophesying. Franklin, however, made his piece a parody, which is a most "questionable" practice.

7   BRIGGS, C[HARLES] F[REDERICK]. "Franklin." In Homes of American Statesmen: With Anecdotal, Personal and Descriptive Sketches, by Various Writers. New York: G.P. Putnam & Co., pp. [65]-76.
     Franklin is remembered and revered by the "popular heart" more than any other great American, for "he was one of us." Most of this essay focuses on Franklin's earlier years and on his modesty, frugality, and inventiveness.

8   COQUELIN, CH[ARLES], and COQUELIN, GUILLAUMIN. "Franklin (B)." In Dictionnaire de l'économie politique contenant l'exposition des principes de la science[,] l'opinion des écrivains qui ont le plus contribué à sa fondation et ses progrès. . . . Vol. 1. Paris: Guillaumin & Cie et L. Hachette & Cie, p. 810.
     Franklin was an excellent economist. See 1852.4.

9   M. "Franklin's Parable." Notes and Queries 10, no. 248 (29 July):82-83.
     Franklin's friend, Lord Kames, published Franklin's "Parable Against Persecution," but his version is incomplete.

10   ROBIQUET, [EDMOND] HENRI. Fermentation gallique Éthérification de l'alcool vinique. Observations au sujet de la théorie de Franklin sur la nature du fluide életrique. Propositions de physique données par la Faculte. Paris: E. Thunot & Cie, 46 pp.
     Defends the Franklinian theory of electricity.

11   W., W. "Telegraphing Through Water, Not a Recent Discovery." Notes and Queries 10, no. 266 (2 December):443.
     Franklin knew that electricity could be carried through water.

12   WASHINGTON, H.A., ed. The Writings of Thomas Jefferson: Being His Autobiography, Correspondence, Reports, Messages, Addresses, and Other Writings, Official and Private. Vol. 8. New York: Riker, Thorne & Co., pp. 497-502.
     Franklin's anecdotes were always appropriate to the occasion and could frequently turn a tense situation into a relaxed, humorous one.

119

1855

1   [ABBOTT, JACOB.] Franklin, The Apprentice Boy. Harper's
    Story Books, no. 11. New York: Harper & Brother,
    Publishers, 160 pp.
        Representative of many early stories of Franklin written
    for American children. Franklin is used as a example of
    limitless possibility in an America that awaits those young-
    sters who practice the virtues he institutionalized in his
    adult life as Poor Richard. Abbott interrupts his narrative
    to discourse at length on the practical benefits of swimming,
    an exercise Franklin enjoyed. Questionable aspects of
    Franklin's conduct are either ignored or glossed over.
    Ralph, for example, "found cause to quarrel with Franklin
    about something connected with the milliner" and so con-
    sidered himself free of all debts he had incurred. Franklin
    is said to have used Vernon's money to pay off Collins's
    debts, and so even this "erratum" is treated as an act of
    generosity and compassion. Bad company, then, hurts even
    the purely motivated. Franklin was not one who could com-
    mit a misdeed without suffering for it. When he had earlier
    run away from Boston and settled in Philadelphia, he felt
    "uneasiness and self-condemnation." Franklin's only real
    fault is that like all boys of talent he was a little "vain
    and self-willed." Nothing is mentioned of his early rejec-
    tion of Christianity, for this book hoped to use Franklin's
    full and successful life to fashion industrious, frugal and,
    on the whole, passive Christian boys.

2   G. "Franklin's Parable." Notes and Queries 11, no. 285
    (14 April):296.
        Franklin borrowed the "Parable Against Persecution" from
    Jeremy Taylor's The Art of Prophesying. We do not know,
    however, in what edition of Taylor's work the original of
    the "Parable" first appeared.

3   JONES, A[BNER] DUMONT. "Benjamin Franklin." In American Por-
    trait Gallery, Containing Correct Portraits and Brief No-
    tices of the Principal Actors in American History. New
    York: J.M. Emerson & Co., p. 4.
        Franklin's portrait is followed by a very brief sketch
    of his life. See 1853.10.

4   MELVILLE, HERMAN. Israel Potter: His Fifty Years of Exile.
    New York: G.P. Putnam & Co., pp. 63-105.
        Melville, believing Franklin devoid of emotion, says that
    in spite of his numerous accomplishments, he lacked the
    poetic qualities necessary to the complete man. (Israel
    Potter was originally published serially in 1854-1855.)

5   SINGER, S.W. "Franklin's Parable and Taylor's 'Liberty of
     Prophecying.'" Notes and Queries 11, no. 288 (5 May):
     344-45.
          Responding in particular to G. (1855.2) Singer points
     out that Taylor's model for Franklin's "Parable Against
     Persecution" appeared first in Taylor's Collection of
     Polemical Discourses (1647). The enlarged version of
     Taylor's piece that is most like the "Parable" did not
     appear until the 1674 edition of the Collection.

6   STAYMAN, JOHN K., and WEILAND, FRANCIS. Ben. Franklin's Grave.
     Philadelphia: Stayman & Brothers, 6 pp.
          A song. Weiland did the music, and Stayman is responsi-
     ble for the lyrics, the second stanza of which follows:

               No flattery of Epitaphs is here
          To mock with idle praise the heart sincere;
               No pride that lurks in monumental show
          Commemorates the dust that sleeps below:
               A simple slab of stone is all that shows
          The spot where thou, O Franklin! dost repose,
               A simple slab of stone whereon are seen
          The names of Deborah and Benjamin.

7   WELKER von GUNTERSHAUSEN, HEINRICH. "Friktionsinstrumente mit
     Glocken und Röhren von Glas. Die Glasharmonika." In Neu
     eröffnetes Magazin musikalischer Tonwerkzeuge. . . .
     Frankfurt: Im Selbst-Verlag des Verfassen, pp. 2-3, 190-92.
     Discusses Franklin's glass armonica.

                              1856

1   ANON. "An Anecdote of Dr. Franklin, Never Before Published."
     In The Year-Book of the Unitarian Congregational Churches,
     for 1856. Annual Serial, no. 6. Boston: American Unitar-
     ian Association, p. 63.
          Among a group of wits and savants in France the question
     arose as to what was the strongest proof of the divine ori-
     gin of Christianity. Different persons asserted various
     proofs, but Franklin's was the best and most practical.
     He is said to have declared that the best evidence of the
     divine origin of Christianity would be true Christians.

2   B[ACHE?], T.H. "Portrait of Franklin." Notes and Queries,
     2d ser. 1, no. 1 (5 January):12.
          In the April 1783 issue of The European Magazine there
     appeared a portrait of Franklin. The author asks what has
     become of the original.

1856

3   [BOSTON CITY COUNCIL.] <u>Order of Exercises at the Inauguration</u>
     <u>of the Statue of Benjamin Franklin, September 17, 1856.</u>
     [Boston]: printed by Geo. C. Rand & Avery for the Boston
     City Council.
         The exercises included music, speeches, the singing of
     the "Ode" by James T. Fields (1857.6), which had been
     adapted to music by Nathaniel Richardson, and various
     other ceremonies.

4   BRIDGMAN, THOMAS. <u>The Pilgrims of Boston and Their Descendants.</u>
     New York: D. Appleton & Co., pp. 323-34, 374.
         A brief account of the Franklin family and extracts from
     the <u>Autobiography</u>; on page 374 is a list of Franklin's
     descendants.

5   BROUGHAM, JOHN. <u>Franklin: A New and Original Historical Drama,</u>
     <u>in Five Acts.</u> French's Standard Drama, no. 166. New York:
     Samuel French, 27 pp.
         Makes no attempt at historical accuracy and is simply an
     effort to show that Franklin was always a philosopher and
     patriot who preferred Yankee simplicity to the honors and
     fashions of the courtier.

6   [CHAMBERS, ROBERT.] "Benjamin Franklin, 1706-1790." In <u>Hand-</u>
     <u>book of American Literature, Historical, Biographical and</u>
     <u>Critical.</u> Philadelphia: J.B. Lippincott & Co., pp. 24-29.
         A brief survey of Franklin's life and achievements and
     selections from his writings.

7   [GROUX, DANIEL E.] <u>Franklin Medallion Struck for the Inaugura-</u>
     <u>tion of the Statue of Franklin, Boston, September 17, 1856.</u>
     [Boston], 4 pp.
         Describes the medal in detail.

8   GROUX, DANIEL E. <u>Prospectus of an Important Work in Three</u>
     <u>Volumes, to Be Called Numismatical History of the United</u>
     <u>States, Comprising a Full Description of its Medals &</u>
     <u>Coins from the Earliest Period to Our Times.</u> . . . Boston:
     press of the Franklin Printing House, 16 pp.
         Groux intended to include Franklin medals and coins.

*9   GRUBE, AUGUST WILHELM. "Benjamin Franklin." In <u>Charakterbilder</u>
     <u>aus der Geschichte und Sage, für einen propädeutschen</u>
     <u>Geschichtsunterricht gesammelt.</u> . . . Vol. 3. Leipzig:
     Brandstetter.
         Source: <u>NUC.</u> See 1865.10.

1856

10 HACKWOOD, R. W. "Portrait of Franklin." <u>Notes and Queries,</u>
    2d ser. 1, no. 6 (9 February):122.
        Referring to the query by T.H.B. (1856.2), says that
    the portrait asked about may have been owned by M. Regnier
    of Paris.

11 HOWE, HENRY. "Benjamin Franklin." In <u>Memoirs of the Most</u>
    <u>Eminent American Mechanics: Also, Lives of Distinguished</u>
    <u>European Mechanics; Together With a Collection of Anecdotes,</u>
    <u>Descriptions, &c. &c. Relating to the Mechanic Arts.</u> New
    York: J.C. Derby, pp. [35]-67.
        Biography that calls particular attention to Franklin's
    scientific achievements. These were a splendid manifesta-
    tion of his democratic qualities and benevolent nature that
    caused him to use his abilities to improve man's lot. Howe
    also praises Franklin for his unaffected simplicity, "im-
    mense stock of common sense" and his greatness in "little
    things." <u>See</u> 1840.3.

12 KNOWLES, [WILLIAM] J. <u>Features of Inauguration of the</u>
    <u>Franklin Statue in Boston, September 17th, 1856.</u> Boston:
    printed for the author, 12 pp.
        Verse celebrates both Franklin and the Greenough statue
    of him in the following manner:

        We love to think of Franklin, when yet he was a youth,
        A mind so very active and always told the truth;
        Obedient to his parents, his duty well discharged,
        With industry and patience, that mind must be enlarged.

13 [LECLERC, E.] "Hommes d'état de l'Amérique du nord. Franklin
    et ses mémoires." <u>La Libre recherche, revue universelle</u>
    3:[391]-405.
        Draws heavily from the Temple Franklin edition of his
    grandfather's works as it summarizes Franklin's achieve-
    ments and calls him immortal and a benefactor of mankind.

14 LOMÉNIE, LOUIS de. <u>Beaumarchais et Son Temps[:] Études sur</u>
    <u>La Société en XVIIIe Siècle[,] D'après Des Documents Inédits.</u>
    Vol. 2. Paris: Michel Lévy Frères, pp. [113]-213.
        Loménie traces Franklin's diplomatic career in France,
    concentrating on his relationship with Beaumarchais and on
    the occasional misunderstandings between the two men with
    respect to the role of France in the American Revolution.
    (There is an English edition of this work translated by
    Henry Sutherland Edwards and published in four volumes in
    London by Addey and Company in 1856. The section dealing
    with Franklin is in volume three, pages 131-237.)

1856

15   [MASSACHUSETTS CHARITABLE MECHANIC ASSOCIATION.] "The Seven-
      teenth of September, 1856." Illustrated Magazine, broadside.
      FCL.
         Praises the statue honoring Franklin, the "most distin-
      guished Son" Massachusetts has ever had. He deserves to
      have his memory perpetuated. (This curious piece appears
      on a sheet entitled "From the Illustrated Magazine of the
      Eighth Exhibition under the direction of the Massachusetts
      Charitable Mechanic Association," part of a packet of mate-
      rials concerning the proceedings at the dedication of the
      Franklin statue in Boston. A reference librarian at the
      Boston Public Library, which was supposed to own this item,
      reports that for each of the Association's Exhibitions there
      was printed a catalog, and that the Illustrated Magazine is
      actually such a catalog. The Boston Public Library owns
      only the nineteenth volume or catalog, which is for 10
      September-1 October 1856, and does not include the above
      noted item.)

16   MITTEIS, HEINRICH. "Abbé Nollet in seiner Stellung gegen
      Benjamin Franklin." In Programm und Jahresbericht des K.k.
      Obergymnasiums zu Laibach für das Schuljahr 1856. Laibach:
      Ign. v. Klemmahr & Fedor Bamberg, pp. [3]-12.
         Discusses Nollet's objections to the Franklinian theory
      of electricity. The attitude of the French preceptor
      toward the new theory was prompted by personal as well as
      intellectual considerations.

*17   RION, ADOLPHE. Découvertes et invention depuis les temps plus
      anciens jusqu'a nos jours. Bibliothèque illustrée des
      familles et des écoles, no. 28. 3d ed. Paris: Dans les
      departments et a l'étranger, 119 pp.
         (I do not find an earlier edition. This book is sup-
      posed to contain a discussion of Franklin. It is listed
      as being in the Smithsonian Institute's Air and Space
      Library, no. DSI T15 R58 1856 RB NASM; however, the
      library reports it missing as of 8 April 1980.)

18   [SAMPER, JOSÉ MARÍE.] Benjamin Franklin. Breve noticia sobre
      su vida. [Bogota?]: 48 pp.
         The work is actually a collection of pieces by Samper,
      the title page of which is missing from the copy inspected.
      The present title, given by persons at the Hispanic Society
      of America, is the title of a biographical sketch. There
      is also a piece by Samper entitled "La ciencia del buen
      Ricardo, ó el camino de la fortuna," pp. 7-16, but this is
      not the same as the work with the identical title, edited

by Samper and published in Caracas in 1858, for the latter
item has eighty-eight pages, according to Antonio Palau y
Dulcet's Manuel, 2d ed., 5, no. 94616, p. 494.

19 SHILLABER, [BENJAMIN PENHALLOW]. A Very Brief and Very Com-
    prehensive Life of Ben: Franklin, Printer, Done into Quaint
    Verse, by One of the Types--September 17, 1856. [Boston?]:
    broadside.
    A few stanzas of this tribute can easily represent the
    whole:

             And then when the bond was rent,
                 And the patriots made resistance,
             He over to France was sent,
                 To ask King Louis' assistance.

             His name before him had gone,
                 And the king was delighted to meet him;
             He even stepped from his throne,
                 In his earnestness to greet him.

             And the queen frowned not in check,
                 When this plain republican Mister
             Threw his arms about her neck
                 And very gallantly kissed her!

20 THOMPSON, N.A. Inauguration of the Statue of Franklin[:]
    Boston, September 17, 1856. Notice to Marshalls. [Boston:
    printed by Rand & Avery, for the Boston City Council],
    broadside.
    The marshalls were part of the procession of those honor-
    ing Franklin.

21 TRIQUETI, H[ENRY] de. Benjamin Franklin. Discours adressé
    aux apprentis. . . . 2d ed. Paris: Ch. Meyrueis et Cie,
    12 pp.
    The author uses Franklin's life and well known virtues
    to show the young apprentices that their present poverty
    need not stand in the way of their attaining great success.
    Franklin's diligence, industriousness, patriotism, and
    benevolence can, one must realize, be emulated by all.
    (The first edition was also published in 1856.)

22 [TUCKERMAN, HENRY THEORDORE.] "The Character of Franklin."
    North American Review 83, no. 173 (October):402-22.
    In addition to being a review of Sparks's edition of
    Franklin's works, this piece is also an appreciative sum-
    mary of Franklin's life, career, and qualities. Tuckerman,

1856

who published the essay in 1857 as the last of his Biographical Essays, asserts that Franklin's "pervading trait" of
character was his complete devotion "to the Practical."
He was not only a great example of self-education, but of
humanitarianism as well.

23 VERD ANTIQUE MARBLE Co. Franklin Statue! [N.p.: printed
for the Verd Antique Marble Co.]
    The Verd Company "furnished the Marble for the Pedestal
of the Franklin Statue." The pedestal was designed by
Henry Greenough, brother of Richard Greenough, who designed
the statue and executed the plaster cast.

*24 WATSON, ELKANNAH. Men and Times of the Revolution; or Memoirs
of Elkannah Watson Including Journals of Travels in Europe
and America From 1777 to 1842, With His Correspondence With
Public Men and Reminiscences and Incidents of the Revolution. . . . Edited by Winslow C. Watson. New York:
Dana & Co.
    Source: NUC. See 1857.19.

25 WINTHROP, ROBERT CHARLES. Oration at the Inauguration of the
Statue of Benjamin Franklin, in His Native City, Sept. 17,
1856. Boston: T.R. Marvin, 28 pp.
    This pamphlet pays tribute to Franklin's achievements
and character. "He has carried with him a native energy,
integrity, perseverance, and self-reliance, which nothing
could subdue or permanently repress. He has carried with
him a double measure of the gristle and the grit which are
the best ingredient and the most productive yield of the
ice and granite of New England."

1857

1 ANON. "Franklin (Benjamin)." In Nouvelle biographie générale
depuis les temps plus reculés jusqu'a nos jours. . . .
Vol. 18. Paris: Firmin Didot Frères, pp. 575-91.
    Relies heavily on the Autobiography for its presentation
of Franklin's early years, but concerns itself chiefly with
his scientific and political achievements.

2 ANON. "Inedited Apologue by Dr. Franklin." Notes and Queries,
2d ser. 1, no. 16 (19 April):305-6.
    Provides background to Franklin's "On Human Vanity,"
which appeared first in the Pennsylvania Gazette of
4 December 1735, and many years later more memorably in
the Ephemera.

3   ANON. "Memorial of the Inauguration of the Statue of
     Franklin." Historical Magazine, 1st ser. 1, no. 11
     (November):351.
     The City Council of Boston published the proceedings of
     the inauguration of the Franklin statue on 17 September 1856.

4   BOSTON (MASS.) CITY COUNCIL. Memorial of the Inauguration of
     the Statue of Franklin. Edited by N[athaniel] B.
     S[hurtleff]. Boston: City Council of Boston, 412 pp.
     This large and long book is a record of the entire pro-
     ceedings, a history of the statue, and various addresses,
     including the "Inaugural Oration" by Robert C. Winthrop.
     The addresses and other relevant pieces are cited separately.

5   CUCHEVAL-CLARIGNY, PHILIPPE ATHANASE. Histoire de la press en
     Angleterre et aux Etats-Unis. Paris: Amyot, pp. 324-67.
     Franklin's career as a journalist was important to him,
     to his country and, indeed, to the world. It was through
     his journalistic writings that he was able to influence
     ideas on morality, economics, education, philosophy, and
     politics.

6   FIELDS, JAMES T[HOMAS]. "Ode." In Memorial of the Inaugura-
     tion of the Statue of Franklin. Edited by N[athaniel] B.
     S[hurtleff]. Boston: City Council of Boston, pp. [2], [5].
     The "Ode" is printed once with the music written for it
     by Nathan Richardson and a second time without music.
     Franklin is praised as an honest working man whose Saxon
     qualities led him to hate injustice. Moreover, his per-
     sonal merit made him great. Boston should be proud of
     its son, as Fields writes in the final stanza:

                Room for the gray-haired patriot sage!
                  For here his genial life began;
                Thus let him look from age to age,
                  And prompt new Thought ennobling Man.

7   GENLIS, STÉPHANIE FÉLICITÉ DUCREST de SAINT AUBIN [Stéphanie
     Félicité Brulard Ducrest de St. Aubin Sillery]. "Franklin."
     In Souvenirs de Félicie par Mme de Genlis[;] suivis des
     souvenirs et portraits par M. le Duc de Lévis [Pierre Marc
     Gaston,] avec avant-propos et notes par M. [Jean] F[rançois]
     Barriere. Paris: Libraire de Firmin Didot Frères, fils et
     Cie, p. 279.
     Franklin was the most versatile man of his time and de-
     serves Turgot's famous tribute.

1857

8 GILPIN, HENRY D[ILWORTH]. The Character of Franklin. Address
  Delivered Before The Franklin Institute of Pennsylvania on
  the Evening of the Fourth of December, 1856. Philadelphia:
  King & Baird, Printers, 50 pp.
   Franklin was very ambitious and desired "honorable dis-
  tinction and respect; yet he sought them by the exercise of
  his talents, by incessant industry, by patient frugality,
  by tenacity of resolution, by an integrity never sullied,
  and a social intercourse that brought to him ready confi-
  dence; above all, by the unwearied pursuit, for himself and
  for those around him, of whatever was useful and true," as
  well as by prudence. He became famous for, among other
  qualities, his benevolent utility and remarkable versatility. Such is the character of Franklin, and it has won him
  a permanent place in the hearts of his countrymen and of
  all good people.

9 [LUBACH, D.?] "Bij Het Portret van Benjamin Franklin" [On the
  portrait of Benjamin Franklin]. In Praktische Volks-Almanak.
  Jaarboekje ter Verspreiding van Kennis der Toegepaste
  Wetenschappen Onder Alle Standen der Maatschappij [Practical
  national almanac. Yearbook of the dissemination of knowledge of applied sciences among all stations of society].
  Haarlem: A.C. Kruseman, pp. 171-74.
   Franklin's penchant for practicality and usefulness was
  a major factor in his greatness, and these qualities are
  just as valuable today as they were in his time. The portrait of Franklin in the fur cap expresses his practical
  nature.

10 MONKBARNS. "Funeral of Dr. Franklin." Historical Magazine,
  1st ser. 1, no. 3 (March):83-84.
   Tells of the large funeral Philadelphia held to honor
  Franklin.

11 N., G. "Benjamin Franklin." Notes and Queries, 2d ser.
  2, no. 30 (28 July):76.
   Points out that the History of a French Louse portrays
  Franklin as parsimonious.

12 _____. "Benjamin Franklin." Notes and Queries, 2d ser.
  2, no. 32 (9 August):118.
   Corrects an error he made in the 26 July 1857 issue of
  Notes and Queries (1857.11), in which the author had dis-
  cussed the unflattering portrayal of Franklin in the
  History of a French Louse.

1857

13   P., W.S. "Dr. Franklin's Account With Georgia." Historical
     Magazine, 1st ser. 1, no. 10 (October):311.
        Franklin received £100 sterling per year as agent for
     Georgia.

14   R., G.H. "Author of American Taxation." Historical Magazine,
     1st ser. 1, no. 2 (February):57.
        Asks if Franklin wrote the song "American Taxation."

15   R., J. "Dr. Franklin." Notes and Queries, 2d ser. 1, no. 26
     (28 June):510.
        Actually asks when and where William Temple Franklin
     died and wants to know whether he left any posterity, for
     anyone connected with Franklin is of interest.

16   SHILLABER, BENJAMIN PENHALLOW. A Very Brief and Very Compre-
     hensive Life of Ben: Franklin, Printer, Done into Quaint
     Verse, by One of the Types--September 17, 1856.
        See 1856.19.

17   TREVELYAN, W.C. "Inedited Letters by Dr. Franklin." Notes
     and Queries, 2d ser. 3, no. 63 (14 March):204.
        Owns two letters of Franklin that had never before been
     printed.

18   TUCKERMAN, HENRY T[HEODORE]. "Benjamin Franklin, the American
     Philosopher." In Essays, Biographical and Critical; or,
     Studies of Character. Boston: Phillips, Sampson & Co.,
     pp. [456]-75.
        Franklin was more than a great philosopher. Born into
     conditions that were hardly promising in terms of formal
     education, he "took his degree in the school of humanity
     before the technical honor was awarded him by Oxford,
     Edinburgh, and the Royal Society."

19   WATSON, ELKANNAH. [Franklin Anecdotes.] In Men and Times of
     the Revolution. . . . Edited by Winslow C. Watson. 2d ed.
     New York: Dana & Co., pp. 140-43, 154-56, 329-30.
        Anecdotes about Franklin. The first concerns humorous
     incidents arising from Mrs. Wright's realistic wax head of
     Franklin; the second is on Franklin's character, which
     Watson found to be naturally graceful and urbane; and the
     third is on Franklin's death, tributes to him and on John
     Adams's dislike of him. See 1856.24.

20   WINTHROP, ROBERT C[HARLES]. "Inaugural Oration." In Memorial
     of the Inauguration of the Statue of Franklin. Edited by
     N[athaniel] B. S[hurtleff]. Boston: City Council of
     Boston, pp. [219]-72.

1857

A recapitulation of Franklin's career which stresses his genius, versatility, and benevolence.

21 WIRT, WILLIAM. "Colloquial Powers of Franklin." In McGuffey's New Sixth Eclectic Reader: Exercises in Rhetorical Reading With Rules and Examples. Eclectic Educational Series. Stereotype ed. Cincinnati: Winthrop B. Smith & Co., pp. 342-44.
    Franklin's powers of persuasion were at their best "in a domestic circle," according to Wirt, who claims to have spent two or three weeks with him at the house of a mutual friend. Franklin made no effort to attain eloquence, but was altogether natural. He had unbounded cheerfulness, wit, and good sense.

1858

1 ANON. [Anecdote about Franklin.] In Hunt's Family Almanac, for 1858. Philadelphia: Uriah Hunt & Son, p. 507.
    A pompous English lady shocked that Franklin, the American ambassador to England, dressed in what seemed to her a shabby manner, was warned that he was the man "that bottles up thunder and lightning."

2 ANON. "The Character of Franklin." Ballou's Dollar Monthly Magazine 7, no. 5 (May):494.
    The young men of America are more interested in Franklin than in any other great man; for while they admire the outstanding public things done by our heroes and pay tribute to them on appropriate occasions, with Franklin the case is different. He was great in small as well as large things, in his private as well as public life, and so our young men are also interested in "the spirit of his actions" and seek to emulate him. "This peculiarity in Franklin which makes him so deep an object of interest to the young, was his naturalness." In public or private, he was himself. Nowadays, though, public figures are stilted and artificial and are unworthy of emulation.

3 ANON. "Das Denkmal Benjamin Franklin's in Boston." In Weber's Volks-Kalendar für das Jahr 1858. Leipzig: Weber, pp. 56-58.
    The Boston statue of Franklin, erected to honor him, is a fitting tribute.

4   ANON. "Franklin and the Church." Historical Magazine,
      1st ser. 2, no. 12 (December):361.
      Franklin held a pew in Christ Church, Philadelphia.

5   ANON. "Galerie berühmter Männer der Wissenschaft aus der
      neueren und neuesten Zeit." In Das Buch der Welt.
      Stuttgart: Hoffmann'sche Verlags-Buchhandlung, pp. 130-36.
      Includes a sketch of Franklin's scientific career.

6   ANON. "The Portraits of Franklin." Crayon 5, no. 11
      (November):329-30.
      Discusses the histories of a number of Franklin por-
      traits. Asserts that the portraits of Franklin by
      Duplessis and Greuze are so similar that one artist must
      have copied from the other.

7   ANON. "A Souvenir of Benjamin Franklin." In Hunt's Family
      Almanac, for 1858. Philadelphia: Uriah Hunt & Son, p. 5.
      Franklin made a musical toy consisting "of seventeen
      pieces of wood, which are swung equi-distantly on two
      cords, and decrease in length from the lowest to the high-
      est; it is played by being struck in the manner of the
      dulcimer, and its compass is two octaves."

8   ANON. "The Tomb of Franklin." Historical Magazine, 1st ser.
      2, no. 10 (October):302-3.
      The wall around Christ Church burying ground will be
      knocked down, and so Franklin's grave will be visible from
      the street.

9   BROWN, HUGH STOWELL. Twelve Lectures to the Men of Liverpool.
      Liverpool: Gabriel Thomson, pp. 4-12.
      These pages make up most of the first lecture in which
      Brown, obviously addressing an audience of working class
      men, uses Poor Richardisms to get them to value their work,
      to work hard, and to get by on what they earn. The maxims
      are represented as the eminently practical philosophy of
      Franklin.

10 D., W. "The Grave of Benjamin Franklin." Historical Magazine,
      1st ser. 2, no. 7 (July):207.
      Persons devoid of principle have been chipping away
      pieces of Franklin's tombstone.

11 HULLFISH, E.E. The Grave of Franklin. Philadelphia: Lee &
      Walker, 5 pp. American Philosophical Society, B F85x
      no. 504.
      A sentimental song, the music for which was composed by
      J.C. Beckel.

1858

12   L. "Dr. Franklin." Historical Magazine, 1st ser. 2, no. 5
     (May):154.
          Identifies the recipient of Franklin's letter to "Dear
     J," 27 August 1745, as James Read. A reader had requested
     the information in the April 1858 issue of the Historical
     Magazine.

13   M., O. "Franklin." Historical Magazine, 1st ser. 2, no. 9
     (September):281-82.
          Referring to the query by Mo. in the April 1858 issue
     of the Historical Magazine, the present author says that
     the letter to "Dear J----" was intended for Jared Eliot.

14   MO. "Frankliniana." Historical Magazine, 1st ser. 2, no. 4
     (April):119-20.
          Franklin had written a letter to "Dear J----" on 17
     August 1745. Mo. asks to whom the letter was written.

15   ____. "Original Letter of Benjamin Franklin." Historical
     Magazine, 1st ser. 2, no. 6 (June):163-64.
          Asks to whom Franklin wrote a letter of 12 April 1753,
     concerning the word "adhesion" and also the ship Argo.

16   MOLA. "Engravings of Washington and Franklin." Historical
     Magazine, 1st ser. 2, no. 6 (June):179-80.
          Parke Custis ordered in Paris "'two colossal statues,
     in marble, of his two great heroes,'" Washington and
     Franklin. The statues were to be for the vestibule of his
     new residence at Bridge Creek, Virginia.

17   SCOUDER, CASPER. "The Tomb of Franklin." Historical Magazine,
     1st ser. 2, no. 11 (November):333-34.
          The improvements undertaken on the graves of Benjamin
     and Deborah Franklin will make it impossible for vandals
     to chip away pieces of the tombstone for souvenirs.

18   SEYMOUR, CHA[RLE]S C.B. "Benjamin Franklin." In Self-Made
     Men. New York: Harper & Brothers, Publishers, pp. [428]-48.
          Biographical tribute to Franklin, who assiduously
     applied his great abilities to projects that benefited
     his countrymen and others throughout the world.

1859

1   ANON. "Franklin." <u>Ballou's Dollar Monthly Magazine</u> 10,
    no. 3 (September):210-11.
      Praises Franklin for his brilliance and patriotism and
asserts that America has produced no man more noble than
he. Yet his sensibility, appropriate to his time, was
decidedly utilitarian, whereas current American thought
is far more "speculative." Franklin's practicality and
his simple, undramatic manner have caused him to be undervalued by history; however, he seems now to be winning
the recognition he deserves.

2   ANON. "Franklin in the Printing Office." <u>Leisure Hour</u> 8,
    no. 367 (January):8-10.
      Describes the Crowe engraving of the young Franklin in
Watts's printing house and praises Franklin's temperate
conduct and efforts to get his fellow workmen to give up
beer.

3   ANON. "Historical and Literary Intelligence." <u>Historical
    Magazine</u>, 1st ser. 3, no. 1 (January):30-31.
      The most important point made is that while the French
court honored Franklin publicly, many of those at court
privately deprecated him and thought of him as "a sort of
half-civilized savage, of the new world."

4   ANON. "A Library for the Town of Franklin." <u>Historical
    Magazine</u>, 1st ser. 3, no. 4 (April):123.
      There exists in Franklin, Massachusetts, "the identical
library that Dr. Franklin gave to it for adopting his name."

5   BACHE, T.H. "Picture in Honor of Franklin." <u>Historical
    Magazine</u>, 1st ser. 3, no. 9 (September):286.
      In response to the query of B.J.L. (1859.11), Bache
says he owns two copies of the famous engraving, <u>Franklin
Crowned by Liberty</u>.

*6 CECIL, E. <u>Life of Franklin. Written for Children</u>. Boston:
    Crosby, Nichols & Co.
      Source: Paul L. Ford's <u>Franklin Bibliography</u>, no. 830
(1889.11).

7   DELTA, pseud. "Dr. Franklin As a Printer." <u>Historical
    Magazine</u>, 1st ser. 3, no. 5 (May):151-52.
      There is no doubt that Franklin, when he worked for his
brother James, helped set the type for <u>English Liberties</u>,

1859

or the Free-Born Subject's Inheritance, a book which was
probably of service to him when he defended his countrymen
against Parliament and the Crown.

8   FALCON, pseud. "Books Printed by Franklin." Historical
    Magazine, 1st ser. 3, no. 5 (May):158-59.
        Referring to the query of B.G. (1859.9), Falcon writes
    that the earliest book printed by Franklin is the 1729 A
    Modest Enquiry into the Nature and Necessity of a Paper
    Currency. A year earlier he printed forty sheets of
    William Sewell's The History of the Rise and Progress of
    the People Called Quakers.

9   G., B. "Books Printed by Benjamin Franklin." Historical
    Magazine, 1st ser. 3, no. 4 (April):121.
        Wants to know about earliest Franklin imprints.

10 HALE, E. W. "What Made Franklin." Christian Examiner, 5th
    ser. 4, no. 2 (March):265-74.
        Ostensibly reviewing Sparks's edition of Franklin's
    Works, Cotton Mather's Bonifacius, and Defoe's Miscella-
    neous Works, Hale goes beyond this assignment, though,
    pointing out what he considers to be the intellectual and
    moral connections among the three men. Franklin, of course,
    had in the Autobiography discussed his reading of Mather
    and Defoe and noted their influence on him. Mather had
    the greater impact. Indeed, Hale says that had the Puritan
    minister not overdone everything in his life and writings,
    he could have been an earlier Franklin, for the sage "lay
    hidden" in the clergyman, as Mather's Franklinian concern
    for good works proves.

11 L., B.J. "Picture in Honor of Dr. Franklin." Historical
    Magazine, 1st ser. 3, no. 8 (August):252.
        Asks if there exists in the United States a copy of the
    French engraving "Dr. Franklin Crowned by Liberty."

12 Le RAY de CHAUMONT, [VINCENT]. Souvenirs de Etats-Unis.
    Paris: Jacques Lecoffre et Cie, pp. [3]-7.
        These pages, which make up about one-third of the
    pamphlet, relate anecdotes about Franklin, and show him
    to be a wise moralist and humorist.

13 LORING, J.S. "The Franklin Manuscripts." Historical Magazine,
    1st. ser. 3, no. 1 (January):9-12.
        Begins by praising Franklin for his role in the Revolu-
    tionary War and for establishing medals for young students,
    but then goes on to discuss his uncle of the same name.

1860

14 SIMPSON, HENRY. "Benjamin Franklin." In <u>Lives of Eminent</u>
   <u>Philadelphians</u>. Philadelphia: W. Brotherhead, pp. 377-79.
   Biographical sketch in which chronology plays a small
   role. Key parts of the sketch are lifted without comment
   from the 1835 work by James Herring and James B. Longacre,
   <u>The National Portrait Gallery of Distinguished Americans</u>
   (1835.4).

15 SMITH, S.F. "An Original Ode." In <u>Boston. The Gift of</u>
   <u>Franklin[.] Order Exercise at the CLIII Anniversary of</u>
   <u>the Birthday of Franklin, by the Association of Franklin</u>
   <u>Medal Scholars, at The Music Hall, Monday Evening, 17th</u>
   <u>January, 1859.</u> [Boston? published for the Association,
   p. 3.]
   Verse tribute to Franklin, whose "glorious fame" will
   live on.

16 WINSLOW. "The Franklin Library, Franklin, Mass." <u>Historical</u>
   <u>Magazine</u>, 1st ser. 3, no. 9 (September):284.
   Lists the books Franklin gave to the library. This is
   in response to the query in (1859.4).

<u>1860</u>

1 ANON. "Benjamin Franklin." <u>Southern Literary Messenger</u> 31,
   no. 3 (September):191-95.
   Franklin, "the benefactor of mankind," exemplified by
   his unaffected and mild manners, expresses "the purity of
   republican democracy." It is a tribute to him that he was
   no narrow sectarian in politics or religion, but in spirit
   he was "a warm advocate of the Christian religion" and an
   example of excellent morality.

2 ANON. <u>Benjamin Franklin, the Printer Boy</u>. Edinburgh:
   William P. Nimmo, 120 pp.
   Though the author of this narrative does not say so, his
   biography of Franklin's youth is highly fictionalized and
   intended to impress upon young readers the view that
   Franklin was always Poor Richard and, in fact, was a serious
   Christian as well and one who learned while very young not
   to pay too much for his whistle. This book contains a number of inaccuracies, and there is scant evidence that the
   author based his account on works other than the <u>Autobiog-</u>
   <u>raphy</u> and perhaps early biographies.

3 ANON. <u>Child's Life of Franklin</u>. Philadelphia: Fisher &
   Brother, 192 pp.

1860

An idealized account of Franklin's life that draws
heavily on the Autobiography.

4   B[ACHE?], T.H. "Portrait of Franklin." Historical Magazine
    4, no. 12 (December):369.
        Asks what happened to the portrait "bequeathed by
    Franklin to the Supreme Executive Council of Pennsylvania."
    No one knows what has become of the portrait, and it is
    only seventy years after Franklin's death.

5   C., O.A. "Benj. Franklin's Visit to His Old Mother." In The
    Forty-Fourth Annual Report of the Directors of the American
    Asylum at Hartford, for the Education and Instruction of
    the Deaf and Dumb. Presented to the Asylum, May 12, 1860.
    Hartford: Case, Lockwood & Co., pp. 25-26.
        Franklin visits his mother, after being away for many
    years. Not recognizing him, she refuses him lodging at
    first and thought him a thief. Franklin later revealed
    himself to her.

6   [COZZENS, FREDERICK SWARTOUT.] "The Character of Franklin."
    Cozzens Wine Press, 6th ser., no. 12 (20 May), p. 93.
        Franklin's chief glory is that he is Bacon's greatest
    student; for like his teacher, he saw philosophy as a
    practical means of doing good.

7   D., J.W. "Notice of Sir Isaac Newton and Benjamin Franklin."
    In The Forty-Fourth Annual Report of the Directors of the
    American Asylum at Hartford, for the Education and Instruc-
    tion of the Deaf and Dumb. Presented to the Asylum, May 12,
    1860. Hartford: Case, Lockwood & Co., p. 25.
        Newton realized that apples fell to the ground because
    of the gravitational attraction of the earth, and Franklin
    "made the profound discovery" that lightning and electricity
    were identical and from this insight invented the lightning
    conductor.

8   FRANKLIN SAVINGS BANK, NEW YORK CITY. A Tribute to Benjamin
    Franklin. . . . [New York: printed for the Franklin
    Savings Bank.]
        A calendar honoring Franklin.

9   [GREEN, SAMUEL ABBOTT.] "Poor Richard's Proverbs."
    Historical Magazine 4, no. 1 (January):16.
        Green, using parallel columns, compares a number of
    Franklin's proverbs with some from J. Ray's Collection of
    English Proverbs, 2d ed. (London, 1678), noting similarities
    and differences.

10   [MAUDUIT, ISRAEL, ed.] "Introduction. Franklin Before the
     Lords in Council." In <u>Franklin Before the Privy Council</u>.
     Philadelphia: John M. Butler, 134 pp.
          Background on Franklin in the cockpit and Wedderburn's
     vicious attack on him. (For Wedderburn's attack, <u>see</u>
     1774.6.)

11   MAYHEW, HENRY. <u>Young Benjamin Franklin. Showing the Princi-</u>
     <u>ples Which Raised a Printer's Boy to First Ambassador of</u>
     <u>the American Republic</u>. New York: G.P. Putnam & Sons,
     534 pp.
          This fictionalized narrative for children has Uncle
     Benjamin, Franklin's godfather, as "expounder of the
     Franklinian philosophy to the boy Benjamin himself."
     Mayhew asserts that this device, though it may reduce
     Franklin's "original, cast-iron economic character, to a
     mere second-rate form of the prudential mind," nevertheless
     gets at the fact that someone taught him his Poor-Richard
     quality of mind. Thus we see emerging from the constant
     lessons taught him by Uncle Benjamin a precocious, shrewd,
     moralistic youngster who is bound to succeed in this world
     by employing Yankee qualities. Neither Uncle Benjamin nor
     his pupil has any clearly defined interior life in this
     rendering of the American character.

12   [ODELL, JONATHAN.] "Inscription for a Curious Chamber Stove,
     in the Form of an Urn, So Contrived As to Make the Flame
     Descend, Instead of Rise, From the Fire: Invented by
     Doctor Franklin." In <u>The Loyal Verses of Joseph Stansbury</u>
     <u>and Doctor Jonathan Odell; Relating to the Revolution</u>.
     Munsell's Historical Series, no. 6. Albany: J. Munsell,
     pp. 5-6.
          Franklin is praised for his real achievements in science
     and philosophy and then satirized sharply for his part in
     the Revolution, which he played for power and fame. Odell,
     in 1776, wrote of Franklin:

               Like a Newton sublimely he soar'd
                 To a Summit before unattained;
               New regions of Science explor'd,
                 And the Palm of Philosophy gain'd.

     Yet from Odell's Tory point of view, things did not work
     out well:

1860

>   But to covet <u>political</u> fame
>   Was, in him, a degrading ambition;
>   A Spark, that from <u>Lucifer</u> came,
>   And kindled the blaze of <u>Sedition</u>.

(William Smith used Odell's poem in his eulogy on Franklin.)

13   TRONCHE, LOUIS. <u>La jeunesse de Franklin[:] drame en cinq</u>
     <u>actes mêlé de chant</u>. . . . Paris: Beck, 31 pp.
         A fictional five-act play which humorously shows that
     even the young Franklin was an intriguing combination of
     philosopher and very human male who was entirely subject
     to female charms.

                           1861

1   ANON. "Books Printed by Franklin." <u>Historical Magazine</u> 5,
     no. 4 (April):125-26.
         Replies to the query by B.G. (1859.9). The author says
     that the forty sheets concerning the Quakers that Franklin
     printed in 1728 made up William Sewell's <u>The History of the</u>
     <u>Rise, Increase and Progress of the Christian People Called</u>
     <u>Quakers</u>.

2   ANON. "Dr. Franklin." In <u>Catholic Youth's Magazine</u>. Vol. 4.
     Baltimore: John Murphy & Co., pp. 32-33.
         Biographical sketch emphasizing Franklin's advancement
     to eminence through hard work and diligence. The author
     also commends the American philosopher-statesman for his
     accomplishments in philosophy and diplomacy.

3   ANON. "The Old Franklin Press." In <u>Continental Almanac, for</u>
     <u>1861</u>. Philadelphia: J. Van Court, p. 31.
         John B. Murray had purchased the printing presses
     Franklin worked on while at Watts's printing house, and
     now he has purchased the one Franklin used when he helped
     his brother turn out the <u>New England Courant</u>.

4   BAFFLED, pseud. "Dr. Franklin and His Mother." <u>Historical</u>
     <u>Magazine</u> 5, no. 8 (August):252.
         Wants to know the origin of the fictional story of
     Franklin's having visited his mother who did not recognize
     him and nearly turned him out of her house.

5   BAKER, PETER C[ARPENTER]. <u>European Recollections. An Address</u>
     <u>Delivered Before the New York Typographical Society on</u>
     <u>Franklin's Birthday, January 17, 1861</u>. New York: published
     for the Society by Baker & Godwin, Printers, 46 pp.

                           138

Though the occasion is the anniversary of Franklin's birth, this piece has nothing to do with him.

6　[CURTIS, GEORGE WILLIAM.] "Editor's Easy Chair." Harper's
　　New Monthly Magazine 22, no. 130 (March):558.
　　　　On titles representing Poor Richard's maxims: "Did our
　　ancestors of the last century really look at these pictures
　　without laughing? Did they not see as plainly as we the
　　absurdity of them? Did they suppose vice is as simple and
　　candid as this . . . ? Yet it was the eighteenth century--
　　so bad that Carlyle thinks there is hardly a man or event
　　worth remembering in the whole of it. And it is Poor
　　Richard who is the moralist! But Poor Richard possibly
　　knew and did more than Mr. Everett tells us in his excel-
　　lent lecture."

7　E., M. "Dr. Franklin." Historical Magazine 5, no. 4
　　(April):117.
　　　　Anecdote concerning Franklin's benevolence with regard
　　to the sick and the Pennsylvania Hospital. One influential
　　Philadelphian did not want the hospital built, fearing that
　　the sick would come from all over. Franklin hoped this
　　would be the case.

8　NORTON, JOHN N[ICHOLAS]. Life of Doctor Franklin. Frankfort,
　　Ky.: S.I.M. Major & Co., 258 pp.
　　　　Franklin is used as splendid proof that the thirteen
　　virtues, if followed diligently, will help one become good
　　and successful. Norton follows the popular nineteenth-
　　century tradition of having the dying Franklin adopt the
　　religion of his birth, spending his final days taking com-
　　fort in viewing a picture of the crucified Christ. A good
　　deal of Norton's Life is made up of quoted passages from
　　Franklin's writings.

9　PRAT, HENRI. "Franklin et l'intervention française en
　　Amérique." In Études historiques. XVIIIe siècle. Pt. 2.
　　Paris: Firmin Didot Frères, fils et cie, pp. [250]-66.
　　　　Franklin had, of course, a major role in establishing
　　Franco-American relations. His reputation and his cause
　　aided him in enlisting French support for America; however,
　　he won the hearts of the French people because of his per-
　　sonal qualities and tact. Since the time of Franklin, the
　　two peoples have enjoyed good relations.

10　S. "Miss Polly Baker." Philobiblion[:] A Monthly Catalogue
　　and Literary Journal, no. 1 (December), p. 24.
　　　　Inquires as to the original date of the Polly Baker
　　story and wants to know the actual author of the piece.

1861

11 THAYER, WILLIAM M[AKEPEACE]. The Printer Boy; or, How Ben
    Franklin Made His Mark. Boston: J.E. Tilton & Co., 261 pp.
        Thayer portrays a Franklin whose instincts and desires
    rose no higher than that of Father Abraham's. What is more,
    the author not only whitewashes Franklin's "errata," but
    makes him a good Christian at last. As Franklin attained
    wisdom, he rejected deism in favor of the faith of his
    parents. There is much invented conversation, as Thayer
    often reports what he would have liked to have happened
    rather than what did happen. There is also a good deal of
    preaching to the young boys who were the intended audience
    of this work.

12 TORELLI, GIUSEPPE. "Beniamino Franklin." In Paesaggi e
    profili. Florence: Felice le Monnier, pp. 260-83.
        Franklin's genius is not only of intellect but of char-
    acter and personality. He represents at once freedom and
    stability, honesty and other sound moral principles, liberty
    and public-spirited benevolence. His philosophy of life is
    expressed in Poor Richard's maxims, and he is treated by
    Torelli as a model for Italians to follow.

                              1862

1   C., H.P. "Grindstone." Notes and Queries, 3d ser. 2
    (2 December):449.
        Asks where he can locate a piece by Franklin called the
    "Grindstone."

2   [CHAMBERS, ROBERT.] "Benjamin Franklin." In The Book of
    Days; a Miscellany of Popular Antiquities in Connection
    With the Calendar. Including Anecdote[,] Biography &
    History, Curiosities of Literature & Oddities of Human
    Life & Character. Pt. 1. Edinburgh: W. & R. Chambers,
    pp. 58-60.
        Sketch of Franklin's character that stresses his desire
    to be useful to mankind.

3   DUYCKINCK, E[VERT] A[UGUSTUS], and DUYCKINCK, G[EORGE] L[ONG].
    "Benjamin Franklin." In American Portrait Gallery. New
    York: pp. 9-26.
        These pages precede the selections from Franklin's
    writings. The authors declare that the Autobiography
    presents the best picture of Franklin to be found, and
    they clearly accept the persona of that work as the actual
    Franklin. Of course, other writings, such as the aphorisms
    of Poor Richard and various pieces in the Pennsylvania

                              140

Gazette reveal more of Franklin's excellent character and
qualities. While the Duyckincks note that Franklin was a
deist, they are quick to point out that his early New England religious upbringing kept him truly pious and at least
nearly a Christian throughout his life. Even the deism of
the French or of Thomas Paine, "that arch-corrupter himself
to religion" failed to turn Franklin away from his religious
beliefs.

4   F., D.W. "Miss Polly Baker." Philobiblion, no. 2 (January),
    pp. 44-46.
        Responds to S. in the December 1861 (1861.10) issue and
    says that the earliest known date of Polly Baker's "Speech"
    is 1749, at which time it appeared in A Collection of Tracts
    of a Certain Free Enquirer Noted by His Sufferings for His
    Opinions. If Franklin, who was widely reported to be the
    author of this piece actually did write it, then it is
    likely that it appeared before 1749 in some magazine.

5   LIVERMORE, GEORGE. "Franklin, an Historical Research Respect-
    ing the Opinions of the Founders of the Republic on Negroes
    As Slaves, As Citizens, and As Soldiers." In Proceedings
    of the Massachusetts Historical Society. Vol. 6. Boston:
    printed for the Society, pp. 119-26.
        Franklin was an ardent opponent of slavery.

6   LUCAS, HIPPOLYTE [JULIEN JOSEPH]. "Franklin, l'électricité."
    In Le panthéon des hommes utiles, by Gustave Chadeuil and
    Hippolyte Ldcas. Paris: E. Dentu, pp. [157]-66.
        The focus of this essay is on Franklin's work in elec-
    tricity within the context of some of the work done in the
    field by his contemporaries and near contemporaries. Lucas
    pays tribute to the excellence of Franklin's vision as one
    of the earliest scientists in the field and to the practi-
    cality of his achievements.

7   R., J.B. "Lost Work of Franklin Recovered." Historical
    Magazine 6, no. 8 (August):253-54.
        James Crossley had reported finding a copy of Franklin's
    Dissertation on Liberty and Necessity, Pleasure and Pain.
    See 1852.6.

8   VENEDEY, J[ACOB]. Benjamin Franklin. Ein Lebensbild. 2 ed.
    Freiburg im Breisgau: Friedrich Wagner'sche Buchhandlung,
    355 pp.
        This rather long biography draws heavily on Franklin's
    own account of events, which is accepted uncritically.
    Franklin is somewhat idealized, especially in his services
    to the developing nation. While focusing on Franklin,

1862

Venedey becomes carried away by his affection for his subject and makes it appear that independence was gained
almost singlehandedly through Franklin's remarkable achievements in France. The book is chiefly interesting because
of the insight it offers into Franklin's standing among
Germans in the second third of the nineteenth century.
(I found no indication of an edition prior to 1862.)

1863

1   ANON. "Aus dem Leben Benjamin Franklins." In Der arme
    Richard oder der Weg zum Wohlstand von Benjamin Franklin.
    Nebst eine kurzen Lebensgeschichte Franklins. Mainz:
    H. Prickarts, pp. [17]-30.
        Franklin's rise in life from obscurity to wealth and
    reputation in the world, his patriotism, goodness, and
    achievements in science, philosophy, and diplomacy are an
    inspiration for all.

2   ANON. "The Celebrated Latin Line on Franklin." Historical
    Magazine 7, no. 11 (November):354.
        Agrees with Charles Sumner's contention in the Atlantic
    Monthly (1863.8) that Turgot wrote the line, "Eripuit coelo
    fulmen, sceptrumque tyrannis."

3   ANON. "Franklin's Imprimatur." Historical Magazine 7, no. 7
    (July):226.
        At a recent sale of books a Franklin imprint of The
    Charters of the Province of Pennsylvania and the City of
    Philadelphia sold for $13.50. "It had no other value than
    bearing an immortal imprint."

4   BRIGHTWELL, C[ECILIA] L[UCY]. "Benjamin Franklin." In Annals
    of Industry and Genius. London: T. Nelson & Sons,
    pp. 123-41.
        A sketch essentially of Franklin's youth and early man-
    hood showing that his Poor Richard qualities, which sur-
    faced early, helped him start on the road to success.
    Furthermore, these traits are as useful in modern times
    as they were in the eighteenth century.

5   HILDEBRAND, RICHARD. Benjamin Franklin als Nationalökonom.
    Jena: Friedrich Mauke, 61 pp.
        Deals extensively with Franklin's writings to show that
    both personal interest and patriotic endeavor made him
    America's most persistent and notable economist. Moreover,
    Franklin established the foundation for the study of

economics in America, gave capitalism its certain foothold there and made it a subject worthy of serious investigation.

6   OERTEL, WILHELM [W.D. Von Horn]. Benjamin Franklin. Lebensbild eines Ehrenmannes aus Amerika. Wiesbaden: Julius Niedner, 112 pp.
    Stressed in this life of Franklin are his famous virtues, especially his industry and drive for self-improvement and his nationalism which did not prevent his becoming a friend to mankind.

7   ROWLANDS, W. BOWEN. [Bequest of Franklin's Walking-Stick.] Notes and Queries, 3d ser. 4 (1 August):92.
    Franklin left his "fine crabtree stick, with a gold head" to Washington.

8   [SUMNER, CHARLES.] "Monograph From an Old Note-Book; With a Postscript." Atlantic Monthly 12, no. 73 (November):648-62.
    Points out that it was Turgot who wrote of Franklin, "Eripuit coelo fulmen, sceptrumque tyrannis." Sumner presents a great deal of evidence to support his assertion.

                              1864

1   ANON. "Benjamin Franklin." Eclectic Magazine 62, no. 3 (July):367-68.
    Brief and general sketch of Franklin's life of service to America and mankind.

2   ANON. "Franklin's House at Passy." Historical Magazine 8, no. 5 (May):176.
    Victor Hugo had sketched Franklin's Passy residence and gave the drawing to the United States Sanitary Commission for the Metropolitan Sanitary Fair.

3   AQUARONE, BARTOLOMEO. Beniamino Franklin: pubblicazione popolare per gli operai delle scuole serali. Siena: Moschini, 25 pp.
    Aquarone's brief biography is intended to instruct his countrymen in the proper conduct for workers, as gleaned from Franklin's life and beliefs. (This is one of the literary attempts to promote an industrious and frugal work force in Italy.)

4   BLACKFORD, JOSEPH H. "Memoranda, Relating to Dr. Franklin's Administration of the Colonial Post Offices." Proceedings of the New Jersey Historical Society, 1st ser. 9:83-85.

1864

A summary of Franklin's post office career and a reprinting of his accounts with the offices of Trenton, Princeton, and Morristown from 1776 through the summer of 1778.

5   De CADOUDAL, M.G. "Franklin." In Les serviteurs des hommes.
    Paris: C. Dillet, pp. [23]-84.
    An account of Franklin's life and career that is often inaccurate and sometimes fictionalized. Loosely based on the Autobiography for its treatment of Franklin's earlier life, De Cadoudal's essay attempts to show that even when the American was a boy in Boston, he was the philosophical, wise, and careful follower of eminent English deists. Yet Franklin was also one who profited from his native intelligence and made opportunities of what other people would consider hindrances. The provinciality of colonial America did not hold back the determined and enterprising young Franklin, and he soon established himself in Philadelphia as a person of unusual merit. That he achieved personal success was not enough for him, though, and he dedicated himself to improving the lives of his fellows in any way he could. This was a characteristic of Franklin throughout his long and remarkably productive life. He always tried to be of service to others, whether in science, philosophy, politics, or diplomacy. He was perhaps most useful and most eminent as the chief American representative and negotiator in France.

6   G., G. "Old Portrait of Franklin." Historical Magazine 8,
    no. 4 (April):147.
    Dr. Edward Vanderpool of New York owns a painting of Franklin by the English artist Stibbs. The artist, perhaps followed Cochin in his representation, but Stibbs shows Franklin aging. The portrait was painted "a year or two" before Franklin's death.

7   GREELEY, HORACE. "Self-Made Men." In Life and Times of
    Benjamin Franklin, by James Parton. Vol. 2. New York:
    Mason Brothers, pp. 677-79.
    The lecture, which Greeley first delivered in 1862, deals with Franklin's successful life.

8   HILL, GEORGE CANNING. Benjamin Franklin. A Biography.
    New York: Butler Brothers, 333 pp.
    Although this narrative follows very closely the Autobiography and borrows freely from earlier accounts, it is one of the better popular nineteenth-century studies. Hill presents an only partly developed thesis: Franklin "was a genuine product of American soil," in his versatility and

desire to improve the condition of his fellowmen. The book
is relatively free of attempts to make Franklin more proper
and less earthy that he was, and Hill avoids the temptation
so common at the time, to make Franklin a solid Christian
at last. Hill does, however, betray a slight prejudice
against American Indians.

9   J., J.H. "The Celebrated Latin Line on Franklin." Historical
    Magazine 8, no. 3 (March):112-13.
        Comments on the anonymous assertion (1863.2) that Sumner
    proved the line to have been written by Turgot. J.H.J.
    says that the entire matter had been cleared up ten years
    earlier in the English Notes and Queries of February 1852
    (1852.13).

*10 JORDAN, THOMAS. Benjamin Franklin and Popular Ethics. A Lec-
     ture Delivered Before the St. Michaus Young Men's Christian
     Association. . . . Dublin: Hodges, Smith & Co., 26 pp.
         Source: see 1889.11, no. 895.

*11 LASCAUX, PAUL DESCUBES de. Benjamin Franklin, sa vie, ses
     ouvrages, ses decouvertes. Mirecourt: Humbert, 89 pp.
         Source: see 1889.11. Paul L. Ford, Franklin Bibliog-
     raphy, no. 899, found this title in Sabin. It is also
     cited in Librarie Française, 1840-1865, vol. 3, p. 165.
     It appears to be unavailable in the United States and,
     over a period of two years, could not be obtained from
     France.

*12 LONGHENA, FRANCESCO. La maniera di farsi ricco o La scienza
     del buon Riccardo e altri opuscoli di pratica economia di
     Beniamino Franklin volgarizzati dal P[rof.] F[rancesco]
     L[onghena] . . . Milan: Barbini
         Source: Pace, pp. 202-3. Franklin was a great practical
     economist and taught his fellow Americans how to prosper
     and how to protect their liberty. He therefore made an
     invaluable contribution to the eventual independence of
     the United States.

13   PARTON, JAMES. Life and Times of Benjamin Franklin. 2 vols.
     New York: Mason Brothers, 1:627 pp.; 2:707 pp.
         A very full, pleasant to read account of Franklin's
     life, beliefs, career, and achievements. While Parton pro-
     vides detail and information either omitted or truncated
     elsewhere, his biography does not pretend to objectivity.
     Franklin is the godlike man whom God fortunately gave to
     the world for a long enough time so that the philosopher
     could accomplish an astonishing array of necessary and
     good things. Parton does mention the well known errata

1864

admitted to by Franklin in the memoirs, but otherwise
Franklin's serious errors and his faults are either sub-
sumed or utterly ignored. Moreover, Parton is guilty of
superficiality in treating Franklin's religion and politics,
and he repeats the Weems invention that has Franklin, on
his deathbed, looking at a picture of Christ on the cross.
Other errors result from a lack of information available
to Parton, but also from scholarship that must be considered
weak by more modern standards.

1865

1   ANDRIESSEN, S[IMON] J[ACOBUS]. "Benjamin Franklin." In Bato,
    Tijdschrift voor Jongens [Bato, magazine for boys]. Vol. 2.
    Amsterdam: Gebroeders Kraay, pp. [276]-83.
        A brief account of Franklin's career that emphasizes
    his rise to eminence. Franklin is portrayed as a model
    for the young to emulate.

2   ANON. "Benjamin Franklin." London Quarterly Review 23,
    no. 46 (January):483-514.
        After summarizing and reviewing Parton's Life, the
    critic treats Franklin harshly. Franklin was deficient
    in morality and sensitivity and dismissed his moral fail-
    ures casually. What he passes off as his morality is
    "essentially mean," for he lacks "deep and generous feel-
    ing," never rising above the level of the pragmatic and
    utilitarian virtue epitomized in the aphorism: "Honesty
    is the best policy." Furthermore, as a young man, at
    least, he was guilty of self-seeking, and later he prac-
    ticed nepotism to such a degree as to tarnish his reputa-
    tion as a patriot. He lacks faith, creativity, and dignity.
    His abilities, many-sided though they were, must be recog-
    nized as the commonest kind. Truth is not well served by
    the efforts of Americans to glorify Franklin.

3   ANON. Benjamin Franklin, "Doer of Good:" A Biography.
    Edinburgh: William P. Nimmo, 326 pp.
        "The present volume has been carefully condensed and
    edited from the celebrated Life by Jared Sparks, and the
    more extensive Life and Times by James Parton."

4   ANON. "Benjamin Franklin, L.L.D., F.R.S." In The National
    Portrait Gallery of Distinguished Americans: With Biograph-
    ical Sketches by Celebrated Authors. Vol. 2. Philadelphia:
    Rice, Rutter & Co., pp. 1-20.
        Franklin was an extraordinary man who "in any age or
    country, would, by the mere force of his native talents,

have made a respectable figure in life." Yet it is hardly
arguable that he achieved his great eminence because he was
born in a provincial and unrefined country that particularly needed men of ability. Though he was guilty of fol-
lies in his youth and retained an aversion to useless
theological dogmatism, Franklin came to be a sincerely
religious man and a believer in general Christian doctrine.

5   ANON. "Benjamin Franklin, Vorbilder." In Franklin.
    Stephenson. Piepenstock. Elberfeld: Bädeker, pp. [3]-20.
        Biographical sketch showing Franklin's rise to inter-
    national fame and relating this success to his inner
    qualities.

6   BAKER, PETER C[ARPENTER]. Franklin. An Address Delivered
    Before The New York Typographical Society on Franklin's
    Birthday, January 17, 1865. New York: Baker & Godwin,
    Printers, 28 pp.
        Printers have special reason to be proud of Franklin,
    for he always considered himself first and foremost a
    printer. Indeed, his career in printing, so intimately
    related to his later careers, was instrumental in his life
    and success. Franklin was one of the "noblest souls" with
    whom God ever blessed mankind. Not all may reach Franklin's
    "Greatness," but all can strive to match his "Goodness."

7   BUTTERY, ALBERT. "Benjamin Franklin." Notes and Queries,
    3d ser. 7 (20 May):409.
        Referring to the query of S.W.P. (1865.11), Buttery
    identifies the place where Franklin lived during his first
    visit to England.

8   C., J.H. "The Franklin Family." Historical Magazine 9,
    no. 9 (September):276.
        Resents Parton's Life and Times of Dr. Franklin which
    makes it seem that "the subject of his book monopolized
    all the talent of the family."

9   DELTA, pseud. "Descendants of Josiah Franklin." Historical
    Magazine 9, no. 11 (November):346.
        Considers the remark made by J.H.C. (1865.8) and calls
    for a complete list of the descendants of Josiah Franklin.

10 GRUBE, AUGUST WILHELM. "Benjamin Franklin." In Charakterbilder
    aus der Geschichte und Sage, für einen propadeutschen
    Geschichtsunterricht gesammelt. . . . Vol. 3. Leipzig:
    Brandstetter, pp. 300-11.
        Biographical account emphasizing Franklin's many talents
    and his remarkable diligence. See 1856.9.

1865

11   P., S.W. "Benjamin Franklin." <u>Notes and Queries</u>, 3d ser.
      7 (6 May):356.
           Franklin lived in Little Britain during his first stay
      in England. "Are there any houses still standing, and
      where?"

1866

1   ANON. "Franklin." <u>Frank Leslie's Chimney Corner</u> 3, no. 63
      (11 August):165.
           Quotes from another source, saying that Franklin's bland,
      commonsensical approach to life, his cheerful humor, shrewd
      perceptions and delicate manners made him a wonderful and
      much sought after companion by the leading intellectuals of
      his age. While his benevolent acceptance of the beliefs of
      others derived from a catholic liberalism, it is nonetheless
      true that he lacked mystical and enthusiastic aspects of
      character "even to a fault." In his character, and in his
      republicanism, we see "the ideal American."

2   ANON. "Franklin, What He Was, and What He Did."
      <u>Phrenological Journal</u> 43:49-50.
           Franklin's phrenological characteristics show him to be
      a man of ability and compassion.

3   BACHE, BENJAMIN FRANKLIN. "Dr. Franklin's Return From France
      in 1785." <u>Historical Magazine</u> 10, no. 7 (July):213-16.
           The residents of Passy were very sorry to see Franklin
      leave forever. They stood around the litter on which he
      was carried and were stonily silent, except for those who
      were sobbing. On the way to the ship that was to take him
      home, Franklin and his party were treated with every cour-
      tesy. (According to the <u>NUC</u>, this piece was written in
      1785 but first published here.)

*4   BARBÈRA, PIERO. <u>Beniamino Franklin. . . .</u> [Florence:
      G. Barbèra], 7 pp.
           Source: Pace, p. 200. Tribute to Franklin on the com-
      pletion of a bust done in his honor. Pace notes that
      Barbèra was an eleven-year-old boy when he composed this
      piece, and he did so after reading Mignet's account of
      Franklin.

5   BESSIÈRE (TABERLY), L. <u>La jeunesse de Franklin[,] racontée
      par un ouvrier et publiée.</u> Senlis: Charles Duriez, 117 pp.
           Depicts a fictional and idealized Franklin whose back-
      ground and experiences led him to the adoption of virtuous
      conduct that make him an example for children to follow.

6   BLADE, WILLIAM. "Franklin Medals." Notes and Queries,
    3d ser. 10 (1 December):431.
        Blade asks if there ever was struck a medal dealing
    with Franklin as a printer.

7   D. "Dr. Franklin's Library." Historical Magazine 10, no. 4
    (April):123.
        Franklin's library was taken by William Temple Franklin
    to London. There it was "pledged for the repayment of
    money borrowed by Temple Franklin" to help his financially
    troubled friend, Robert Morris, Jr.

8   HAYDEN, SIDNEY. Washington and His Masonic Compeers. 4th ed.
    New York: Masonic Publishing & Manufacturing Co.,
    pp. 281-99.
        On Franklin, particularly as a devoted Mason. (I find
    no indication of an edition prior to 1866.)

9   LEONI, CARLO. "Vita di Beniamino Franklin." In Libro pegli
    operai. Venice: P. Naratovich, pp. [11]-68.
        Based entirely on published accounts of Franklin's life,
    this piece makes the point that Franklin had the philo-
    sophic perspective to remain calm and patient even in
    very difficult times.

10 McCLEARY, SAMUEL [F.], comp. A Sketch of the Origin, Object
    and Character of the Franklin Fund, for the Benefit of
    Young Married Mechanics of Boston. Boston: published
    by order of the Board of Aldermen, 38 pp.
        In 1866 the Boston Franklin Fund was worth $110,166.56.

11 NEW YORK (CITY), The METROPOLITAN MUSEUM of ART. THE LIBRARY.
    Collection of Books Relating to Benjamin Franklin and Other
    Prominent Men of Colonial Times[,] Presented by John Bigelow.
    [New York: Metropolitan Museum of Art], 95 pp. American
    Philosophical Society.
        Lists primary and secondary sources.

12 P., R. "The Last Love-Episode in the Life of a Philosopher."
    Once a Week 14 (16 June):653-58.
        Fictionalized account of Madame Helvétius's reasons
    for not marrying Franklin. (This is the same sketch that
    appeared in Every Saturday 2, no. 27 (7 July 1866):34-36.)

13 Y., M.S. "Dr. Franklin and His Mother." Historical Magazine
    10, no. 4 (April):122-23.
        Replies to the query of Baffled (1861.4) and says that
    he first came across the anecdote of Franklin's mother

1866

failing to recognize him and nearly turning him out of her
house "more than thirty years ago" in "the 'Percy Anecdotes,' Vol. ii, p. 140, and, I think, also, in some
school books." (The anecdote does not appear in any of
the twenty volumes of the Percy Anecdotes. The piece may,
however, appear in some edition I have been unable to
examine.)

1867

1   ANON. "Franklin, Benjamin." In Chambers's Encyclopaedia:
A Dictionary of Universal Knowledge for the People. Vol. 4.
Philadelphia: J.B. Lippincott & Co., pp. 492-93.
Straightforward summary of Franklin's life.

2   ANON. "Franklins erste Erscheinung in einer englischen
Druchkerei." In Neuer Gemeinnütziger pennsylvanischer
Calender . . . 1867. . . . Lancaster, Pa.: Johann Bar's
Sohnen, p. [28].
Fictional account of Franklin as the new hand at the
printing shop, where he must prove his worth.

3   AQUARONE, BARTOLOMEO. Vita di Beniamino Franklin, aggiuntovi
racconti e massime dello stess. Piccola biblioteca pei
comuni italiani, no. 13. Milan: P. Carrara, 64 pp.
Calls attention to Franklin's unpromising beginnings
and his astonishing rise in life which was brought about
not only because of his natural abilities, but also because
of his diligence and good works. Franklin is further acclaimed for his patriotism and achievements in diplomacy.
Much of this account is taken from the Autobiography, and
Aquarone sees Franklin as a model for Italians to emulate.
(The Vita is an expansion of Aquarone's 1864 account of
Franklin.)

4   CANTÙ, CESARE. "Beniamino Franklin." In Vite parallele di
Mirabeau e Washington. Milan: Corona e Caimi Editori,
pp. [273]-93.
Uncritical portrait of Franklin as Poor Richard.
Quotes extensively from Franklin to show that he lived
by the famous thirteen virtues.

5   [CANTWELL, EDWARD.] Benjamin Franklin. A Lecture Delivered
Before the Franklin Society at the Academy, Oxford, N.C.,
on Friday, 14th December, 1866. Oxford, N.C.: Franklin
Society, 32 pp.

Also known as the "Life and Character of Franklin."
Traces Franklin's career and comments on those personal
qualities that made him great. Franklin probably has no
superior as a citizen, philosopher or statesman and, in
fact, "every theory of the wonderful power of an individual
mind, gains new strength and illustration by the mention of
his name." He rose to eminence by the force of his own
abilities and drive, but he has won the love of men because of his benevolence. The message of Franklin's life,
so closely aligned to his love of America, has great rele-
vance to Southerners and to all Americans of the post-Civil
War era, who must put aside passions and unite to restore
hope and peace to the Union.

6 CYRIL, pseud. "Franklin's Prayer-Book." Notes and Queries,
3d ser. 11 (22 June):496.
Asks title and whereabouts of the prayer book revised
by Franklin and Despencer.

7 FERRARI, PIETRO. La vita di Beniamino Franklin, il grande,
operaio americano ad uso del popolo raccontata dall
avvacato. . . . Spezia: Tipografia Artistica, 32 pp.
Italian workers are urged to practice the virtues of
Franklin, particularly those virtues that are designed to
make people hard working and financially independent.

*8 FONVIELLE, WILFRID de. "Franklin and Frederick the Great."
In Thunder and Lightning. Translated and edited by T.L.
Phipson. New York: C. Scribner & Co.
Source: NUC. See 1869.3.

9 RAMAGE, C.T. "Franklin." Notes and Queries, 3d ser. 11
(29 June):515.
Franklin was too modest to permit Turgot's Latin epigram, especially the part dealing with the defeat of England, to be taken seriously.

10 SISYPHUS, pseud. "Wedderburn and Franklin." Notes and
Queries, 3d ser. 11 (5 January):12.
Asks if there is any explanation for Wedderburn's
severity toward Franklin and then condemns Franklin's
conduct as "base and dishonest" and deserving the treatment he received at Wedderburn's hands.

11 UNEDA, pseud. "Franklin's Prayer Book." Notes and Queries,
3d ser. 12 (7 December):468.
Refers to the query of Cyril (1867.6) and says that the
prayer book revised by Franklin and Despencer is rare but
can be seen in Philadelphia.

<u>1868</u>

1   ANON. "Benjamin Franklin." <u>Historical Magazine</u>, 2d ser.
    4, no. 11 (November):234.
        Very favorable career sketch introduces two Franklin
    letters from Passy. Franklin's services in science and
    diplomacy justify Turgot's epigram.

2   ANON. "Franklin." In <u>Les bons exemples cent-et-un récits</u>
    <u>instructifs, moraux, religieux</u>. <u>Hommes utiles de tous les</u>
    <u>pays</u>. Les bon livres, no. 32. Paris: Chez tous les
    libraires, pp. 49-50.
        Sketch identifying Franklin with Poor Richard.

3   BIGELOW, JOHN, ed. Introduction to <u>Autobiography of Benjamin</u>
    <u>Franklin</u>. <u>Eidted from His Manuscript, with Notes and an</u>
    <u>Introduction</u>. . . . Philadelphia: J.B. Lippincott & Co.,
    pp. 7-59.
        Bigelow read the le Veillard manuscript of the memoirs
    and, comparing it with the version published by William
    Temple Franklin, found "twelve hundred separate and dis-
    tinct changes"; therefore, a new edition seemed necessary.
    Some of the differences are discussed, the story of the le
    Veillard version is related in detail, and Temple Franklin
    is criticized for delaying his edition.

4   CARR, ROBERT. "Personal Recollections of Benjamin Franklin."
    <u>Historical Magazine</u>, 2d ser. 4, no. 8 (August):59-60.
        These are the "crude reminiscence of a thoughtless
    school-boy of eleven or twelve years of age," who lived
    near Franklin. Carr describes the house and is able to
    remember that Franklin was sick in his last years but
    always had a word of advice or encouragement for people.

5   DOBELLI, F[ERDINAND]. <u>Gli uomini illustri, biografie</u> . . .
    <u>Beniamino Franklin</u>. Vol. 1. Fasc. 12. Milan: Giovanni
    Gnocchi di Giacomo, 32 pp.
        Laudatory, uncritical biography which depicts Franklin
    as the selfless, generous friend to the human race.

6   EVERETT, EDWARD. "Franklin the Boston Boy." In <u>Orations and</u>
    <u>Speeches on Various Occasions</u>. Vol. 4. Boston: Little,
    Brown & Co., pp. [108]-29.
        The occasion of the speech was the awarding of Franklin
    school medals in 1859. Everett tells his audience that
    Franklin is a fine example to the young of how to live well
    and succeed in spite of obstacles.

1869

7 SCHMIDT, FERDINAND. Benjamin Franklin. Ein Lebensbild für
Jung und Alt. Berlin: Hugo Kastner, 136 pp.
Franklin is praised for his virtue, humanitarianism,
wisdom, and many accomplishments. The biographical sketch
is followed by selections from Franklin's writings, and
both are intended to show that his life is worthy of emula-
tion. The readers, who is spite of the title must have
been children, are also told that the virtues Franklin
preached can, if followed, enable nineteenth-century young
people to improve their lives.

8 WILLIS, WILLIAM. "Dr. Franklin, Charles Thompson and
Mrs. Logan." Historical Magazine, 2d ser. 4, no. 6
(December):280-82.
Deborah Logan had a high opinion of Franklin and
Thompson.

1869

*1 [BARBÈRA, PIERO.] "Beniamino Franklin." Arte della stampa
(Florence), 1:76-77.
Source: Pace, p. 305. Italian workers are called upon
to follow the example of the illustrious Franklin and endeavor to attain virtue and prosperity.

2 CADET, FELIX. "Franklin." In Histoire de l'economique
politique. Le précurseurs[:] Adam Smith--Franklin.
Reims: H. Gérard, pp. 39-73.
Extensive quoted passages from Franklin's writings show
that his economic thought was of a piece with his general
political and social liberalism and humanitarianism.

3 FONVIELLE, WILFRID de. "Franklin and Frederick the Great."
In Thunder and Lightning. Translated by T.L. Phipson.
New York: C. Scribner & Co., pp. 275-80.
A chapter dealing with Franklin's work in electricity.
See 1867.8.

4 LABOULAYE, ÉDOUARD. "La jeunesse de Franklin." In Discours
populaires. Paris: Charpentier et Cie, Libraires-Editeurs,
pp. [161]-81.
Originally a lecture before the first general meeting
of the Franklin Society in Paris, this appreciative essay
pays tribute to Franklin's goodness, love of liberty, wisdom, skill, and versatility. By virtue of his philosophical and scientific writings, his fame preceded him in
France, and he was instrumental in making Frenchmen

153

1869

unstinting supporters of America in the Revolutionary War.
Today Franklin lives on in the hearts and minds of the
French people.

5   LAWRENCE, EUGENE. "The Progress of Electricity." Harper's
    New Monthly Magazine 39, no. 232 (September):548-60.
        Recounts Franklin's central role in the development of
    electrical science.

6   PEZUELA, LUIS ROBLES. "Benjamin Franklin." Boletin de la
    Sociedad Mexicana de Geografia y Estaolistica, Segunda
    Epoca, 1:532-36.
        Brief biographical sketch which treats Franklin as
    representing typical American qualities.

7   S., E.L. "Dr. Franklin." Notes and Queries, 4th ser. 4
    (25 December):558.
        Confuses William Franklin with William Temple Franklin
    and also relates an anecdote of an electrical experiment
    performed by Franklin in which he intended to electrocute
    a live "duck" but nearly succeeded instead in killing
    himself.

8   S., M.B. "Did Doctor Franklin Write Two Autobiographies?"
    Historical Magazine, 2d ser. 5, no. 5 (May):336-37.
        Questions why there are different versions of Franklin's
    Autobiography and wants to know which is the correct text.

9   SHIRLEY, E.P. "Dr. Franklin on the Voyage of Admiral
    Bartholomew de Fonte." Notes and Queries, 4th ser. 4
    (13 November):406-7.
        On Franklin's reasons for believing de Fonte's 1640
    voyage genuine and accurately reported.

187-

1   ANON. "Benjamin Franklin." In Record of Unitarian Worthies.
    London: pp. 193-94. FCL.
        Franklin's life and ideas teach us that religious vener-
    ation is entirely "compatible with a sound, practical under-
    standing." Franklin, in fact, can be said to have been a
    Unitarian Christian. On 17 April 1774, he attended services
    at the opening of the first British Unitarian congregation,
    that of the Essex-street Chapel, London. More important,
    Franklin's views concerning God and His relationship with
    mankind are definitely Unitarian.

1870

1 A., L.T. "Dr. Franklin." Notes and Queries, 4th ser. 5
(28 May):519.
Asserts that William Franklin was illegitimate, but that
William Temple Franklin was legitimate and that Franklin
and William were "easily reconciled" after the War of Independence because "it is doubtful if either was sincere or
cared for any opinion."

2 ANON. "Benjamin Franklin." Demorest's Young America 4, no. 5
(March):182.
A very brief biographical sketch.

3 B., H.P. "William Temple Franklin." Notes and Queries,
4th ser. 6 (8 October):311-12.
Neither William Franklin nor William Temple Franklin was
illegitimate. This note responds to that of E.L.S.
(1869.7).

4 BARNES, JOHN KAY. "Dr. Franklin." Notes and Queries,
4th ser. 5 (15 January):70.
Corrects E.L.S. (1869.7) who, confused William Franklin
with William Temple Franklin.

5 CANTÙ, CESARE. "Racconto[:] Franklin." In Buon senso e buon
cuore[:] Conferenze popolari. Milan: Giacomo Agnelli,
pp. [193]-201.
Franklin's morality, particularly as expressed in his
famous thirteen virtues, is workable and worth following.

6 CLEMENS, SAMUEL LANGHORNE [Mark Twain]. "Memoranda: The
Late Benjamin Franklin." Galaxy 10, no. 1 (July):138-40.
Satirizes the Franklin of the maxims and well known
frugality and industry. Twain writes: "The subject of
this memoir was of a vicious disposition and early prosti-
tuted his talents to the invention of maxims and aphorisms
calculated to inflict suffering upon the rising generation
of all subsequent ages." Twain gives Franklin general
credit for his services to America, but he calls upon
parents to stop using the philosopher as an impossible
example for their children. (This piece is more readily
available in Mark Twain's Sketches New and Old, 1875.)

7 D'ADDA, GIROLAMO. Preface to Vita di Franklin per M. Mignet:
nouva versione dal francese col consenso dell'autore,
preceduta da brevi cenni bibliografici. . . . Milan:
Brigola, pp. vii-xii.

1870

Italians can help themselves through the difficult
period of unification, for which they are unprepared, by
emulating the life of the prudent, patriotic, and honest
Benjamin Franklin.

8   [DUANE, WILLIAM.] Remarks upon a Speech Delivered by Mrs. E.
     Cady Stanton! During the Summer of 1870. Philadelphia:
     Merrihew & Son, Printers, 7 pp.
     The well-known agitator for women's rights attacked
     Franklin for being a bad husband and father, going abroad
     and leaving his wife at home alone with two infants who,
     over the years he was gone, caught various children's dis-
     eases. Duane points out that Franklin did not expect to be
     gone for eleven years; that his children, far from being
     infants, were adults; that Deborah was left in comfortable
     circumstances; and that Franklin was a very good father.
     Moreover, Franklin was deeply involved abroad in the most
     important affairs of American colonial history. "Where
     can we find so great an amount of ignorance crowded into
     the same space as is exhibited in this portion of Mrs.
     Stanton's harrangue? The display of such ignorance may
     confirm some persons in their opposition to female poli-
     ticians. If Mrs. Stanton, who is a bright and shining
     light (not to say a torch) among these female agitators,
     knows so little, what must be expected from the rank and
     file of her followers?" Duane goes on to rebuke these
     "mannish women [who] mistake a strong will for a strong
     understanding," and who relinquish their "proper duties"
     and try to get their names in the newspapers.

9   GASTINEAU, BENJAMIN. "La Physique [:] Benjamin Franklin.--
     Galvani." In Les genies de la science et de l'industrie.
     Paris: Pagnerre, pp. [67]-79.
     Franklin was an outstanding philosopher in many ways.
     We should remember, however, that he was a major scientist
     as well.

10   HUTCHINSON, P. "Dr. Franklin." Notes and Queries, 4th ser.
     5 (15 January):70.
     Corrects E.L.S. (1869.7) on the confusion between
     William Franklin and William Temple Franklin, but points
     out that both were the illegitimate offspring of "street
     women." (Hutchinson's great grandfather was Thomas
     Hutchinson, the last royal governor of Massachusetts.)

11   L., P.A. "Dr. Franklin." Notes and Queries, 4th ser. 5
     (15 January):70-71.

Asserts that E.L.S. (1869.7) is wrong, and that William Franklin and William Temple Franklin are both legitimate offspring.

12   LENIHAN, MAURICE. "The Pennsylvania Gazette." Notes and Queries, 4th ser. 6 (1 October):272.
Franklin may have worked as a printer on the Pennsylvania Gazette of 29 April 1756.

13   McC[OY], R[OBERT]. "Franklin, As a Mason." Historical Magazine, 2d ser. 7, no. 3 (March):198.
Asks who made Franklin a Mason and when and where the ceremony took place.

14   PARKER, THEODORE. "Franklin." In Historic Americans. Boston: Horace B. Fuller, pp. [13]-72.
Franklin was a great philosopher and statesman whose powers were used for the betterment of mankind. Parker sketches Franklin's life and career to describe his many abilities and his sincere desire to help men help themselves.

15   SMITH, LLOYD P. "The Franklin Statue." Historical Magazine, 2d ser. 7, no. 4 (April):253-54.
The statue of Franklin still stands in front of the Library Company of Philadelphia.

16   UNEDA, pseud. "Dr. Franklin." Notes and Queries, 4th ser. 5 (19 February):217.
Corrects E.L.S. (1869.7) on the identities of William Franklin and William Temple Franklin.

17   WYLIE, CHARLES. "The Pennsylvania Gazette." Notes and Queries, 4th ser. 6 (22 October):356.
Responds to Maurice Lenihan (1870.12) and says that Franklin could not have worked on the Pennsylvania Gazette after 1723.

1871

*1   ANON. Franklin Memorial Window for the New University Building. [Philadelphia.]
Source: Paul L. Ford, in his Franklin Bibliography, no. 870, says that this is a "report by the Committee, asking for money." See 1889.11.

1871

2 ANON. "Franklin's <u>Cato Major</u>." <u>Historical Magazine</u>, 2d ser.
9, no. 2 (February):118-19.
The Franklin imprint of Cicero's <u>Cato Major</u> is an extremely sought after book.

3 BONISTABILE, G. "Biografia di Beniamino Franklin." In
<u>Risparmio: tre conferenze d'economia popolare ad uso</u>
<u>speciale degli operai. . . .</u> Milan: Tipografia della
Società Cooperativa, pp. 87-92.
Emphasizes Franklin's industry and frugality, qualities
that helped lead him to eminence and that should be adopted
by Italian workers.

4 D[UANE, WILLIAM ?]. "Dr. Franklin and Mrs. Stanton." <u>Histor-</u>
<u>ical Magazine</u>, 2d ser. 9, no. 1 (January):50.
Defends Franklin from the charge by the feminist,
Elizabeth Cady Stanton, who asserted that he was a poor
husband and father because he went to England in 1757,
leaving Deborah Franklin alone to care for the children.
Duane points out that of the two living Franklin children
in 1757, William had been married two years and Sally was
seventeen years old.

5 D[UANE], W[ILLIAM]. "Theodore Parker and Benjamin Franklin."
<u>Historical Magazine</u>, 2d ser. 9, no. 2 (February):123-24.
Attacks errors in Parker's essay (1870.14).

6 GREEN, SAMUEL A[BBOTT]. <u>The Story of a Famous Book: An</u>
<u>Account of Dr. Benjamin Franklin's "Autobiography."</u>
Boston: for private distribution, 14 pp.
Presents the history of the <u>Autobiography</u> based on the
information available to him at the time. Green holds that
the <u>Autobiography</u> is the greatest and most enduring historical work published in America. Moreover, it "has
passed through many editions among all civilized nations,
and the demand for it still continues." (Also published
in the <u>Atlantic Monthly</u> 27 (February 1871).)

7 HUGENHOLTZ, P[ETRUS] H[ERMANUS]. <u>Benjamin Franklin</u>.
Bibliotheek van Volks voordrachten, no. 2. Amsterdam:
G.L. Funke, 24 pp.
Franklin's life proves that a workman can rise in the
world and can even accomplish great things.

8 SHEARES, ISAAC. "Benjamin Franklin's 'Laurel Wreath': A
Picture." <u>Notes and Queries</u>, 4th ser. 7 (4 March):189.
Asks who is the artist of the picture of Franklin being
crowned by a wreath of laurel at the court of Louis XVI.

1872

1 ANON. "Franklin's Grave." <u>Old Curiosity Shop</u> 1, no. 9
   (March):455-57.
   Franklin's greatness is well appreciated in the United
   States, and it is only his modesty that permits his grave
   to be marked simply by a plain stone rather than by a
   grand monument erected by his grateful countrymen.

2 BAKER, PETER CARPENTER. [Speech on Franklin.] In <u>Record of</u>
   <u>the Proceedings and Ceremonies Pertaining to the Erection of</u>
   <u>the Franklin Statue in Printing-House Square, Presented by</u>
   <u>Albert De Groot, to the Press and Printers of the City of</u>
   <u>New-York</u>. New York: Francis Hart & Co., pp. 69-71.
   If the sculptors of the past fashioned men after the
   gods, De Groot was absolutely correct in fashioning a
   Franklin who represents the fully human man that was the
   original.

3 BATES, WILLIAM. "Franklin's Epitaph." <u>Notes and Queries</u>,
   4th ser. 9 (25 May):419-21.
   Discussing earlier and later versions of the epitaph
   Franklin wrote for himself, Bates argues that Franklin
   cannot be said to have copied the piece from any source,
   for he made it distinctly his own.

4 BEECHER, HENRY WARD. [Speech on Franklin.] In <u>Record of the</u>
   <u>Proceedings and Ceremonies Pertaining to the Erection of</u>
   <u>the Franklin Statue in Printing-House Square, Presented by</u>
   <u>Albert De Groot, to the Press and Printers of the City of</u>
   <u>New-York</u>. New York: Francis Hart & Co., pp. 58-60.
   Franklin was a man who loved the truth, and his maxim
   asserting that honesty is the best policy is a practical,
   realistic approach to getting men to recognize the importance of honesty.

5 BROOKS, ERASTUS. [Speech on Franklin.] In <u>Record of the Pro-</u>
   <u>ceedings and Ceremonies Pertaining to the Erection of the</u>
   <u>Franklin Statue in Printing-House Square, Presented by</u>
   <u>Albert De Groot, to the Press and Printers of the City of</u>
   <u>New-York</u>. New York: Francis Hart & Co., pp. 65-68.
   Franklin lauded for his contributions to journalism,
   printing, intellectual and civic life.

6 CHAPIN, E.H. [Speech on Franklin.] In <u>Record of the Proceed-</u>
   <u>ings and Ceremonies Pertaining to the Erection of the</u>
   <u>Franklin Statue in Printing-House Square, Presented by</u>
   <u>Albert De Groot, to the Press and Printers of the City of</u>
   <u>New-York</u>. New York: Francis Hart & Co., pp. 62-64.

1872

Franklin was a representative American and proof that in this country any man can rise through his own exertions.

7   [De VINNE, THEODORE L., ed.] <u>Record of the Proceedings and Ceremonies Pertaining to the Erection of the Franklin Statue in Printing-House Square, Presented by Albert De Groot, to the Press and Printers of the City of New-York.</u> New York: Francis Hart & Co., 104 pp.
      A collection of speeches, records, and pieces from the press concerning the preparations for and reaction to the erection of the statue. The important speeches have been cited separately, and these are by Horace Greeley, Charles C. Savage, S. Irenaeus Prime, A. Oakey Hall, Henry Ward Beecher, E.H. Chapin, Erastus Brooks, Peter Carpenter Baker, and Thomas N. Rooker.

8   GREELEY, HORACE. "Presentation Speech." In <u>Record of the Proceedings and Ceremonies Pertaining to the Erection of the Franklin Statue in Printing-House Square, Presented by Albert De Groot, to the Press and Printers of the City of New-York.</u> New York: Francis Hart & Co., pp. 45-46.
      It is "appropriate" that the statue of Franklin be located in Printing-House Square, among workers at the trade he loved, for his entire life "was devoted to practical hard work, rather than to the ornamental and recreative."

9   HALL, A. OAKEY. [Speech on Franklin.] In <u>Record of the Proceedings and Ceremonies Pertaining to the Erection of the Franklin Statue in Printing-House Square, Presented by Albert De Groot, to the Press and Printers of the City of New-York.</u> New York: Francis Hart & Co., pp. 56-57.
      Franklin is lauded for his contributions to Boston.

*10   JANET, PAUL [ALEXANDRE RENÉ]. <u>Histoire de la science politique dans ses rapports avec la morale.</u> Bibliothèque de philosophie contemporaine. Paris: Felix Alcan.
      Source: <u>NUC</u>. <u>See</u> 1887.11.

11   JASPER, pseud. "Jasper's Preface to the Sketches of Franklin's Life and Character." In <u>The Young Franklinsonian. Grandfather's Story: Written for the Children of Mechanics and Farmers, by Their Wellwisher.</u> Hartford: W[illia]m L. Mott, pp. [72]-111.
      Emphasizes the Poor Richard qualities that made Franklin both personally successful and a benefactor to mankind. Following the biographical sketch there are excerpts from Franklin's writings.

12 KEYDAN, J[OH]N KAY. "Benjamin Franklin's 'Laurel Wreath':
    A Picture." Notes and Queries, 4th ser. 10 (6 July):16.
    Responds to Isaac Sheares (1871.8) and says that the
    artist of the painting of Franklin being crowned by a
    wreath of laurels at the French court is Baron Jolly of
    Brussels.

13 PRIME, S. IRENAEUS. [Speech on Franklin.] In Record of the
    Proceedings and Ceremonies Pertaining to the Erection of
    the Franklin Statue in Printing-House Square, Presented by
    Albert De Groot, to the Press and Printers of the City of
    New-York. New York: Francis Hart & Co., pp. 54-55.
    Franklin's success, while the result of many factors,
    certainly speaks to the usefulness of printing in helping
    one rise in life.

14 ROOKER, THOMAS N. "The Kite, the Key, and the Telegraph."
    In Record of the Proceedings and Ceremonies Pertaining to
    the Erection of the Franklin Statue in Printing-House Square,
    Presented by Albert De Groot, to the Press and Printers of
    the City of New-York. New York: Francis C. Hart & Co.,
    pp. 77-82.
    Elaborate praise for Franklin, the man who bottled
    lightning and by doing so carried civilization forward.

15 SAVAGE, CHARLES C. "Acceptance Speech." In Record of the
    Proceedings and Ceremonies Pertaining to the Erection of
    the Franklin Statue in Printing-House Square, Presented by
    Albert De Groot, to the Press and Printers of the City of
    New-York. New York: Francis Hart & Co., pp. 46-50.
    Praises Franklin and printing for their usefulness and
    greatness.

1873

1 ANON. "Franklin." La Mosaique 1:287-88.
   Sketch using Franklin's rise in life as a model for
   others to follow.

2 ANON. "Franklin's Printing Office." American Historical
   Record 2, no. 16 (April):165-67.
   Describes Franklin's printing office and reprints James
   Parker's valuation of it in 1766, when David Hall took
   over the business.

3 ANON. "Franklin's Statue." American Historical Record 2,
   no. 2 (August):381.

1873

Notes that the marble statue of Franklin by Hiram Powers
was given to the city of New Orleans in June 1873.

4   ANON. "Genio di Franklin: statua di Giulio Monteverde."
     Illustrazione popolare (Milan) 6:342.
          This tribute praises both the sculptor and the subject.

5   ANON. "A Memento of Franklin." Historical Magazine, 3d ser.
     2, no. 10 (October):253-54.
          On the "Ben Franklin watch," which Franklin may have
     purchased when he "represented the independent Colonies
     at the British Court, in London." There is an inscription
     which reads: "Ben Franklin, 1776."

6   APPLETON, W[ILLIAM] S[UMNER]. "Medals of Franklin." American
     Journal of Numismatics 7, no. 3 (January):[49]-52.
          Appleton points out that just in his collection there
     are thirty-nine medals honoring Franklin.

7   BRANDON, CHARLES. "Benjamin Franklin. Né en 1706, mort en
     1790." In L'ami de la jeunesse ou livre d'or illustré.
     Vol. 2. Leipzig: Otto Spamer, pp. [209]-18.
          Franklin is a model of purposeful human activity, and
     the virtues he popularized and followed helped him to be-
     come a good and very useful man.

*8   De CASTRO, GIOVANNI. "Chi Fosse Benjamin Franklin." In La
     morale dell'operaio desunta dalla vita e dai pensieri di
     Beniamino Franklin. Turin: G.B. Paravia.
          Source: Catologo generale dell liberaria italiano
     (1847-1899), vol. 1. See 1874.3.

9   HUDSON, FREDERIC. "Benjamin Franklin As a Journalist." In
     Journalism in the United States, From 1690 to 1872. New
     York: Harper & Brothers, pp. 77-79.
          Summary of Franklin's career on the Pennsylvania Gazette.

10   ____. "The Franklins As Journalists." In Journalism in the
     United States, From 1690 to 1872. New York: Harper &
     Brothers, pp. 66-71.
          On the Courant's efforts to be satirical and urbane.
     Hudson says that even at the age of sixteen Franklin
     "seemed to combine, in petto, all the elements of a modern
     newspaper establishment--brains, steam, courage, and
     electricity."

*11 PINELLI, L.P. "All'illustre autore del Genio di Franklin:
     sonetto." Illustrazione popolare (Milan) 8:274.

Source: Pace, pp. 296-99. Pinelli's poem was inspired
by Giulio Monteverde's statue, "Genius of Franklin."

12   SPAMER, FRANZ OTTO [Franz Otto und H. Schramm]. "Benjamin
     Franklin, freier Bürger Stolz und Vorbild. Geb. 1706,
     gest. 1790." In Vier grosse Burger. Vorbilder fur die
     Jugend. Otto Spamer's Illustriert Jugend und Hausbibliothek,
     X. Serie. Leipzig: Otto Spamer, pp. [47]-74.
        An idealized presentation of Franklin's life and charac-
     ter, which depicts the American philosopher as one who not
     only preached virtuous conduct but, in fact, acted virtu-
     ously at all times. His intelligence and perserverance
     helped him succeed in his many enterprises, and those who
     knew of his work recognized in him nobility and goodness.
     Franklin cared far less for personal gain than to be help-
     ful to mankind. It is therefore just that his memory con-
     tinues to be honored. (I have used an abbreviated version
     of the title on the cover; however, the book is sometimes
     cited, as it is at the Regenstein Library of the University
     of Chicago, as follows: Zum 4. Juli 1876. Hundert Jahre
     in der Entwicklung der grossen transatlantischen Republik.
     Vier grosse Bürger der neuen Welt: George Washington und
     Benjamin Franklin . . . , Friedrich Wilhelm v.
     Steuben . . . , Abraham Lincoln. This is the title on the
     second title page.)

                              1874

1   ANON. "Franklin's Unabhängigkeit." In Neuer Gemeinnütziger
     pennsylvanischer Calender . . . 1874. . . . Lancaster, Pa.:
     Johann Bar's Sohnen, p. [4].
        Fictional anecdote showing the adult Franklin to be
     wise and to deserve his prominence in Pennsylvania.

2   BRUCE, W.J. "The Death and Funeral of Franklin." American
     Historical Record 3, no. 25 (January):13-16.
        Bruce sends accounts from the Brunswick Gazette (New
     Brunswick, N.J.) for 4 May 1790, of Franklin's funeral and
     of "A Monody" on him which asserts that even when time on
     earth ends, "In heaven's glad courts thy name shall still
     stand high,/With angels join'd, sure it can never die."

3   De CASTRO, GIOVANNI. "Chi Fosse Benjamin Franklin." In La
     morale dell' operaio desunta dalla vita e dai pensieri di
     Beniamino Franklin. Rome: G.B. Paravia e comp., pp. 1-31.
        Franklin's well-known writings on virtue and success and,
     indeed, his own life are one and point the way for all

1874

people to live successfully and usefully. Franklin is
thought of as Poor Richard, and De Castro points out that
this kind of person, in the public arena, is necessarily a
benefactor to mankind. See 1873.8.

4   FRANÇOIS, L. Franklin[:] sa vie et ses oeuvres. Instruction
republicaine, no. 18. Paris: A. Le Chevalier, 36 pp.
A biographical study that treats Franklin's life and
literary works as indications of his brilliance, dedication,
and virtue. His concern for mankind led Franklin to devote
nearly his entire life to improving the conditions of his
fellows. Whether as a writer, philosopher, scientist or
diplomat, he was prompted by his humanitarianism.

5   [FRANKLIN TYPOGRAPHICAL SOCIETY, BOSTON.] Proceedings of the
Franklin Typographical Society at the Observance of the
Semi-Centennial of Its Institution, January 17, 1874: With
a Brief Historical Sketch. Boston: published by the
Society, 60 pp.
The celebration included addresses praising Franklin as
a printer, molder of public opinion, and statesman.

6   G[REEN], S[AMUEL] A[BBOTT]. "Boston School Medals." American
Journal of Numismatics 9, no. 2 (October):[25]-26.
On the origin and continuing purpose of the Franklin
school medals.

7   H., H.W. "Franklin Medals." American Journal of Numismatics
9, no. 1 (July):4-5.
From his own collection, the author adds to the list of
Franklin medals presented by W.S. Appleton in the January
1873 issue of this journal (1873.6).

8   NEW YORK TYPOGRAPHICAL SOCIETY. Printers' Festival. Celebra-
tion of the 168th Anniversary of the Birthday of Benjamin
Franklin, by the New York Typographical Society (in Aid of
the Library Fund), at New York Turn Hall, 64, 66, 68 East
4th St., Near 2d Ave., Friday Evening, Jan. 16, 1874.
[New York: published for the New York Typographical
Society], 60 pp.
The celebration included an address by William Cullen
Bryant and a performance of John Brougham's Scenes From the
Life of Franklin. The play is discussed separately.
(1856.5).

9   SOLGER, HEINRICH. "Benjamin Franklin." In Ausgewählte
Lebensbeschreibungen berühmter Personen. Der deutschen
Jugend gewidmet. Würzburg: A. Stuber's Buchhandlung,
pp. [35]-51.

The Franklin presented in this appreciation is an idealized Poor Richard.

10   STONE, HORATIO. "Freedom and Franklin." In Ecce Homo
     (Morality Personified) and Freedom (Science Applied)[:]
     Two Bronze Vases. Washington: Republican Book & Job
     Office Print., pp. 10-11.
         Franklin is represented on a three-foot bronze vase
     designed to illustrate how science serves and liberates
     mankind. "Franklin sits between his press and his elec-
     trical machine, and rests his one hand on the kite . . . ,
     and in the other hand holds the key" not only to the exper-
     iment, but to all of science.

                              1875

1   ANON. "Als der bekannte Buchdrucker Franklin." In Neuer
     Gemeinnütziger pennsylvanischer Calender . . . 1875. . . .
     Lancaster, Pa.: Johann Bar's Sohnen, p. [32].
         Franklin withstood the trial in the cockpit and
     Wedderburn's insults with dignity.

2   ANON. "Benjamin Franklin." La abeja, revista bisemanal
     concoimientos dedicada a la clase obrera e industrial 1,
     no. 6:7.
         A brief sketch of Franklin's life which, paying tribute
     to him for a number of achievements, calls him a benefactor
     to mankind.

3   ANON. "Benjamin Franklin and William Cowper." Leisure Hour
     24, no. 1215 (10 April):229-31.
         Discovers a letter of 1782 showing that Franklin, having
     received a volume of William Cowper's poetry, wrote to the
     then unknown poet praising his work. This letter may have
     helped Cowper overcome his despondency and encourage him
     to continue writing.

4   ANON. "Early Newspapers." Potter's American Monthly 4,
     no. 37 (January):7-13.
         Brief account of Franklin's undertaking the Pennsylvania
     Gazette and the immediate improvements he made in the news-
     paper. Begun under Keimer on 24 December 1728, it continued
     "until the death of Sellers, in 1804." Included is a sample
     issue of the Gazette for 25 September to 2 October 1729.

5   ANON. "Memorial de la mano izquiauda." In Almanaque-aquinaldo
     de la Isla de Puerto Rico, pp. 54-55.

1875

Biographical sketch of Franklin highlighting his rise in life and his steadfast patriotism.

6   R., L. "Les savants illustres, Benjamin Franklin." La science illustrée, no. 2 (25 October), pp. 9-12.
Describes the Bartholdi statue of Franklin and praises him as a scientist whose careers in science and politics both show him to be a liberator of mankind.

7   SMITH, C.C. "Bigelow's Life of Franklin." Unitarian Review 3 (January):41-49.
In addition to reviewing Bigelow's edition of the Life, Smith analyzes and defends Franklin's conduct in early life, his basic religious views, and his handling of the Hutchinson and Oliver letters. Franklin stands second only to Washington among the heroes of the Revolution.

1876

1   ABBOTT, JOHN S[TEVENS] C[ABOT]. Benjamin Franklin. American Pioneers and Patriots. New York: Dodd, Mead & Co., 373 pp.
Abbott's biography is filled with inaccuracies. Its value is as a document expressing the way in which an earlier religious and moralizing America wanted to see a national hero who was second only to Washington in the hierarchy of saints. Abbott finds disturbing Franklin's inability to accept Christianity and contends that the reason for this failure is "unexplained." Franklin is therefore, at least until the end of his life, a secular saint who unstintingly struggled for moral perfection and the betterment of mankind. The author later repeats the story that Franklin had a painting of Christ on the cross at his bedside during his last illness. Franklin, we are told, had faults, but these were imperfections bred of limitations in perception and imagination rather than born of indifference. The Franklin that emerges here is the patron saint of capitalism and is nearly devoid of ideas. Yet his life is considered to be typically American.

2   ANON. "Benjamin Franklin." Le Rayon De Soleil, no. 10 (October), pp. 165-66.
A biographical sketch.

3   ANON. "Franklin at the Court of France, and the French Court." Carnival of Authors. Women's Centennial Commission. February 22d & 23d [1, no. 2]:4-5.

Presents the basic story line, characters, symbolism,
and stage directions for a theatrical scene depicting the
crowning of Franklin "with laurels by the Countess Diana
Polignac, in honor of his genius, and in recognition of
his country's advent among the nations."

4   ANON. "Sketch of Benj. Franklin's Life." In The National
    Eagle. Claremont, N.H.: Robert L. Smiley & Co.,
    unpaginated.
        Emphasizes Franklin's wisdom and its importance in his
    becoming "the greatest diplomat of the 18th century."

5   ANON. "Werth der Zeit." In Neuer Gemeinnütziger
    pennsylvanischer Calender . . . 1876. . . . Lancaster,
    Pa.: Johann Bar's Sohnen, p. [28].
        Anecdote of Franklin's method of pricing books according
    to how much time the customer took to buy.

6   BAR-POINT, [pseud]. "'The Little Postmaster of Philadelphia.'"
    Notes and Queries, 5th ser. 5 (1 April):266.
        In The Virginians, Thackeray speaks of Franklin as short.
    Actually, he was five feet nine inches tall, which was
    above the average height of men at that time.

7   CHAPLIN, JEREMIAH. The Life of Benjamin Franklin. Boston:
    D. Lothrop & Co., 398 pp.
        This book, though unreliable by modern standards and
    clearly superseded by later works, is nevertheless one of
    the better nineteenth-century biographies of Franklin. It
    intends, with some success, to present a balanced and accu-
    rate account of Franklin rather than one designed to in-
    spire appropriate morality or patriotism in the readers.

8   De COSTA, B[ENJAMIN] F[RANKLIN]. Introduction to Soldier
    and Sage. Memorials of George Washington and Benjamin
    Franklin. Philadelphia: McCalla & Stavely, pp. 6-7.
        Introduces two Franklin letters to Bouquet in 1764 and
    points out that Franklin was "a devoted servant of the
    Crown[,] and so he would always have remained, if the
    Crown had remained worthy of his devotion."

9   KAPP, FRIEDRICH. "Benjamin Franklin." In Aus und über
    Amerika. Tsatsachen und Erlebnisse. Vol. 1. Berlin:
    Julius Springer, pp. [37]-89.
        Franklin is the founder and chief representative of
    what has come to be regarded as the American character.
    Yet, he is also a most remarkable man; achieving greatness
    in science and guiding his country to freedom and independ-
    ence, he still retained his broad human sympathy.

1876

10   _____. Introduction to Benjamin Franklin. Ein Leben von ihm
      selbst beschreiben. Stuttgart: Berth[old] Auerbach,
      pp. 9-99.
           These pages constitute an uncritical appreciation of
      Franklin's life, career, virtues, and achievements. Kapp
      is especially impressed by Franklin's ability to remain a
      balanced human being of very generous sympathies while
      achieving much in a long life remarkably filled with
      importance.

11   McFARLAND, H[ORACE] H[ENRY]. "Franklin (Benjamin)." In
      Johnson's New Universal Cyclopaedia: A Scientific and
      Popular Treasury of Useful Knowledge. Edited by
      Frederick A.P. Barnard and Arnold Guyot. Vol. 2. New
      York: A.J. Johnson & Son, pp. 294-95.
           Favorable summary of Franklin's career.

12   POLKO, ELISE VOGEL. "The Invention of the Harmonica." In
      Musical Tales, Phantasms, and Sketches. Translated by
      Mary P. Mandslay. London: Samuel Tinsley, pp. 103-15.
           A fictional account of Franklin, whose sensitivity to
      English ballads causes him to swoon when he hears one sung
      beautifully by a young English girl, Mary Davies. When she
      saw the effect of her singing on Franklin, she went into
      shock and lost her voice. To compensate her for her loss,
      Franklin invented the glass harmonica so that Mary could
      sing, "though not with your lips." (Marianne Davies per-
      formed on the harmonica made according to Franklin's speci-
      fications. She taught Marie Antoinette, among others, to
      play the instrument.) See 1852.12.

13   PUIG, JOAQUIN OLMEDILLA y. "Franklin." Revista Europa 7,
      no. 121 (March-June):638-40.
           Franklin is considered against the state of science in
      his time and is praised for his contributions which, fit-
      tingly, have made him immortal.

14   SAWCZYŃSKI, ZYGMUNT. Benjamin Franklin. Jerzy Wasyngton.
      Lwów: Nakladem Towarzystwa pedagogicznego, pp. 1-66.
           An account of Franklin's life that follows closely the
      Autobiography and Mignet. Sawczyński deals more fully with
      Franklin's young manhood as a printer than with any other
      period of his life.

15   SCUDDER, H[ORACE] E[LISHA?], ed. "An Evening with Franklin."
      In Men and Manners in America One Hundred Years Ago.
      Sans-Souci Series. New York: Scribner, Armstrong, & Co.,
      pp. 86-88.

The author's evening with Franklin proved memorable not only because the philosopher played Scottish tunes on his armonica, but because the next morning after his performance he had the pleasure of announcing Cornwallis' surrender.

16 ____. "Mrs. Wright and Franklin's Head." In Men and Manners in America One Hundred Years Ago. Sans-Souci Series. New York: Scribner, Armstrong, & Co., pp. 83-86.
Mrs. Wright had made a head of Franklin, and he presented for it a suit of clothes he had worn in 1778 to make the likeness complete. A series of misadventures follow Mrs. Wright when she carries the head around with her.

1877

1 ANON. "Benjamin Franklin." Barnard's American Journal of Education 27, no. 6 (April):[409]-31.
These pages of a longer piece, which includes selections from Franklin's memoirs and other writings, are a sketch of his life and character.

2 BALCH, THOMAS. "Dr. William Shippen, the Elder." Pennsylvania Magazine of History and Biography 1:212-16.
Notes that Franklin's junto helped shape the life of the elder Dr. William Shippen.

3 BLY, ARMAND. L'arte de faire sa fortune de l'acquérir de l'augmenter, de la conserver par un ancien ouvrier devenu millionaire ou[,] la vie de Benjamin Franklin en exemples imite de la science du Bonhomme Richard. Paris: Se vend chez l'auteur, 16 pp.
Assumes that Poor Richard's views are identical with those of his creator. Moreover, the philomat's maxims will still enable one to get ahead morally, intellectually, and especially financially.

4 BUTTRE, LILLIAN C. "Benjamin Franklin." In The American Portrait Gallery. With Biographical Sketches of Presidents, Statesmen, Military and Naval Heroes, Clergymen, Authors, Poets, Etc., Etc. Vol. 1. New York: J.C. Buttre, Publisher, unpaginated.
A summary of Franklin's career, noting especially his versatility, philanthropy, and patriotism. The piece on Franklin is the eighth item in the book.

1877

5 DANA, RICHARD H[ENRY, Jr.]. "Francis Dana." Pennsylvania
   Magazine of History and Biography 1:86-95.
   Shows that Francis Dana supported John Adams rather than
   Franklin in Adams's contentions with Vergennes.

*6 De VARA, A. [A. Ravà]. "Considerazioni generali-Sentenze di
   Franklin e di S. Agostino--La dignità dell'operaio, etc." In
   Consigli agli operai. Milan: Tipografia Editrice Lombarda,
   pp. 7-18, passim.
        Source: Pace, p. 434, no. 254; p. 304. Franklin, the
   arduous workingman, is discussed along with Saint Augustine
   to prove that ordinary workers have true dignity.

7 HILLARD, GEORGE STILLMAN. The Franklin Fifth Reader for the
   Use of Public and Private Schools. New York: Taintor
   Bro's, Merrill & Co., pp. 62-63.
   Biographical sketch of Franklin.

8 HOADLEY, CHARLES J. "Silas Deane." Pennsylvania Magazine of
   History and Biography 1:96-100.
   Praises Franklin for defending Silas Deane.

9 KLEE, E. George Washington und Benjamin Franklin, die
   Begründer der "Vereinigten Staaten." Geschichtsbilder für
   Jugend und Volk, 11 Bdchen. Leipzig: Ferdinand Hirt und
   Sohn, pp. [537]-96.
   Franklin is treated as an architect of American inde-
   pendence, but very little of this career study gets beyond
   the years covered in the Autobiography.

10 NORRIS, GEORGE W. "Isaac Norris." Pennsylvania Magazine of
   History and Biography 1:449-54.
   Norris points out that his ancestor opposed Franklin's
   plan to bring Pennsylvania under the Crown.

11 TERRIGI, GUGLIELMO. Il parafulmine e Beniamino Franklin[:]
   lezione popolare e sperimentale fatta nell'aula massima
   della R. Università di Roma nel giorno 26 marzo 1871. . . .
   Rome: Tipografia Romana, 24 pp.
   Reviews Franklin's career and achievements in electrical
   science in a relatively objective manner rather than with the
   unbounded enthusiasm that other Europeans treated Franklin
   and his contributions to science and other areas.

1878

1   DICKINSON, JOHN, et al. The Reasons on Which Were Founded the
    Protest Offered by Certain Members of the Assembly to That
    Body Concerning the Sending of Mr. Franklin to England As
    Assistant to Our Agent There. Philadelphia, 4 pp.
       The protestors object because of Franklin's desire to
    bring royal government to Pennsylvania, because of his in-
    flexible hostility toward the proprietors of Pennsylvania,
    and because "several of his Majesty's ministers" think
    poorly of him. Moreover, Franklin is thoroughly disliked
    by many "of the most serious and reputable inhabitants of
    this Province of all denominations, and societies," and in
    the past he has proved an unworthy servant of the public,
    having misused its funds. Franklin's allies have pushed
    through his appointment with unseemly haste so that he can
    continue abroad the mischief which he has begun in the
    colonies. See 1764.12.

2   HILLARD, GEORGE STILLMAN. "Anecdote of Franklin's Boyhood."
    In The Webster-Franklin Intermediate Reader for the Use of
    Public and Private Schools. New York: Taintor Brothers,
    pp. 44-55.
       Fictional account of the time when Franklin led the
    neighborhood boys of Philadelphia in taking the masons'
    stones, which were intended for a house, and using them to
    build a wharf so that he and his friends could fish more
    conveniently. As one might expect, the anecdote is quite
    moralistic.

3   LEVRAY, ALPH[ONSE]. Benjamin Franklin. Petite bibliothèque
    de l'enfance. Paris: J. Bonheure et cie, 72 pp.
       Makes much of the influence of Josiah and Abiah
    Franklin and of the Quakers on the young Franklin, whose
    life is an example of how one can live successfully and
    usefully by constant effort and self-examination. While
    Levray does invent conversations between Franklin and
    others, his book follows closely the Autobiography. In
    fact, only about twenty percent of Benjamin Franklin deals
    with the years after 1757, and most of these pages have to
    do with Franklin's years in France. The critical decade
    prior to the War of Independence is merely touched upon in
    a few pages. Levray is less interested in presenting a
    complete and balanced account than in providing a moral,
    religious, patriotic, and benevolent Franklin who should
    inspire children to rise in life as he did.

1878

4   LITTEL, CHARLES WILLING. "Major William Jackson, Secretary
    of the Federal Convention." Pennsylvania Magazine of
    History and Biography 2:353-69.
        Confirms Franklin's wisdom in handling American funds
    in France and his judgment of the character of Captain
    Alexander Gillon.

5   MICHEELS, J[AN JOZEF MATTHIJS]. Benjamin Franklin, een
    levensbeeld [Benjamin Franklin, a biography]. Gent:
    Boekhandel W. Rogghé (J. Vuylsteke), 120 pp.
        A brief biography based largely on the memoirs. The
    Franklin that emerges is sanitized in the manner of many
    nineteenth-century biographies.

*6 RICHARDSON, CHARLES FRANCIS. "Benjamin Franklin." In A
    Primer of American Literature. Boston: Houghton, Osgood &
    Co.
        Source: NUC. See 1884.4.

7   STUDENT, pseud. "An Epitaph on Franklin." Magazine of
    American History 2, no. 5 (June):365.
        On Turgot's epigram and d'Alembert's poem praising
    Franklin.

8   TYLER, MOSES COIT. "Benjamin Franklin." In A History of
    American Literature. Vol. 2. New York: G.P. Putnam's
    Sons, pp. 251-53.
        Franklin's "pure, pithy, racy, and delightful diction"
    has made him a master of English style. It is nevertheless
    true that his works were written for a practical and "imme-
    diate purpose," and so he did not have the leisure to
    polish his works. He cannot really be considered, then,
    a man of letters.

                            1879

1   ANON. "Benjamin Franklin." Harper's Young People 1, no. 4
    (25 November):28.
        Very brief, fragmented sketch of a few of the highlights
    of Franklin's early years.

2   BERSOT, [PIERRE] ERNEST. "Oeuvres morales de Franklin." In
    Études et discours (1868-1878). . . . Paris: Hachette et
    cie, pp. [30]-34.
        Franklin was both a liberal and a moralist; however, he
    was also without illusions or naïveté, which made him even
    more effective.

3   BIGELOW, J[OHN]. "Franklin, Benjamin (1706-1790)." In <u>The</u>
    <u>Encyclopaedia Britannica. A Dictionary of Arts, Sciences,</u>
    <u>and General Literature.</u> 9th ed. American Reprint. Vol. 9.
    Philadelphia: J.M. Stoddart Co., pp. 626-33.
        A biographical account focusing attention on Franklin's
    political and diplomatic activities, but also noting that
    the accomplishment of his difficult mission to France was
    helped considerably by his reputation as a scientist and
    moral philosopher. Franklin, though he wrote much, Bigelow
    says, was never fragmentary or dull; therefore, all his
    works have "permanent interest." His greatest achievement,
    in a life filled with notable deeds, is that by his own
    splendid example he dignified manual labor.

4   BIGELOW, JOHN. <u>Franklin. A Sketch.</u> Boston: Little, Brown,
    & Co., 30 pp.
        Emphasizes Franklin's virtues. Though he was hardly
    free from worldly considerations, he never used his public
    position to advance his own fortune. There is hardly a
    person who will not find the encouragement to strive for
    excellence by reading some part of Franklin's life that is
    relevant to his own.

5   EGLE, WILLIAM H. "The Constitutional Convention of 1776.
    Biographical Sketches of Its Members." <u>Pennsylvania Maga-</u>
    <u>zine of History and Biography</u> 3:327-28.
        Egle offers a brief sketch of Franklin's career.

6   G., J.J. "Pierres Gravées representant Voltaire et
    Franklin." <u>Nouvelles archives de l'art français; recueil</u>
    <u>de documents inédits relatifs à l'histoire des arts en</u>
    <u>France,</u> 2d ser. 1:[433]-36.
        The author comments essentially on the background of the
    likeness rather than on the work itself.

7   GUERRIER, HENRI. "Franklin." In <u>Petites biographies</u>
    <u>littéraires et historiques pouvant servir de lectures et</u>
    <u>dictées a l'usage de écoles primaires et de cours d</u>
    <u>l'enseignment special. . . .</u> Paris: Ch. Delgrave,
    pp. 145-46.
        Franklin was loved both in France and America.

8   HUGHES, THOMAS. "English Views of Franklin." <u>Lippincott's</u>
    <u>Magazine</u> 24 (July):108-17.
        Comments on the Bigelow edition of Franklin's life and
    attacks "the prejudices, political and religious, which
    have obscured Franklin's fame in England." Contrary to
    popular English opinion, Franklin's Crown office did not

1879

make it necessary for him to follow anti-American Crown
policies or to lessen his efforts in behalf of his countrymen. The arguments against Franklin on religious grounds
are more understandable but nevertheless unreasonable.
Franklin joined Christ Church after his marriage and remained a member all his life. In truth, though, he was a
Christian on fundamentals rather than a sectarian. In this
sense he anticipated the "ideal American," the man who has
learned to divest himself "of definite creeds, while retain-
ing their moral essence, and finds the highest sanctions
needed for the conduct of human life in experience tempered
by common sense." (This piece also appears in the Library
Magazine 2 (July 1879):1-14.)

9   MELISH, THOMAS J. "Brother Benj. Franklin." Masonic Review
     and the Masonic Journal of Louisville, Kentucky 52:[337]-43.
          Recounts Franklin's career as a Mason and suggests that
     his beliefs, which he developed while still very young,
     were very similar to those held by Masons, and so it was
     natural that he would become a member of the Society.

10   QUINCY, ELIZA SUSAN. "Josiah Quincy, Senior." Pennsylvania
     Magazine of History and Biography 3:182-86.
          Franklin helped Quincy in his appeal before the Pennsyl-
     vania Assembly for funds to enable Massachusetts to erect a
     fortress near the French fortress at Crown Point. The
     Assembly, of which Franklin was a leading member, granted
     £10,000.

11   REBOLLEDO, JOSE A[NTONIO]. "Benjamin Franklin." In Los
     héroes de la Civilización. Ensayo historico-critico.
     Madrid: J.A. García, pp. 238-81.
          Laudatory, uncritical survey of Franklin's career and
     character. Clearly, Franklin represents allegiance to
     broad, humane principles and to a nation that offers the
     hope of a good life for average people.

12   SMITH, HORACE WEMYSS. Life and Correspondence of the Rev.
     William Smith, D.D. 2 vols. Philadelphia: S.A. George &
     Co.
          This is still the most complete account of Provost Smith
     and is also a valuable source for many of his writings.
     Nevertheless, it has all the faults of a family biography
     of a great grandfather for whom the author still felt "youth-
     ful veneration." H.W. Smith is completely biased in dealing
     with the political hostility that developed between Smith
     and Franklin, who enters prominently in this work. The
     author points out that Franklin and his supporters tried

1880

to "break down" the College of Philadelphia, because of
their intense hatred for the Provost.

13   STONE, FREDERICK D.   "Philadelphia Society One Hundred Years
      Ago, Or the Reign of Continental Money." Pennsylvania
      Magazine of History and Biography 3:361-94.
          This article tells of Franklin's astonishment and anger
      at the concern of his countrymen, including his daughter,
      with luxuries in the midst of war.

14   WALLER, J[AMES] B[RECKENRIDGE]. Reminiscences of Benjamin
      Franklin As a Diplomatist. Chicago: Jameson & Morse,
      Printers, 39 pp.
          A rather biased sketch of Franklin's diplomatic achieve-
      ments in which John Adams and Arthur Lee are reduced to mere
      envious and malicious schemers against Franklin.

15   [WINTHROP, ROBERT CHARLES.] "Remarks by the President." In
      Proceedings of the Massachusetts Historical Society.
      Vol. 16. Boston: published by the Society, pp. 41-50.
          Franklin is the center of Winthrop's concern, yet the
      "Remarks" do point out that none of the patriots considered
      making public the Hutchinson letters anything other than an
      act of high principle. It seems clear to Winthrop that
      Wedderburn's vicious attack on Franklin two years after
      the American agent sent the Hutchinson letters to Boston
      was undertaken to punish and defame Franklin for the gen-
      eral deterioration in Anglo-American relations and not
      simply because of the Hutchinson affair. (The "Remarks"
      was delivered at the February 1878 meeting of the Society.)

188-

1   SCHUBART, C[HRISTIAN] F[RIEDRICH] D[ANIEL]. "Franklins
     Grabschrift." In Gedichte. Edited by Gustav Hauff.
     Leipzig: Recalm.
         A eulogy on Franklin which notes that his simple epitaph
     expresses the qualities of the man. (Apparently the first
     book publication of the piece. Schubart died in 1791.)

1880

1   ANON. "Franklin[,] 1706-1790." In The Hundred Greatest Men[.]
     Portraits of the One Hundred Greatest Men of History Repro-
     duced From Fine and Rare Engravings. Vol. 8. London:
     Sampson Lowe, Marston, Searle & Rivington, unpaginated.

1880

Franklin is a great man because he stands preeminently
for "Industry-- that is, for Invention, Discovery and
Philanthropy."

2   ANON.   "Review of Bigelow's The Life of Benjamin
    Franklin . . . , 1879." Edinburgh Review 151, no. 310
    (April):321-58.
       A balanced and quite thorough discussion of Franklin's
    career, concentrating on the period of 1763-1783. The re-
    viewer calls the memoirs "one of mankind's greatest liter-
    ary possessions" and considers many of Franklin's letters
    and papers to be of the first importance. Rebuking incom-
    petent British legislators and condemning the many corrupt
    ones who befouled the early years of the reign of George III,
    the reviewer nevertheless believes that Franklin had long
    been testing to discover the weak links in the chain that
    tied America to the British Empire, and by virtue of his
    experience in the cockpit, if not before 1774, Franklin
    actively sought independence for his countrymen.

3   DANA, RICHARD H[ENRY, Jr.]. "Sketch of American Diplomacy."
    Scribner's Monthly 20, no. 4 (August):616-19.
       These pages of a somewhat longer piece deal with the
    birth of American diplomacy at Paris and Franklin's role
    in securing the alliance with France.

4   DRAPER, J[OHN] W[ILLIAM]. "Franklin's Place in the Science of
    the Last Century." Harper's New Monthly Magazine 61,
    no. 362 (July):265-75.
       As a scientist Franklin perceived new truths and, over-
    coming superstition and other obstacles, turned the specula-
    tions of lesser philosophers into scientific truths. So
    great and versatile was he, however, that his brilliant
    scientific work is overshadowed by his political
    accomplishments.

5   [GREENE], F.B. The Benjamin Franklin Primer. Boston: Boston
    School Supply Co., 24 pp.
       A satire on primers and on Poor Richardisms.

6   JONES, WINSLOW. "Benjamin Franklin." Notes and Queries, 6th
    ser. 2 (14 August):127-28.
       Asks the location of the cenotaph of Franklin based on
    the epigram of Turgot, "Eripuit caelo fulmen, sceptrumque
    tyrannis."

*7 MORSE, JOHN T[ORREY], Jr. Benjamin Franklin. American
    Statesmen. Boston: Houghton Mifflin & Co.
       Source: NUC. See 1889.16.

*8 SHAW, THOMAS BUDD. "Benjamin Franklin." In Shaw's New His-
    tory of English Literature. Prepared on the Basis of
    "Shaw's Manual," by Truman J. Backus. New York: Sheldon &
    Co.
    Source: NUC. See 1887.16.

1881

1 ANON. "Benjamin Franklin und die Spotter." In Neuer
   Gemeinnütziger Calender. . . . Lancaster, Pa.: Johann
   Bar's Sohnen, pp. [23, 25].
        A fiction in which Franklin plays a trick on an ignorant
   loudmouth and defends the worth of the Bible.

2 BLAINE, JAMES G. "Letter from the Secretary of State Trans-
   mitting a Report on the Papers of Benjamin Franklin Offered
   for Sale by Mr. Henry Stevens, and Recommending Their Purchase by Congress." In 47th Congress, 1st Session. Senate.
   Misc. Doc. No. 21. [Washington: Government Printing
   Office], 99 pp.
        "Believing that in the failure to acquire these papers
   the national archives might sustain an irreparable loss,
   I caused the librarian of this Department . . . , to make,
   at London, an examination of them, and upon his report took
   steps to induce Mr. Stevens again to withdraw them from
   sale, and give the United States another opportunity to
   secure them." The above mentioned librarian's report was
   made by Theodore Frelinghuysen Dwight, on 30 November 1881,
   and is cited separately (1881.4).

3 DEMOULIN, [ANAIS GILLET]. "Mme. Gustave Demoulin." In
   Franklin. Bibliothèque des écoles et des familles. Paris:
   Hachette, 36 pp.
        Brief biography in which Franklin's life, especially his
   excellent character and well-known Poor Richard virtues,
   are used to guide school children to better, more useful,
   and successful lives. Franklin's scientific accomplishments and his splendid reputation in France are used to
   inspire French children to try and model their lives after
   his.

4 DWIGHT, THEODORE F[RELINGHUYSEN]. ["Letter to James G. Blaine,
   Secretary of State."] In 47th Congress, 1st Session.
   Senate. Misc. Doc. No. 21. [Washington: Government
   Printing Office], 99 pp.
        Dwight recommends the purchase of the Henry Stevens
   Franklin collection. Dwight, the Librarian of Congress,
   had responded to an inquiry made by Blaine (1881.2).

1881

5   HERDER, JOHANN GOTTFRIED von. "Fragen zu Errichtung einer
     Gesellschaft der Humanität von Benjamin Franklin." In
     Herders Sämmtliche Werke. Herausgegeben von Bernhard
     Suphan. Vol. 17. Berlin: Weidmannsche Buchhandlung,
     pp. 10-18.
         Analyzes the questions in depth to show the excellence
     of Franklin's character, his humanitarianism and his prac-
     tical approach toward human betterment.
         Franklin's self-scrutiny, which was a habit with him,
     was an important factor in his leading a successful and
     most useful life. (Written in 1793 but apparently first
     published in 1881.)

6   _____. [On Franklin's Life.] In Herders Sämmtliche Werke.
     Herausgegeben von Bernhard Suphan. Vol. 17. Berlin:
     Weidmannsche Buchhandlung, pp. 16-18.
         Tribute to Franklin, who was a true original. (Written
     in 1792 but apparently first published in 1881.)

7   _____. "Ueber Benj. Franklins Lebensbeschreibung von ihm
     selbst." In Herders Sämmtliche Werke. Herausgegeben von
     Bernhard Suphan. Vol. 17. Berlin: Weidmannsche
     Buchhandlung, pp. 7-10.
         Franklin's remarkable success story is particularly
     valuable to young people who are starting out in life.
     (Written in 1792 but apparently first published in 1881.)

8   ROSAVO, NARISSA. "Benjamin Franklin." Argosy 32 (August):
     123-29.
         A sketch of Franklin's life, particularly of his youth.

9   SJÖGREN, [KARL AUGUST] OTTO. Benjamin Franklin. Lefnadsbilder
     af märkvärdiga personer, 2. Stockholm: J. Seligmann &c:
     24 pp.
         A brief sketch apparently intended for young readers.
     Franklin is portrayed as the model of the virtuous and
     self-made man. The cover of this work is dated 1882.

10   STEVENS, HENRY. Benjamin Franklin's Life and Writings: A
     Bibliographical Essay on the Stevens' Collection of Books
     and Manuscripts Relating to Doctor Franklin. London: printed
     b6 Messrs. Davy & Sons for the Dryden Press, 40 pp.
         In his bibliographical essay Stevens hopes to "present
     to view some of the new, hitherto unused materials for the
     history of the life and remarkable career of Franklin. In
     doing this a vindication of the British government and
     Franklin's grandson from the oft repeated charge of

conspiring to destroy or suppress the old philosopher's papers follows as a matter of course." Stevens next offers a bibliographical essay on, and a list of, the Franklin materials he collected. He also tries to rescue Franklin from the attacks of his enemies and their descendants.

11 ____. "Henry Stevens Franklin Collection." In Stevens Historical Collections[.] Catalogue of the First Portion of the Extensive & Varied Collections of Rare Books and Manuscripts Relating Chiefly to the History and Literature of America . . . Sold by Auction, by Messrs. Sotheby, Wildinson & Hodge. . . . [London: Dryden Press], pp. 159-60, 160A-60L, 161-76.

Pages 159-76 constitute the catalogue dealing with the Franklin material and with Stevens's essay in which he defends William Temple Franklin from charges that he destroyed Franklin manuscripts. Stevens also remarks that Franklin, like Shakespeare, was remarkably careless of his literary reputation and thus did not see most of his writings through the press or attempt to write an account of his critical role in the American Revolution and the peace treaty. He "trusted loyally to posterity" to care for his papers and his reputation. Unfortunately, he has not been well served. The lack of a comprehensive account of his activities such as the completed memoirs would have furnished, might have protected his reputation from enemies. The Franklin papers offered by Stevens for sale will, however, do much to foil his enemies and prove that William Temple Franklin was a loyal and honest guardian of his grandfather's papers.

12 TOWLE, GEORGE MAKEPEACE. "Franklin, the Boston Boy." In Memorial History of Boston, Including Suffolk County, Massachusetts. 1630-1830. Edited by Justin Winsor. Vol. 2. Boston: James R. Osgood & Co., pp. [269]-96.

Sketch of Franklin's life which asserts that although he had troubles in the Boston of his youth, he always retained his affection for the city and benefited all his life from the Yankee virtues he learned in Boston.

1882

1 ANDERSON, RICHARD. The Lightning Rod. On "The Necessity for a Regular Inspection of Lightning Conductors." Being Abstract of Papers Read Before the British Association, 1878-80. London: Grattan Marshall & Co., Sanderson & Co., & Leadenhall House, pp. 3-17.

1882

Recounts Franklin's experiments with electricity and
presents in some detail the intellectual process by which
Franklin concluded that a "charge of electricity could be
drawn off by means of a sharp-pointed conductor." In terms
of his own kite experiment, it is fortunate he did not know
more about metals as conductors, for he then would have
used wire on his kite instead of twine and been killed.
Franklin lived to be honored in America and Europe; however, "the use of lightning conductors even in America
spread with surprising slowness." A number of ministers
in America looked upon Franklin as a free-thinker and on
his discovery as an effort to avoid one of God's punish-
ments of sinful men. In Europe the opposition to Franklin's
work was even greater. The problem here was not only religious but intellectual bigotry and vanity, witness the conduct of the Abbé Nollet, who refused at first to believe
that Franklin existed, and of the French mob "at St. Omer
[that] tore down a lightning rod which had been erected"
by a manufacturer who had seen Franklin's rods in America.
This man, though, persisted, for he "appears to have had
English blood in his veins." (Anderson does not point out
that the Royal Society refused at first to take Franklin's
work seriously. He does later mention that the Society's
acceptance of the discoveries was "half-hearted," and that
a century afterwards England, like France, had done little
to improve lightning rods. This section constitutes nearly
half of the pamphlet.)

2 [BACHE, RICHARD MEADE.] "The Lost Papers of Benjamin
   Franklin." Penn Monthly 13 (May):333-50.
      Tells the story of Temple Franklin's trunk of Franklin
   papers, defends Temple's honesty and calls upon Congress to
   purchase these papers rather than let them fall into private hands. Purchasing them would be doing justice to
   Franklin, who was too busy in behalf of his countrymen
   to bring out an edition of his papers himself.

3 BATES, WILLIAM. "'Eripuit Caelo Fulmen, Sceptrumque Tyrannis':
   Letter of Walter Savage Landor: Turgot: Franklin." Notes
   and Queries, 6th ser. 5 (15 April):288-90.
      Implies that this is the verse Turgot actually wrote
   and quotes a letter of Landor to show that the Englishman
   knew Turgot had written the words. Also quotes the poem,
   "Franklin," by James Montgomery (1852.11), a piece which
   praises Franklin's efforts in science and in behalf of a
   free press.

4 BEARD, GEORGE M[ILLER]. "A Few Extracts From a Paper on the
   Medical Use of Statical Electricity." In Franklinism; or

the Treatment of Disease by Statical Electricity, With a
Discription [sic] of the Necessary Apparatus and Appliances.
Compiled by H.D. Hall. New York: J. & H. Berge,
unpaginated.

One of the three forms of electricity is "franklinism,"
which was the earliest to be used by the medical profession.
After "a history of tremendous promise and tremendous disap-
pointment," it is returning to use. In fact, it may well
prove more useful to doctors than the other two forms of
electricity, "faradism" and "galvanism." The publisher of
this pamphlet manufactured electrical machines and other
electrical apparatus.

5   CAMPBELL, HELEN. "A Master Builder." Our Continent 2, no. 22
     (6 December):[673]-80.

     The Folgers of Nantucket, so closely identified with the
     sea and early simple virtues, left their mark on young
     Benjamin Franklin. This is especially true of the manly,
     honest, courageous and intelligent father of Abiah,
     Franklin's mother. The qualities represented by the
     Folgers were especially useful to Franklin as he corrected
     his life and struggled to rise from apprentice to eminently
     successful master.

6   DESCHANEL, ÉMILE [AUGUSTE ETIENNE MARTIN]. Benjamin Franklin.
     Bibliothèque des écoles et familles. Paris: Librairie
     Hachette et Cie, 191 pp.

     A quite derivative biography which calls attention to
     French enthusiasm for Franklin as a thinker, scientist,
     statesman, writer, and humanitarian. His personal qualities
     were an important factor in effecting the alliance with
     France.

7   GENEVAY, A[NTOINE]. "Benjamin Franklin." In La fin de
     l'esclavage aux Etats-Unis derniers jours d'une guerre
     civile. Franklin. Paris: Ch. Delagrave, pp. [149]-89.

     A fictionalized piece showing that the wise and benevo-
     lent Franklin, minister to France from the United States of
     America, rose in life and achieved great success through
     steady hard work, sobriety, and frugality.

8   [JOHNSTON, HENRY? P.] "The Franklin, Rochambeau, and Force
     Papers." Magazine of American History 8, no. 4 (May):
     [346]-48.

     These pages of a longer piece deal with the purchase by
     the Library of Congress of the Stevens collection of
     Franklin papers.

1882

9   LUBIMOFF, ALEKSANDR N.   Veniam Franklin, ego zhĭzn' i ego
     pravila samousover.   Shenstvovania, biograficheskii ocherk
     [Benjamin Franklin, his life and self-disciplinary rules].
     Moscow: Katkoff, 70 pp.
          Franklin's moralistic writings represent the actual man
     and constitute a sound guide to the good and useful life.
     (In Russian.   Published separately from Dietskiĭ Otdykñ.)

10   MARINI, G.   Franklin: libriccino pei figli del lavoro.   Forli:
     Marini.
          Young Italian workers are reminded that the great
     Franklin was also a worker and that, like him, they can
     improve their lives by practicing his virtues.

11   ROCKWELL, A.D.   [On the Therapeutic Value of Franklinic Elec-
     tricity.]   In Franklinism; or the Treatment of Disease by
     Statical Electricity, With a Discription [sic] of the Neces-
     sary Apparatus and Appliances.   Compiled by H.D. Hall.   New
     York: J. & H. Berge, unpaginated.
          Testimony that "franklinic electricity as a therapeutic
     agent is, without question, very great."   It is on occasion
     a reliever of pain in cases unaffected by faradic electric-
     ity.   Moreover, franklinic electricity, unlike other forms,
     produces sedative and tonic effects on patients.   Other
     uses are noted.

1883

*1   BARBÈRA, GASPERO.   Memorie di un editore.   Florence: Barbèra,
     pp. 58ff.
          Source: Pace, pp. 195-96.   Barbèra, an eminent Italian
     printer, attributes his reformation from evil to virtue and
     prosperity to his reading Franklin's Autobiography and
     other works and to following, as well as he could, the
     illustrious American's example.

2   BOSTON PUBLIC LIBRARY.   Bulletins Showing Titles of Books
     Added to the Boston Public Library [,] with Bibliographical
     Notes, etc.   2d ser., nos. 60-66.   Boston: printed by
     order of the Trustees by Rockwell and Churchill, City
     Printers, pp. 217-31, 276-84, 420-33.
          This list of works by and about Franklin and items
     printed by him is somewhat more complete than the similar
     list by Lindsay Swift (1833.10).

3   COCHRANE, ROBERT.   "Benjamin Franklin."   In Risen by Perse-
     verance: or, Lives of Self-Made Men.   New York:
     R. Worthington, pp. 5-50.

Franklin was not born into a family that could afford
to have him educated at Harvard; however, he was a man of
great ability and determination and so undertook to educate
himself. He realized that education was a lifelong affair
and became probably the greatest example of a self-educated
man in colonial America.

4   CURTIS, GEORGE TICKNOR. "The Treaty of Peace and Independ-
    ence." Harper's New Monthly Magazine 66, no. 395 (April):
    [666]-82.
        On Franklin's critical role and shrewdness in the nego-
    tiations that ended the Revolutionary War. The conclusion
    of the article, which is in two parts, appears in no. 396
    (May):[833]-44, of the same volume; however, it merely
    touches upon Franklin.

5   DWIGHT, THEODORE F[RELINGHUYSEN]. "Lost and Found Manuscripts
    of Benjamin Franklin." Magazine of American History 9,
    no. 6 (June):428-39.
        That Congress approved the purchase of the Stevens col-
    lection of Franklin's papers is testimony to the services
    of this least adequately honored of the heroes of the Amer-
    ican independence. Describes some of the collection.

6   GROFF, LEVI W. A Statement Concerning My Rare Old Relic.
    Lancaster, Pa., broadside.
        A broadside asserting that Groff's "relic," a watch, did
    at one time belong to Franklin. Groff's claim was corrob-
    orated by William Duane.

7   HERDER, JOHANN GOTTFRIED von. "Franklin's Fragen." In
    Herders Sämmtliche Werke. Herausgegeben von Bernhard
    Suphan. Vol. 18. Berlin: Weidmannsche Buchhandlung,
    pp. [503]-8.
        Franklin posed for himself questions about his character
    and his conduct. These searching questions led not only to
    self-improvement, but to virtue and benevolence as well.
    (This piece was written in 1792, but apparently first pub-
    lished here.)

8   MOON, W[ILLIA]M. Life of Benjamin Franklin, Embossed in
    Dr. Moon's Type for the Blind. 2 vols. Brighton, Eng.:
    Moon's Institute, 82 pp.
        A raised typed account of Franklin's life.

9   SOLLY, EDWARD. "Benjamin Franklin, Printer." Bibliographer
    3, no. 1 (December):3-4.
        Concludes that Franklin worked on the third edition of
    Wollaston's The Religion of Nature Delineated.

1883

10   [SWIFT, LINDSAY.] Catalogue of Works Relating to Benjamin
      Franklin in the Boston Public Library. Boston: published
      by order of the Trustees, 42 pp.
          The collection, which had been greatly increased in 1881
      by the gift of Samuel A. Green, is listed with an annotation.
      There are actually three sections to this Catalogue: works
      by Franklin, relating to him, and printed by his printing
      house.

1884

1   B., O.A. "Franklin and John Paul Jones." Magazine of American
      History 12, no. 1 (July):81-82.
          Their correspondence shows that Franklin and Jones were
      in close communication, and that Franklin counseled the
      younger man.

2   HUNTINGTON, W[ILLIAM] H[ENRY]. Benjamin Franklin--France.
      Francis Bacon. Portraits in Limoges Enamel, Painted by
      F. de Courcy of Paris. Paris, 1 p.
          Bacon was the promoter of the experimental method used
      so well by Franklin, and so the two de Courcy pendants
      belong together.

3   MAALDRINK, D[ANIEL] M[ARTINUS]. Benjamin Franklin. Een die
      zich zelven hielp [Benjamin Franklin and those who help
      themselves]. Amsterdam: Tj. van Holkema, 52 pp.
          Franklin's life is certain proof that through self-help
      one can accomplish a great deal.

4   RICHARDSON, CHARLES FRANCIS. "Benjamin Franklin." In A
      Primer of American Literature. Boston: Houghton, Osgood &
      Co., pp. 18-21.
          Contends that Franklin is a genuine man of letters and
      surveys his accomplishments. See 1878.6.

5   SCHARF, J. THOMAS, and WESTCOTT, THOMPSON. "Benjamin Franklin
      and Philadelphia." In History of Philadelphia, 1609-1884.
      Vol. 1. Philadelphia: L.H. Everts & Co., pp. 218-43.
          Franklin was a great rather than good man, for his
      morals, in some respects are so bad as to border on "little-
      ness." This summary sets Franklin's career to 1765 against
      the background of Philadelphia history.

6   TRÉVERRET, [ARMAND de GERMAIN]. "Conférence sur Benjamin
      Franklin (la science du bonhomme Richard)." Bulletin de
      la société philomatique de Bordeaux, 3d ser., pp. 6-23.

Tribute to the philosophy of good sense and the sound
morals Franklin, in the guise of Poor Richard and Father
Abraham, upheld.

7   TYPOTHETAE of [the CITY of] NEW YORK. Annual Dinner . . . in
     Honor of the Birth-day of Benjamin Franklin[,] at the
     Metropolitan Hotel[,] Thursday, January 17th, 1884. [New
     York: printed for the Typothetae of the City of New York.]
     Franklin is praised in toasts, speeches, and telegrams.

                              1885

*1   ANON. "Uso dell'olio per calmare l'agitazione del mare."
     Rivista marittima (Rome) 18, no. 1:162-63.
        Source: Pace, p. 309. Later in the nineteenth century
     Italians were becoming more concerned about Franklin as a
     scientist and less about him as a moralist. This piece
     debates scientifically the results of Franklin's experiment
     in calming rough waves by pouring oil on them.

2   BELOT, [ÉMILE JOSEPH]. Benjamin Franklin[,] chief de la
     démocratie américaine. Discours de réception à l'Académie
     des science, belles-lettres et arts de Lyon lu dans la
     seance publique de 22 décembre 1885. Lyon: Association
     typographique, 21 pp.
        France knows Franklin as a scientist, economist, author,
     and diplomat. It is, though, Franklin the representative
     of American democracy and of the promise his nation holds
     for mankind that has most appealed to Frenchmen. (This
     piece is an extract from the Academy's Memoires de la
     classe des lettres, volume 23.)

3   BRENNAN, MARTIN S. "Benjamin Franklin." In A Popular Exposi-
     tion of Electricity[,] With Sketches of Some of Its Dis-
     coverers. New York: D. Appleton & Co., pp. [63]-80.
        Brief retelling of Franklin's basic work in electricity.

4   CIPANI, G.B. "Beniamino Franklin." In Eroi del lavoro;
     raccoltina di dodici biografie popolari offerta ai giovani
     operai italiani. Milan: Agnelli, pp. 12-18.
        Young Italian workers are told that they can prosper by
     following the example of Franklin, who was also a worker.
     In particular, they should be industrious and frugal.

5   [EDITORS, PUBLISHERS, REPORTERS and PRINTERS of DUBUQUE, IOWA.]
     Proceedings of the Commemoration of the 177th Anniversary of
     the Birth of Benjamin Franklin . . . , January 17, 1865.

1885

[Dubuque? printed for the Editors, Publishers, Reporters and Printers of Dubuque, Iowa.]
Franklin extolled for his rise in life, which has become a symbol of hope for others.

6   HALE, EDWARD EVERETT. "Benjamin Franklin." In Stories of Invention, Told by Inventors and Their Friends. Boston: Roberts Brothers, pp. [97]-118.
Among Franklin's inventions were his system of morals, the lightning rod, and musical glasses.

7   MACKAY, CHARLES. "Benjamin Franklin." In The Founders of the American Republic[.] A History and Biography With a Supplementary Chapter on Ultra-democracy. Edinburgh: William Blackwood & Sons, pp. 293-322.
A biography that emphasizes Franklin's "plebian" origins, his genius, and his services to America and to mankind.

8   STILLÉ, CHARLES J[ANEWAY]. "Religious Tests in Provincial Pennsylvania." Pennsylvania Magazine of History and Biography 9, no. 4:405-6.
Testimony of religious orthodoxy was a requirement of all who would hold public office in colonial Pennsylvania. Franklin, too, had to sign his Declaration of Faith many times. He must have been literally forced to take such a test, for we find him on the first opportunity, when the people of this Commonwealth determined to declair their independence "of proprietary government and the Crown both," "raising his voice against the imposition of such tests as had been taken during the Provincial Period." Franklin's influence on the state constitution resulted in "the very mild form of test" which replaced the old one. Franklin proved to be the champion of liberty of conscience.

9   TOMKINSON, E.M. Benjamin Franklin. The World's Workers. London: Cassell & Co., 128 pp.
Repeats some inaccuracies about Franklin, but tries to present a balanced account of his life. Sees him as a good man with faults who accomplished many outstanding and useful things.

10   [TULOU, FRANÇOIS.] "Franklin (1706-1790)." In [Galerie des enfants célèbres, ou Panthéon de la jeunesse.] Paris: [Garnier Frères], pp. [137]-52.
Familiar story, with some errors, of Franklin's youth and young manhood, though his latter years are also mentioned very briefly.

186

1886

11   TYPOTHETAE of [the CITY of] NEW YORK. Annual Dinner . . . in
      Honor of the Birthday of Benjamin Franklin[,] at the
      Hoffman House[,] Saturday, January 17, 1885. [New York:
      printed for the Typothetae of the City of New York.]
          Franklin is extolled for his private as well as public
      character and for his many accomplishments. He was, as
      one speaker, Dr. Charles F. Deems, put it, "An Upper-Case
      Type of Manhood."

                              1886

*1   ANON. "Treaty of 1782-'83 With Great Britain: Franklin."
      In A Digest of the International Law of the United Sates,
      Taken From Documents Issued by Presidents and Secretaries
      of State, and From Decisions of Federal Courts and Opinions
      of Attorneys-General. Edited by Francis Wharton.
      Washington: Government Printing Office.
          Source: NUC. See 1887.3

2   BROWN, W. SYMINGTON. Benjamin Franklin, a Lecture . . .
      Delivered in the Unitarian Church, Stoneham, Nov. 20, 1881,
      and in Paine Memorial Hall, Boston, Feb. 28, 1886.
      Stoneham, Mass.: R.W. Barnstead, Printer, 36 pp.
          Franklin was great in many ways; however, it is as a
      statesman that he was greatest. He was helped in this as
      in his other careers by his open-mindedness and by the com-
      bination of humor and zest that were characteristic of him.

3   BUTLER, JAMES D. "Franklin's Grace Over the Whole Pork Barrel."
      Notes and Queries, 7th ser. 1 (19 June):489.
          Asks the origin of the anecdote that Franklin asked his
      father to say grace over the entire pork barrel at once
      rather than at each meal.

4   DONIOL, HENRI. "Franklin à Paris." In Histoire de la
      participation de la France à l'établissement des Etats-
      Unis d'Amérique[,] corresspondance diplomatique et documents.
      Vol. 2. Paris: Imprimerie Nationale, pp. 98-143
          Deals with the reasons for sending Franklin to France,
      the complexity of the French position with regard to America
      and England, and with French support for the new nation be-
      fore the alliance was formed. A good deal of the piece is
      based on documents. While Doniol does not try to denigrate
      Franklin's accomplishments in France, he does emphasize the
      affection of the French people and the importance of inter-
      national affairs in France's decision to help America.

1886

5   DURR, GEORGE J.C. "Benjamin Franklin, A Commentary."
    Franklin Review 1, no. 1 (February):[5]-7.
        Franklin is one of the great men whose lives are worthy
    of emulation because he was raised by pious and cautious
    parents.

6   FORD, PAUL L[EICESTER]. "History of a Newspaper." Magazine
    of History 15, no. 5 (May):[452]-56.
        Tells the familiar story of how Franklin, with Meredith,
    took over the Gazette, made it a success and used it as a
    means to benefit both the public and himself. The history
    of the newspaper after Franklin relinquished it to Hall is
    summarized briefly.

7   MARSHALL, EDWARD H. "Franklin." Notes and Queries, 7th ser.
    2 (10 July):37.
        Replies to the query of James D. Butler (1886.3).
    Concerns the story of the young Franklin asking that grace
    be said over the whole pork barrel at once instead of going
    through the ritual of saying grace at each meal.

8   MOTTAY, F. Benjamin Franklin et la philosophie pratique.
    Paris: Imprimerie Maçonnique du F. Louis Hugonis, 28 pp.
        Franklin is a model of the virtuous citizen whose phi-
    losophy is to bring his learning to bear for the public
    good. Whether as a writer, educator, politician, scientist,
    or great diplomat in France, Franklin sought practical ways
    of improving the condition of his fellow men.

9   SMITH, HELEN AINSLIE. "Benjamin Franklin." In One Hundred
    Famous Americans. New York: George Routledge & Sons,
    pp. 42-46.
        Concentrates on the achievements of Franklin the states-
    man, and these were great. Moreover, Franklin was not only
    a wise and competent man, but a very noble one. What is
    most impressive, perhaps, is that he was a self-made man.

10 TYPOTHETAE of [the CITY of] NEW YORK. Annual Dinner . . . in
    Honor of the Birthday of Benjamin Franklin[,] at Hotel
    Brunswick[,] Monday, January 18, 1886. [New York: printed
    for the Typothetae of the City of New York.]
        While Franklin was praised in speeches and telegrams by
    the typothetae, the main speaker, Mark Twain, barely men-
    tioned Franklin and spoke instead about his early days as
    a printer's devil. He (1870.6) had satirized Franklin for
    the Poor Richard qualities with which he was identified.

1887

*1 ANON. "Effetti dell'olio sul mare agitato: estratto da una
    lettera di Franklin diretta a M. de Brownring [sic] di
    Londra in data 7 novembre 1773." Rivista marittima (Rome)
    20, no. 2:287-96.
        Source: Pace, p. 435, no. 268. A scientific debate on
    the results of Franklin's experiment of trying to calm
    rough waves with oil.

2   ANON. "Portraits of Benjamin Franklin." Pennsylvania Maga-
    zine of History and Biography 11, no. 2:173.
        Listed here are the then known portraits of Franklin
    along with the individuals and institutions that owned
    them. The list encouraged reader response and was added
    to in 11, no. 3:365; 11, no. 4:504-5; 12, no. 2:256; and
    12, no. 3:376.

3   ANON. "Treaty of 1782-'83 With Great Britain: Franklin."
    In A Digest of the International Law of the United
    States. . . . Edited by Francis Wharton. 2d ed., Vol. 3.
    Washington: Government Printing Office, pp. 912-23.
        A brief survey of Franklin's role in the peace treaty
    that ended the Revolutionary War. Wharton asserts that
    Franklin was actually very little influenced by French
    interests and proved himself the ablest model of simple
    republican virtue. See 1886.1

4   BIGELOW, JOHN. Preface to The Complete Works of Benjamin
    Franklin. Vol. 1. New York: G.P. Putnam's Sons,
    pp. vii-xxxii.
        Defends William Temple Franklin from the charge of having
    sold his grandfather's papers to the English government for
    £7000, but charges him with great neglect and irresponsibil-
    ity in delaying publication of the papers for so long.

5   ELLIS, GEORGE. "Franklin's Magic Picture." Notes and Queries,
    7th ser. 4 (16 July):48.
        The picture "was produced by means of a square pane of
    glass covered in part with leaves of metal, with a print
    over them, which, when electrified and properly touched"
    produced a shock. Asks about the subject and size of the
    picture.

6   FISCHER, HEINRICH. Benjamin Franklin als unermüdlicher
    Arbeiter. Leipzig: Osker Peters, 22 pp.
        A summary of Franklin's career which focuses on his in-
    volvement with the art of printing, so central to his suc-
    cess, and with his reading and writing.

1887

7   GILDER, JEANETTE LEONARD. "Books That Have Helped Me."
    Forum 4 (October):[207]-12.
        The author as a child was inspired by Franklin's memoirs
    and has tried to emulate him in a number of ways.

8   HALE, EDWARD EVERETT, and HALE, E[DWARD] E[VERETT], Jr.
    Franklin in France. 2 vols. Boston: Roberts Brothers,
    1:478 pp.; 2:470 pp.
        The narrative is heavily interspersed with documents and
    letters, and it is not always possible for the casual reader
    to differentiate between the authors' remarks and those of
    the original participants.
        Franklin's early connections in France and his reputa-
    tion as a moral philosopher and scientist, coupled with the
    overwhelming sympathy for the American cause, helped
    Franklin in his efforts to gain aid in the Revolutionary
    War. Vergennes and especially Louis XVI, however, were
    most reluctant to form an open alliance with the rebellious
    Americans for reasons of self-interest and honor. By 1778,
    though, mounting pressure in France, Franklin's diplomacy,
    and American victories in the field brought first the min-
    ister and then the king to favor the alliance. Franklin's
    tasks were made more difficult by the unstable Arthur Lee
    and later by Jay and Adams, who "formed a party in opposi-
    tion to Franklin" and in effect "compelled" him to adopt
    their less pro-French policy and their pragmatic disregard
    of some Congressional instructions. The authors carefully
    examine the motives and conduct of each nation in the nego-
    tiations, the complexities of the efforts for peace, which
    ranged from the condition of the Tories and the opinions
    regarding Oswald's commission, to the status of the respec-
    tive nations toward each other and toward the terms of peace.
    All parties had to accept the final peace terms because
    they were clearly the best that could be worked out. Once
    the treaty was signed, Franklin was able to spend less time
    on diplomatic affairs and indulged his interest in science
    again until his final return to Philadelphia.

9   HALLIWELL-PHILLIPPS, J.O. "Anecdote of Dr. Franklin." Notes
    and Queries, 7th ser. 4 (26 November):427.
        Anecdote is about the sign made by "John Thompson
    hatter." He made the mistake of listening to the opinions
    of people regarding the sign until it said almost nothing.

10 HARRISON, MARY. "B." Sunday Magazine 16:239-45.
        Franklin was fortunately born into a home that reflected
    "incarnate Christianity," and he remained broadly and truly
    Christian all his life.

1887

11 JANET, PAUL [ALEXANDRE RENÉ]. Histoire de la science politique
    dans ses rapports avec la morale. Bibliothèque de
    philosophie contemporaine. 3d ed. Vol. 2. Paris:
    Felix Alcan, pp. 696-702.
        Franklin is one of the most original figures of modern
    time, as an analysis of his moral and political writings
    will show. See 1872.10.

12 McMASTER, J[OHN] B[ACH]. Benjamin Franklin As a Man of Letters.
    Boston: Houghton Mifflin & Co., 293 pp.
        Nearly all of what Franklin wrote is characterized by
    simple, vigorous English, "hard common sense and wit."
    These qualities give "his later writings a popularity and
    influence beyond those of any American author since his
    day." Franklin is at his best in works that combine use-
    fulness with humor, witness his "Rules by Which a Great
    Empire May Be Reduced to a Small One" and "An Edict by the
    King of Prussia." His other political efforts can be
    largely dismissed. Those written in England in behalf of
    the American cause, while then "effective," are "now for-
    gotten." The essays written in France and designed to
    raise money for the war "did not bring forth one groat"
    because they are devoid of "a single reason which could
    persuade a capitalist to lend money to the rebellious sub-
    jects of King George."
        Franklin's place in American letters is "among that giant
    race of pamphleteers and essayists most of whom went before,
    but a few of whom came immediately after the war for inde-
    pendence. And among them he is easily the first," for his
    style is better than theirs. He has left behind two great
    works, The Way to Wealth and his Autobiography. It is un-
    fortunate that his multiplicity of business and his "sloth"
    have joined to render his output small. Further, it is
    most regrettable that so great a man "should, long after
    he had passed the middle life, continue to write pieces so
    filthy that no editor has ever had the hardihood to print
    them."
        (This early treatment of Franklin as a writer provides
    historical contexts for the writings rather than analyses
    and supported evaluations. The analysis is confined to the
    final few pages, and readers should watch out for serious
    errors concerning historical and literary matters.)

13 McMASTER, JOHN BACH. "Franklin in France." Atlantic Monthly
    60, no. 359 (September):318-26.
        Franklin's tasks and trials in France were many, but so
    were his successes. His personal popularity among the
    French led to their support for "des insurgens," and to
    their esteem for America.

1887

14 PEPPER, WILLIAM. <u>An Address on Benjamin Franklin</u>. <u>Delivered</u>
    <u>at Franklin and Marshall College, Lancaster, Pa., on the</u>
    <u>Centennial Anniversary of Its Foundation, 1787-1887</u>.
    [Philadelphia: Dando Printing & Publishing Co], 26 pp.
       Franklin was not only a great teacher of morality, reli-
    gious toleration, and practicality, he taught us also to
    enlarge and enlighten our notions of self-interest. Were
    he alive today, he would take real pride in the progress
    his country has made and is making in all areas of human
    endeavor; however, he would caution us against the "social
    and economic dangers" that beset us. (This piece also
    appears in the <u>Reformed Quarterly Review</u> 9, no. 4
    (October 1887):413-28.)

15 RICHARDSON, CHARLES F[RANCIS]. "Benjamin Franklin." In
    <u>American Literature, 1607-1885</u>. New York: G.P. Putnam's
    Sons. Vol. 1. <u>The Development of American Thought</u>,
    pp. 154-76.
       Franklin had his personal failings and he was "intellec-
    tually limited"; however, his greatness, versatility, and
    humaneness are beyond dispute. He still inspires unusual
    enthusiasm "largely because he was a product character-
    istically American." As a writer, he must not be over-
    estimated. He had a "pleasant style" and wrote sensibly,
    but his performances are not to be measured by the best
    works of his time. In fact, they are commonplace, save
    only his <u>Autobiography</u>, his papers on electricity, and his
    <u>Poor Richard's Almanacks</u>. In these we see at best the wise,
    practical guide through everyday affairs.

16 SHAW, THOMAS BUDD. "Benjamin Franklin." In <u>Shaw's New History</u>
    <u>of English Literature in America[,] by Truman J.</u>
    <u>Backus</u>. . . . Rev. ed. New York: Sheldon & Co.,
    pp. 404-7.
       Brief account of Franklin as a writer. See 1880.8.

17 STEBBING, WILLIAM. "An American Revolutionist and an English
    Radical. Benjamin Franklin, 1706-1790. William Cobbett,
    1763-1835." In <u>Some Verdicts of History Reviewed</u>. London:
    John Murray, pp. 257-99.
       Franklin, along with Washington, was one of the archi-
    tects of the United States of America. Franklin's sagacity
    and his years in England enabled him to see and to report
    to his countrymen that English politics had become rotten
    because foolish and evil men had perverted the institutions
    of government to their own selfish ends. Yet England was
    not so bad as Franklin had supposed. Moreover, "he chose
    to be for the most part utterly blind to the more radical

1887

vices of French government and society." This was one of a
number of his faults, but withal he was an outstanding and
good man and a great patriot and liberator. The essay on
Cobbett is not included within these pages.

18   STILLÉ, CHARLES J[ANEWAY]. "Comte De Broglie, the Proposed
     State-holder of America." Pennsylvania Magazine of History
     and Biography 11, no. 4:369-405.
         The eccentric spy, Comte de Broglie, visionary and self-
     seeking professional soldier, offered to aid the United
     States during the Revolution in return for enormous power
     and wealth. Franklin and Silas Deane came across many such
     ridiculous schemes in France and had to humor their origina-
     tors for the sake of their delicate mission. Franklin in
     particular was a master at making the impractical French
     think he acquiesed in their plans, even that of making
     America a French protectorate. At the same time he had
     to work diligently and cautiously to bring about the alli-
     ance. Franklin's skill in adopting the mask of simplicity
     was of particular value for this purpose.

19   TYPOTHETAE of [the CITY of] NEW YORK. Annual Dinner . . . in
     Honor of the Birthday of Benjamin Franklin[,] at Hotel
     Brunsiwck[,] Monday, January 17, 1887. [New York: printed
     for the Typothetae of the City of New York.]
         Traditional praise of Franklin as a printer, statesman,
     philosopher, and humanitarian.

                              1888

1   ANON. Benzhamen Franklin. Moscow.
         Russian text biography that praises Franklin as a
     scientist, philosopher, and friend to mankind.

2   ANON. "Franklin, Benjamin." In Appleton's Cyclopaedia of
     American Biography. Edited by James Grant Wilson and John
     Fiske. Gale Facsimile Edition. Vol. 2. New York:
     D. Appleton & Co., pp. 526-34.
         Surveys Franklin's career and praises him for his human-
     itarianism and versatility.

3   ANON. "The Two Great Franklins." Harper's Young People 9,
     no. 457 (31 July):692-93.
         Biographical sketches of Benjamin Franklin and Sir John
     Franklin.

1888

4   BENJAMIN, S.G.W. "Unpublished Letters of Franklin to Strahan."
    Atlantic Monthly 61, no. 363 (January):21-36.
        The letters cover the period of 1743 to 1783, and
    Benjamin's introduction and commentary provide a framework
    that helps illuminate the letters and the relationship be-
    tween the two successful printers. Their friendship, which
    is "remarkable," appears "to have called into action the
    best qualities of Franklin's character," for he is seen as
    not only a shrewd Yankee--a quality in him too much empha-
    sized--but rather "as a man of feeling."

5   BIGELOW, JOHN. "Franklin's Home and Host in France." Century
    Magazine 35, no. 5 (March):[741]-54.
        Franklin's time at Passy was, if hectic, pleasant, and
    Le Ray de Chaumont, his host at the Hôtel Valentinois, was
    a good and helpful friend to him.

6   BOLTON, SARAH K[NOWLES]. "Benjamin Franklin." In Famous
    American Statesmen. New York: Thomas Y. Crowell & Co.,
    Publishers, pp. 38-66.
        An idealized biographical account that focuses most of
    its attention on Franklin's American years.

7   BUTLER, JAMES D. "Anecdote of Dr. Franklin." Notes and
    Queries, 7th ser. 5 (21 January):57.
        Praises Franklin's anecdote of the hatter's sign and
    points out that it was published in Jefferson's Works and
    in Franklin's Writings. Butler is replying to the query
    of J.O. Halliwell-Phillipps (1887.9).

8   HALE, EDWARD EVERETT. "Franklin and Junius Brutus." Harvard
    Monthly 6, no. 3:91-94.
        English Captain Harry Asgill was nearly executed in an
    American prisoner of war camp to retaliate for the execu-
    tion by the English of an American prisoner. Franklin was
    asked to intervene and have Asgill spared, but in a sharp
    letter he refused. He did not know at the time that
    William Franklin, president of the Board of Associated
    Loyalists, was in part responsible for the execution of
    the American.

9   HUNEEUS, ROBERTO. "Oda a Benjamin Franklin[.] (Leida en el
    'Ateneo de Santiago' en la sesion del 10 de setiembre)."
    Revista del progresso, pp. [198]-204.
        Franklin is lauded in the highest terms as one of the
    truly great liberators and benefactors of mankind. (The
    poem is bound with a number of other miscellaneous items
    in the University of Texas, Benson Latin American

Collection, G983. L568, no. 10. Since the "Oda" was cut out of a magazine, there is no title page for it.)

10 McMASTER, JOHN BACH, and STONE, FREDERICK D., eds. Pennsyl-vania and the Federal Convention[,] 1787-1788. Lancaster, Pa.: Historical Society of Pennsylvania, pp. 699-701.
A biographical account of Franklin.

11 MANSERGH, J.F. "Franklin's Press." Notes and Queries, 7th ser. 5 (26 May):407.
Asks if there exist any editions other than the one Mansergh himself owns of a particular Franklin imprint.

12 MARSHALL, JULIAN. "Anecdote of Dr. Franklin." Notes and Queries, 7th ser. 5 (5 May):352-53.
Relates Franklin's anecdote of the hatter's sign.

13 MEIDINGER, HEINRICH. "Franklin." In Geschichte des Blitzableiters. Karlsruhe: G. Braun'schen, pp. 9-25.
Tells the story of Franklin's entrance into the world of electrical science and describes his writings in the field and his thinking on the design and value of lightning rods. Meidinger continues, in a rather discursive manner, to dis-cuss Franklin's work in light of later experiments for the next twenty pages.

14 TRENEY, XAVIER. "Franklin." In Extraits des économistes des XVIIIe et XIX siècles. Bibliothèque de l'enseignement secondaire special. Paris: Quantin, A. Picard & Kaan, pp. 65-73.
After a short account of Franklin's life in which Treney praises him for his success and usefulness, the author dis-cusses Franklin's thoughts on economics. Considering his maxims, his plan to achieve virtue as well as his more philosophical ideas on economics, Treney points out that Franklin believed money was of a proliferating nature, that a plentiful supply of money was necessary to financial growth, that honesty was essential to commercial success, that credit could be useful, and that luxury was detrimental to the character of individuals and nations.

15 TYPOTHETAE of [the CITY of] NEW YORK. Annual Dinner . . . in Honor of the Birthday of Benjamin Franklin[,] at Hotel Brunswick[,] Tuesday, January 17, 1888. [New York: printed for the Typothetae of the City of New York.]
John Bigelow and others praise Franklin as a printer, writer, scientist, and philosopher. The audience was told that Franklin exemplifies the highest standards of his art,

1888

for he loved printing and recognized the important role printers play in society.

1889

1   ANON. "Benjamin Franklin." Spectator 63, no. 3188 (3 August): 149.
    In addition to congratulating Bigelow on the completion of Franklin's Works, the critic asserts that while Franklin's Autobiography is extraordinary, he must still be ranked as an author of the second class. The majority of his writings show him clearly to be the American parallel to the English Cobbett, that is, a writer of ephemeral things. And while his style is admirable, it lacks the "raciness" of Cobbett's, and Poor Richard's "diction will not bear comparison with the Authorised Version of Solomon's Proverbs."

2   ANON. Celebration[.] The One Hundred Eighty-Third Anniversary Birthday of Benjamin Franklin[,] Tremont House, Chicago, January 17, 1889. N.p. FCL.
    A booklet recording the dinner and speeches.

3   ANON. "Concerning Voltaire and Franklin." Atlantic Monthly 64, no. 386 (December):858-59.
    It appears that Franklin repaid Princess Dashkoff, president of the Imperial Academy of Sciences at St. Petersburg, Russia, for his election as a member by having her made a member of the American Philosophical Society. Princess Dashkoff was at the time "not then in good repute in polite or learned circles outside of Russia."

4   ANON. "Franklin, Washington, Lincoln." Atlantic Monthly 64, no. 385 (November):707-9.
    Franklin was a remarkably diverse man. His accomplishments enable him to be included among statesmen, men of letters, and even religious leaders (if the term includes men of benevolence and morality). And, of course, Franklin the private, charming man has been the subject of biography. Praises Morse's biography of Franklin in these pages of a longer piece.

5   ANON. [Frankliniana. University of Pennsylvania, Rare Books Room, Special 973.3D F85 Fr.]
    A bound collection. Some of the material may have been compiled by the American Art Association and consists of portraits of Franklin and others connected with him, Henri Bouchot's "Franklin at Passy," and various reprints.

6   ANON. "Yours, B. Franklin." Atlantic Monthly 64, no. 386
     (December):855-56.
        On Franklin's letter to his old friend and fellow
     printer, William Strahan. Franklin's ostensible charge
     that Strahan helped bring about war with America and made
     Franklin his enemy is really a rhetorically excellent "jest."
     Franklin positioned the words "I am Yours, B. Franklin" on
     three different lines and so conveyed not only his bitterness
     but the fact that he was still Strahan's friend. The author
     of the Atlantic piece believes the letter was mailed.

7   BEAMAN, CHARLES C[OTESWORTH]. "Address." In Eighth Annual
     Festival of the New England Society of Pennsylvania, at the
     Continental Hotel, Philadelphia, December 22, 1888. Phila-
     delphia: printed by the Times Printing House for the Soci-
     iety, pp. 39-47.
        Tribute to Franklin.

8   BOUCHOT, HENRI [FRANÇOIS XAVIER MARIE]. "Franklin at Passy[,]
     1777-1785." Art and Letters 1 (Feburary):[177]-200.
        A pleasant, chatty, sentimental and, at times, inaccurate
     narrative of Franklin's years in France. Franklin's great
     reputation and French idealization of him as "a personifica-
     tion" of liberty certainly helped him in his mission. Yet
     it was his personality and character than won over the na-
     tion and its love.

9   FAKHRI. Benjamen Franklen. Constantinople: Dept. of Public
     Instruction.
        A brief life of Franklin in Turkish.

10   FIGUIER, LOUIS. Le mariage de Franklin, comédie en un
     acte. . . . Paris: Tresse en Stock, 58 pp.
        Fictionalized treatment. Franklin marries Deborah Read
     in spite of many obstacles occasioned by her past and his.

11   FORD, PAUL LEICESTER. Franklin Bibliography. A List of Books
     Written by, or Relating to Benjamin Franklin. Brooklyn,
     N.Y., 467 pp.
        The first attempt at a relatively comprehensive primary
     and secondary bibliography of Franklin. The complete List
     contains nearly one thousand items, and nearly two hundred
     of these are works on Franklin.

12   _____. Who Was the Mother of Franklin's Son? An Historical
     Conundrum Hitherto Given up Now--Partly Answered. Brooklyn,
     N.Y., 15 pp.

1889

Ford relies on the claim in the political pamphlet,
What Is Sauce for a Goose Is also Sauce for a Gander
in holding that William Franklin's mother was "Barbara,"
the "Kitchen Wench and Gold Finder" whom Franklin allegedly
supported on "The pitiful Stipend of Ten pounds per Annum"
until she died. It was charged that Franklin then had her
buried in an unmarked grave.

13 FORD, W[ORTHINGTON] C[HAUNCEY]. "Franklin's Articles of Confederation." Nation 48, no. 1239 (28 March):261-63.
In 1775 Franklin presented to Congress a plan for the
confederation of the colonies. His experience at the Albany
Congress twenty years earlier had convinced him of the wisdom of such a union. Congress, though, was not yet ready
to accept Franklin's suggestion and ignored the plan.

*14 GOVI, G. "Di un precursore italiano del Franklin." Atti della
R. Accademia dei Lincei: rendiconti (Rome), 4th ser. 5:
138-42.
Source: Pace, pp. 309, 435 n. 272. Asserts that in
1746 an anonymous Venetian developed a number of the basic
ideas on electricity that were later to make Franklin inter-
nationally famous and admired.

15 JORDAN, JOHN W. "Franklin As a Genealogist." Pennsylvania
Magazine of History and Biography 23, no. 1:1-22.
The author publishes correspondence and documents that
reveal Franklin's keen interest in his family's history and
provides an introduction and brief commentary to the subject.

16 MORSE, JOHN TORREY, Jr. Benjamin Franklin. American Statesmen. Boston: Houghton Mifflin, 428 pp.
More than three-fourths of the book deals with Franklin's
life after the period covered by the Autobiography, and
about half of it treats his efforts in France. Relies very
heavily on secondary sources and yet still lapses into
errors of fact. David Hall, for example, is made to be
one of the beer-guzzling printers whom Franklin converts
to water during his first trip to England. Morse does
handle Franklin's religion honestly, if superficially.
Without discussing deism, he acknowledges that Franklin,
while believing in a God "substantially" like that wor-
shipped by Christians, was himself no Christian. Moreover,
the author points out that Franklin rejected the dogma in
Christianity and in all other religions and adopted their
morality. Morse also defends Franklin from the charge of
duplicitous conduct in France, arguing that he worked bril-
liantly and cautiously, and lesser men, unable to follow
him, saw duplicity where there was none. Franklin, in fact,

1889

once he matured, acted consistently upon the most generous
and humane principles. Though a great patriot, he was the
least parochial of men, having always in mind the betterment
of mankind. See 1880.7.

17   STARBUCK, CHARLES C.   Review of Benjamin Franklin, by John T.
      Morse.   Andover Review 12, no. 71 (November):556-57.
         Less a review than a lament that the American character
      could not have been formed by one with a loftier moral and
      religious vision than Franklin, whose undeniable greatness
      was of the practical and material kind.

18   THAYER, WILLIAM M[AKEPEACE].   From Boyhood to Manhood.   The
      Life of Benjamin Franklin.   New York: Hurst & Co., 497 pp.
         Most of this book is a rehash of Thayer's 1861 fiction-
      alized and moralistic account of Franklin's early life.
      Here Thayer insists that the virtues of Poor Richard, the
      sound religion that Franklin turned to as an adult, and a
      healthy bank account are found together in the horn of
      plenty that is available to all who follow Franklin's
      example.

19   [The TYPOTHETAE of CHICAGO.]   Celebration.   The One Hundred
      Eighty-Third Anniversary Birthday of Benjamin Franklin,
      Tremont House, Chicago, January 17, 1889.   [Chicago?
      printed for the Typothetae of Chicago?], 8 pp.
         A record of the celebration which notes that speeches on
      Franklin were given by members and guests.

20   TYPOTHETAE of [the CITY of] NEW YORK.   Annual Dinner . . .
      Commemorating the Birth of Benjamin Franklin.   Hotel
      Brunswick, Thursday, January 17, 1889.   [New York:
      printed for the Typothetae of the City of New York.]
         Franklin was the ideal public and political man.   He
      never sought office, but he served brilliantly when elected.
      He was greatest, however, as a private man and wrote for
      the benefit of his fellows.

21   WHARTON, FRANCIS, ed.   The Revolutionary Diplomatic Corre-
      spondence of the United States.   6 vols.   Washington:
      Government Printing Office.
         Commentary on Franklin's character, activities, achieve-
      ments, and reputation runs throughout the text and notes.
      While much of the commentary is explanatory, a good deal
      of it is intended to support Wharton's contention in the
      tenth chapter of the first volume, his major discussion of
      Franklin.   He argues that Franklin was one of the greatest
      men of the Revolution and that his unique abilities and

1889

steadfast patriotism enabled him to make the most significant diplomatic contributions of the war. His efforts
characterized his lifelong work in behalf of his fellow
men. Wharton predictably defends Franklin from the charges
of the vain and tactless John Adams, the "puritanic" Samuel
Adams, and the "monomanical[ly]" envious Arthur Lee.
Lacking Franklin's sophistication and experience, these
men did not understand his diplomacy.

189-

1   WIJNAENDTS FRANCKEN, C[ORNELIUS] J[OHANNES]. Benjamin
    Franklin. [s'Gravenhage?], 31 pp.
        Considers Franklin's personal qualities and different
    facets of his career. Franklin had an outstanding mind and
    many valuable talents; however, he achieved great success
    and international fame because of other factors. He dili-
    gently brought to bear his abilities on significant human
    problems and often changed life for the better. Then, too,
    he was a dedicated patriot and was instrumental in America's
    independence. Among other attributes was his ability as a
    writer who could work in various forms to promote useful
    causes and win support for them and respect for himself.
    (Attribution of date and place by Yale University.)

1890

1   AMERICAN PHILOSOPHICAL SOCIETY. "The Commemoration of the One
    Hundredth Anniversary of the Decease of Benjamin Franklin.
    April 17, 1890." Proceedings of the American Philosophical
    Society 28, no. 3 (April):161-226.
        The commemoration included addresses by Talcott Williams,
    John Bach McMaster, Frederick Fraley, G. Brown Goode, J.W.
    Holland, and Henry M. Baird. All the addresses are cited
    separately. The Society's Committee on Arrangements recom-
    mended on 17 April 1890, that Franklin's memory be cele-
    brated in an appropriate way. The recommendation was
    accepted.

2   ANON. "Benjamin Franklin." Nature 43, no. 1098 (13 November):
    39-40.
        Tribute to Franklin and to the American Philosophical
    Society for commemorating the one hundredth anniversary of
    his death.

3   ANON. "The Library Table: A Curio From Benjamin Franklin's
     Will." Chautauquan 11, no. 1 (April):120-22.
        Franklin's motive in establishing funds to help mechanics
     begin their careers was noble, but the results have been
     disappointing.

*4   [ANON.?] [A Piece on Franklin?] Preacher's Assistant and the
     Preacher's Magazine [2?] (November).
        Source: Union List of Serials, volume 4, page 3425.
     The November 1890 issue, though, is missing at the reposi-
     tories cited as owning it.

5   APPLETON, WILLIAM S[UMNER]. Augustin Dupré, and His Work for
     America. Remarks Made Before the Massachusetts Historical
     Society, March 13, 1890. Cambridge, Mass.: John Wilson &
     Son, University Press, 6 pp.
        Describes Dupré's "American medals," including those of
     Franklin. (The piece also appears in the Proceedings of
     the Massachusetts Historical Society, 2d ser. 5
     (March 1890):348-52.)

6   B.H., H. de. "Plagiarism From Franklin." Notes and Queries,
     7th ser. 9 (10 May):366-67.
        Asserts that Havelock Ellis, in The New Spirit, uninten-
     tionally plagiarized from Franklin. Ellis said that Whitman
     has been placed alongside of Jesus and Socrates, a remark
     which leads H. de B.H. to think of Franklin's famous pre-
     scription for humility, in his list of thirteen virtues.

7   BAIRD, HENRY M. "The Diplomatic Services of Benjamin
     Franklin." In Proceedings of the American Philosophical
     Society 28, no. 3 (17 April):209-25.
        Franklin the diplomat was Franklin the man. His many
     notable achievements in France were a development of his
     sincere desire to serve humanity by adding to its happiness
     and comfort.

8   BOLLES, ALBERT S[IDNEY]. "The Presidencies of Franklin and
     Mifflin." In Pennsylvania Province and State[.] A History
     From 1609-1790. Vol. 2. Philadelphia: John Wanamaker,
     pp. 98-116.
        Praises Franklin as a humanitarian and man "of the
     present." America has not seen his equal.

9   CARR, WALTER (Mrs.). "Franklin, Benjamin." In A Dictionary of
     Music and Musicians (A.D. 1450-1889). Edited by George
     Grove. Vol. 1. London: Macmillan & Co., p. 559.

1890

Franklin is listed because of the glass armonica "which
he invented or so far improved as to make it practically
available."

10 DUANE, RUSSELL; PEPPER, GEORGE WHARTON; and BIDDLE, A. SYDNEY
for PETITIONERS. In the Orphans Court of Philadelphia
County. Estate of Benjamin Franklin, Dec'd. Argument sur
demurer. Paper Book of the Petitioner. No. 214. July
Term, 1890. Philadelphia: Maurice H. Power.
The petitioners claim the money in the Franklin Fund of
Philadelphia has been so poorly handled that the Trustees
have lost the legal right to control the money, which is
only one-sixth of what it would have been with competent
management.

11 FOA, EUGÉNIE (RODRIGUES-GRADIER). "Benjamin Franklin (dix-
huitième siècle)." In Les petits savants. Contes
historiques dédiés a la jeunesse. Paris: Librairie
d'éducation[,] Paul Delarue, pp. [85]-108.
Fictional account of the young Franklin, who already as
a youth possessed those famous qualities that would make
him a great and good man. Foa also tells his own version
of Benjamin's apprenticeship on James's Courant.

12 FRALEY, FREDERICK. "Benjamin Franklin's Association With the
Society." Proceedings of the American Philosophical Society
28, no. 3 (17 April):173-75.
Tribute to Franklin. The Society originated in his
junto.

13 GOODE, G[EORGE] B[ROWN]. "The Literary Labors of Benjamin
Franklin." Proceedings of the American Philosophical
Society 28, no. 3:177-97.
While Franklin's memory still shines brightly among his
educated countrymen, they do not accord him quite the same
stature as Europeans do. Franklin's "easy-going freedom of
speech, his liberal views in theological questions and his
irreverence, coupled with a certain coarseness, almost
Rabelasian, in his early writings, have lessened his literary popularity among educated Americans." Then, too, his
subjects were not generally literary. Yet the range of his
writings reveals more than mere originality. The greatness
of his mind has made his writings very popular among lovers
of literature. Goode then breaks down Franklin's writings
into categories and comments on them briefly. His purpose
is to suggest the scope of Franklin's efforts rather than
to analyze his literary achievements in any depth. He does,
however, point out that while Poor Richard "was a

kindergarten teacher," Franklin is no crass utilitarian. "Whoever studies Franklin in a generous spirit, will find no lack of generous thought and principle."

14   HART, CHARLES HENRY. "Franklin in Allegory." Century Maga-zine 41, no. 2 (December):197-204.
The French habit of sanctifying those whom they love and admire was given free play when Franklin went to France. Hart describes and discusses a number of allegories dealing with Franklin as the liberator, democrat, philosopher, and scientist.

15   HOLLAND, J[AMES] W[ILLIAM]. "The Scientific Work of Benjamin Franklin." Proceedings of the American Philosophical Society 28, no. 3 (17 April):199-207.
Topical arrangement of Franklin's work in science shows that his concern is not theoretical but, given his benevo-lent character, useful to mankind.

16   LEFEBVRE, ALPH[ONSE]. Benjamin Franklin[,] savant et diplomate[.] Causerie faite au Harve, en 1868. Boulogne-Sur-Mer: Ch[ez] Brinck-Lefebvre, 30 pp.
A survey and an appreciation of Franklin concentrating on his scientific and diplomatic accomplishments and his relationships in Europe.

17   McMASTER, JOHN BACH. "A Short Biography of Benjamin Franklin." Proceedings of the American Philosophical Society 28, no. 3 (17 April):166-72.
Emphasizes Franklin's diverse talents and active life. The Franklin that emerges here is one who was determined to succeed and did.

18   MUNRO, J[OHN]. "Benjamin Franklin." In Pioneers of Electric-ity[,] or Short Lives of the Great Electricians. London: Religious Tract Society, pp. 45-76.
Surveys Franklin's career in general but deals in some depth with his work in electricity.

19   RIDLER, CHARLES E. "Poor Richard." Education 10, no. 8 (April):493-501.
The celebration at the erection of the Franklin statue in Boston did honor to a great man that every schoolboy knows through Poor Richard's sayings. One person, appar-ently a teacher, conceived of a contest in which school children would memorize as many maxims of Poor Richard as they could. The child who memorized the greatest number would win a book valued at five dollars. The winner, a

1890

Franklin Medalist, committed to memory about 350 of the sayings.

20 TYPOTHETAE of [the CITY of] NEW YORK. Annual Dinner . . . in Honor of the Birthday of Benjamin Franklin[,] at Hotel Brunswick[,] Friday, January 17, 1890. [New York: printed for the Typothetae of the City of New York.]
Franklin lauded for his character and versatility.

21 WILLIAMS, TALCOTT. [Remarks on Franklin at the Commemoration of the One Hundredth Anniversary of His Decease.] Proceedings of the American Philosophical Society 28, no. 3 (17 April):162-65.
Unlike Lincoln, who is a tragic figure because he was taken away before his mission could be completed, Franklin's life shows that he left nothing undone.

1891

1 ABRAMOV, ÎAKOV VASILÉVICH. Franklin: His Life, Social and Scientific Achievements. Lives of Famous People. [St. Petersburg: Public Utility Printing House Co.], 79 pp.
Popular biography written for adults. The emphasis of the book is on Franklin's overall contributions to society in the fields of printing, science, practical inventions, and philanthropy. Abramov keeps before his readers throughout the book evidence of Franklin's remarkable inner drive for self-improvement and his desire to help his fellows. For this reason, the tone of the book is largely inspirational. In Russian.

2 ANON. "Franklin, Benjamin." In The National Cyclopedia of American Biography[,] Being the History of the United States. . . . Vol. 1. New York: James T. White & Co., pp. 328-37.
Franklin is the greatest American of all because his services to his country surpass those of anyone else. Moreover, he was intellectually among the chief people of any time. Happily, as he grew older he came more nearly to accept Christianity and may safely be called a "liberal Christian."

3 BAUDRILLART, HENRI [JOSEPH LÉON]. "Franklin (Benjamin), né à Boston en 1706, mort à Philadelphie le 17 avril 1790." In Nouveau dictionnaire d'économie politique, publié sous la direction de Léon Say et de Joseph Choilley. Vol. 1. Paris: Guillaumin et Cie, pp. 1087-91.

1891

Biographical sketch emphasizing Franklin's belief in individual effort, self-improvement, free trade, and life-long education.

4   BEERS, HENRY A[UGUSTUS]. "The Colonial Period, 1607-1765." In Initial Studies in American Letters. New York: Chautauqua Press, pp. 37-40.
    Sees Edwards and Franklin as opposite poles of American experience. Franklin "illustrates the development of the New England Englishman into the modern Yankee." Beers pays tribute to Franklin's abilities and accomplishments but holds that in spite of his "admirable" and occasionally "great" literary qualities, he was "hardly a great writer." Franklin the utilitarian causes Franklin the writer to meddle too much with lower level subjects that are inappropriate to significant literature, though they are important to human happiness.

5   [CURTIS, GEORGE WILLIAM.] "Editor's Easy Chair." Harper's Monthly Magazine 84, no. 499 (December):[149]-50.
    The secret of Poor Richard's success, of both the almanacs and of Franklin himself, is that Franklin "was full of the Christmas spirit, good sense, and good humor." And by "Christmas spirit" Curtis means "good nature and generosity of sentiment." As Poor Richard, Franklin never placed himself above his readers, but was one of them.

6   FORD, PAUL LEICESTER. Note to To the Good People of Ireland, by Benjamin Franklin. In Winnowings in American History. Revolutionary Broadsides. Brooklyn, N.Y.: Historical Printing Club, pp. 2, 5-6.
    Tells the story of Franklin's address, which was intended to exploit dissatisfaction in Ireland over English rule and identify the American cause with that of the Irish.

7   FORNARI, P. "Beniamino Franklin." In Dizionario illustrato di pedagogia. Edited by A. Martinazzoli and L. Credaro. Vol. 1. Milan: Vallardi, p. 713.
    Franklin is praised as the ideal educator of the masses.

8   GREEN, SAMUEL A[BBOTT]. "The New England Courant." Proceedings of the Massachusetts Historical Society, 2d ser. 6 (June). Boston: published by the Society, pp. 516-18.
    A small pamphlet that touches briefly on Franklin's work on the newspaper and also provides information on Josiah Franklin's first wife and their infant son.

1891

9   MANSERGH, J.F. "Benjamin Franklin." <u>Notes and Queries</u>, 7th
     ser. 12 (26 September):253.
          Replies to R. (1891.10) that Franklin's <u>Autobiography</u>
     "contains full particulars of his life and work" during the
     time of his first London stay.

10   R. "Benjamin Franklin." <u>Notes and Queries</u>, 7th ser. 12
     (29 August):167.
          Claims to own the composing stick used by Franklin when
     he first went to London. Asks where Franklin was employed
     then.

11   SCHWARTZ, ALEXANDER. <u>Benjamin Franklin. Sein Leben</u>. Vienna:
     published by the author, 25 pp.
          Concentrates on Franklin's career as a printer and on
     his lifelong love and respect for the art. A good deal of
     this piece treats Franklin's early career and follows
     closely the memoirs.

12   TYPOTHETAE of [the CITY of] NEW YORK. <u>Annual Dinner . . . in</u>
     <u>Honor of the Birthday of Benjamin Franklin[,] at Hotel</u>
     <u>Brunswick[,] Saturday, January 17, 1891</u>. [New York:
     printed for the Typothetae of the City of New York.]
          Next to Washington, Franklin is the greatest American.
     While he was not a formal student, as a printer he read as
     much as scholars do and developed "one of the most grandly
     furnished minds of his age."

                              1892

1   ANON. "The World's Fair Franklin Statue." <u>Scientific American</u>
     66, no. 4 (23 January):55.
          The statue by Carl Rohl Smith honors Franklin as an
     electrician.

2   ALLISON, YOUNG E[WING]. "The Franklin Statue." <u>Engineering</u>
     <u>Magazine</u> 2, no. 6 (March):827-28.
          On the statue of Franklin at the entrance to the Elec-
     trical Building at the World's Fair in Chicago. Allison
     notes that visitors to the fair were very impressed by the
     statue.

3   BOSTON PUBLIC LIBRARY. "Franklin Portraits." <u>Bulletin Showing</u>
     <u>Titles of Books Added to the Boston Public Library[,] With</u>
     <u>Bibliographical Notes, Etc</u>. 11, no. 2 (July):139-50.
          There are 239 Franklin items in the list of portraits,
     allegories, and medals.

4 BOWEN, CLARENCE WINTHROP. "Portrait of Benjamin Franklin."
   Magazine of American History 27, no. 6 (June):472-73.
   "The portrait of Franklin owned by the Boston Public
   Library and claimed to be by Greuze, is said to have belonged to Mr. Oswald, and was the portrait which Franklin
   gave to Oswald when the two men exchanged portraits. As
   the portrait now in Scotland in the family of Oswald,
   painted by Duplessis, is also said to be the portrait
   which Franklin gave to Oswald, it seems that a mistake has
   been made."

5 CAVERNI, RAFFAELE. Storia del metodo sperimentale in Italia.
   Vol. 2. Florence: Civelli, pp. 262-93.
   Caverni pays tribute to the central role played by
   Franklin in the development of electrical science in Italy.

6 CHAPMAN, T.J. "The Earlier Years of Benjamin Franklin."
   National Magazine 15, no. 3 (January):[258]-66.
   Sets the Puritan scene of the Boston into which Franklin
   was born, touches upon Franklin's career in his brother's
   printing office, tells again the story of his arrival in
   Philadelphia, and points out that Franklin's "skill, industry, and enterprise" led to his success in Philadelphia and
   in later life.

7 _____. "Franklin and Wedderburn." National Magazine 17,
   no. 1 (November):[35]-38.
   It is unfair to single out Wedderburn for criticism,
   since his abusive attack on Franklin expressed the views
   of most Englishmen.

8 McGOVERN, JOHN. "Benjamin Franklin." In The Golden Legacy:
   A Thousand Aids to Thought. Chicago: F.C. Smedley & Co.,
   pp. 756-57.
   Neither Socrates nor Epictetus could "boast" of a more
   apt pupil than Franklin. "Let Philosophy herself grow
   proud as she spreads his career before us!" for he mastered
   science and diplomacy in the service of mankind.

9 NEILL, EDWARD [DUFFIELD]. "The Ideal Versus the Real Benjamin
   Franklin." Macalester College Contributions: Department
   of History, Literature and Political Science, 2d ser.,
   no. 4:[97]-108.
   Franklin portrayed himself in his memoirs as a "placid
   Deist"; however, though he was no Christian, he was nevertheless a sincere believer in God and prayer. Many of his
   writings attest to his genuine concern about the obligations
   of men to God and to each other.

1892

10 POND, GEORGE EDWARD? [Philip Quilbert]. "Our Two Franklins."
    Galaxy 14, no. 3 (March):412-13.
        The statue of Franklin in Printing-house Square is at
    least "inoffensive" and acceptable.

11 SNYDER, JOHN. Benjamin Franklin[.] A Paper Read Before the
    St. Louis Typothetae[,] January 16, 1892. [St. Louis:
    published for the St. Louis Typothetae], 12 pp.
        A sketch of Franklin's life pointing out his achieve-
    ments and noting that he loved printing all his life and
    recognized its importance in his success. Snyder, a min-
    ister, is very favorably disposed to Franklin and quite
    readily admits that the "color" in Franklin's life includes
    a youth in which he sowed "his sceptical wild oats." Snyder
    follows the Weems tradition, through Parton, however, and
    makes Franklin at least an ethical Christian, if not a
    theological one, at the end.

12 [TYPOTHETAE of the CITY of NEW YORK.] Annual Dinner . . . in
    Honor of Benjamin Franklin[,] at Hotel Brunswick[,] Monday,
    January 18, 1892. [New York: printed for the Typothetae
    of the City of New York.]
        Those who think of Franklin as a materialist have seri-
    ously misunderstood him. His chief characteristic is
    "kindness of the heart," according to the main speaker,
    the Rev. Dr. Charles F. Deems.

1893

1   ADAMS, HERBERT B[AXTER]. "Sparks' Edition of Franklin." In
    The Life and Writings of Jared Sparks[,] Comprising Selec-
    tions From His Journals and Correspondence. Vol. 2.
    Boston: Houghton Mifflin & Co., pp. [334]-59.
        Extensive quotations from Sparks indicate that he hoped
    to rescue Franklin's reputation from the harm it had re-
    ceived by Pennsylvania aristocrats and their descendants.

2   ANON. "Celebration of Franklin's Birthday." Inland Printer
    10, no. 5 (February):411-12.
        The Old Time Printer's Association of Chicago and the
    Typothetae of Chicago celebrated Franklin's birthday with
    separate affairs.

3   ANON. "The Gazette of the United States, Philadelphia, 1792."
    Pennsylvania Magazine of History and Biography 17, no. 2:
    234.

A reprint from the Gazette notice reporting the place-
ment on 7 April 1792, of François Lazzarini's statue of
Franklin "in its niche over the door in the new library
on Fifth Street."

4 BRÜSCHWEILER-WILHELM, J. Benjamin Franklin. Lebensgeschichte
   eines Nordamerikaners. Deutsche Jugend und Volksbibliothek.
   Stuttgart: J.F. Steinkopf, 136 pp.
       Biography commending Franklin for his virtues, abilities,
   and patriotism. His qualities, though excellent and many,
   are made to seem within the reasonable aspirations of the
   young readers.

5 [CHASE, WALTER G.] "Color and Warmth--Dr. Franklin's Experiment." In The Colors You Should Wear. Boston: Walter G.
   Chase, pp. 31-32.
       Recounts Franklin's experiment on the relationship be-
   tween heat and color.

6 ELLIS, EDWARD S. "American Boys Who Became Famous: Benjamin
   Franklin." Blue & Gray (July), pp. 99-102.
       A survey of Franklin's early life in particular to show
   boys the characteristics that made him famous.

7 EPES, SARGENT. Memoir of Benjamin Franklin, With Notes.
   Classics for the Home and School. Boston: Lee & Shepard,
   Publishers.
       Picks up where the Autobiography leaves off and shows
   Franklin to be a liberator and philanthropist. Epes,
   however, does not idealize Franklin.

8 GREEN, SAMUEL ABBOTT. [The Career of Benjamin Franklin.]
   In A Paper Read Before the American Philosophical Society[,]
   Philadelphia, May 25, 1893, at the Celebration of the One
   Hundred and Fiftieth Anniversary of Its Foundation in That
   City. Groton, Mass.: [printed by the University Press:
   John Wilson & Son, Cambridge], 14 pp.
       Traces Franklin's career, pointing out his multifaceted
   interests and achievements. His successes, of course, resulted from his abilities and determination; yet, it is also
   true that "he had a knack of doing the right thing at the
   right time, which is epitomized by the American people as
   horse-sense,--a quality which justly assigns him to a high
   place among men of worldly wisdom."

9 GREEN, SAMUEL A[BBOTT]. "Remarks on the Bequest of the
   Rev. Robert C. Waterston and on an Original Portrait of
   Franklin." In Proceedings of the Massachusetts Historical

1893

Society, 2d ser. 8. Boston: published by the Society, pp. 171-73.
On the discovery of a privately owned Duplessis portrait of Franklin.

10 HENKELS, STAN[ISLAUS] V[INCENT], firm. "Franklin." In The Valuable Private Library of Mr. Charles Henry Hart of Philadelphia[.] Catalogue No. 702. Philadelphia: [Stan. V. Henkels], pp. 23-26.
Twenty-one items for sale, including Franklin's Plain Truth, Some Account of the Pennsylvania Hospital and William Smith's Eulogium on Benjamin Franklin.

11 _____. "Franklin Portraits." In Engraved Portraits (An Unique Collection)[:] Washington, Lafayette, Franklin and Other Noted Americans and Europeans[.] Also Historical Scenes and Rare Maps. Catalogue No. 709. Philadelphia: [Stan V. Henkels], pp. 6-9.
Offers for sale thirty-one works which include "Au Genie de Franklin" and L'Amérique Independante."

12 HOWARD, CONWAY ROBINSON. "Extracts from the Diary of Daniel Fisher, 1775." Pennsylvania Magazine of History and Biography 17, no. 3:263-78.
Fisher came to Philadelphia seeking employment. Franklin befriended him and hoped to accommodate him, but Fisher, who lived in Franklin's house, was made very uncomfortable by Deborah Franklin's "turbulence and jealousy and pride of her disposition." Her hostility toward William Franklin was well known in the community, and she berated him to Fisher "in the foulest terms I ever heard from a Gentle-woman." Her conduct was one reason for Fisher's decision to leave Philadelphia.

13 HUBERT, PHILIP G[ENGEMBRE]. "Benjamin Franklin." In Inventors. Men of Achievement. New York: Charles Scribner's Sons, pp. [9]-44.
A survey of Franklin's theories, experiments, and inventions, all of which were of a piece with his practical philosophy of life and were thus geared to promoting the greatest degree of comfort for the largest number of people.

14 LOSSING, BENSON J[OHN]. "Franklin, Benjamin, L.L.D." In Harper's Popular Cyclopaedia of United States History From the Aboriginal Period[,] Containing Brief Sketches of Important Events and Conspicuous Actors. Vol. 1. New York: Harper & Brothers, pp. 532-33.
Franklin lauded as a humanitarian and statesman.

1893

15 POWELL, E.P. "A Study of Benjamin Franklin." <u>Arena</u> 8, no. 46
    (September):477-91.
       The period of the Revolution is one in which words were
    mightier than swords for Americans, and the tongue and pen
    of Franklin the diplomat were more critical to American
    success than even the great sword of Washington.

16 THORPE, FRANCIS NEWTON, ed. <u>Benjamin Franklin and the Univer-
    sity of Pennsylvania</u>. Bureau of Education Circular of
    Information, no. 2, 1892. Washington: Government Printing
    Office, 450 pp.
       A collection of essays which essentially concentrates on
    the University of Pennsylvania rather than on Franklin's
    relationship with the institution. The first two essays,
    which are by Thorpe, however, do deal with Franklin's role
    in the university and his views on education as these are
    expressed in his writings. "Franklin's Self-Education"
    (pp. 9-132) is an able documentary treatment of Franklin's
    success in educating himself and a summary of how the views
    on education at which he arrived influenced the university.
    The second, "Franklin's Ideas of Education As Seen in His
    Writings" (pp. 133-203), points out that his background led
    him to favor a practical education designed to provide good
    and useful citizens. Thorpe admits to some dismay that in
    his writings on education Franklin expressed no apprecia-
    tion of the beautiful. His influence is felt primarily in
    the practical side of American education. Of the remaining
    chapters, only part of the fourth (pp. 205-18), deals with
    Franklin, and this is a sketchy account of his role as
    founder of the university. The author, John L. Stewart,
    avoids mentioning the unpleasant hostility between Franklin
    and Provost William Smith and his supporters. Thorpe's
    first and second essays are cited separately.

17 _____. "Franklin's Ideas in Education As Seen in His Writings."
    In <u>Benjamin Franklin and the University of Pennsylvania</u>.
    Bureau of Education Circular of Information, no. 2, 1892.
    Washington: Government Printing Office, pp. 133-203.
       The democracy that was the essence of Franklin's polit-
    ical and social thinking also informs his ideas on education.
    He sought an education that, like his practical English
    School, would help poor boys become rich and make all boys
    enlightened and good citizens.

18 _____. "Franklin's Self-Education." In <u>Benjamin Franklin and
    the University of Pennsylvania</u>. Bureau of Education Circu-
    lar of Information, no. 2, 1892. Washington: Government
    Printing Office, pp. 9-132.

1893

Franklin's ideas on education bear the stamp of his own
self-education, his utilitarianism, and his concern with
the welfare of his fellow men. Thorpe says that Franklin's
life and career, his intellectual curiosity, skepticism,
practicality, and benevolence influenced all his activities.

19   [TYPOTHETAE of the CITY of NEW YORK.] Annual Dinner . . . in
      Honor of the Birthday of Benjamin Franklin[,] at Hotel
      Brunswick[,] Tuesday, January 17, 1893. [New York:
      printed for the Typothetae of the City of New York.]
          It is fortunate that Franklin was human rather than
      saintly, according to orthodox standards, for he had much
      work to do in secular human affairs. Yet it is also true
      that "wherever he went he became at once a radiating centre
      of wholesome influences."

20   UNDERWOOD, FRANCIS HENRY. "Benjamin Franklin." In The
      Builders of American Literature; Biographical Sketches of
      American Authors Born Previous to 1826. 1st ser. Boston:
      Lee & Shepard, pp. 44-46.
          Summary of the highlights of Franklin's life.

21   WENDELL, BARRETT. "American Literature:" [Franklin]. In
      Stelligeri and Other Essays Concerning America. New York:
      Charles Scribner's Sons, pp. 129-30.
          Wendell's point is that Franklin was too great to be
      merely a literary man.

*22   WHARTON, ANNE HOLLINGSWORTH. "The American Philosophical
      Society." In Through Colonial Doorways. Philadelphia:
      J.B. Lippincott Co.
          Source: NUC. See 1900.19.

                              1894

1   ALLEN, FRANCIS OLCOTT. "The Provincial or Colonial Flag of
      Pennsylvania." Pennsylvania Magazine of History and Biog-
      raphy 18, no. 2:249-52.
          Allen discovered that in 1747 Franklin designed the
      first provincial flag of Pennsylvania.

2   ANON. "Franklin's 'Our Lady of Auteuil.'" Atlantic Monthly
      74, no. 446 (December):858-60.
          On the sincere regard Franklin and Madame Helvétius had
      for each other.

1894

3   BIGELOW, JOHN. Introduction to Facsimile of Poor Richard's
    Almanack for 1733. N.p.: Duodecimos, pp. 9-106.
        A survey of Franklin's career leading especially to his
    publication of the almanacs, which Bigelow discusses at
    length. He considers them in light of other humorous
    Franklin pieces and provides background to some of Poor
    Richard's fictions.

4   C[ARRUTH], H[AYDEN]. "New York to Philadelphia--1723."
    Harper's Weekly 27, no. 1921 (14 October):983.
        Recounts Franklin's difficult voyage from New York to
    Philadelphia to remind Harper's readers how much more
    arduous life in general was for Americans of Franklin's
    day. (Author attribution by Nineteenth Century Reader's
    Guide to Periodical Literature, 1892-1899, vol. 2 (New
    York: H.W. Wilson Co., 1944), p. 988.)

5   DUANE, RUSSELL. An Oration at the Unveiling of the Statue of
    Dr. Benjamin Franklin, Presented by the Commissioners of
    the World's Fair to the University of Pennsylvania, and
    Erected in the City of Philadelphia. June 6th 1894.
    Philadelphia: Maurice H. Power, 8 pp.
        Franklin loved education and the University of Pennsyl-
    vania. It is therefore appropriate that the university
    should receive the statue.

6   FORD, PAUL LEICESTER. "Franklin's 'Explanatory Remarks.'"
    Nation 59, no. 1517 (26 July):60-61, 76-77.
        Cites a copy of Franklin's "Explanatory Remarks" on the
    resolutions of the Pennsylvania Assembly concerning the
    proprietor's refusal to submit to taxation of his lands.
    The resolutions together with the "Remarks" form the best
    "platform of grievances" Ford had seen "on the whole pro-
    prietary dispute in Pennsylvania." Eventually the problem
    led to the move to make Pennsylvania a royal colony.

7   _____. "A New Portrait of Franklin." Scribner's 15, no. 62
    (April):[617]-18.
        The medallion by Jean Martin Renaud catches Franklin's
    humorous side.

8   FRANKLIN FUND. Report of the Trustees of the Franklin Fund
    Upon Their Visit and Observations of the Workings and Bene-
    fits of Trade Schools in Different Parts of the Country.
    Document 165. [Boston: published by the City of Boston.]
        The Trustees of the Franklin Fund of Boston decided that
    establishing a trade school would prove to be the most
    efficient and useful way of spending the money accumulated

1894

over the years. It was therefore ordered that $322,490.20
be used to buy land on which would be built the Franklin
Trades School.

9   GREEN, SAMUEL A[BBOTT]. "Benjamin Franklin, Printer, Patriot
     and Philosopher." Proceedings of the American Philosophical
     Society 32, no. 143:42-54.
         "Whether considered as a printer, a patriot, or a phi-
     losopher, Franklin challenges our highest regard. . . ."
     Intellectually and morally, he is the most complete Ameri-
     can of all. (This piece derives from Green, 1893.8.)

10   HAYDEN, HORACE EDWIN. An Autograph of Benjamin Franklin.
     [Wilkes-Barre, Pa.], 8 pp.
         Hayden owned a promissory note of Franklin to John
     Phillips, a bookseller, and used this fact as the opportu-
     nity to recount briefly Franklin's life to 1724, the date
     of the note. (Appeared originally in the Library News-
     Letter, Wilkes-Barre, Pa., Nov. 1894.)

11   HORNE, CHARLES F., ed. "Benjamin Franklin (1706-1790)." In
     Great Men and Famous Women. Vol. 4. New York: Selmar
     Hess Publishers, pp. 231-36.
         Franklin was a man of "moderate" but "useful" ability
     and thought. He was certainly not a genius, but he became
     eminent through "industry and perseverance." While it is
     true that he was deficient in imagination, he did make im-
     portant contributions to the world.

12   LEVIN, MENDEL. Sefer Heshbōn ha-nefesh. [Warsaw], 144 pp.
         Franklin's ethics were of the practical rather than
     theoretical kind. He was chiefly concerned with bettering
     the human condition, which he was able to do because of his
     benevolence and persistent effort. First, however, Franklin
     worked to improve himself so that he could help others. In
     Hebrew.

13   TEGGART, FREDERICK J. "Franklin and Torrey." Nation 67,
     no. 1741 (10 November):350-51.
         Replies to the assertion by an anonymous author in the
     20 October 1898, issue of the Nation, that Franklin "cer-
     tainly did not establish a free library supported by taxa-
     tion either in Franklin, Mass., or elsewhere."

14   [TYPOTHETAE of the CITY of NEW YORK.] Annual Dinner . . . in
     Honor of Benjamin Franklin at Hotel Brunswick[,] Wednesday,
     January 17, 1894. [New York: printed for the Typothetae
     of the City of New York.]

Franklin represents the best features of the American
character and patriotism, says the Rev. Dr. Maynard, the
featured speaker of the night. We must try, he warned, to
return to the individualism, originality, shrewdness, and
determination of Franklin even in these comparatively
"settled and methodical" times.

15 WATKINS, MILDRED CABELL. "Benjamin Franklin, the Practical
Thinker." In <u>American Literature</u>. Literature Primers.
New York: American Book Co., pp. 18-22.
It is difficult to detect in Franklin's writings the
qualities that have caused him to be considered great, for
he wrote not to create literature but for practical ends
while engaged in public affairs.

<u>1895</u>

1 ANON. "Anecdotes of Mary H." <u>Pennsylvania Magazine of
History and Biography</u> 19, no. 3:408-9.
Dying, Franklin had placed at the foot of his bed an old
picture of the Day of Judgment, so that he could keep it in
view. This seeming change of heart encouraged Mary H. to
hope that Franklin had converted on his deathbed and therefore gained salvation.

2 ANON. "Franklin's 189th Birthday Celebrated." <u>Critic</u>,
n.s. 23, no. 675 (26 January):69-70.
The New York Typothetae were told that Franklin "was a
man of poetic imagination."

3 HENKELS, STAN[ISLAUS] V[INCENT], firm. "Franklin Imprints."
In <u>A Valuable Collection of Rare and Scarce Americana[,]
Including Franklin Imprints Belonging to M. Polock, Esq.,
of Philadelphia. Catalogue No. 748, Pt. 1</u>. Philadelphia:
[Stan. V. Henkels], pp. 28-41.
Fifty-one Franklin imprints were offered, and these
included <u>Cato Major, A Narrative of the Late Massacres</u> and
<u>Poor Richard Improved</u> for 1757.

4 JAMES, EDMUND J. "A Neglected Incident in the Life of
Dr. Franklin." <u>Nation</u> 60, no. 1555 (18 April):296-97.
Deals with Franklin's trip to Germany in 1766 but
focuses attention on some of the German commentary on
Franklin and America. Much of the response was precipated
by Achenwall (1768.1). Perhaps the most interesting reaction came from J.T. Koehler, who edited Achenwall. Koehler
was openly hostile toward the rebellious Americans, and

1895

Pennsylvanians in particular. Moreover, he charged Franklin
with inflating the importance of Pennsylvanians, and he
asserted that the Quakers were cowards because of their
pacifist beliefs.

5   _____. [On Franklin's 1766 Trip to Germany.] Proceedings of
     the American Philosophical Society 34, no. 149:482-83.
          James made copies of Franklin's letter housed in the
     university library in Leipzig. One of them proved that
     Franklin visited the Pyrmont area and Göttingen in 1766.

6   [NISBIT, HAZEL.] Benjamin Franklin. Young Folks Library of
     Choice Literature, no. 29. Vol. 2. Boston: Educational
     Publishing Co.
          An account of Franklin's life for very young children.

7   SCHUSTER, ARTHUR. "On Some Remarkable Passages in the
     Writings of Benjamin Franklin." Memoirs and Proceedings
     of the Manchester Literary and Philosophical Society,
     4th ser. 9:152-64.
          Franklin's writings on science, which are quoted at
     length, reveal the brilliance of his mind.

8   THORPE, FRANCIS N[EWTON]. "The University of Pennsylvania."
     Harper's New Monthly Magazine 91, no. 542 (July):285-87.
          These pages of a longer piece deal with Franklin's
     pioneering role in the school. A summary of Thorpe's
     findings in his booklength and far more detailed history
     of the University is cited separately (1893.16).

9   [TYPOTHETAE of the CITY of NEW YORK.] Annual Dinner . . . in
     Honor of Benjamin Franklin at Hotel Brunswick[,] Thursday,
     January 17, 1895. [New York: printed for the Typothetae
     of the City of New York.]
          Franklin praised by different speakers for his contribu-
     tions to American liberty, his deathless maxims of Poor
     Richard, his generally overlooked poetic nature and imagi-
     nation, and for his achievements in science and other areas.

10   WETZEL, W[ILLIAM] A[CHENBACH]. Benjamin Franklin As an
     Economist. Johns Hopkins Studies in Historical and
     Political Science. Edited by Herbert B[axter] Adams.
     13th ser. Vol. 9 (September). Baltimore: Johns Hopkins
     Press, 58 pp.
          Wetzel provides a careful discussion of Franklin as an
     economist and argues forcefully that he was a good deal
     more than a teacher of crass materialism or a crude specu-
     lator about economics. Franklin, in fact, must be taken
     seriously by those interested in the science.

1896

1   ANON. "Benjamin Franklin." Illustrierte Jugenblätter 12
    (April):[43]-46.
       A sketch of Franklin's life.

2   ANON. "Benjamin Franklin." Proofsheet 2, no. 21 (June):
    [209]-11.
       On 6 June 1896, "at Lincoln Park, in the city of Chicago,
    will be unveiled a bronze statue of Benjamin Franklin.
    This statue is the gift of Hon. Joseph Medill, editor of
    the Chicago Tribune, to the printers of Chicago." It is
    fitting that Franklin, as great an American who has ever
    lived, should be so honored by a fellow printer.

3   ANON. "Probating Franklin's Will." Electrical Engineer 21,
    no. 414 (8 April):376.
       "The will of Benjamin Franklin was allowed in the
    Suffolk County, Massachusetts, Probate Court to-day by
    Judge Grant on petition of Mayor Quincy, of Boston, as
    a foreign will, having been probated a century ago in the
    Orphans' Court in Philadelphia."

4   AXON, WILLIAM E.A. "Benjamin Franklin As a Derbyshire Miner."
    Notes and Queries, 8th ser. 9 (22 February):145.
       Quotes from a bookseller's catalogue noting a letter
    from Franklin "on the Mineral Customs of Derbyshire, in
    which the Question relative to the Claim of the Duty of
    Lot on Smitham is occasionally considered, by a Derbyshire
    Miner, post 8vo., 1766." This alleged Franklin letter,
    which presumably was listed in the November 1895 catalog
    "of Mr. William Downing" is apparently not by Franklin.
    It does not appear in the Papers for 1764-1766. Franklin
    had been in England from the late autumn of 1764 and con-
    tinued there for nearly eleven years.

5   BALDWIN, JAMES. The Story of Benjamin Franklin for Young
    Readers. The Werner Biographical Booklets. Chicago:
    Werner School Book Co., 56 pp.
       An account of Franklin's career which stresses his prac-
    tical morality and many achievements. Central to Franklin's
    full and successful life were the industry, frugality, and
    other virtues he helped make popular.

6   BECK, J.A. "First Franklin Prize Essay." Self Culture 3,
    no. 1 (April):51-54.
       On the numerous achievements of a self-made man, whose
    abilities were used in behalf of the public good.

1896

7   BIGELOW, JOHN. "Benjamin Franklin (1706-1790)." In <u>Library</u>
    <u>of the World's Best Literature[,] Ancient and Modern.</u>
    Vol. 15. New York: International Society, pp. 5925-36.
       A sketch commenting on Franklin's beliefs and qualities,
    especially pointing out that he was no agnostic.

8   BOARDMAN, GEORGE DANA. "Early Printing in the Middle Colo-
    nies." <u>Pennsylvania Magazine of History and Biography</u> 10,
    no. 1:15-32.
       Pays tribute to Franklin's role in the development of
    printing in the Middle Colonies before 1800.

9   CHANDLER, ALBERT B. "Benjamin Franklin, the Patriot." In
    <u>Sons of the Revolution. Missouri Society. Prize Medal</u>
    <u>Essay Contest by the High School Scholars and the Schools</u>
    <u>of Equal Grade in the State of Missouri.</u> Subject:
    <u>"Benjamin Franklin, the Patriot."</u> . . . Kansas City, Mo.:
    published by the Society, pp. 15-19.
       The cockpit affair was actually the high point in
    Franklin's great career as a patriot.

10 CURTIS, MATTOON MONROE. "Franklin." In <u>An Outline of Philoso-</u>
    <u>phy in America.</u> [Cleveland], pp. 4-6.
       Franklin was influenced considerably by Shaftesbury,
    Collins, the "French <u>Illuminatti</u>," and Hume, as he was by
    English deism; however, he acknowledged "Locke as his
    master." Franklin's writings do not make up a coherent
    philosophical system, nor did he strive for one. "The
    enthusiasm of Franklin was for humanity, for self-mastery
    and the mastery of nature." (Originally published in the
    March 1896 issue of <u>The Western Reserve Bulletin.</u>)

11 ESTABROOK, H.D. "Benjamin Franklin." <u>Inland Printer</u> 17,
    no. 5 (August):531-35.
       An oration delivered 6 June 1896, at the unveiling of
    the statue of Franklin in Lincoln Park in Chicago. Calls
    Franklin one "of nature's noblemen," a patriot, philosopher,
    friend, and guide whose accomplishments in so many different
    areas must make us reflect on his greatness. Moreover,
    Franklin was also remarkable in that he remained calm and
    happy during his early poverty; for he realized that all
    circumstances contributed to the making of a virtuous man
    in a universe controlled by God. The statue was given to
    the city by Joseph Medill.

12 FAYE, [HERVÉ]. [Address.] "Cérémonie de la pose et de
    l'inauguration de plaque commémorative Franklin." <u>Société</u>

1896

historiques de Auteuil et de Passy. <u>Bulletin</u>, no. 15,
1st trimester (31 March), pp. 98-99.
Tribute to Franklin as a scientist.

13   FLINN, J.J. "Franklin." <u>Inland Printer</u> 18, no. 1 (October):
87.
The ode was written as part of the celebration of the
unveiling of the Franklin statue in Lincoln Park, Chicago,
6 June 1896. Of Franklin, Flinn writes:

Wherever truth prevails, throughout the earth,
Wherever reason reigns and minds are free,
Wherever toil commands a cheerful hearth,
Wherever plenty smiles on industry,
Wherever honor's paid to honest worth,
And manhood's robed in manhood's dignity,
Wherever Franklin's words and deeds are known,
The millions claim and love him as their own.

14   GUILLOIS, ANTOINE. [Address.] "Cérémonie de la pose et de
l'inauguration de plaque commémorative Franklin." <u>Société</u>
<u>historiques de Auteuil et de Passy. Bulletin</u>, no. 15,
1st trimester (31 March), pp. 99-103.
It is clear from French writings, portraits, and actions
that the country perceived Franklin not so much as a revolutionary than as a sage and friend of liberty. This love
of Franklin certainly helped create widespread sympathy for
America, with which he was so closely identified.

15   HENKELS, STAN[ISLAUS] V[INCENT], firm. <u>Catalogue of Rare and</u>
<u>Choice Engravings . . . [,] Including an Extraordinary</u>
<u>Collection of Portraits of Washington and other Noted</u>
<u>Americans. . . . [Catalogue no. 768.]</u> Philadelphia:
[Stan. V. Henkels], pp. 13-15.
Offered nearly fifty portraits of Franklin for sale,
including "L'Apôtre de la Liberté Immortalisé."

16   _____. <u>Rare and Scarce Americana[.] Early Almanacs, Maga-</u>
<u>zines and Poetry[,] Franklin and Other Imprints[,] Works</u>
<u>Relating to the Quakers, Local and General American His-</u>
<u>tory, etc. . . . Catalogue No. 753.</u> Philadelphia:
[Stan. V. Henkels], pp. 9, 14, 16.
Offerings included <u>Poor Richards</u> for 1752, 1753, and
1755.

*17   HULBERT, P.G. [A piece on Franklin?] <u>Inventors</u>.
There is a card for this book in the Van Pelt Library of
the University of Pennsylvania, and the number is 926 C H86;
however, the book has been missing since at least 1977.

1896

18   [JAMES, JOHN HOUGH.] "Third Franklin Prize Essay." <u>Self
      Culture</u> 3, no. 1 (April):56-59.
           Franklin as a great politician and statesman who,
      though beset by problems in ending the war and winning a
      sound peace in France, continued his literary and intellec-
      tual activity and always remained an excellent human being.

19   JONES, ELINOR. "Benjamin Franklin, the Patriot." In <u>Sons of
      the Revolution. Missouri Society. Prize Medal Essay Con-
      test by the High School Scholars and Schools of Equal Grade
      in the State of Missouri. Subject: "Benjamin Franklin,
      the Patriot."</u> . . . Kansas City, Mo.: published by the
      Sons of the Revolution, Missouri Society, pp. 5-9.
           The essay that won the first prize calls Franklin "the
      plain American" who represents his plain countrymen.

20   LAY, GEORGE C. "Benjamin Franklin." <u>Godey's Magazine</u> 133,
      no. 796 (October):[339]-54; no. 797 (November):[458]-69;
      no. 798 (December):[626]-39.
           A detailed life of Franklin dividing his career into
      three stages. The first traces his career to about 1751,
      showing his rise from poor beginnings through his appren-
      ticeship, success as a printer and achievements as a
      scientist-philosopher. The second part deals with
      Franklin's political career to the Revolution, pointing
      out that through his ability and, just as important, his
      consistently faithful and honorable conduct in trying cir-
      cumstances, he moved from a local politician to a statesman.
      The final section of this account of Franklin's life high-
      lights his diplomatic achievements in France. Here is pre-
      sented the full ripeness of the philosopher-patriot who
      inspired the French people, won the support of the king
      and ministers, and proved a major factor in the founding
      of the United States. His service continued upon his return
      to Pennsylvania and, through his will, continues to the
      present. His life was brilliant, but his reputation grows
      ever more brilliantly.

21   MANUEL, EUGÈNE. [Address.] "Cérémonie de la pose et de
      l'inauguration de la plaque commémorative Franklin."
      <u>Société historiques de Auteuil et de Passy. Bulletin,</u>
      no. 15, 1st trimester (31 March), pp. 97-98.
           Though the setting up of honorary plaques in France is
      normally reserved for Frenchmen, Franklin was loved through-
      out France. He therefore deserves this singular honor.

22   MATTHEWS, BRANDER. "Benjamin Franklin." In <u>An Introduction
      to the Study of American Literature</u>. New York: American
      Book Co., pp. 21-39.

1896

Franklin was a "typical American," but like another
typical American, Lincoln, he was humorous almost to a
failing. His chief limitation, though, was his lack of
"spirituality, the faith in the ideal, which was at the
core of Lincoln's character." Franklin could not perceive
what lay beyond the limits of common sense, and most likely
he did not care to see beyond. Still he had many virtues
and did great and valuable things. Moreover, he wrote what
is worth reading.

23 MEDILL, JOSEPH. A Typical American. Benjamin Franklin.
    Chicago: Ben Franklin Co., 38 pp.
        An address delivered before the Old-Time Printers' Asso-
    ciation of Chicago. Franklin was one of the greatest, most
    brilliant, and humane men who ever lived, and he never
    ceased to identify with working people or to try and help
    them as well as "the poor and the weak." The story of his
    rise in life is a typical American success story.

24 [MOORHEAD, F.G.] "Second Franklin Prize Essay." Self Culture
    3, no. 1 (April):54-56.
        Tribute to Franklin as a scientist, statesman, philoso-
    pher, and patriot.

25 MORZYCKA, F[AUSTYNA]. Wielki charakter czyli Życie Beniamina
    Franklina [The great character and life of Benjamin
    Franklin]. Warsaw: A. Rzażewskiej, 74 pp.
        An idealized Franklin is made the epitome of morality
    and good will as well as brilliant, versatile, and self-
    lessly patriotic. The biographer commits a number of errors
    concerning Franklin's scientific experiments and political
    activities in a book intended for people who had little or
    no knowledge of Franklin. In Polish.

26 PHILLIPS, F. "Franklin's House at Passy." Notes and Queries,
    8th ser. 9 (30 May):428.
        Inquires about the exact location of Franklin's Passy
    house, "which disappeared in 1830."

27 PHILOMATH, Jr., pseud. "Third Franklin Prize Essay." Self
    Culture 3, no. 1 (April):56-59.
        Franklin as a great politician and statesman.

28 [POTIN, ÉMILE.] [Address.] "Cérémonie de la pose et de
    l'inauguration de la plaque commémorative Franklin."
    Société historiques de Auteuil et de Passy. Bulletin,
    no. 15, 1st trimester (31 March), pp. 95-108.

1896

The plaque commemorated Franklin's years at the Hôtel Valentois. Included in this piece on the ceremony are addresses by Eugène Manuel, Hervé Faye, and Antoine Guillois, all of which are cited separately.

29 SONS of the REVOLUTION, MISSOURI SOCIETY. Prize Medal Essay Contest by the High School Scholars and Schools of Equal Grade of the State of Missouri. Subject: "Benjamin Franklin, the Patriot." . . . Kansas City, Mo.: published by the Society, 19 pp.
A collection of the winning essays, which are cited separately.

30 STEPHENS, KATE. "Was Benjamin Franklin a Plagiarist?" Bookman 4, no. 1 (September):24-30.
Franklin might have been indebted to Swift at times; however, because Franklin's hoax on Titan Leeds is far rougher than Swift's Bickerstaff joke predicting the death of Partridge, it seems unlikely that Franklin knew of the earlier work.

31 SWOFFORD, RALPH P. "Benjamin Franklin, the Patriot." In Sons of the Revolution. Missouri Society. Prize Medal Essay Contest by the High School Scholars and Schools of Equal Grade of the State of Missouri. Subject: "Benjamin Franklin, the Patriot." . . . Kansas City, MO.: published by the Society, pp. 10-14.
The winner of the second prize points out that America owes a great deal to Franklin.

32 [TOWNE, EDWARD C.] "Benjamin Franklin Medals and Prizes for Essays on This Subject to Be Prepared by Members of the Home University League." Self Culture 3, no. 4 (January):702-3.
The Home University League, desiring to "stimulate special study" offers a variety of medals for the best essays on Benjamin Franklin.

33 WAHL, E. "Communications écrites." Société historiques de Auteuil et de Passy. Bulletin, no. 15, 1st trimester (31 March), pp. 103-5.
A fair treatment of Franklin, who was indeed a very great man, will take into account the criticism of Sainte-Beuve that Franklin lacked spirituality and refinement. Compared in particular to the other American commissioners, Franklin did not lack these qualities, and he certainly was improved by his association with his female friends at Passy.

34 YOUMANS, WILLIAM JAY. Pioneers of Science in America. New
    York: D. Appleton & Co., pp. 1-23.
       An account of Franklin's life that surveys his accom-
    plishments in science.

                              1897

1   ANON. "Franklin's House in Passy." Scientific American 77,
    no. 4 (24 July):58.
       On events commemorating Franklin's residence in Passy.

2   BACHE, RICHARD MEADE. "Franklin's Grave." Red and Blue of
    the University of Pennsylvania 10, no. 3 (December):4-9.
       Someone had charged that Franklin's grave and tombstone
    were utterly neglected and in diplorable condition, an un-
    fitting memorial to so great a man. Bache refutes the
    charge.

3   _____. "The So-Called 'Franklin Prayer-Book.'" Pennsylvania
    Magazine of History and Biography 21, no. 2 (July):225-34.
       The revision of the Anglican liturgy by Franklin and
    Dashwood in 1785 may have had some influence on those who
    were revising it officially. An additional very brief note
    on the book appears on page 502 of this volume of the
    journal.

4   BELLOW, BESSIE RAYNER. "Franklin's America." In A Passing
    World. London: Ward & Downer, pp. 155-94.
       On the Anglo-Saxon virtues which made early America
    "resistant," honorable, and "firmly-knit." These admirable
    qualities Franklin had in full measure.

5   [BROOKS, ELBRIDGE STREETER.] "Benjamin Franklin, the Candle-
    maker's Son, Who with His Kite Discovered That Electricity
    is the Cause of Lightning." In True Stories of Great
    Americans. . . . Philadelphia: John C. Winston & Co.,
    pp. 90-111.
       A survey of Franklin's life for children. Stresses
    Franklin's resourcefulness, dedication, and concern for
    human welfare.

6   BUTTERWORTH, HEZEKIAH. True to His Home[:] A Tale of the
    Boyhood of Franklin. New York: D. Appleton & Co., 322 pp.
       This fictionalized account is generally arranged topi-
    cally, according to the lessons to be taught young readers.
    One of these is that by the time he was twenty-two, Franklin
    rejected his earlier deism and, if he did not become a

1897

Christian, did adopt a kind of spiritual moralism as his guide through life. The historical facts in this book come from Parton.

7 CONWAY, MONCURE D[ANIEL]. "Letter of Thomas Paine to Dr. Franklin." Athenaeum 110, no. 3367 (10 July):65.
Provides the context for Paine's letter thanking Franklin for recommending him to Richard Bache and, through him, to other influential Americans in the Philadelphia area.

8 GOUILLY, AL[EXANDRE]. Vie et travaux de B. Franklin. Montévrain: Imprimerie Typographique de L'École D'Alembert, 68 pp.
Provides a detailed biography of Franklin and then, after praising him for his many qualities and achievements, says that Franklin's life is a tribute to the ability of a man to raise himself morally and intellectually. Gouilly also relates Franklin's working class background to his success in science and other areas.

9 HART, CHARLES HENRY. "Life Portraits of Great Americans . . . Benjamin Franklin." McClure's Magazine 8, no. 3 (January): [263]-72.
Reproduces and comments on fifteen life portraits of Franklin done by such artists as Pratt, Chamberlin, Cochin, Nini, and Charles Willson Peale. Furthermore, Hart condemns portraits falsely claimed to have been painted from life.

10 _____. "An Unpublished Life Portrait of Franklin." McClure's Magazine 8, no. 5 (March):[459].
On the Nini medallion of Franklin sans the famous fur cap. The portrait, executed in 1778, is the first to make use of the inscription: "He snatched the thunderbolt from heaven and the sceptre from tyrants."

11 JAMESON, J. FRANKLIN. "Franklin, Benjamin." In Dictionary of United States History, 1492-1898. Boston: Puritan Publishing Co., pp. 245-46.
Praises Franklin as a statesman, writer, scientist, and philanthropist.

12 JEAKES, THOMAS J. "Benjamin Franklin." Notes and Queries, 8th ser. 12 (21 August):158.
Replies to Student (1897.20) and tells him where to find printed copies of "'Dr. Franklin's Moral Code.'" By the Moral Code, Jeakes means Franklin's "Articles of Belief and Acts of Religion."

1897

13 McADIE, ALEXANDER. "Franklin's Kite Experiment With Modern
    Apparatus." Popular Science Monthly 51, no. 6 (October):
    739-47.
        Given improvements in kites, it is possible to realize
    Franklin's dream "of harnessing the electricity of the air."

14 McCLEARY, SAMUEL F. "The Franklin Fund." Pennsylvania Maga-
    zine of History and Biography, 2d ser. 12 (October):17-29.
        On the origin, purpose, and continuing usefulness of the
    fund.

15 MITCHELL, DONALD G[RANT]. "Benjamin Franklin." In American
    Lands and Letters[,] the Mayflower to Rip Van Winkle. New
    York: Charles Scribner's Sons, pp. 98-112.
        Franklin was a great man and generally a good writer.
    Whatever moral and literary deficiencies he had, and these
    became pronounced when he was in France, derive from the
    same problem. Simply put, he "was never a man of nice
    delicacies--of thought or action; he had never a bringing-
    up at the impressionable age, among ladies of dignity and
    refinement. He lacked appreciation in that direction;
    lacked too, perhaps, a large and fine moral sense." Yet
    he was our first internationally recognized great thinker,
    author, and worker and was truly wise.

16 PAINTER, F.V.N. "Benjamin Franklin." In Introduction to
    American Literature[,] Including Illustrative Selections
    and Notes. Boston: Sibley & Co., pp. 41-50.
        On Franklin's "extraordinary" and always interesting
    life. Offers almost nothing on him as a writer other than
    his use of the Spectator Papers.

17 [RIDPATH, JOHN CLARK.] "Franklin." Arena 18, no. 96
    (November):716.
        Verse tribute calling Franklin "the first/Of all
    Americans!"

18 SMITH, JESSIE R. "The Story of Benjamin Franklin." In Four
    True Stories of Life and Adventure. New York: William
    Beverley Harrison, pp. 95-125.
        Franklin made perfect for very young children. Smith
    emphasizes Franklin's goodness, morality, faith, diligence,
    independence, and self-sacrificing patriotism.

19 STILLÉ, CHARLES J[ANEWAY]. "Some Recent Books on Pennsylvania
    History." Pennsylvania Magazine of History and Biography
    21, no. 1:92-93.

1897

Reviewing the updated edition of George B. Wood's <u>Early</u>
<u>History of the University of Pennsylvania to the Year 1827</u>,
which was brought down to the end of the century by
George D. Stone, Stillé notes as important the fact that
Franklin was the school's founder in a limited, though
significant sense. He disapproved of the traditional
classical education for any but those few who intended
"to follow the learned professions." For all others he
desired the practical English education he outlined. His
plan was not the dominant one in the school, however.

20 STUDENT, pseud. "Benjamin Franklin." <u>Notes and Queries</u>, 8th
ser. 12 (31 July):88–89.
Asks where Franklin's "liturgy" is to be found. By the
liturgy, he means the "Articles of Belief and Acts of
Religion."

21 TRENT, W[ILLIAM] P[ETERFIELD]. "The Makers of the Union:
Benjamin Franklin." <u>McClure's Magazine</u> 8, no. 3 (January):
[273]-77.
Franklin lives for us because "he is a typical and in
many respects unapproachable product of true Americanism,"
and because "he is the most complete representative of his
century that any nation can point to."

22 TYLER, MOSES COIT. "Franklin in the Literature of the Revolution." In <u>The Literary History of the American Revolution,</u>
<u>1763-1783</u>. Vol. 2. New York: G.P. Putnam's Sons,
pp. 359–81.
Notes that although Franklin was abroad for most of the
period of the Revolution, he likely had more to do with
"shaping" its thought and even bringing it about than any
other person. In the imagination of men he seemed to direct
American events from England and France. Franklin always
wrote to achieve some useful end rather than to gain fame
as a writer. Although much of what he wrote in his earlier
years is good, "his best work was done after the year 1764,
and thenceforward down to the very year of his death. . . ."
This later work shows the touch of a master of letters as
well as benevolence and a sense of humor which makes his
work irresistibly charming. It is remarkable that in the
midst of his labors in behalf of the Revolution, Franklin
could write perhaps his greatest work, the <u>Autobiography</u>,
as well as the bagatelles and other pieces that have nothing
to do with the war. Tyler shows that Franklin moved over
the years from the genial friend to both England and America
who hoped to prevent the dissolution of the Empire to a
great, biting satirist. "It is only by a continuous reading

of the entire body of Franklin's Revolutionary writings . . . that any one can know how brilliant was his
wisdom, or how wise was his brilliance, or how humane and
gentle and helpful were both."

23   WALKER, LEWIS BURD, ed. The Burd Papers. Extracts From Chief
     Justice William Allen's Letter Book . . . Together With an
     Appendix Containing Pamphlets in the Controversy With
     Franklin. [Pottsville, Pa.: Standard Pub. Co.],
     pp. 81-131, passim.
         Nearly half the book is made up of anti-Franklin docu-
     ments and Allen's letters to David Barclay and Sons, in
     which he loses no opportunity to discredit Franklin.

24   WARREN, C.F.S. "Benjamin Franklin." Notes and Queries, 8th
     ser. 12 (21 August):158.
         Replies to Student (1897.20) and corrects him on his use
     of theological terms in regard to Franklin's alleged "li-
     turgy" or "Articles of Belief and Acts of Religion."
     Warren clearly doubts that Franklin wrote such a piece.

                              1898

1   ANON. "Franklin Anniversary Celebrations." Inland Printer 20,
     no. 5 (February):655.
         Nearly "all printers' associations" in America honored
     the memory of the patron saint of printing on January 17th.
     In Chicago, there was a gathering of 300 people at the Old
     Time Printers' Association.

2   ANON. "Notes." Nation 67, no. 1738 (20 October):297.
         Franklin was not only the first advocate of free public
     libraries, he established such a library in Massachusetts.

3   ANON. "The Oldest Paper in America[,] Founded A.D. 1728 by
     Benjamin Franklin." [Advertising Supplement.] Cosmopolitan
     25, no. 5 (September):unpaginated.
         The Saturday Evening Post claims to be descended from
     Franklin's Pennsylvania Gazette.

4   BAKER, HERBERT L. "What Franklin Did to Canada." Inland
     Printer 20, no. 6 (March):762-65.
         When Franklin went to Canada in 1775 to try and persuade
     Canadians to join the American cause, he took with him
     enough type to start a newspaper. Though the Canadians
     remained loyal to the Crown, the type was used to start
     the Montreal Gazette.

1898

5   BATES, KATHERINE. "The Revolutionary Period: Benjamin
    Franklin." In American Literature. New York: Macmillan
    Co., pp. 52-68.
        Surveys Franklin's career, especially as a man of letters,
    and calls the Autobiography his best work because of the
    candid and delightful revelation of his personality.

6   BENJAMIN, PARK. "Benjamin Franklin." In A History of Elec-
    tricity. (The Intellectual Rise in Electricity) from
    Antiquity to the Days of Benjamin Franklin. New York:
    John Wiley & Sons, pp. 537-47, 555-64, 575-93.
        A survey of Franklin's theories, experiments, and his
    impact on electrical research.

7   BROOKS, ELBRIDGE S[TREETER]. The True Story of Benjamin
    Franklin[:] the American Statesman. Boston: Lothrop, Lee
    & Shepard Co., 250 pp.
        A children's version of Franklin that emphasizes the
    Poor Richard virtues he learned and which, with his native
    intelligence and concern for the common good, he used to
    save America during the French and Indian War, the Revolu-
    tion, and again at the Constitutional Convention. Asserts
    that Franklin had been an Abolitionist "all his life" and
    that the continuation of slavery in the republic was his
    only regret as he neared the end of his long life.

8   CHOULLIER, ERNEST. "Voltaire et Franklin à l'Académie des
    Sciences. . . ." Extrait des Mémoires de la Société
    académique de l'Aube. Vol. 61. Troyes: Paul Nouel,
    pp. 3-7.
        On the respect accorded Franklin by his fellow philoso-
    phers and scientists and of his meeting with Voltaire.
    (This was written in 1897, but first published here.)

9   D[AVIS, N.]D. "Franklin and the Royal Society." Nation 66,
    no. 1708 (24 March):222-24.
        The story of and correspondence concerning the Royal
    Society's "slighting" of Franklin and its "subsequent
    recognition" of him.

10 FISHER, SYDNEY GEORGE. The True Benjamin Franklin.
    Philadelphia: J.B. Lippincott, 369 pp.
        Claims at the outset that his intention is to demytholo-
    gize Franklin, to present him as a full human being and thus
    to rescue him from earlier attempts to make him less earthy
    than he was. Fisher does indeed avoid, rather self-
    consciously avoid, the softenings and evasions of the
    Parson Weems school of fictionalized biography passed off

1898

as fact. He treats Franklin's hostility toward the clergy and toward the Massachusetts religious establishment in an honest if incomplete manner and calls Franklin, rather apologetically and inaccurately, something of a socialist or Populist. No attempt is made to disguise Franklin's lifelong deism, and Fisher deals at length with Franklin's affairs with women. He asserts, in fact, that Franklin also had an illegitimate daughter, who eventually married John Foxcroft. This error results from Fisher's misreading of certain Franklin letters. The author pays tribute to Franklin's literary skill and says that it contributed a great deal to his fame and success. While he might actually share credit with others for discoveries and plans, he wrote so much better than most men that his report became the standard one and those of his competitors were lost or ignored. In dealing with Franklin's life, Fisher makes some minor errors, but he is guilty of serious misunderstanding and superficiality in treating Pennsylvania politics. He succeeds better with Franklin's activities in England and France before and during the Revolution. While he does not understand the degree to which Franklin worked on French fears of a reunited England and America, he offers a detailed explanation of what he sees as the personal reasons for Franklin's success in France.

11   FORD, PAUL LEICESTER. "Franklin and the Rattlesnakes." Nation 67, no. 1731 (1 September):165-66.
    Identifies as Franklin's the piece suggesting that American rattlesnakes be sent to England in exchange for the English felons being sent to America.

12   _____. "The Many-Sided Franklin." Century Magazine 57, no. 1 (November):30-47; no. 2 (December):284-304; no. 3 (January 1899):395-414; no. 4 (February 1899):502-19; no. 6 (April 1899):803-17; 58, no. 2 (June 1899):288-303; no. 3 (July 1899):410-27; no. 4 (August 1899):606-20; no. 5 (September 1899):750-63; no. 6 (October 1899):881-98.
    To emphasize Franklin's multiplicity of interests, activities and accomplishments, Ford presents a series of essays dealing with Franklin's family background; his build, illnesses, and theories about health and medicine; his self-education, concern with sound, practical public education, and his library; his religion; career as printer and publisher; his successes as a writer and journalist; his relations with women; his outstanding ability as a generalist or remarkable factotum; his contributions to the world as a scientist; and his great diplomatic services. (These essays were published in book form by The Century Company in 1899. The book also contains pieces on Franklin's humor

229

1898

and social life, not included in the magazine. See 1899.17
and 18.)

13   HALE, EDWARD E[VERETT]. "Ben Franklin's Ballads." New
     England Magazine, n.s. 18, no. 4 (June):505-7.
        Asserts that "The Downfall of Piracy," which appeared in
     a volume entitled Some Real Sea-Songs, and was edited by
     John Ashton, is actually Franklin's juvenile ballad on the
     pirate Teach.

14   HALE, [EDWARD EVERETT]. [On a Supposed Franklin Ballad.]
     Proceedings of the American Antiquarian Society, n.s. 12
     (April). Worcester, Mass.: published by the Society,
     pp. 215-16.
        Hale believes he has found Franklin's youthful ballad
     on Blackbeard.

15   HALE, EDWARD EVERETT. [On the Franklin Ballads.] In Proceed-
     ings of the American Antiquarian Society, n.s. 11, pt. 3.
     Worcester, Mass.: published by the Society, pp. 255-56.
        Hale believes that the ballads Franklin wrote as a youth,
     The Lighthouse Tragedy, and the piece on Blackbeard the
     pirate, still exist.

16   HENKELS, STAN[ISLAUS] V[INCENT], firm. Catalogue of Rare and
     Scarce American Early Laws and Charters of the Colonies[,]
     Bradford, Keimer, Zenger, Franklin and Other Imprints. . . .
     Catalogue No. 819. Philadelphia: [Stan. V. Henkels],
     passim.
        Items for sale included imprints and An Historical Review
     of the Constitution and Government of Pennsylvania, which
     was thought at the time to have been written by Franklin.

17   _____. A Description of an Extraordinary Collection of Rare
     Bradford, Zenger, Franklin, Keimer and Other Early American
     Imprints. . . . Catalogue No. 819. Philadelphia: [Stan. V.
     Henkels], passim.
        Franklin imprints, including the Cato Major, appear
     throughout the catalogue.

18   _____. "Frankliniana." In Valuable Private Library of a Well
     Known Philadelphia Collector[,] Embracing Rare and Scarce
     Americana. . . . Catalogue No. 815. Philadelphia:
     [Stan. V. Henkels], pp. 92-108.
        Offers for sale nearly eighty items, including Franklin's
     abridged Common Prayer book, his edition of Cato Major, a
     number of Franklin imprints, and the edition of Wollaston's
     Religion of Nature Delineated on which the young Franklin
     worked while at Samuel Palmer's printing establishment in
     London.

19   HUBBARD, ELBERT. Benjamin Franklin. Little Journeys to the
     Homes of American Statesmen, vol. 4. New York: G.P.
     Putnam's Sons, pp. [39]-70.
        Praises Franklin as a patriot, practical moralist, and
     scientist. Filled with errors.

20   JONES, ADAM LEROY. "Early American Philosophers: Benjamin
     Franklin, 1706-1790." Columbia University Contributions
     to Philosophy, Psychology and Education 2, no. 4 (June):
     12-17.
        While Franklin's "direct contribution to philosophy was
     small," he did encourage education in many important ways
     and thereby helped to advance learning of all kinds. In
     his personal life, he was typically American in that he
     eschewed metaphysics and adopted a pragmatic attitude
     toward experience.

21   LABANDE, L[ÉON] H[ONORÉ]. "Notes sur le peintre Joseph-
     Sifferd Duplessis et sur les portraits de Franklin
     exécutes par lui." Mémoires de l'Académie de Vaucluse 17:
     [393]-402.
        Describes the paintings and discusses the relationship
     between the artist and Franklin.

22   OGDEN, H[ENRY] A[LEXANDER]. "A Great Republican at Court."
     St. Nicholas Magazine 25, no. 96 (July):774-80.
        Franklin's republican manners helped him succeed as
     ambassador in France. His genuine simplicity was a remark-
     able contrast to the style of the French court.

23   PANCOAST, HENRY S. "The Beginnings of Nationality: Benjamin
     Franklin (1706-1790.)" In An Introduction to American Litera-
     ture. New York: Henry Holt & Co., pp. 80-92.
        Franklin wrote a good deal and wrote rapidly; therefore,
     he had little time to think of literature as an end in it-
     self. His chief literary contribution is his Autobiography,
     a worthy representative of "the unambitious class of writing
     to which it belongs." Yet in his writings and private life,
     though he can be credited with numerous virtues, he is seen
     to lack "some of the highest qualities." He is too prac-
     tical and materialistic. In his cool rationalism, he is
     the product of Old rather than of New England. Those who
     see Franklin as the epitome of the American character are
     only partly correct. He is doubtless typically American in
     his patriotism; however, his limitations and intellectual
     characteristics show him to be a figure of England under
     Queen Anne more than of eighteenth-century America.

1898

24 [PARTON, JAMES?] "Franklin, Benjamin." In <u>The National
    Cyclopaedia of American Biography</u>[:] <u>Being the History
    of the United States As Illustrated in the Lives of the
    Founders, Builders, and Defenders of the Republic, and
    of the Men and Women Who Are Doing the Work and Moulding
    the Thought of the Present Time</u>. Vol. 1. New York:
    James T. White, pp. 328-37.
    Appreciative biography highlighting Franklin's personal
    qualities, and a career sketch that calls particular atten-
    ion to his achievements in science and diplomacy.

25 ROBINS, EDWARD. <u>Benjamin Franklin</u>[:] <u>Printer</u>[,] <u>Statesman</u>[,]
    <u>Philosopher and Practical Citizen</u>[,] <u>1706-1790</u>. American
    Men of Energy. New York: G.P. Putnam's Sons, 354 pp.
    A detailed survey of Franklin's career which emphasizes
    his kinship with ordinary good citizens. This sympathetic
    identification is a source of his efforts to improve the
    conditions of his fellowmen. Moreover, Franklin's writings
    can be read, enjoyed, and profited from by all; for like
    him, they are wise in their simplicity.

26 SACHSE, JULIUS FRIEDRICH. <u>Franklin's Account with the "Lodge
    of Masons</u>[,]" <u>1731-1737</u>[:] <u>As Found Upon the Pages of His
    Daily Journal</u>. [Philadelphia: Lippincott Press], 21 pp.
    Sachse uses Franklin's "Mason Book" to support the
    earlier assertion by Clifford P. MacCalla that Philadelphia
    is "the 'Mother City of Freemasonry in America.'"

27 STRONG, FRANK. <u>Benjamin Franklin</u>[.] <u>A Character Sketch</u>.
    Dansville, N.Y.: Instructor Publishing Co., 120 pp.
    A generally sound account of Franklin's life and career,
    focusing on his political achievements. Guilty of some pro-
    Anglo-Saxon bias and concentrating on heredity as the shap-
    ing force in Franklin's life almost to the exclusion of
    environment, Strong nevertheless presents a basically real-
    istic sketch of Franklin's strengths and weaknesses. The
    author makes it clear, for example, that Franklin, who had
    been abroad for many years, was slow to recognize the temper
    of the colonists in the decade before the Revolution, and
    that he had too high "a personal regard for King George,
    and a remarkable and unfounded faith in his purposes toward
    America." Intended for teachers and students, this book
    provides a good deal of material for class discussions,
    additional reading, and even a "School or Club Programme."

28 TRENT, WILLIAM P[ETERFIELD]. "Benjamin Franklin." In <u>American
    Prose</u>. Edited by George Rue Carpenter. New York:
    Macmillan Co., pp. 27-30.

Franklin lacks spirituality and is at times "ludicrous"
in his optimism, but his clear, straightforward prose and
good humor make him read and admired.

1899

1   ANON. Annual Dinner of the Typothetae of the City of New York
    in Honor of the Birthday of Benjamin Franklin[,] Hotel
    Savoy[,] Tuesday, January 17, 1899. [New York.]
        On this occasion Joseph Howard, Jr. delivered a toast
    to "Benjamin Franklin, the Printer."

2   ANON. "Benjamin Franklin." Inland Printer 24, no. 1
    (October):67.
        Franklin is an example of a man who recognized that his
    first calling in life was to the trade of printing. Such a
    recognition of what one must do promotes success.

3   ANON. "Benjamin Franklin[,] 1706-1790." In Travailleurs et
    hommes utiles. Limoges: Ardant et cie, pp. 279-316.
        A biography that makes particular mention of Franklin's
    wide range of abilities and, to substantiate this point,
    discusses in some detail many of his ideas and accomplish-
    ments. The author also notes that Franklin loved France in
    addition to his native country.

4   ANON. "Book Reviewing With a Stiletto. Concerning the
    Daughter of Benjamin Franklin." Lippincott's Monthly
    Magazine 63 (May):712-20.
        Not only attacks the assertion of Sydney George Fisher,
    in The True Benjamin Franklin (1898.10), that Franklin had
    fathered an illegitimate daughter, but marshalls evidence
    to refute the claim as "nonsense." Franklin had, on occa-
    sion, referred to young ladies to whom he felt close as
    daughter; however, as the reviewer pointed out, this was
    just a fatherly expression and should not be construed as
    evidence of wrongdoing.

5   ANON. Ceremonies Attending the Unveiling of the Statue of
    Benjamin Franklin[,] June 14, 1899[.] Presented to the
    City of Philadelphia by Mr. Justus C. Strawbridge.
    Philadelphia: Lane & Scott, 58 pp.
        This commemorative volume includes addresses (cited
    separately) by Charles C. Harrison, James M. Beck, Josiah
    Quincy, Charles Emory Smith, and Samuel H. Ashbridge. An
    introduction describes the ceremonies.

1899

6   ANON. "Memoirs of John Ross, Merchant of Philadelphia."
    Pennsylvania Magazine of History and Biography 23, no. 1:
    77-85.
        A granddaughter of Ross offers anecdotes concerning him
    and Franklin. During the Revolution Ross feared financial
    ruin because of the Government's failure to pay him £20,000
    for goods it purchased from him. He repeatedly asked
    Franklin for the money, but Franklin, in Paris, had none
    for this purpose. He did, however, try to see to it that
    Ross was repaid. Eventually Franklin became irritated with
    the pleas. Another anecdote tells of the time that Franklin
    gave a letter of introduction to Robert Fulton, then a poor
    young man, and sent him to Ross, hoping that the merchant
    would help him with employment.

7   ANON. "'A Note for Mr. Franklin.'" Pennsylvania Magazine of
    History and Biography 22, no. 4:458-61.
        Franklin was quite well known in France for his achieve-
    ments; nevertheless, a contemporary of his offered advice
    on how Franklin could most readily win French support for
    the American Revolution.

8   ARNOLD, HOWARD PAYSON. Historic Side-Lights. New York:
    Harper & Brothers, 330 pp.
        Franklin is the center of this loosely connected book.
    Arnold relates what is now generally known information,
    often of a very trivial nature, on Franklin as a writer,
    scientist, patriot, and statesman. Also discusses
    Franklin's reputation after 1790.

9   ASHBRIDGE, SAMUEL H. "Address." In Ceremonies Attending the
    Unveiling of the Statue of Benjamin Franklin[,] June 14,
    1899[.] Presented to the City of Philadelphia by Mr.
    Justus C. Strawbridge. Philadelphia: Lane & Scott,
    pp. 56-58.
        Franklin's "career through life was typical of the push
    and energy of American youth" and their self-reliance.

10 BACHE, RICHARD MEADE. "Franklin's Ceremonial Coat."
    Pennsylvania Magazine of History and Biography 23, no. 4:
    444-52.
        Franklin wore a red velvet suit when he was assaulted
    by Wedderburn in the cockpit. He wore the same suit again
    not at the peace treaty, as has often been asserted, but at
    the treaty of commerce and alliance between the United
    States and France.

11 BARDEEN, C[HARLES] W[ILLIAM]. "January 17[,] Benjamin
    Franklin." In Authors' Birthdays. Standard Teachers
    Library. 3d ser. Syracuse, N.Y.: C.W. Bardeen, Publisher,
    pp. 11-39.
       Franklin was in many ways a great representative of the
    self-made man. Circumstances forced him to educate him-
    self; nevertheless, he became justly admired for his learn-
    ing. As the Autobiography tells us, he also had to teach
    himself how to write, yet Franklin's memoirs is one of the
    best such works and one of the most enduring in the English
    language. Outstanding in a number of areas, he was most
    great as a human being.

12 BECK, JAMES M[ONTGOMERY]. "Address." In Ceremonies Attending
    the Unveiling of the Statue of Benjamin Franklin[,] June 14,
    1899[.] Presented to the City of Philadelphia by Mr.
    Justus C. Strawbridge. Philadelphia: Lane & Scott,
    pp. 17-48.
       The major speech of the ceremony, it is a very full
    tribute to Franklin's greatness and achievements. Accord-
    ing to Beck, Franklin had the greatest intellect of any
    American, yet he is the "most typical" of all Americans.
    He "typifies, as none other, that product of our institu-
    tions, the self-made man. He was incarnate democracy,"
    a simple "man of the people" without class prejudices.
    Philadelphia, however, has been slow in appreciating him
    and in honoring his memory.

13 BROOKS, ELBRIDGE S[TREETER]. "The Story of Benjamin Franklin,
    of Philadelphia, Called by All Europe 'Le Grand Franklin.'"
    In Historic Americans[:] Sketches of the Lives and Char-
    acters of Certain Famous Americans Held Most in Reverence
    by the Boys and Girls of America, for Whom Their Stories
    Are Here Told. New York: Thomas Y. Crowell & Co.,
    pp. 18-33.
       Picks up Franklin's life from the kite experiment,
    summarizes his achievements, and calls him the greatest
    of all Americans and the architect of American democracy.

14 CAFFIN, CHARLES H., ed. "The American Survey: John J. Boyle's
    Statue of Benjamin Franklin." Artist (April):lvi-lviii.
       Boyle sculpted the statue that Strawbridge presented as
    a gift to the people of Philadelphia. The statue captures
    Franklin's qualities--dignity, homeliness, and individuality.

15 EDMUNDS, CHARLES K. "The Character of Benjamin Franklin."
    Self Culture 8, no. 5 (January):563-68.

1899

> Franklin was a self-made man who did more than
> Washington or anyone else to create the United States
> of America. While Franklin was somewhat deficient in
> spirituality, and though he was not Christian, he was
> nevertheless a great man and great American.

16   FORD, PAUL LEICESTER. "Franklin's 'Anecdote.'" Nation 68
     no. 1754 (9 February):108.
         Ford identifies as Franklin's "The Intended Speech for
     the Opening of the First Session of Parliament viz. Nov.
     29, 1774."

*17   _____. "The Humorist." In The Many-Sided Franklin. New
     York: Century Co., pp. 388-417.
         Source: NUC. While Franklin had displayed his wit and
     humor in the Silence Dogood essays which he wrote in Boston
     while an apprentice on his brother's New England Courant,
     he can be said to have launched American humor with Poor
     Richard's Almanack. And it should be pointed out that
     Franklin could do more than joke at the expense of others;
     he could just as readily enjoy a good joke on himself.

*18   _____. "Social Life." In The Many-Sided Franklin. New
     York: Century Co., pp. 467-509.
         Source: NUC. People were attracted to Franklin, and
     he sincerely enjoyed the company of others of diverse
     backgrounds and opinions. At once simple and wise in the
     ways of the world, Franklin was at home in colonial America,
     Great Britain, and in France where, during the tense days
     of the American Revolution, he captivated the French people
     and won support for his country.

19   GRANDGENT, C[HARLES] H. "From Franklin to Lowell[:] A Century
     of New England Pronunciation." Publications of the Modern
     Language Association 14, no. 2:207-39.
         This study of dialect considers changes in New England
     pronunciation in the century between the death of Franklin
     and the death of Lowell. A number of assertions are made
     concerning the way in which Franklin pronounced words,
     judging from his time and place.

20   HARRISON, CHARLES C. "Address." In Ceremonies Attending the
     Unveiling of the Statue of Benjamin Franklin[,] June 14,
     1899[.] Presented to the City of Philadelphia by
     Mr. Justus C. Strawbridge. Philadelphia: Lane & Scott,
     pp. 15-17.
         The institutions and philosophical society Franklin
     founded endure, just as his spirit endures.

1899

21 HENKELS, STAN[ISLAUS] V[INCENT], firm. American History[.] Genealogies, Early Imprints, American Newspapers and Historical Pamphlets[.] Duplicates From the Historical Society of Pennsylvania[,] Tuesday and Wednesday, Dec. 19 and 20, 1899. Catalogue No. 835. Philadelphia: [Stan. V. Henkels], passim.
Among the items for sale were Condorcet's eulogy on Franklin, delivered 13 November 1790, before the Academy of Science, various Franklin German imprints, and copies of his works.

22 PERRINE, WILLIAM. "Franklin As an Editor." Saturday Evening Post 171, no. 29 (14 January):460-61.
Praises Franklin as an editor and writer for the liveliness and integrity of the Pennsylvania Gazette. Also asserts that the Post is descended from the Gazette.

23 QUINCY, JOSIAH. "Address." In Ceremonies Attending the Unveiling of the Statue of Benjamin Franklin[,] June 14, 1899[.] Presented to the City of Philadelphia by Mr. Justus C. Strawbridge. Philadelphia: Lane & Scott, pp. 49-50.
Quincy, the Mayor of Boston, argues that Boston and Philadelphia can lay equal claims to Franklin.

24 SACHSE, JULIUS F[RIEDRICH]. "The First German Newspaper Published in America." Pennsylvania German Society 10 (20 October):41-46.
Franklin's Philadelphische Zeitung began publication on 10 June 1732. While Franklin thought that the Germans of Philadelphia and Germantown needed a newspaper in their own language, they failed to support the venture, and it apparently ended with the second issue.

25 SMITH, CHARLES EMORY. "Address." In Ceremonies Attending the Unveiling of the Statue of Benjamin Franklin[,] June 14, 1899[.] Presented to the City of Philadelphia by Mr. Justus C. Strawbridge. Philadelphia: Lane & Scott, pp. 53-55.
Franklin was a citizen of the world, but he has a special meaning for Philadelphians.

26 UPHAM, A.E. "Franklin As an Inventor." Outline, no. 44, pp. [1]-4.
Surveys Franklin's accomplishments as an inventor and discoverer.

1899

27 _____. Talks About Our Country [New York]: 4 pp.
The author was an instructor, apparently in the New York
public school system, and addressed an audience on Sunday,
22 January, on Franklin "as a business man and citizen."
Franklin the prudential go-getter and public spirited man
are stressed in this presentation. (It seems that Upham
had given a talk on Franklin's youth the first week in
January. His "last talk" on Franklin's achievements as an
inventor is 1899.26.)

19--

1 ANON. The Life of Benjamin Franklin Told in Glass Murals in
the Lobby of the Benjamin Franklin Hotel, Philadelphia,
Penna. Philadelphia.
The murals depict four aspects of Franklin's life: his
career as a printer; his achievements as a humanitarian;
his scientific work; and his diplomatic accomplishments.

2 ARMINE, C. Franklin. [Chicago? printed for the Franklin
Glass & Mirror Co.]
Errors mar this booklet sketching Franklin's career and
pointing out that in spite of his many great abilities, he
remained a plain, simple man.

3 [BEAN, HAROLD J.] There Before My Desk. . . . . N.p.
Franklin is used to puff the Saturday Evening Post.

4 BERÈS, PIERRE, firm. Livres rares[,] autographes. New York:
Pierre Berès.
Franklin items for sale cover his private life as well
as his work in science, politics, and diplomacy.

5 CASEY, ROBERT E. The Declaration of Independence[:] Illustrated Story of Its Adoption, With the Biographies and Portraits of the Signers and of the Secretary of the
Congress. . . . New York: Illustrated Publishers, p. 51.
A brief sketch of Franklin's career. Near the end of
the book are excerpts from the Autobiography and
illustrations.

6 GREENLEE, ROBERT. B. Franklin, Printer. Ames, Iowa: Old
Colony Press.
Franklin was not a great printer; however, he loved his
trade and all his life considered himself a printer.

1900

190-

1 ANON. Benjamin Franklin. Vidas de hombres celebres. Colección infantil. 2d ser., no. 11, Barcelona: Ramon Sopena, 15 pp.
A biography of Franklin for children. The author emphasizes Franklin's Poor Richard qualities and shows how these helped his subject lead a remarkably useful and successful life.

2 GODDARD, DWIGHT. A Short Story of Benj. Franklin. Worcester, Mass.: Wyman & Gordon, 7 pp.
Franklin's other outstanding achievements have overshadowed his skill as an inventor, yet he was an excellent one. Goddard recounts Franklin's contributions as an inventor. (Reprinted in Goddard's Eminent Engineers (New York: Hill Publishing Co., 1905), pp. 9-16. This work is more easily available than A Short Story of Benj. Franklin.)

3 VENARD, HENRI. "Benjamin Franklin, homme d'état Américain (1706-1790)." In Les contemporains. [Paris: P. Feron-Vrau], pp. [1]-16.
About half this account of Franklin's career and character deals with his life between 1770 and 1790, especially with his role in France. Franklin is praised as a great moralist, liberator, a friend to mankind, and as an example for the young to follow.

1900

1 ADAMINA, J. Benjamin Franklin[:] ou un homme qui réussi et comment il s'y est pris pour réussir. Lausanne: George Bredel & Cie, 103 pp.
An account of Franklin's character, his criteria for successful living, and his own successful life. There are a number of misprintings and numerous errors in this book.

2 ANON. "Dr. Franklin's Parable Against Persecution." William and Mary Quarterly 8, no. 4 (April):231-36.
Franklin lifted his parable from some source, probably a translation of Boostan by the eminent Persian poet, Saadi.

3 ANON. "The First German Newspaper Published in America." Pennsylvania Magazine of History and Biography 24, no. 3: 306-7.

1900

While it is true that Franklin's Philadelphische
Zeitung was discontinued in 1732 after only a few numbers,
it is important historically because of its position as the
first German newspaper published in the colonies.

4   ANON. "Franklin, Benjamin." In Lamb's Biographical Dictionary
    of the United States. Edited by John Howard Brown. Vol. 3.
    Boston: James H. Lamb Co., pp. 174-78.
        Biography noting Franklin's many services to his country
    and to mankind. (There is a list of contributors at the
    beginning of the first volume, and it is possible, but by
    no means certain, that the author of this sketch is either
    Francis Newton Thorpe or John McGovern.)

5   BACHE, RICHARD MEADE. "The Two Rival Autobiographies of
    Franklin." Pennsylvania Magazine of History and Biography
    24:195-99.
        In exchanging his copy of the Autobiography for that
    owned by Madame Veillard, Temple was not trying to suppress
    information but rather was exposing his incompetence to
    carry out his editorial tasks. The version Temple owned
    originally did contain some material not found in the
    Veillard manuscript. It would seem, then, that the most
    authentic text of the memoirs would be Temple's published
    version with the addition of the supplementary matter of
    the Veillard version. This was the one published by
    Bigelow for the first time.

6   CLARK, THOMAS ARKLE. "Benjamin Franklin, 1706-1790." In
    Benjamin Franklin[:] Biography and Selections From His
    Writings[,] Written Especially for School Reading.
    Taylorville, Ill.: C.M. Parker, Publisher, pp. 347-62.
        Franklin was certainly "a great and noted man, but he
    was simple and unostentatious as a child, and his writings
    reveal his character."

7   GRIFFIN, APPLETON P[RENTISS]. "Franklin's Daughter, Mrs. John
    Foxcroft." In Publications of the Colonial Society of
    Massachusetts. Vol. 3. Transactions, 1895-1897. Boston:
    Published by the Society, pp. 267-71.
        Because of a very literal reading of the Franklin-
    Foxcroft letters, Griffin erroneously concludes that Mary
    Osgood Foxcroft was really Franklin's daughter. Franklin
    had referred to her, as he affectionately did to other
    young ladies, by the name of "Daughter." Griffin's paper
    was read in April 1896.

1900

8 HENKELS, STAN[ISLAUS] V[INCENT], firm. The Library of Chas. B. Rogers, Esq . . . .[,] Bibliotheca Americana et Curiosa. . . . Catalogue No. 848. Philadelphia: [Stan. V. Henkels], passim.
Offers for sale Franklin imprints and other items related to him.

9 _____. Rare Broadsides, Early Imprints[,] Colonial Laws and Other Interesting Items[,] Many from Benjamin Franklin's Own Papers[,] to Be Sold Friday and Saturday, April 27 and 28, 1900. Philadelphia: [Stan. V. Henkels].
Only a few of the items relate directly to Franklin.

10 LAMAS, G. EDUARDO. "Benjamin Franklin." Reviste de Chile 5 [no. 60? (November?)]:268-72.
Franklin knew well that one had to show his faith by his works, and that prayer should give one the grace to understand his own condition. Moreover, when one does understand his own condition, he realizes that the most fundamental drive of human beings is to be free. Lamas is carefully but obviously calling on his countrymen to emulate the life of Franklin and lead lives of useful activity rather than continuing to practice servile obedience to established theological views ("una resignacion evanjélica incomparable").

11 _____. "Benjamin Franklin." Reviste de Chile 5, no. 59 [October]:244-48.
In reviewing a translation of the Autobiography, Lamas praises Franklin as one of the founders of America who, in fact, changed the vision of men in his country. Franklin and the other nation builders, from the beginning of American colonization of the New World on, sought religious liberty rather than wealth. Their idealism distinguishes them from those men who remained in Europe. The earliest American settlers planted the seeds of Puritanism that are realized in Franklin, the moralist. Of course, there were changes in that character, and Franklin is the pragmatic, very human philosopher in action. Lamas's point is clearly that his Chilean readers can do what the North Americans have done: they can rise through their earnest endeavors. First, however, they must devote themselves, like Franklin, to a life of useful activity in which rewards are sought in human rather than in traditional religious terms that confuse virtue with the suppression of legitimate human needs and desires. Franklin's life shows unmistakably that one does not have to live in this way to be good.

1900

12   MONTGOMERY, THOMAS HARRISON. "Benjamin Franklin." In A His-
     tory of the University of Pennsylvania From Its Foundation
     to A.D. 1770. Philadelphia: George W. Jacobs, pp. 73-82.
        A biographical sketch focusing on Franklin's accomplish-
     ments in science.

13   _____. A History of the University of Pennsylvania from Its
     Foundation to A.D. 1770. Philadelphia: George W. Jacobs,
     pp. [11]-40.
        A very detailed history of the university and of
     Franklin's relationship with it. Montgomery also makes
     extensive use of primary source material, much of which
     is reproduced, and so the work is virtually a source book.
     Nevertheless, he ignores the religious-political tensions
     within the school and asserts that the hostility between
     Franklin and Provost Smith had no affect on the institution.

14   MORE, PAUL ELMER. Benjamin Franklin. Riverside Biographical
     Series, no. 3. Boston: Houghton Mifflin Co., 139 pp.
        Franklin's remarkably versatile mind joined with circum-
     stances to prevent him from devoting his energies to any
     one field, yet he became outstanding in many. If he lacks
     "the fervid insight of Jonathan Edwards, who was his only
     intellectual equal in the colonies, or the serene faith of
     an Emerson," he was nevertheless a truly great man. "In
     his shrewdness, versatility, self-reliance, wit, as also
     in his lack of the deeper reverence and imagination, he,
     I think, more than any other man who has yet lived, repre-
     sents the full American character." These points and others
     dealing with Franklin's benevolence, equable temper, and
     ability to bring together opposing sides are emphasized in
     More's biography.

15   SONNECK, O.G. "Benjamin Franklin's Relation to Music."
     Music (Chicago) 19:1-14.
        Contends that musical taste in the colonies was more
     sophisticated than is commonly thought. In fact Franklin,
     who was interested in the art, could have learned about
     European music in Philadelphia. That Franklin built his
     armonica attests to his genuine and continuing interest
     in music.

16   SWIFT, LINDSAY. "Our Literary Diplomats: Benjamin Franklin."
     Book Buyer 20, no. 4 (May):[285]-87.
        The qualities that made Franklin a great man--his good
     sense, cosmopolitanism and humor--made him a successful
     diplomat in France.

17 TOURTOURAT, CH[ARLES]. Benjamin Franklin et la médecine à la
    fin du XVIIIᵉ siècle. Paris: Société de editions
    scientifiques.
      A survey of Franklin's lifelong interest in medical
    science and health care. Tourtourat makes the point that
    Franklin's interest was genuine, and his concern with the
    care patients received was a manifestation of his advanced
    mind and general sympathy for his fellows.

18 WENDELL, BARRETT. "Benjamin Franklin." In A Literary History
    of America. The Library of Literary History. New York:
    Charles Scribner's Sons, pp. [92]-103.
      "The contemporary of Edwards who best shows what Amer-
    ican human nature had become, is Benjamin Franklin." The
    great Franklin, that is, the diplomat, is not Wendell's
    concern. He is rather here interested in "the shrewd
    native American whose first fifty years were spent in
    preparation for his world-wide career." Franklin is
    treated as an archetypal Yankee who tested all theories--
    religious as well as secular--for their everyday usefulness.
    His is the American success story of one's rise in life
    through his own abilities and exertions.

19 WHARTON, ANNE HOLLINGSWORTH. "The American Philosophical
    Society." In Through Colonial Doorways. Philadelphia:
    J.B. Lippincott Co., pp. 97-146.
      This chapter tells the familiar story of Franklin's
    relationship with the American Philosophical Society and
    his reasons for desiring such an organization. See 1893.22.

                              1901

1   ANON. "Franklin Birthday Celebrations." Inland Printer 26,
    no. 5 (February):828-30.
      Reports on tributes to Franklin in Chicago, New Haven,
    Buffalo, and St. Louis.

2   ANON. [On the Franklin Fund.] Chautauquan 32, no. 5
    (February):469-70.
      Commends Franklin for his generosity and foresight in
    establishing the funds for young married mechanics.

3   BRANSCOMBE, ARTHUR. "The Home of the Franklins." In The
    Cradle of the Washingtons & the Home of the Franklins.
    London: Anglo-American Exchange (Publishing Department),
    pp. [30]-43.
      On Ecton and Franklin's English ancestors.

1901

4   CASTLE, HENRY ANSON. Address at Annual Banquet of Minnesota
     Commandery Military Order of the Loyal Legion, Minneapolis,
     Minnesota, February 12, 1901. Typical Americans. N.p.,
     23 pp.
          From Franklin on, the typical American has always been
     capable of leading America.

5   DUVAL, A[LEXANDRE]. "Marat et Franklin." Chronique médicale
     8, no. 2 (15 January):53-54.
          Franklin and the young Marat were interested in many of
     the same areas of science, including electricity and
     medicine.

6   HURWITZ, SHMARYA LOEB. Lebensbeschreibung von Benjamin
     Franklin und die bafryying von Amerika [Benjamin Franklin:
     his life and the liberation of America]. Warsaw: Progress
     Publishing Co., 64 pp.
          Based on secondary sources and the memoirs, this book
     treats Franklin as the diligent, resourceful wise man whose
     rise in life offers hope for people throughout the world
     and shows the value of Franklin's Poor Richard qualities.
     (The book is clearly intended to provide, first of all,
     appropriate values for people intending to emigrate to
     the United States and, second, to show those who were re-
     maining in Eastern Europe that one could succeed almost
     anywhere if he were truly hard working, honest, and frugal.
     Hurwitz also uses Franklin as proof that an individual can
     create significant political and social change, if he is
     determined to do so. This theme, however, is necessarily
     muted.) In Yiddish.

7   ROSENGARTEN, J[OSEPH] G[EORGE]. "Franklin's Bagatelles."
     Proceedings of the American Philosophical Society 40,
     no. 166:87-135.
          Reprinted here are a few bagatelles and some correspond-
     ence concerning them. Rosengarten's fifteen-page discussion
     of the pieces printed at Passy includes a useful summary of
     scholarship on them, and he claims that the bagatelles
     "were no inconsidered trifles."

8   SPARKS, EDWIN ERLE. "Formative Incidents in American
     Diplomacy." Chautauquan 34, no. 2 (November):[139]-55.
          Deals with Franklin's diplomacy in France and his rela-
     tionships with Deane, Adams, Lee, Laurens, and others.

9   TRENT, WILLIAM P[ETERFIELD], and WELLS, BENJAMIN, eds.
     "Benjamin Franklin." In Colonial Prose and Poetry: The
     Growth of the National Spirit[,] 1710-1775. Vol. 1.
     New York: Thomas Y. Crowell & Co.[,] Publishers, pp. 190-92.

These pages, which offer a brief survey of Franklin as
a writer and call him "thoroughly American, and an ideal
citizen," constitute a preface to the selection of
Franklin's writings which follows. The editors do assert,
however, that Franklin is less a man of his nation than of
his "century."

10 WALZ, JOHN A. "The American Revolution and German Literature."
    Modern Language Notes 16, no. 6 (June):336-51; no. 7
    (November):411-18; no. 8 (December):[449]-62.
    Focuses on how Franklin and Washington were perceived
    by Germans. Franklin was highly regarded by many Germans;
    however, those who were seriously troubled by the defeat of
    England, were hard on "'Den alten Franklin.'" The final
    section of the history does not deal directly with Franklin.

11 WILSON, WOODROW. Introduction to The Autobiography of
    Benjamin Franklin. New York: Century Co., pp. v-xix.
    Franklin's life and writings express the American char-
    acter. Yet though he had literary gifts, his writing is
    of "the ordinary world," lacking any note of distinction.
    In this lack he is also typically American, for American
    letters reveal our necessary preoccupation with settling
    the continent and with business.

1902

1 ANON. "Franklin Celebrations." Inland Printer 20, no. 5
   (February):764-68.
   Franklin honored at celebrations in Chicago, Boston,
   New York, New Haven, Atlanta, St. Louis, and Dayton.

2 ANON. Reply to the Toast at the Dinner Given April 4, 1902,
   Upon the One Hundred and Fiftieth Anniversary of the Amer-
   ican Philosophical Society[.] To the Memory of Our Founder.
   [Philadelphia? American Philosophical Society?]
   It is almost impossible to praise Franklin adequately,
   so remarkable was he. (This work was presented to Yale
   University by Sydney George Fisher, who may have been the
   author.)

3 ANON. Ye Merrie Songs of ye Disciples of Benjamin Franklin[,]
   Jan 17[,] MCMII[.] N.Y. Typothetae[,] Savoy Hotel. [New
   York], 11 pp. FCL.
   Included in the entertainment were a toast to Franklin
   by Theodore Low Devinne and a general toast by Paul L. Ford.

1902

4   BALDWIN, ERNEST H.   "Joseph Galloway, the Loyalist Politician."
    Pennsylvania Magazine of History and Biography 26, no. 2:
    161-90; no. 3:289-321; no. 4:417-42.
        Baldwin stresses the importance of Galloway and says
    that while Franklin was in England, Galloway assumed con-
    trol of the Quaker or popular party in Pennsylvania. Though
    the two men were close allies, Franklin was no longer the
    leader of the Assembly; Galloway was. When Franklin went
    to England to present the petition that would take Pennsyl-
    vania away from the proprietor and place it under the con-
    trol of the Crown, Galloway again worked with Franklin and
    urged him to press the matter. Franklin thought Galloway's
    services to the province so valuable that he encouraged him
    to stay on after Galloway wanted to retire because of polit-
    ical disappointments. Franklin continued to respect and
    defend Galloway's character even after politics had placed
    them in opposite camps.

5   BOSTON. History of the Franklin Fund. Boston: Municipal
    Printing Office.
        The management of the Fund caused litigation, contrary
    to Franklin's intentions. Especially ironic is that the
    litigation was initiated by his descendants.

6   BUTLER, JAMES D. "Frankliniana." Notes and Queries, 9th ser.
    10 (25 October):329.
        N.E.D. says that the phrase "To have axes to grind"
    comes from a story by Franklin. Asks what story. Also
    asks where he can find the source of the anecdote about
    the young Franklin asking his father to bless the entire
    barrel of pork at one time instead of saying grace at each
    meal.

7   CLOYD, DAVID EXCELMONS. Benjamin Franklin and Education. His
    Ideal of Life and His System of Education for the Realiza-
    tion of That Ideal. Boston: D.C. Heath & Co., 104 pp.
        Franklin worked for an education that would create
    virtuous and useful citizens, practical men of affairs
    capable of improving life in America. He also favored
    practical education for women so that, if necessary, they
    could be self-supporting. Franklin's educational ideal,
    however, was also directed at turning out humane and toler-
    ant people who would achieve unity while respecting diver-
    sity. Though in his own life he fell considerably short
    of perfection, he did leave us a vivid picture of the ideal
    education and the kind of citizens it should fashion.

1902

8   FLEISCHER, CHARLES. "The Common Sense of Franklin and the
      Vision of Jefferson." In The Free Religious Associaton[:]
      Proceedings at the Thirty-Fifth Annual Meeting Held in
      Boston, Mass.[,] Thursday and Saturday[,] May 29 and 31[,]
      1902. Boston: Free Religious Association, pp. 57-64.
          Draws parallels "between the faith and teachings of
      Isaiah, Malachi, and Jesus on the one hand and the vision
      of Jefferson and the common sense of Franklin on the other."
      More specifically, Franklin's common sense and Jefferson's
      vision led them to the position of the Orientals: the love
      and encouragement of peace.

9   FORD, WORTHINGTON CHAUNCEY. "Franklin's Advice to a Young
      Tradesmen. Two Unique Impressions." Bibliographer 1,
      no. 3 (March):[89]-96.
          A lengthy bibliographical discussion, quite speculative,
      in which Ford suggests that Franklin's "Necessary Hints to
      Those Who Would Be Rich" was published by Daniel Humphreys
      in 1784. Humphreys had published his "Advice" in his re-
      vived Pennsylvania Mercury and Universal Advertiser. He
      included Franklin's "Necessary Hints" to fill up the sheet
      on which the "Advice" appears. Ford considers another edi-
      tion of Franklin's "Advice," which is perhaps of an even
      earlier date than the one by Humphreys. Internal evidence
      seems to indicate that the piece was printed by Benjamin
      Mecom some time after he left Antigua and returned to
      Boston. Ford's opinion is that it was printed by Mecom
      between 1758 and 1762.

10   HAMM, MARGHERITA ARLINA. "Benjamin Franklin." In Builders of
      the Republic[:] Some Great Americans Who Have Aided in the
      Making of the Nation. New York: James Pott & Co.,
      pp. 19-35.
          Franklin is the chief representative "of Anglo-Saxon
      genius." While he was far broader and more international
      than the other founding fathers, he was also more typically
      American.

11   HENKELS, STAN[ISLAUS] V[INCENT], firm. "Franklin Almanacs
      and Imprints." In Rare Americana[.] Original Manuscript
      Laws of Pennsylvania, and Other Papers From the Foundation
      of the Government in 1682 to 1774. . . . Catalogue No. 886.
      Philadelphia: [Stan. V. Henkels], pp. 49-50.
          Seven Franklin items for sale, including copies of Poor
      Richard's Almanack for 1748, 1749, and 1750.

12   KOHUT, GEORGE ALEXANDER. "Abraham's Lesson in Tolerance."
      Jewish Quarterly Review, o.s. 15 (October):104-11.

1902

> Kohut asserts that the source of Franklin's "Parable
> Against Persecution" is Jeremy Taylor's version of the
> story. The actual origin of the piece, though, is Persian
> and can be traced back to the Būstān of Sa'dī, who lived
> approximately from 1184 to 1291.

13 LAWTON, WILLIAM CRANSTON. "Benjamin Franklin." In Introduction to the Study of American Literature. New York:
Globe School Book Co., pp. 50-55.
Franklin lacked idealism, but he was personally charming,
vigorous, sincere, and useful, qualities that are all revealed in his writings.

14 LEES, FREDERIC [ARNOLD]. "The Parisian Suburb of Passy. Its
Architecture in the Days of Franklin." Architectural
Record 12, no. 7 (December):[669]-83.
Describes Franklin's Passy residence, the Hôtel de
Valentinois and the neighborhood, both of which he liked.

15 OBERHOLTZER, ELLIS PAXSON. "Franklin's Philosophical Society."
Popular Science Monthly 60, no. 5 (March):430-37.
On Franklin's contribution in founding the American
Philosophical Society, which is a most valuable organization.

16 ROSENGARTEN, JOSEPH G[EORGE]. "The Gainsborough Franklin."
Alumni Register 6, no. 6 (March):294-99.
The college graduating class of 1852 presented the portrait to the University of Pennsylvania. The remembrance
of this occasion provides Rosengarten the opportunity of
tracing Franklin's relationship with the university. He
asserts that the "great development of the University has
largely followed the lines laid down by Franklin" in his
plans for it as well as for the Library Company of Philadelphia and The American Philosophical Society. (Journal
title later is changed to The General Magazine and Historical Chronicle.)

17 [ROSENGARTEN, JOSEPH GEORGE.] Reply to the Toast at the Dinner Given April 4, 1902, Upon the One Hundred and Fiftieth
Anniversary of the American Philosophical Society[.] To
the Memory of Our Founder. [Philadelphia? American
Philosophical Society?]
First the toastmaster praised Franklin's versatility
and curiosity, and then, apparently, Rosengarten replied.

1903

1 ABERNETHY, JULIAN W. "Benjamin Franklin[:] 1706-1790."
   In American Literature. New York: Maynard, Merrill & Co.,
   pp. 67-79.
   Franklin's life epitomizes "Americanism throughout its
   progress from colonialism to nationality." He wrote well
   and interestingly, but he was essentially a man of affairs,
   not a literary figure.

2 ADAM, G[RAEME] MERCER. "Benjamin Franklin (1706-1790)." In
   Benjamin Franklin[.] A Character Sketch, by Frank Strong.
   Milwaukee: H.G. Campbell Publishing Co., pp. [103]-24.
   This later edition of Strong's biography includes sup-
   plementary material of which Adam's essay is one piece.
   Adam borrows heavily from Jeffrey, Sparks, and Bigelow
   in evaluating Franklin's career and determining his beliefs,
   powers, and limitations.

3 ANON. "Benjamin Franklin." In Stories of Great Men. Young
   Folks Library of American Literature. New York: Educa-
   tional Publishing Co., pp. 133-57.
   Even as a youngster, Franklin embodied the virtues of
   Poor Richard.

4 ANON. "Benjamin Franklin's Birthday Commemorated." Old Penn
   Weekly Review of the University of Pennsylvania 1, no. 9
   (10 January):3.
   S. Weir Mitchell gave a dinner for authors in honor of
   Franklin's birthday.

5 ANON. "The Franklin Fund." Atlantic Monthly 91, no. 547
   (May):716-19.
   The spirit of Franklin returns to express its opinion
   on such matters as the use of the Franklin Fund, govern-
   mental borrowing, and modern inventions. Franklin approves
   or disapproves on the basis of common sense.

6 ANON. "The Franklin Papers in the Library of the American
   Philosophical Society." Popular Science Monthly 63
   (August):382-83.
   General description of the papers.

7 ANON. "Frankliniana." Notes and Queries, 9th ser. 11
   (3 January):16.
   Replies to Butler (1902.6) and points out that the
   phrase "To have axes to grind" is from Poor Richard's
   Almanack. Does not know for which year.

1903

8   ANON. "Where Even Franklin Failed." Charities 11, no. 23
    (5 December):520-21.
      In establishing funds for Boston and Philadelphia,
    Franklin failed to account adequately for changes in the
    value of money.

9   BRADLEY, ARTHUR GRANVILLE. "English Home of the Franklins."
    Nation 77, no. 1992 (3 September):187-88.
      At the time Josiah Franklin emigrated to America, the
    Franklin ancestral home was in the village of Ecton in
    Northamptonshire. Given the connection of the Ecton church
    with Franklin's family, Bradley asks Americans for contribu-
    tions toward its restoration.

10 CHOATE, JOSEPH HODGES. Benjamin Franklin, an Address Delivered
    in the Town Hall, Birmingham, on Friday, 23rd October, 1903.
    [Birmingham, Eng.:] printed by order of the Council of
    the Birmingham Midland Institute, for circulation among
    the Members of the Institute, 102 pp.
      Choate, American Minister in London, stresses Franklin's
    intense loyalty to Great Britain and his devotion to the
    imperial greatness of the Empire. It was with genuine re-
    luctance, Choate asserts, that Franklin became a revolu-
    tionary. (While Choate ignores the fact that Franklin's
    opinion toward England in particular changed radically by
    1775, he does offer a good summary of Franklin's political
    career.) The piece was reprinted in The Critic 48, no. 1
    (January 1906):51-67.

11 D. "Franklin's Oxford Degree." Nation 76, no. 1982 (25 June):
    514-15.
      In granting Franklin a D.C.L., the "dons" of Oxford
    insulted him by having him accompanied by a person of lower
    rank than the one who accompanied William Franklin, who was
    awarded a degree at the same ceremony.

12 DOLE, NATHAN HASKELL. Introduction to Autobiography of
    Benjamin Franklin. New York: Thomas Y. Crowell & Co.,
    pp. v-xxxix.
      Discusses Franklin's life, particularly the years not
    covered in the Autobiography, and says that Franklin "stands
    out as the typical American, good-natured, quick-witted, and
    successful in his rise from poverty and obscurity to wealth
    and station."

13 HENKELS, STAN[ISLAUS] V[INCENT], firm. The Robert Proud
    Papers[,] Letters, Manuscripts, Books and Newspapers. . . .
    Catalogue No. 893. Philadelphia: [Stan. V. Henkels],
    pp. 227-29.
      Mostly Poor Richard and other Franklin imprints for sale.

14   HIGGINSON, THOMAS WENTWORTH and BOYNTON, HENRY WALCOTT.
      "Benjamin Franklin." In A Reader's History of American
      Literature. Boston: Houghton Mifflin Co., pp. 59-65.
         It is unfortunate but true that Franklin lacked spirit-
      uality, the essence of creativity. Instead he had "the
      ability to state homely truths in such an effective form
      as to offer unimaginative minds a practical rule for liv-
      ing," which is utilitarianism.

15   LEWIS, ALFRED HENRY. "Great Days in Great Men's Lives."
      Everybody's Magazine 8, no. 2 (February):[135]-44.
         A fictionalized account of the signing of the peace
      treaty in 1783. Franklin is made to seem the wise and
      cosmopolitan man working between the arrogant and too
      bold Adams and the backward, almost useless Jay.

16   MITCHELL, S[ILAS] WEIR. Verses Read to the Franklin Inn Club
      on the Birthday of Franklin, January 6, O.S. [Philadel-
      phia: J.B. Lippincott & Co.], 6 pp.
         Verse tribute to Franklin, whose spirit welcomes the
      celebrants.

17   MURRAY, JAMES A.H. "Franklin's Oxford Degree--a Correction."
      Nation 77, no. 2003 (19 November):403.
         Oxford had been accused of trying to slight Franklin
      even while awarding him a D.C.L. (1903.11). This was not
      at all the case, as Murray proves.

18   ROSENGARTEN, J[OSEPH] G[EORGE]. "The American Philosophical
      Society, 1743-1903." Pennsylvania Magazine of History and
      Biography 27, no. 3:329-36.
         At the convention on the 160th anniversary of the Amer-
      ican Philosophical Society, Rosengarten pays tribute to its
      founder, Franklin, and calls for a "Franklin Memorial Hall"
      to be erected in time for the bicentennial of the philoso-
      pher's birth.

19   _____. "Franklin in Germany." Lippincott's Monthly Magazine
      71, no. 5 (January):128-34.
         In this survey of Franklin's trip to Germany with Sir
      John Pringle in the summer of 1766, Franklin made a number
      of friends among the faculty at Göttingen. Some of these
      men, as well as other Germans, were to be very favorably
      impressed by Franklin and later proved to be friends to
      American independence.

1903

20   _____. "The 'Franklin Papers' in the American Philosophical
        Society." Proceedings of the American Philosophical
        Society 42, no. 173 (April-May):165-70.
            Rosengarten offers a brief description of some of the
        Papers, praises the undertaking of Hays's Calendar, and
        says that more Franklin material should be published.

21   _____. "Some New Franklin Papers." Alumni Register 7, no. 10
        (July):498-503.
            Rosengarten describes in general the Franklin manu-
        scripts "recently added" to the library of the University
        of Pennsylvania and reprints a few of them. (Journal
        title later becomes General Magazine and Historical
        Chronicle.)

22   SMYTH, ALBERT H[ENRY]. Benjamin Franklin. [Philadelphia:
        American Philosophical Society], 15 pp.
            Summary focusing on Franklin's optimistic and philo-
        sophical nature and on his usefulness.

23   THORPE, FRANCIS NEWTON. "Franklin's Influence in American Edu-
        cation." Report of the Commissioner of Education for the
        Year 1902. 1, whole no. 329:91-190.
            The discussion is divided into five parts, which are as
        follows: 1. "The Artisan and the Art." Franklin was
        self-educated and therefore had to create his own successes
        based on his reading and other experiences. These led him
        to stress the humanitarian, practical and useful life, a
        view reflected in his plans for the academy and for the
        education of orphans. 2. "The Practice of the Art in a
        Democracy." If his junto was intended to educate America,
        Franklin himself, as an agent in England for Pennsylvania
        and other colonies, educated the English about America by
        using the press and by "exemplifying in his own character"
        what kind of man his country "could produce." His success
        can be measured by the general esteem in which he was held
        in Europe and in America and also by the fact that among
        his friends were many of the chief men of the age. 3. "The
        Law of Living." Franklin's conviction that each person
        could help educate and improve himself and be of value to
        his nation and to mankind led him to promote the general
        welfare. Whether we consider schools, his ideas on the
        importance of labor, science, politics, or nearly any area
        of his concern, we see that he is guided by a keen desire
        to be useful and to help others to be useful. It is unfor-
        tunate that he "was somewhat of a Philistine" and never
        recognized the human value of beauty. 4. "Three Inter-
        preters." Franklin, John Adams, and Jefferson had different

views of education. Franklin's emphasis on self-education
led him to think of education as a private and individual
enterprise. His influence on American education is therefore seen in terms of our having "the means of self-
education, books, business, factories, libraries, learned
societies, nature, and the human soul capable of making use
of these opportunities." From John Adams we receive the
modern tax supported public school educational system, and
Jefferson's contributions are the ideas that education must
be professional, that there should be technical schools and
universities. 5. "For the Sake of the Whole." Franklin's
ideas of individualism in education do not appear in important modern educational thought because thinking about
the nature of the State has changed. In 1776 the entire
nation had been organized to serve the individual. Since
then there has been a change in emphasis from the individual's rights to the welfare of the whole. Yet Franklin's
ideas of education led him to Plato's position that learning was for citizenship and not for the mere accumulation
of facts. Modern education also strives for this goal,
but it recognizes too that the safety of the individual
rests in the welfare of the democratic state.

24 TRENT, WILLIAM P[ETERFIELD]. "Later Colonial Prose (1701-
    1764)." In A History of American Literature. Short His-
    tories of the Literature of the World, no. 12. Edited by
    Edmund Gosse. London: William Heinemann, pp. 98-130.
        The most relevant section of this chapter consists of
    pages 122-30. Franklin's "practical learning, shrewd
    mother-wit, honesty, and patriotism" make him the embodi-
    ment of "'true Americanism'" and a continually influential
    character. Moreover, he represents the eighteenth century's
    love of reason, science, and humanitarianism "over poetry
    and faith." Franklin was great, and therefore what he did
    was great. The quality of his writing, especially his
    Autobiography, derives not from any unique literary merits
    but from his personal traits.

1904

1 ANON. Benjamin Franklin Expresses His Views on the Pending
   Campaign. New York: Allied Printing Trades Council,
   16 pp.
       A long verse propaganda piece in which "a bronze statue
   of Benjamin Franklin," is interviewed by a reporter and
   made to support Theodore Roosevelt's candidacy.

1904

2   ANON. "Franklin Bi-Centennial." <u>Old Penn Weekly Review of</u>
     <u>the University of Pennsylvania</u> 2, no. 13 (9 January):6.
        Pleased that Congress appropriated $350,000 to celebrate
     the 200th anniversary of Franklin's birth, but is disap-
     pointed Congress did not include the University of Pennsyl-
     vania in the celebration. Yet the University is largely
     responsible for this oversight, since "nowhere on campus"
     or in any hall is there "any fitting monument to commemorate
     [Franklin's] services."

3   ANON. "Franklin's Birthday To Be Celebrated by Franklin Inn
     Club." <u>Old Penn Weekly Review of the University of Pennsyl-</u>
     <u>vania</u> 2, no. 12 (2 January):3.
        The celebration included a dinner, toasts, and speeches
     commemorating Franklin.

4   BAER, GEORGE F[REDERICK]. <u>Response . . . to the Toast "The</u>
     <u>Memory of Benjamin Franklin" . . . at the Dinner of the</u>
     <u>American Philosophical Society[,] Hotel Philadelphia[,]</u>
     <u>Eighth of April 1904.</u> [Philadelphia: published for the
     Society], 6 pp.
        Franklin is the second greatest American and one of the
     chief men of all time.

5   BOSTON, TRUSTEES of the FRANKLIN FUND. <u>The Will of Benjamin</u>
     <u>Franklin and Proceedings of Managers and Courts Relating</u>
     <u>Thereto.</u> Boston: Municipal Printing Office, 59 pp.
        The Fund is, as Franklin had hoped, of continuing
     usefulness.

6   CHOATE, JOSEPH H[ODGES]. "Benjamin Franklin." <u>Working Men's</u>
     <u>College Journal</u> 8, no. 137 (April):[289]-98.
        Franklin was a working man all his life, at first for
     himself as well as for his fellow Philadelphians, but later
     largely for mankind. As a worker, Franklin remained inter-
     ested in working men all his life.

7   CLEMENS, WILLIAM MONTGOMERY. <u>Benjamin Franklin; a Biographical</u>
     <u>Sketch.</u> Akron, Ohio: Werner Co., 30 pp.
        Traces Franklin's career from his days in Boston to his
     final years and shows that his life was one of achievement.

8   CUSHING, HENRY K. "Notes Suggested by the Franklin-Heberden
     Pamphlet of 1759." <u>Johns Hopkins Hospital Bulletin</u> 15,
     no. 162 (September):1-16.
        Background of Franklin's <u>Some Account of the Success of</u>
     <u>Inoculation for the Small-Pox in England and America and of</u>
     <u>Heberden's Plain Instructions for Inoculation in the Small-</u>
     <u>Pox. . . .</u> The pieces are also reprinted.

1904

9 HAYS, I[SAAC] MINIS. The Chronology of Benjamin Franklin.
   Philadelphia: American Philosophical Society, 32 pp.
       Not merely a list of dates, for Hays provides extensive
   commentary, particularly on Franklin's political career.

10 HENKELS, STAN[ISLAUS] V[INCENT], firm. The Hampton L. Carson
    Collection of Engraved Portraits of Jefferson, Franklin,
    and Lafayette[.] Catalogue No. 906[,] Part 2. Philadel-
    phia: [Stan. V. Henkels], pp. 21-93.
        Lists more than 550 portraits of Franklin according to
    the type of likeness it is, such as the "Charles Willson
    Peale Type" and the "C.N. Cochin Type."

11 LEARNED, M[ARION] D[EXTER]. "Herder and America [part] 2.
    Herder and Franklin." German American Annals 6, no. 9
    (September):550-70.
        Herder knew of Franklin and his achievements in science,
    moral philosophy, and diplomacy before 1769. Hoping to
    establish in Germany a society like Franklin's junto,
    Herder translated Franklin's "Rules for a Club" and com-
    mented on the questions asked the junto at every meeting.
    So much did Herder admire Franklin that he called him "one
    of my favorites in this century," a man of goodness, "sound
    reason," activity, and unfailing good sense.

12 An OBSERVER, pseud. "Mr. Choate's Talk to Workingmen."
    Nation 78, no. 2020 (17 March):206-7.
        Corroborates Choate's praise of Franklin (1904.6). It is
    unfortunate that, beginning in the nineteenth century, Eng-
    lishmen failed to treat Franklin justly. In part because,
    like Carlyle, they have been guilty of "sentimentality,"
    they have accused Franklin and his century of moral coarse-
    ness. Franklin was often enough "prosaic" in his ideals,
    to be sure; however, he tried earnestly to live up to those
    ideals. Furthermore, Franklin accomplished and helped
    others to accomplish great things which we now take for
    granted. For example, he encouraged toleration and the
    splendid belief, to which his own life attests, that aver-
    age people can be virtuous, successful, and useful if they
    work hard.

13 PIDGIN, CHA[RLE]S FELTON. A Nation's Idol[.] A Romance of
    Franklin's Nine Years of Happiness at the Court of France.
    Philadelphia: Henry Altemus Co., 348 pp.
        This historical novel, while it does make unacknowledged
    use of the work of Franklin scholars and, it would seem of
    Franklin's papers, nevertheless ignores his true French
    social experiences and invents others that at times are
    not credible.

1904

14 ROSENGARTEN, J[OSEPH] G[EORGE]. "American History From German
    Archives[,] With Reference to the German Soldiers in the
    Revolution and Franklin's Visit to Germany." Proceedings
    of the Pennsylvania-German Society 13:1-93.
        The relevant section is chapter 7, pp. 50-61, which
    deals with Franklin's tour of Germany in the summer of
    1766. Franklin made influential friends there and they
    later helped to create support for the American cause in
    the Revolution.

15 SPARKS, EDWIN ERLE. "Benjamin Franklin, the Colonial Agent in
    England." In The Men Who Made the Nation. New York:
    Macmillan Co., pp. 1-46.
        During his last ten-year residence in England, Franklin
    tried earnestly to prevent the tragic breach between the
    two countries he loved, but his efforts proved futile. It
    was therefore a sad patriot who returned to America in 1775.
    Sparks also deals with Franklin's religious and racial views
    and the Paxton riots. Errors mar these latter discussions.

16 TROWBRIDGE, JOHN. "Two Early American Letters on Electricity."
    Nation 78, no. 2025 (21 April):303-9.
        Trowbridge introduces both a Franklin letter on elec-
    tricity to John Winthrop of Harvard and Winthrop's notes
    on electricity. The many-sidedness of Franklin's experi-
    ments in the field have yet to be fully appreciated.

17 UNITED STATES SENATE. Senate Bill 5691. (7 December.) 58th
    Congress, 3d Session.
        Senator Hale offered a bill to erect a monument to
    Franklin in Washington, D.C. "not to exceed one hundred
    thousand dollars."

18 WILLIAMS, SHERMAN. "Benjamin Franklin: Printer, Inventor,
    Scientist, Author, Politician, and Diplomat." In Some
    Successful Americans. Boston: Ginn & Co., pp. 173-94.
        Franklin's great public career reflects his personal
    qualities and the opportunities for success in America.

1905

1   ANON. "In Honor of Franklin's 200th Birthday." Publishers'
    Weekly 68, no. 1768 (16 December):1808.
        The Pennsylvania Society celebrated the occasion with
    speeches on various aspects of Franklin's career.

1905

2   ANON. The Life and Services of Benjamin Franklin With Some of
     the Proverbs of Poor Richard and a Catalogue of the Benjamin
     Franklin Pattern of Sterling Silver Tableware. Newburyport,
     Mass.: Towle Mfg. Co., 88 pp.
         An attractive book of Franklin odds and ends and a promo-
     tion for silverware and a chest of drawers.

3   ANON. "A Sculptor of American Primitive Life." Current
     Literature 39, no. 5 (November):507-8.
         Essentially on John J. Boyle's statue of Franklin.

4   ANON. "To the Memory of Franklin and His Disciples." Inland
     Printer 36, no. 3 (December):402.
         The United States should prepare for the celebration of
     the 200th anniversary of Franklin's birth, for his numerous
     achievements deserve tribute.

5   [AYER, N.W. & SON.] In the Land of Benjamin. [Philadelphia:
     N.W. Ayer & Son], 23 pp.
         This pamphlet tribute to Franklin, on Independence Day,
     1905, consists of an illustrated sketch of his life, espe-
     cially as a Philadelphian, a list which proves "Ben Franklin
     a Good Advertiser" and explains how self-advertising helped
     Franklin succeed, and finally a promotion for the advertis-
     ing agency of N.W. Ayer & Son of Philadelphia.

6   BOWEN, EDWIN W. "The Franklin Bi-centenary." South Atlantic
     Quarterly 4, no. 4 (October):[352]-64.
         Franklin was the "pioneer of American letters," but he
     did not at all care about literary fame. His chief work,
     and it is outstanding and popular, is the Autobiography;
     however, some of his best things appear in the almanacs.
     Franklin's weakness as an author is the same as his weak-
     ness of character. He lacked "singleness of purpose." As
     a writer he finished little, and in his career he had the
     unhappy "habit of shifting from one pursuit in life to
     another, and not sticking to any one pursuit very long."
     He therefore is a great man, but not of the first order.

7   HENKELS, STAN[ISLAUS] V[INCENT], firm. Catalogue No. 943[.]
     Books Relating to Benjamin Franklin Collected by the Hon.
     Samuel W. Pennypacker[,] Governor of Pennsylvania. 8
     Parts in 2 vols. [Philadelphia: Stan. V. Henkels.]
         Part 1, also known as The Extraordinary Library of the
     Hon. Samuel W. Pennypacker, lists for sale 500 items, which
     brought about $9,500.

1905

8   _____. "Franklin's Pennsylvania. Boards Uncut." In <u>Valuable</u>
     <u>Library of Rare and Scarce American History Belonging to</u>
     <u>a Well-Known Philadelphia Collector</u>[.] To Be Sold Tuesday
     and Wednesday, February 28 and March 1, 1905[.] Catalogue
     No. 925. Philadelphia: [Stan. V. Henkels], pp. 25-26.
         Lists seven Franklin items for sale, including the 1754
     edition of <u>Experiments and Observations on Electricity</u> and
     the eulogies on Franklin by Fauchet and Smith.

9   KRAUSKOPF, JOSEPH. <u>The Bi-Centenary of the Birth of Benjamin</u>
     <u>Franklin</u>[,] <u>a Discourse</u>. 19th ser., no. 23. Philadelphia:
     J.B. Lippincott Co., 10 pp.
         Franklin's name inspires few today; however, had he died
     a martyr his glory and reputation would have been greater.
     Reverence, it seems, requires some kind of sacrifice, if
     not martyrdom. Yet had he been martyred to the American
     cause, Franklin would not have been able to accomplish the
     great work that made him distinguished in Europe as well
     as in America. And as significant as were his accomplish-
     ments in America's struggle for independence, "his greatest
     distinction lay in preparing the American people for the
     proper use of that freedom once it was obtained." Franklin,
     in other words, was greatest as a broad, humane, and liberal
     educator.

10   LUZENBERGER, AUGUST von. <u>Die Franklinische Elektrizität in</u>
     <u>medizinischen Wissenschaft und Praxis</u>. Zwanglose
     Abhandlungen aus dem Gebiete der Elektrotherapie und
     Radiologie und verwandter Disziplinen der medizinischen
     Elektrotechnik, no. 4. Leipzig: Johann Ambrosius Barth,
     98 pp.
         On the uses of the Franklinian theory in medical science.

11   MACDONALD, WILLIAM. "The Fame of Franklin." <u>Atlantic Monthly</u>
     96, no. 4 (October):450-62.
         Franklin and Washington are the two greatest American
     heroes and are complementary. Each was absolutely neces-
     sary to American victory, and each was perfect in his role.
     Yet, on a national level, Franklin, for a number of reasons,
     has not received his fair share of fame for his achievements.
     While it is clear that Washington's contributions are in
     some ways without parallel, it is also true that Franklin
     has been too complex to be fully perceived, much less fully
     appreciated, by his fellow Americans. To be sure, Franklin
     has received acclaim; still in the popular rendering of his
     life and career, we find almost completely overlooked his
     qualities "of devotion, and endurance, magnanimity and
     strength," as if they were no part of him rather than

central to his being. In effect, then, Franklin's reputation has suffered because he cannot be easily synthesized as can most great men, including Washington.

12   MACDONALD, WILLIAM, ed. Preface to The Autobiography of Benjamin Franklin[,] Now First Printed in England From the Full and Authentic Text. . . . London: J.M. Dent & Co., pp. ix-xxiv.
      There was great anticipation of Franklin's memoirs, though they were never published during his lifetime, Macdonald says.

13   _____. "Some Account of Franklin's Later Life[,] Principally in Relation to the History of His Time." In The Autobiography of Benjamin Franklin[,] Now First Printed in England From the Full and Authentic Text. . . . London: J.M. Dent & Co., pp. 205-314.
      Franklin, the "Complete Citizen," lived a life that can be appropriately divided into three parts: his years as an apprentice, as a journeyman, and as a master. The first period deals with his youth; the second with his rising years in Philadelphia, and the last with his greatest period as a philosopher-statesman. The United States has never expressed enough official gratitude for Franklin's services.

14   [PENNSYLVANIA, LEGISLATURE of.] File of the Senate. No. 233. Session of 1905. An Act.
      Appropriates $35,000 for the American Philosophical Society to celebrate the bicentennial of Franklin.

15   [PENNSYLVANIA SOCIETY of NEW YORK.] A Dinner Given by the Pennsylvania Society in the City of New York in Commemoration of the Two Hundredth Anniversary of the Birth of Benjamin Franklin. New York: printed and distributed at the Waldorf Astoria[,] December 12, 6 pp.
      This was the seventh annual dinner honoring Franklin.

16   RUSH, BENJAMIN. "Excerpts from the Papers of Dr. Benjamin Rush: Conversation With Dr. Franklin." Pennsylvania Magazine of History and Biography 29, no. 1:23-30.
      Rush had frequent occasion to visit Franklin between 1785 and 1789. They discussed a variety of matters, including politics and Franklin's claim to have recognized the seeds of separation between America and England in the 1750s. Rush also reports Franklin's vehement opposition to slavery, his dislike of tobacco, his advice on American trade and industry, interest rates and labor, French habits,

1905

the medical profession, practical education, his experience
in the cockpit, the patriotism of ethnic groups in America,
and the career of John Dickinson.

17   SMYTH, ALBERT HENRY, ed. The Writings of Benjamin Franklin
Collected and Edited With a Life and Introduction. . . .
10 vols. New York: Macmillan Co., 1:1-217, 10:141-493.
In the first volume Smyth discusses Franklin's recorded
legacy: his manuscripts, which are scattered and very
difficult to pull together, and the printed editions of
his writings, which too often do him little justice. As
for the character of Franklin's works in general, they are
fundamentally of two kinds: those concerned with science
and those with philosophical matters. The scientific writings are important, but it is only the philosophical works
that have literary matter. This latter group shows Franklin
to have been a "utilitarian" and an important economist.
The last two categories of Franklin's writings are the satires
and bagatelles and the general correspondence. Smyth points
out, with respect to the first, that American humor begins
with Franklin's efforts in Poor Richard's Almanacks and in
the Pennsylvania Gazette. As for the correspondence, it is
"immense in range and volume," thus reflecting the scope of
Franklin's mind and interests. The tenth volume contains
Smyth's "Life" of Franklin. Actually, it is his career
that is recorded, since the years covered in the memoirs
are here dealt with in two chapters, leaving Smyth free to
concentrate on Franklin's achievements in statesmanship and
diplomacy as well as in political and economic philosophy.

18   STEPHENS, KATE. "Plagiarizing Humors of Benjamin Franklin."
In American Thumb-Prints, Mettle of Our Men and Women.
Philadelphia: J.B. Lippincott Co., pp. 285-343.
Franklin plagiarized much of what is considered his best
writing from British authors, particularly Swift. Stephens
rebukes Franklin for this and criticizes those who applaud
Franklin's honesty and originality; however, she points out
that there is in Franklin "a certain grace . . . , a human
feeling, a genial simplicity and candor, a directness of
utterance and natural unfolding of his matter which are his
perennial value in a literary way" and which make him "the
most readable writer yet known on the western side of the
Atlantic."

19   TRENT, WILLIAM P[ETERFIELD]. "Benjamin Franklin." In A Brief
History of American Literature. New York: D. Appleton &
Co., pp. 30-35.

1906

A brief survey of Franklin's career which asserts that
while Franklin represents his time in his diversity and
brilliance, he does so too in his lack of poetic imagination and spirit.

20 UNITED STATES LIBRARY of CONGRESS. List of the Benjamin
    Franklin Papers in the Library of Congress. Compiled by
    Worthington Chauncey Ford. Washington: Government Print-
    ing Office, 322 pp.
       Lists items from 1726 to 1818 and includes a section of
    anonymous letters and documents. The List is made up basic-
    ally of the Henry Stevens collection, though other Franklin
    pieces in the Library of Congress are noted in appropriate
    places.

1906

1 ABBE, CLEVELAND. "Benjamin Franklin as Meteorologist." In
   Proceedings of the American Philosophical Society 45,
   no. 183 (May-September):117-28.
      Franklin was America's "first meteorologist" because he
   was the first person to study the weather in a scientific
   manner. From at least 1726 to the end of his life he
   showed a keen interest in meteorology.

2 ABBE, CLEVELAND, and BURGESS, GEORGE K. [Address of] "The
   Philosophical Society of Washington." In Record of the
   Celebration of the Two Hundredth Anniversary of Benjamin
   Franklin. Vol. 1. Philadelphia: printed for the American
   Philosophical Society, p. 292.
      Tribute to Franklin, "Promoter of Science and Friend of
   Humanity."

3 ABBOTT, C. YARNALL. An Anniversary Masque . . . Composed for
   the Franklin Inn Club on the Occasion of Its Dinner Commemorative of the Two Hundredth Anniversary of the Birth
   of Benjamin Franklin, January 6, 1906, and Enacted by
   Edward Childs Carpenter as Franklin [and] E. Marshall Scull,
   as Penn. Philadelphia: J.B. Lippincott Co., 10 pp.
      Franklin tells an astonished William Penn about life in
   twentieth-century Philadelphia. Franklin is clearly made
   to seem the modern man who is not surprised by progress and
   accepts it as natural and good. Penn is used as a contrast
   by which one can measure the greatness and modernity of
   Franklin.

1906

4   ALGER, GEORGE W[ILLIAM]. "Franklin: The Citizen." American
    Illustrated Magazine 61, no. 3 (January):317-22.
        It is unfortunate that most Americans learn about
    Franklin from school books that made his life seen unevent-
    ful, almost trivial. In truth, he led a very dramatic and
    significant life of service to his country and mankind.

5   ALT, ADOLF; OLSHAUSEN, ERNEST P.; and HUNICKE, H. AUG[UST].
    [The Address of] "The Academy of Sciences of St. Louis."
    In Record of the Celebration of the Two Hundredth Anniver-
    sary of Benjamin Franklin. . . . Vol. 1. Philadelphia:
    printed for the American Philosophical Society, p. 279.
        Franklin "was above all, and in the highest sense, the
    friend of man."

6   The AMERICAN PHILOSOPHICAL SOCIETY. Record of the Cele-
    bration of the Two Hundredth Anniversary of Benjamin
    Franklin. . . . Vol. 1. Philadelphia: printed for the
    American Philosophical Society, pp. 310-21.
        Cablegrams and telegrams paying tribute to Franklin.

7   _____. The Record of the Celebration of the Two Hundredth
    Anniversary of the Birth of Benjamin Franklin, Under the
    Auspices of The American Philosophical Society Held at
    Philadelphia for Promoting Useful Knowledge, April the
    Seventeenth to April the Twentieth, A.D. Nineteen Hundred
    and Six. Vol. 1. Philadelphia: printed for the American
    Philosophical Society.
        The Record includes a preface which relates the plans
    for the celebration and contains the following: Horace
    Howard Furness, "Franklin as a Citizen and Philanthropist";
    Charles William Eliot's "Franklin as Printer and Philoso-
    pher"; Joseph Hodges Choate's "Franklin as Statesman and
    Diplomatist"; "Presentation to France of the Gold Medal
    Authorized by The Congress of the United States" by Elihu
    Root; "Reception of the Medal" by J.J. Jusserand; Edward L.
    Nichols's "Franklin's Researches in Electricity"; Ernest
    Rutherford's "The Modern Theories of Electricity and Their
    Relation to the Franklinian Theory"; addresses by Hampton L.
    Carson and Andrew Carnegie in behalf of the Universities of
    Pennsylvania and St. Andrews respectively; and "Addresses
    from Sister Societies and Institutions of Learning." These
    works are all cited separately. Volumes 2-6 of the tribute
    make up the Calendar of Franklin's papers by I Minis Hays.
    The Hays Calendar is supplemented by Mrs. Lightner Witmer's
    Calendar of the Papers of Benjamin Franklin, published in
    1908 by the University of Pennsylvania. (The supplement
    will be dealt with in the second volume of this bibliography.)

8   ANON. "American Philosophical Society[,] Present Officers
     Reelected.--The Franklin Celebration." <u>Old Penn Weekly
     Review of the University of Pennsylvania</u> 4, no. 16
     (13 January):[1].
          Beginning of plans to celebrate the 200th anniversary
     of Franklin's birth.

9   ANON. "Benjamin Franklin." <u>Electrical World</u> 47, no. 3
     (20 January):[137]-38.
          The magazine joins in celebrating the 200th anniversary
     of Franklin's birth by publishing articles on him. The
     author of the present piece calls Franklin "the greatest
     American who has yet lived" because he was outstanding in
     more ways than any other of his countrymen.

10   ANON. "Benjamin Franklin: A Typical American Citizen."
     <u>Scrap Book</u> 1, no. 1 (March):[156]-59.
          Franklin was great in many areas: as a manager of people,
     a scientist, man of letters, statesman, and practical phi-
     losopher. Moreover, though he was indifferent to the sec-
     tarian divisions that plagued Christians, he was essentially
     a religious man.

11   ANON. "Benjamin Franklin et la médecine de son temps."
     <u>Chronique médicale</u> 13, no. 9 (1 May):280-82.
          Franklin's interest in medical science was intense and
     continued even during the eventful hectic years of the
     American Revolution.

12   ANON. "Benjamin Franklin, the First American Heating and
     Ventilating Engineer." <u>Scientific American Supplement</u>
     94, no. 1574 (3 March):217-18.
          On the Pennsylvania fireplace.

13   ANON. "Bicentenary of Benjamin Franklin's Birth." <u>American
     Printer</u> 42, no. 3 (May):321.
          Reports on the celebration of Franklin's 200th birthday
     conducted by the American Philosophical Society.

14   ANON. "Bi-Centenary of Franklin." <u>Old Penn Weekly Review of
     the University of Pennsylvania</u> 4, no. 29 (14 April):[1]-2.
          Announces the four-day celebration of Franklin's 200th
     birthday. The event, under the auspices of the American
     Philosophical Society, includes addresses intended to ex-
     press the range of Franklin's curiosity and his versatility.

15   ANON. <u>Bi-Centennial of Benjamin Franklin[,] 1706-1906.</u>
     Philadelphia: printed for the University of Pennsylvania
     by the John C. Winston Co., 4 pp.

1906

A program praising Franklin and the University in
song.

16   ANON. Books Printed by Benjamin Franklin, Born January 17,
1706. New York: Dodd, Mead & Co.
The title of this pamphlet is not quite correct, for
the list includes also works written by Franklin but
printed by others and items on which Franklin may have
worked as a printer, as well as pieces certainly printed
by him.

17   ANON. Catalogue of an Exhibition Commemorating the Two
Hundredth Anniversary of the Birth of Benjamin Franklin.
[New York]: Grolier Club of the City of New York.
The Catalogue lists 458 items of Frankliniana.

18   ANON. "Doctor Walter T. Taggart Lectures on Franklin." Old
Penn Weekly Review of the University of Pennsylvania 4,
no. 29 (14 April):7.
Taggart spoke on "Benjamin Franklin and His Relations
to the University of Pennsylvania." The speech was accompanied by about fifty slides made especially for the occasion. Moreover the "words of the song, 'Ben Franklin,'
were thrown on the screen and at the same time a talking
machine gave an excellent rendering of it by a male quartet."
The record was made by the Victor Talking Machine Company.

19   ANON. "Franklin and Paine." To-morrow[.] For People Who
Think (January), pp. [4-5].
Like Paine, Franklin is a hero. Moreover, he is "the
greatest intellect ever produced in America."

20   ANON. "Franklin and the Germans." Old Penn Weekly Review of
the University of Pennsylvania 4, no. 29 (14 April):3.
The author noted that M.D. Learned delivered a paper on
Franklin's relations to Germans in America and Germany.
Learned, who addressed the Germanic Association, pointed
out that Franklin disliked Germans because of their insist-
ence on remaining apart from English society and traditions.

21   ANON. "The Franklin Bi-Centenary." American Journal of
Science, 4th ser. 21, no. 125 (May):406-7.
Reports on the celebration conducted by the American
Philosophical Society in honor of the 200th anniversary
of Franklin's birth.

22   ANON. "The Franklin Bi-Centenary." Science, n.s. 23,
no. 599 (22 June):[929]-43.

Describes the events and lists the papers read at the
celebration of Franklin's two hundredth birthday.

23   ANON. "Franklin Bicentenary Exercises at Philadelphia."
      Electrical World 47, no. 16 (21 April):812.
      The American Philosophical Society celebration of the
      200th anniversary of Franklin's birth was international in
      scope and very impressive.

24   ANON. "The Franklin Bicentenary in Philadelphia." Electrical
      World 47, no. 17 (28 April):862.
      The American Philosophical Society celebration paid
      particular attention to Franklin as a scientist.

25   ANON. "The Franklin Celebration." Alumni Register 10, no. 8
      (May):369-75.
      On Philadelphia's four days' celebration of the 200th
      anniversary of the birth of its most famous son. (The
      journal title later becomes The General Magazine and
      Historical Chronicle.)

26   ANON. "The Franklin Celebration." Old Penn Weekly Review of
      the University of Pennsylvania 4, no. 17 (20 January):2.
      On the elaborate plans to celebrate the 200th anniversary
      of Franklin's birth. Invitations were sent by the Univer-
      sity of Pennsylvania to some 600 institutions throughout
      the world to send representatives to take part in the event.

27   ANON. "The Franklin Celebration." Old Penn Weekly Review of
      the University of Pennsylvania 4, no. 23 (3 March):3.
      On plans for the University of Pennsylvania and the
      American Philosophical Society to celebrate the 200th
      anniversary of Franklin's birth.

28   ANON. "The Franklin Celebration." Old Penn Weekly Review of
      the University of Pennsylvania 4, no. 28 (7 April):2.
      The program celebrating the 200th anniversary of
      Franklin's birth will be international in scope, for
      Franklin himself had a number of international involvements.

29   ANON. "The Franklin Celebration. Old Penn Weekly Review of
      the University of Pennsylvania 4, no. 30 (21 April):1-2, 5.
      On the sessions of the American Philosophical Society's
      celebration of the bicentennial of Franklin's birth.

30   ANON. "The Franklin Celebration." Outlook 82 (28 April):
      914-16.
      On the American Philosophical Society's celebration of
      the 200th anniversary of Franklin's birth.

1906

31 ANON. "The Franklin Celebration of Rochester Alumni." <u>Old</u>
<u>Penn Weekly Review of the University of Pennsylvania</u> 4,
no. 18 (27 January):2.
Franklin's 200th birthday celebrated with a banquet and
speeches.

32 ANON. "Franklin Day Celebration." <u>American Printer</u> 41, no. 6
(February):629.
Special programs celebrated the 200th anniversary of
Franklin's birth.

33 ANON. "Franklin Dinner in Buffalo." <u>American Printer</u> 41,
no. 6 (February):625.
The dinner featured a skit in which Franklin is made to
extol printing and hard work.

34 ANON. "Franklin Echoes." <u>Old Penn Weekly Review of the Uni-</u>
<u>versity of Pennsylvania</u> 4, no. 31 (28 April):2.
Scattered bits of information about Franklin and about
the 200th anniversary of his birth.

35 ANON. "The Franklin Program." <u>Old Penn Weekly Review of the</u>
<u>University of Pennsylvania</u> 4, no. 25 (17 March):5.
Plans of the American Philosophical Society to honor
Franklin on his bicentennial. President Theodore Roosevelt
was to head the list of dignitaries at the celebration.

36 ANON. "Franklin Relics." <u>Old Penn Weekly Review of the Uni-</u>
<u>versity of Pennsylvania</u> 4, no. 24 (10 March):3.
The Masonic Temple of Pennsylvania presented an exhibit
of Frankliniana, with the help of the Historical Society of
Pennsylvania and the American Philosophical Society.

37 ANON. "Franklin Relics at Masonic Temple." <u>Old Penn Weekly</u>
<u>Review of the University of Pennsylvania</u> 4, no. 23
(3 March):[1].
Announcement that the library of the Masonic Temple
would have an exhibition of Frankliniana from throughout
the world.

38 ANON. "Franklin the Citizen." <u>Review of Reviews</u> 33, no. 1
(January):107-8.
In addition to reviewing George W. Alger's "Franklin:
The Citizen" (1906.4), the author praises Franklin as a
staunch patriot and broad humanitarian.

39 ANON. "Frankliniana." <u>Old Penn Weekly Review of the Univer-</u>
<u>sity of Pennsylvania</u> 4, no. 17 (20 January):3.

Essentially lists bits of widely known information about Franklin.

40   ANON. "Franklin's Desk." Old Penn Weekly Review of the University of Pennsylvania 4, no. 24 (10 March):7.
The desk at which Franklin wrote much of the material for his almanacs "is now in the possession of Dr. Roland G. Curtin" and will probably be given to the Franklin Institute.

41   ANON. "Franklin's Grave." Electrical World 47, no. 3 (20 January):151.
Franklin's grave is being neglected, according to a report in the New York Sun.

42   ANON. "Franklin's Scientific Work." Scientific American 94, no. 17 (28 April):350-51.
Franklin had no reliable measuring devices and so must be considered "an experimental philosopher rather than . . . a scientist"; however, there is no doubting his scientific and mechanical genius.

43   ANON. "The Grave of Franklin." Electrical World 47, no. 3 (20 January):142-43.
The complaints that Franklin's grave had been ill attended are not longer valid.

44   ANON. "Héroes de la ciencia[.] Benjamin Franklin." Pagines illustradas 3, no. 123 (2 December):175-76.
Brief summary of Franklin's achievements.

45   ANON. "Il secondo centenario di B. Franklin." Nuova ontologia (Rome):205, 964-6.
A perfunctory notice of the 200th anniversary of Franklin's birth; it reflects the diminished state of interest in him among Italians. (See also Pace, p. 308.)

46   ANON. Introduction to The Autobiography of Benjamin Franklin. Boston: Houghton Mifflin & Co., pp. [vii]-xx.
The years covered in the memoirs are the most important because they formed Franklin's character. The second half of his adult life was only "an elaborate Sequel" of the first half.

47   ANON. Introduction to Proceedings of the Right Worshipful Grand Lodge of the Most Ancient and Honorable Fraternity of Free Masons of Pennsylvania . . . [,] at Its Celebration of the Bi-Centenary of the Birth of . . . Benjamin Franklin. . . . Philadelphia: Grand Lodge of Pennsylvania, pp. 9-14.

1906

On the plans to celebrate the 200th anniversary of the
birth of Franklin, "the fourth Grand Master of Masons in
Pennsylvania."

48   ANON. Introduction to The Two-Hundredth Anniversary of the
      Birth of Benjamin Franklin[.] Celebration by the Common-
      wealth of Massachusetts and the City of Boston[,] in Sym-
      phony Hall, Boston[,] January 17, 1906. [Boston]:
      printed by order of the State of Massachusetts and the
      Boston City Council, pp. 7-14.
           History of the plans for the celebration and the program.

49   ANON. "List of Works in the New York Public Library by or
      Relating to Benjamin Franklin." Bulletin of the New York
      Public Library 10, no. 1 (January):29-83.
           Pages 43-50 deal with works about Franklin, and there
      are also sections on bibliography, manuscripts, his pub-
      lished works, and works published by him, as well as a
      section on likenesses of Franklin.

50   ANON. "The Loan Exhibition of Frankliniana." In Proceedings
      of the Right Worshipful Grand Lodge of the Most Ancient and
      Honorable Fraternity of Free Masons of Pennsyl-
      vania . . . [,] at Its Celebration of the Bi-Centenary
      of the Birth of . . . Benjamin Franklin. . . .   Philadel-
      phia: Grand Lodge of Pennsylvania, pp. 319-41.
           Listed are hundreds of items, including art work,
      Franklin imprints, and books relating to him.

51   ANON. "The Magnetic Club and Franklin." Electrical World 47,
      no. 16 (21 April):813.
           One indication of Franklin's "universal genius" is
      that he was "the first American electrician."

52   ANON. "Neglect of Franklin's Grave." American Printer 41,
      no. 6 (February):628.
           If no one else will act, American printers should do
      something about the shocking neglect of Franklin's grave.

53   ANON. "New York's Franklin Banquet." American Printer 41,
      no. 6 (February):616.
           At the annual celebration, Franklin was called one of
      the ordinary or "common" people rather than one of the
      elite. His "vagaries," so well known and often discussed,
      might shock refined people of a later time, but they show
      Franklin to be entirely human.

54   ANON. Note to Books Printed by Benjamin Franklin[,] Born
      January 17, 1706[,] for Sale by Dodd, Mead & Company.
      New York, pp. [5]-6.
          Encourages the collecting of Franklin imprints and com-
      ments briefly on the relative availability of various im-
      prints. The catalogue itself lists the asking prices of
      the Franklin items for sale.

55   ANON. "Notes." Nation 82, no. 2122 (1 March):179.
          Exhibitions of Frankliniana in "various cities" honor
      Franklin on the 200th anniversary of his birth.

56   ANON. "Notes by the Way." American Printer 42, no. 2
      (April):187.
          The New York Typothetae did not hold its annual Franklin
      banquet in 1906 because of the typographer union's strike
      and because there had been too many banquets for the year.
      An informal evening without speeches honoring Franklin or
      anyone else was held instead.

57   ANON. Programme de la cérémonie du bi-centenaire de la
      naissance de Benjamin Franklin au Palais du Trocadéro[,]
      le 27 Avril 1906[,] à 2 heures. N.p., 4 pp.
          The program included music and various speeches, one of
      which was by Albert Henry Smyth, and the unveiling of the
      Boyle statue of Franklin.

58   ANON. "To the Memory of Franklin and His Disciples." Inland
      Printer 36, no. 4 (January):594.
          Intends to honor Franklin with a regular column in the
      Inland Printer keeping his name before printers. Also
      eulogizes recently deceased members of the craft.

59   ANON. "Two Centuries After Franklin." Scientific American
      94, no. 4 (27 January):86-87.
          While the world is not remiss in praising Franklin's
      achievements in most areas, it fails to understand his
      greatness as a theoretical and practical scientist.

60   ANON. "Two Famous Franklin Medals." Bookman[,] an Illustrated
      Magazine of Literature and Life 22 (January):443-46.
          Discusses the meaning of Augustin Dupré's two medals,
      "the Libertas Americana, 1783, for which Franklin was
      responsible, and the medal of 1784, upon which Franklin
      was honoured." Dupré had depicted America as the infant
      Hercules in the Libertas Americana, and this idea was
      Franklin's.

1906

61   ANON. "University Honors Franklin." Old Penn Weekly Review
      of the University of Pennsylvania 4, no. 30 (21 April):
      [1], 5-7.
           The University celebrated the bicentennial event by
      granting honorary degrees to Edward VII (accepted by the
      ambassador), Andrew Carnegie, and others. There was also
      an oration by Hampton L. Carson which expresses Franklin's
      greatness, his faith in God and in mankind.

62   ANON. "Vice-Provost Smith Eulogizes Franklin." Old Penn
      Weekly Review of the University of Pennsylvania 4, no. 17
      (20 January):3.
           Franklin lauded as a man of science and as founder of
      the American Philosophical Society. "The Vice-Provost said
      he had always regretted that the old University of Pennsyl-
      vania song 'Ben Franklin' had died out and no longer ex-
      isted as a college song." Franklin was also praised for
      his work in France.

63   ARRILLAGA, F. de P. [Address of the] "Real Academia de
      Ciencias Exactas Fisicas y Naturales." In Record of the
      Celebration of the Two Hundredth Anniversary of Benjamin
      Franklin. . . . Vol. 1. Philadelphia: printed for the
      American Philosophical Society, p. 269.
           Tribute to Franklin, founder of the American Philosoph-
      ical Society.

64   AUTRAND, [AUGUSTE]. "Discours." In Ceremony Held in Paris
      to Commemorate the Bi-Centenary of the Birth of Benjamin
      Franklin, April 27, 1906. [Compiled by Theodore Ayrault
      Dodge.] Paris: Imprimerie Universelle, English Printers,
      pp. 58-63.
           One of the reasons Franklin is so beloved in France is
      that he represents the enduring friendship between the two
      countries.

65   BACHE, RICHARD MEADE. "Smoky Torches in Franklin's Honor."
      Critic 48, no. 6 (June):561-66.
           Attempts to correct generally minor but common errors
      concerning Franklin.

66   BAILEY, W.H.; JONES, FRANCIS; and LEES, CHARLES H. [Address
      of the] "Manchester Literary and Philosophical Society."
      In Record of the Celebration of the Two Hundredth Anniver-
      sary of Benjamin Franklin. . . . Vol. 1. Philadelphia:
      printed for the American Philosophical Society, p. 240.
           "As a philosopher, statesman, and diplomatist, and as a
      pioneer in the scientific fields of capillarity, acoustics,

electricity and meteorology, Dr. Franklin will long be remembered. . . ."

67 BARTHOU, [LOUIS?]. "Discours." In Ceremony Held in Paris to Commemorate the Bi-Centenary of the Birth of Benjamin Franklin, April 27th, 1906. [Compiled by Theodore Ayrault Dodge.] Paris: Imprimerie Universelle, English Printers, pp. 39-47.
On Franklin's career and great popularity in France.

68 BATES, JOHN L. "Address." In Bicentenary of Benjamin Franklin's Birth[,] January Seventeen[,] Nineteen Hundred and Six. Franklin, Mass.: Sentinel Press, pp. 36-48.
Franklin was a typical Yankee, and his Boston heritage shaped his life.

69 BEARE, T. HUDSON, and CARTER, W[ILLIA]M ALLAN. [Address of] "The Royal Society of Arts." In Record of the Celebration of the Two Hundredth Anniversary of Benjamin Franklin. . . . Vol. 1. Philadelphia: printed for the American Philosophical Society, p. 253.
"The name of Franklin is, with reason, respected wherever the light of Science has reached. . . ."

70 BENTLEY, RICHARD. [Address of] "The Royal Meteorological Society." In Record of the Celebration of the Two Hundredth Anniversary of Benjamin Franklin. . . . Vol. 1. Philadelphia: printed for the American Philosophical Society, pp. 272-73.
Franklin made significant meteorological investigations.

71 BERTHELOT, M., and DARBOUX, G. [Address of] "L'Académie des Sciences de Paris." In Record of the Celebration of the Two Hundredth Anniversary of Benjamin Franklin. . . . Vol. 1. Philadelphia: printed for the American Philosophical Society, pp. 214-16.
All of mankind is in debt to Franklin for his scientific achievements.

72 BIGELOW, JOHN. "Franklin As the Man." Independent 60, no. 2980 (11 January):69-72.
A brief, very laudatory sketch of Franklin's career and beliefs which stresses his benevolence. "It has been the fashion of a certain class of critics who are always wishing to appear wiser than him they criticise, to say that Franklin never dwelt upon any of the higher planes of spiritual life. If not, where did he get the secret of that supernatural wisdom which always led him to seek the good

of each in the advantage of all." It is the spiritual side
of Franklin that contributed mightily to his success and to
the great degree of love and respect in which he has so
long been held.

73 ____. "Letter from Hon. John Bigelow on the Authorship of
the Bishop of St. Asaph's 'Intended Speech,' of 1774."
Bulletin of the New York Public Library 10, no. 1 (January):
23-28.
Cites internal and external reasons for believing that
it was Franklin and not the bishop who was substantially
or entirely the author of the "Intended Speech."

74 [BIGELOW, JOHN.] "Letter from the Hon. John Bigelow on a
Franklin Statuette Supposed to Be the Work of Nini."
Bulletin of the New York Public Library 10, no. 1
(January):9-12.
Describes the statue, which was owned by a descendant
of the French printer, Fournier le Jeune, an acquaintance
of Franklin. Bigelow secured photographs of the statue,
presented them to the Library and explained why he believed
it was by Nini.

75 BORGMANN, I. et al. [Address of the] "Imperatorskij S.
Peterburskij Universitet." In Record of the Celebration of
the Two Hundredth Anniversary of Benjamin Franklin. . . .
Vol. 1. Philadelphia: printed for the American Philosophical Society, p. 251.
Franklin was a "famous public worker, true patriot and
great scholar . . . , who gave mankind a weapon of defence
against the formidable force of Nature--lightning, and by
his remarkable researches greatly advanced the study of
electric phenomena."

76 BOSS, HENRY R. "What Franklin Did and Did Not." American
Printer 42, no. 2 (April):164.
Franklin accomplished many notable and even great things;
however, "there is no record of anything he ever did for
his own craft."

77 BOSTON PUBLIC LIBRARY. "North America." In A List of Books
on the History and Art of Printing and Some Related Subjects
in the Public Library of the City of Boston and the Libraries of Harvard College and the Boston Athenaeum. Published
in Commemoration of the Two Hundredth Anniversary of the
Birth of Benjamin Franklin. Boston: published by the
Trustees of the Boston Public Library, pp. 18-21, 38.

Lists works on Franklin and an unpaginated final section of the book following p. 38 offers a chronology of Franklin's life and reproduces a number of likenesses of him.

78   BOURGEOIS, ARMAND. <u>Benjamin Franklin en France</u>. Paris: Le Soudier, 41 pp.
This brief and somewhat idealized account sketches Franklin's career and achievements in France and tells of the sincere affection the French people have always had for him. Bourgeois's narrative, in fact, was part of the celebration of the 200th birthday of Franklin, on which occasion a statue of him was unveiled in Paris.

79   BROWN, JAMES W. "Franklin As a Freemason and As a Man." In <u>Proceedings of the Right Worshipful Grand Lodge of the Most Ancient and Honorable Fraternity of Free Masons of Pennsylvania . . . [,] at Its Celebration of the Bi-Centenary of the Birth of . . . Benjamin Franklin. . . .</u> Philadelphia: Grand Lodge of Pennsylvania, pp. 179-84.
Franklin's benevolence, dignity, and simplicity enabled him to contribute as much as any person in history "to this world's progress." And Franklin, like other great men, was influenced by Freemasonry.

80   BROWN, T. STEWART. "Benjamin Franklin." In <u>Franklin Lodge, No. 134, F. & A.M. Celebration of the 200th Anniversary of the Birth of Brother Benjamin Franklin[,] January 31, 1906.</u> [Philadelphia], pp. 3-7.
It is astonishing to consider how much Franklin achieved in his life and how much good he did. Brown agrees with those who rank Franklin above Washington as the greatest example of a colonial American.

81   BRUNHES, LOUIS, and L'HOEST, G. [Address of the] "Association des Ingénieurs Électriciens Sortis-de L'Institut Électro-Technique Montefiore." In <u>Record of the Celebration of the Two Hundredth Anniversary of Benjamin Franklin. . . .</u> Vol. 1. Philadelphia: printed for the American Philosophical Society, pp. 299-300.
Praises for Franklin as a philosopher, scientist, and patriot.

82   BURDOCK, Jr. "Andre and the Franklin Portrait." <u>Magazine of History</u> 4, no. 4 (October):241-42.
It was Captain John Andre who, when the British occupied Philadelphia, took Franklin's portrait from his house.

1906

83 BUTLER, NICHOLAS MURRAY; RIVES, G.L.; and PINE, JOHN B.
[Address of] "Columbia University." In Record of the
Celebration of the Two Hundredth Anniversary of Benjamin
Franklin. . . . Vol. 1. Philadelphia: printed for the
American Philosophical Society, pp. 233-34.
Recognition of Franklin's "eminent services . . . to the
advancement of education[,] the encouragement of Scientific
research and the cultivation of higher thought."

84 CAMBRIDGE UNIVERSITY. [Address.] In Record of the Celebra-
tion of the Two Hundredth Anniversary of Benjamin
Franklin. . . . Vol. 1. Philadelphia: printed for the
American Philosophical Society, pp. 202-3.
Tribute to Franklin and the Society.

85 CARNEGIE, ANDREW. [Address on Conferring] "The Honorary Degree
of LL.D." In Record of the Celebration of the Two Hundredth
Anniversary of Benjamin Franklin. . . . Vol. 1. Philadelphia: printed for the American Philosophical Society,
pp. 189-92.
Carnegie, the Lord Rector of the University of St.
Andrews, says it is fitting for the university that first
made Franklin "Doctor Franklin" to honor him again.

86 CARR, JAMES. "Franklin's Grave." American Printer 41, no. 6
(February):616.
Franklin's grave is disgracefully neglected.

87 CARSON, HAMPTON LAWRENCE. "Benjamin Franklin and the University of Pennsylvania." In Record of the Celebration of the
Two Hundredth Anniversary of Benjamin Franklin. . . .
Vol. 1. Philadelphia: printed for the American Philosophical Society, pp. 167-88.
An appreciative survey of Franklin's many careers and of
his connection with the University of Pennsylvania. At the
heart of Franklin's success and greatness was his dedication to practical virtue.

88 CARY, A.A. "Benjamin Franklin's Contributions to the Art of
Heating and Ventilation." In American Society of Heating
and Ventilating Engineers, Transactions. Vol. 12. New
York: published by the Society, pp. 36-38.
Franklin actually originated the practice in America of
heating and ventilation. It is therefore proper that he be
honored by the Society and have, reprinted "in our next
Proceedings" his paper on Pennsylvania fireplaces. The
motion was passed, and the paper appears on pp. 160-94 of
the Society's Proceedings.

89 CHAUTARD, [PAUL-HENRI-JOSEPH]. "Discours." In <u>Ceremony Held</u>
    <u>in Paris to Commemorate the Bi-Centenary of the Birth of</u>
    <u>Benjamin Franklin, April 27, 1906</u>. [Compiled by Theodore
    Ayrault Dodge.] Paris: Imprimerie Universelle, English
    Printers, pp. 53-57.
    On the love which the French people have always felt for
    the great American philosopher and diplomat. (The identi-
    fication of Chautard's full name is based on the 1908 edi-
    tion of <u>Qui Êtes-Vous</u>? and on the article, "Statue of
    Franklin Presented to Paris," <u>New York Times</u>, 28 April
    1906, p. 7, c. 4, the eighth paragraph.)

90 CHOATE, JOSEPH HODGES. "Franklin As Statesman and Diplomatist."
    In <u>Record of the Celebration of the Two Hundredth Anniver-</u>
    <u>sary of Benjamin Franklin</u>. . . . Vol. 1. Philadelphia:
    printed for the American Philosophical Society, pp. 71-95.
    Throughout nearly all of his adult life Franklin "was
    always the statesman, and generally quite in advance of his
    times." His remarkable career in politics was founded on
    his personal virtue and patriotism, and these qualities he
    possessed in such a degree as to set a standard of excel-
    lence for all future American statesmen.

91 COATES, FLORENCE EARLE. "Benjamin Franklin." <u>Reader</u> 7,
    no. 4 (March):[418-19].
    A verse tribute, part of which reads:

        Franklin! <u>our</u> Franklin! America's loved son!--
          Loved in his day, and now, as few indeed:
        Franklin! whose mighty genius allies won,
          To aid her in great need!

92 CORTELYOU, GEORGE B. "Franklin the Postmaster-General." In
    <u>Year Book of the Pennsylvania Society[,] 1906</u>. Edited by
    Barr Ferree. New York: Pennsylvania Society, pp. [23]-28.
    Traces Franklin's career as postmaster and says that
    were he alive in 1906, he would be happy with the post
    office as a model of efficiency.

93 CRAWFORD, MARY CAROLINE. "Franklin and the French Intriguers."
    <u>Appleton's Booklovers' Magazine</u> 7, no. 2 (February):
    [220]-31.
    No other man could have accomplished what Franklin did
    in France. Silas Deane had failed sadly in the artful game
    of diplomatic intrigue with French friends and spies for
    Great Britain. Franklin was not only a master at such
    diplomacy, but captivated the minds and hearts of the
    French people.

1906

94 _____. "An Important Franklin Discovery." <u>Outlook</u> 82
(20 January):117-21.
On the discovery of Franklin correspondence and documents that he brought back with him from France in 1785
and of earlier pieces. Crawford describes a number of
them and reports that the collection was purchased by the
University of Pennsylvania.

95 DANIELSSON, O.A., and DUNER, N.C. [Address of the] "Kongliga
Vetenskaps-Societen." In <u>Record of the Celebration of the</u>
<u>Two Hundredth Anniversary of Benjamin Franklin. . . .</u>
Vol. 1. Philadelphia: printed for the American Philosoph-
ical Society, pp. 227-28.
Franklin as a scientist and philosopher commands the
praise of mankind.

96 DARWIN, G[EORGE] H[OWARD]. [Address of] "The British Association for the Advancement of Science." In <u>Record of the</u>
<u>Celebration of the Two Hundredth Anniversary of Benjamin</u>
<u>Franklin. . . .</u> Vol. 1. Philadelphia: printed for the
American·Philosophical Society, pp. 254-55.
Franklin "was equally great as a Statesman . . . and as
an Investigator of Nature. . . ."

97 _____. "The Bicentenary Celebration of the Birth of Benjamin
Franklin." <u>Nature</u> 74, no. 1906 (10 May):36-37.
An account of the celebration.

98 DAVIS, REBECCA HARDING. "The Every-Day Franklin." <u>St.</u>
<u>Nicholas</u> 34, pt. 1, no. 2 (December):158, 160.
Franklin is a great American not because of his accomplishments in science and diplomacy but by virtue of his
"little homely deeds," which reveal best his great
qualities.

99 DAVIS, WILLIAM MORRIS. "Was Lewis Evans or Benjamin Franklin
the First to Recognize that Our Northeast Storms Came from
the Southwest?" <u>Proceedings of the American Philosophical</u>
<u>Society</u> 45, no. 183:129-30.
It would seem that Franklin was the first. He conveyed
the information to Evans without any concern for receiving
credit for the discovery. Evans, a leading geographer,
made use of this information in his 1747 work on the British
colonies, giving no credit to Franklin.

100 DIXON, R.F. "Some Sidelights on the Character of Benjamin
Franklin." <u>Canadian Magazine [of Politics, Science, Art</u>
<u>and Literature]</u> 28, no. 1 (November):71-73.

Franklin was a man of great talent, probably the most able person ever born in North America. What is more, he had other virtues too, but sadly he lacked a "high-minded" character and is "morally unworthy of being mentioned in the same breath with George Washington, who is the only heroic figure in the American Revolution." Dixon cites as corroboration for his view of Franklin the criticisms made of him in Jonathan Boucher's View of the American Revolution (1797.3). (Boucher opposed the patriots, as Dixon knows; however, he seems unaware that, among other things, Boucher feared Franklin as a revolutionary more than he did anyone else, including Washington, and preached the sermons before the Revolution in the hope of forcing Franklin to retire or give up the patriotic cause.)

101   [DODGE, THEODORE AYRAULT, comp.] Ceremony Held in Paris to Commemorate the Bi-Centenary of the Birth of Benjamin Franklin, April 27, 1906. Paris: Imprimerie Universelle, English Printers, 66 pp.
      To honor Franklin on the 200th anniversary of his birth, a committee of prominent Americans and Frenchmen had built a statue of him and unveiled it on 27 April 1906. This book is a collection of the tributes to Franklin for the occasion, and these are cited individually. In commentary throughout the book, Dodge provides a sketch of the efforts that went into the celebration as well as the background of the speakers and commentary on Franklin. The French speakers show that France had retained its affection and respect for the first American ambassador, the man who did so much to develop enduring Franco-American friendship.

102   DONALDSON, JAMES. [Address of the University of St. Andrews.] In Record of the Celebration of the Two Hundredth Anniversary of Benjamin Franklin. . . . Vol. 1. Philadelphia: printed for the American Philosophical Society, p. 205.
      Tribute to Franklin, "Journalist, Statesman, Diplomatist, and man of Science," who, like the American Philosophical Society itself, represents "the spirit of freedom and intelligence."

103   DRAPER, EBEN S. "Address." In Bicentenary of Benjamin Franklin's Birth[,] January Seventeen[,] Nineteen Hundred and Six. Franklin, Mass.: Sentinel Press, pp. 33-34.
      Franklin was a great and most useful patriot, and we must continue to live by his ideals.

104   DURAND, TH[OMAS]. [Address of the] "Jardin Botanique de l'Etat." In Record of the Celebration of the Two Hundredth

1906

Anniversary of Benjamin Franklin. . . . Vol. 1. Philadelphia: printed for the American Philosophical Society,
p. 283.
    Praise for Franklin as the founder of the Society.

105   ELIOT, CHARLES WILLIAM. "Franklin As Printer and Philosopher."
      In Record of the Celebration of the Two Hundredth Anniver-
      sary of Benjamin Franklin. . . . Vol. 1. Philadelphia:
      printed for the American Philosophical Society, pp. 55-70.
          Franklin's printing office was of great use to him "as
      an author, editor, and publisher." The press, then,
      helped importantly to bring Franklin the philosopher of
      science, education, politics, and morals before the world,
      and in each of these areas he made a contribution. Franklin
      was indeed a versatile, great, and good man; however, he
      "never seems to have perceived that the supreme tests of
      civilization are the tender and honorable treatment of
      women as equals, and the sanctity of home life. There was
      one primary virtue on his list which he did not always
      practice. His failure in this respect diminished his in-
      fluence for good among his contemporaries, and must always
      qualify the admiration with which mankind will regard him
      as a moral philosopher and an exhorter to a good life."

106   ENKLAAR, J.E. "Benjamin Franklin." In Album der Natuur.
      Haarlem: n.p., pp. [193]-239.
          A survey of Franklin's life, concentrating especially
      on his work in electrical science and placing him in the
      historical context of his scientific contemporaries. (The
      title page of the volume is incorrectly dated 1905.)

107   FISCHER, E. [Address of the] "Naturforschende Gesellschaft
      Freiburg I. Breisgau." In Record of the Celebration of the
      Two Hundredth Anniversary of Benjamin Franklin. . . .
      Vol. 1. Philadelphia: printed for the American Philosoph-
      ical Society, p. 256.
          Tribute to Franklin.

108   FISH, FREDERICK P. "Franklin the Scientist." In Year Book
      of the Pennsylvania Society[,] 1906. Edited by Barr
      Ferree. New York: Pennsylvania Society, pp. [40]-53.
          Franklin was greatest of all as a natural philosopher.
      The "merit" of his work was and is clear, and he had the
      skill necessary to present that work before the world.
      Whether in electrical science, medical science, economics,
      or music, Franklin was both a man of his own time and one
      full of curiosity and anticipation about the future.

1906

109 FITZGERALD, JOHN FRANCIS. "Remarks." In The Two-Hundredth
Anniversary of the Birth of Benjamin Franklin[.] Celebration by the Commonwealth of Massachusetts and the City of
Boston[,] in Symphony Hall, Boston[,] January 17, 1906.
[Boston]: printed by order of the Massachusetts General
Court and the Boston City Council, pp. 35-37.
Although Boston has changed significantly in the past
200 years, if Franklin were alive today he would remain
essentially the same and work for the well being of mankind. Of all Americans, Franklin is first "in the arts of
peace."

110 FORD, WORTHINGTON CHAUNCEY. "Franklin and Chatham." Independent 60, no. 2980 (11 January):94-97.
In 1757 Franklin tried unsuccessfully to meet Chatham.
The great Englishman, though an admirer, was apparently
too busy to concern himself with colonial matters. After
1774, however, Chatham proved himself to be a friend to
America as well as to English Whigs and, while trying to
effect a reconciliation between the colonies and the Mother
country, counseled the Americans to remain firm. In plead-
ing the American cause in the House of Lords, Chatham came
to seek the advice of Franklin, and the two men developed
a great mutual respect.

111 _____. "One of Franklin's Friendships[.] From Hitherto Unpublished Correspondence Between Madame De Brillon and
Benjamin Franklin--1776-1789." Harper's Monthly Magazine
113, no. 676 (September):[626]-33.
Franklin helped to relieve the frequent unhappiness of
his much younger friend, and she offered him many hours of
amusement and comfort.

112 FOSTER, JOHN W[ATSON]. "Franklin as a Diplomat." Independent
60, no. 2980 (11 January):84-89.
Franklin had the perfect temperament to be a great
diplomat, and he remains "the representative American
diplomat." His success in France, however, bore testimony
not only to his conciliatory temper, but to his great intellectual powers and to the regard in which he was held in
Europe.

113 [FRANKLIN BICENTENNIAL COMMITTEE, BOSTON.] The Two-Hundredth
Anniversary of the Birth of Benjamin Franklin[.] Celebra-
tion by the Commonwealth of Massachusetts and the City of
Boston[,] in Symphony Hall, Boston[,] January 17, 1906.
[Boston]: printed by order of the Massachusetts General
Court and the Boston City Council, 113 pp.

1906

> The relevant parts of the book are the addresses by
> Samuel Abbott Green, Curtis Guild, Jr., J.J. Jusserand,
> John F. Fitzgerald, Henry S. Pritchett, and Carroll D.
> Wright and a poem by James Jeffrey Roche. These pieces
> are cited individually.

114   FRANKLIN BUSINESS ASSOCIATION, FRANKLIN MASSACHUSETTS. The
      Two-Hundredth Anniversary of the Birth of Benjamin Franklin.
      1706-1906. Franklin, Mass.: Sentinel Press, 67 pp.
         The town honored Franklin by adopting his name and
      asked him for a bell for the church steeple. Franklin sent
      instead books, preferring sense to sound. This pamphlet
      also includes a list of important dates in Franklin's life,
      a number of Poor Richard's maxims, and ten selected virtues
      of his list of thirteen. A copy of the program celebrating
      the anniversary and a brief history of the town complete
      the work.

115   FRAZER, PERSIFOR. [Address of] "The Geological Society of
      America." In Record of the Celebration of the Two Hun-
      dredth Anniversary of Benjamin Franklin. . . . Vol. 1.
      Philadelphia: printed for the American Philosophical
      Society, pp. 301-2.
         Franklin "was perhaps the greatest man this Continent
      has produced."

116   _____. [Address of the] "Sociedad Cientifica 'Antonio
      Alzate.'" In Record of the Celebration of the Two Hundredth
      Anniversary of Benjamin Franklin. . . . Vol. 1. Philadel-
      phia: printed for the American Philosophical Society,
      pp. 295-96.
         The Sociedad expresses "the Pan-American feeling which
      hails Franklin as a great Western Continent patriot" and
      fellow scientist.

117   _____. [Address of the] "Société Géologique de Belgique."
      In Record of the Celebration of the Two Hundredth Anniver-
      sary of Benjamin Franklin. . . . Vol. 1. Philadelphia:
      printed for the American Philosophical Society, pp. 293-94.
         Franklin "reached the summit in each of the departments
      in which his great abilities served mankind" and his memory
      "commands the reverence of all ages."

118   FREEMASONS, GRAND LODGE of PENNSYLVANIA. Proceedings of the
      Right Worshipful Grand Lodge of the Most Ancient and Honor-
      able Fraternity of Free Masons of Pennsylvania, and Masonic
      Jurisdiction Thereunto Belonging[,] at Its Celebration of
      the Bi-Centenary of the Birth of Right Worshipful Past

1906

Grand Master Brother Benjamin Franklin[,] Held in the
Masonic Temple, in the City of Philadelphia on Wednesday,
March the Seventh[,] A.D. 1906--A.L. 5906[,] Together With
an Account of the Memorial Service at His Tomb, on Thurs-
day, April the Nineteenth[,] A.D. 1906--A.L. 5906.
Philadelphia: Grand Lodge of Pennsylvania, 352 pp.
This book consists of various addresses on Franklin, an
account of Philadelphia's St. John's Lodge, the one to which
Franklin belonged, an exhibition of Frankliniana, and other
items concerning the celebration. Substantive pieces are
cited separately; the very long title of the book has been
abbreviated somewhat but will be easily recognizable.

119   FURNESS, HORACE HOWARD. "Franklin As Citizen and Philanthro-
       pist." In Record of the Celebration of the Two Hundredth
       Anniversary of Benjamin Franklin. . . . Vol. 1. Philadel-
       phia: printed for the American Philosophical Society,
       pp. 31-53.
       There is a "divinity that hedges this Franklin, this
       king of men." Franklin was the ideal citizen, and just
       the one Philadelphia and later America needed. His thirst
       for knowledge, wisdom, and compassion joined with a temper
       "so equable that the sight of injustice could alone disturb
       its poise"; and his honesty serves as a lesson to us all.
       In his Autobiography he shows himself as the "jocund youth"
       he was and even "presents the worse side of his own charac-
       ter." Yet it is clear that even in youth and young manhood
       he had the qualities and character that were later to make
       him great and benevolent. Furness traces Franklin's career,
       pointing out his many accomplishments; however, he notes, it
       is Franklin's self-sacrificing goodness and usefulness, his
       perfect citizenship and philanthropy, that make him the
       smiling "demi-god of peace" and the greatest of all "our
       citizens."

120   GAVEY, J.; PATCHELL, WILLIAM H.; and LLOYD, G.C. [Address of
       the] "Institution of Electrical Engineers." In Record of
       the Celebration of the Two Hundredth Anniversary of
       Benjamin Franklin. . . . Vol. 1. Philadelphia: printed
       for the American Philosophical Society, p. 289.
       Franklin praised for scientific work and for founding
       the Society.

121   GIGLIO-TOS, E. [Address of the] "Instituto di Zoologia e
       Anatomia Comparata Della R. Università di Cagliari." In
       Record of the Celebration of the Two Hundredth Anniversary
       of Benjamin Franklin. . . . Vol. 1. Philadelphia:
       printed for the American Philosophical Society, p. 213.
       Praise for Franklin as a scientist and philosopher.

1906

122 GOLDIE, GEORGE TAUBMAN. [Address of] "The Royal Geographical
    Society." In Record of the Celebration of the Two Hundredth
    Anniversary of Benjamin Franklin. . . . Vol. 1. Philadel-
    phia: printed for the American Philosophical Society,
    pp. 262-63.
       Franklin attained distinction in "many directions."

123 GOLGI, C. [Address of the University of Pavià.] In Record
    of the Celebration of the Two Hundredth Anniversary of
    Benjamin Franklin. . . . Vol. 2. Philadelphia: printed
    for the American Philosophical Society, p. 204.
       Tribute to Franklin.

124 GOODWIN, WILLIAM W., and DAVIS, W[ILLIAM] M[ORRIS]. [Address
    of] "The Academy of Arts and Sciences." In Record of the
    Celebration of the Two Hundredth Anniversary of Benjamin
    Franklin. . . . Vol. 1. Philadelphia: printed for the
    American Philosophical Society, pp. 236-39.
       Franklin lives on in the "present freshness" of the
    American Philosophical Society and "in the hearts of his
    countrymen."

125 [GORDON, GEORGE A.] "The Prayer." In The Two-Hundredth Anni-
    versary of the Birth of Benjamin Franklin[.] Celebration
    by the Commonwealth of Massachusetts and the City of
    Boston[,] in Symphony Hall, Boston[,] January 17, 1906.
    [Boston]: printed by order of the Massachusetts General
    Court and the Boston City Council, pp. 17-18.
       The Rev. Mr. Gordon, "a lineal successor to Mr. Willard,
    who baptized the young Franklin," was cautious. While pay-
    ing tribute to Franklin's achievements, benevolence, and
    typically American "passion for self-improvement" and "dig-
    nity before kings," he prayed "that our people may consider
    and continue in their lives all that was honorable and
    worthy in this famous career, and that whatever in it was
    weak or unworthy they may cover with reverent regret and
    shun."

126 GREEN, SAMUEL ABBOTT. "Introductory Remarks by the Chairman."
    In The Two-Hundredth Anniversary of the Birth of Benjamin
    Franklin[.] Celebration by the Commonwealth of Massachu-
    setts and the City of Boston[,] in Symphony Hall, Boston[,]
    January 17, 1906. [Boston]: printed by order of the
    Massachusetts General Court and the Boston City Council,
    pp. 21-22.
       In no matter what capacity we consider him, Franklin
    demands our admiration. He was "brilliant" in whatever he
    undertook. Perhaps, however, his greatest achievement is
    that he always "kept in close touch with the popular heart."

127 GREENE, JEROME DAVIS. [Address of] "Harvard University."
In Record of the Celebration of the Two Hundredth Anniversary of Benjamin Franklin. . . . Vol. 1. Philadelphia:
printed for the American Philosophical Society, pp. 217-18.
Franklin recognized the chief importance of advancing
learning.

128 GROLIER CLUB of the CITY OF NEW YORK. Catalogue of an Exhibition Commemorating the Two Hundredth Anniversary of the
Birth of Benjamin Franklin. [New York]: printed for the
Grolier Club of the City of New York by the De Vinne Press,
100 pp.
A catalogue of portraits, medals, and other art work
depicting Franklin as well as works he wrote, printed, or
with which he was otherwise associated.

129 GROWOLL, A[DOLPH]. "The Franklin Bi-Centenary." Magazine of
History 3, no. 1 (January):44-46.
Franklin remained interested in all aspects of printing
and proud of his connection with the trade.

130 GUILD, CURTIS, Jr. "Remarks by His Excellency." In The Two-
Hundredth Anniversary of the Birth of Benjamin Franklin[.]
Celebration by the Commonwealth of Massachusetts and the
City of Boston[,] in Symphony Hall, Boston[,] January 17,
1906. [Boston]: printed by order of the Massachusetts
General Court and the Boston City Council, pp. 25-28.
Franklin had only one equal in patriotic services to
America during the Revolution: Washington. Yet Boston has
until now done too little to pay tribute to its great
native son.

131 GUMMERE, AMELIA M. "An International Chess Party." Bulletin
of the Friends Historical Society of Philadelphia 1, no. 1
(October):3-22.
Dr. John Fothergill was a friend to Franklin and supported his diplomatic and scientific efforts. Fothergill,
in fact, was the first man to understand the significance
of Franklin's scientific discoveries, and in later years
he worked with the American and David Barclay to prevent
the Revolution. The title of this article refers to
Fothergill's role in having Franklin, Lord Howe, and
Mrs. Howe meet ostensibly to play chess but actually to
try and resolve the hostilities between America and England.

132 GUNSAULUS, FRANK W. "A Unique Franklin Letter." Outlook 83
(5 May):28-30.

1906

A Franklin letter to Darmouth, written less than four
years before American independence, show that Franklin could
yet refresh himself from political concerns by becoming
fully absorbed in writing about electrical theory.

133 HADLEY, ARTHUR TWINING. [Address of] "Yale University." In
Record of the Celebration of the Two Hundredth Anniversary
of Benjamin Franklin. . . . Vol. 1. Philadelphia: printed
for the American Philosophical Society, p. 226.
Franklin lauded for his scientific and political
achievements.

134 HALE, EDWARD EVERETT. "Franklin As Philosopher and Moralist."
Independent 60, no. 2980 (11 January):89-93.
During Franklin's lifetime the word "philosopher" referred to one we would call a physicist. While later generations recognize him as a scientist, they often demean
him as a philosopher, considering him to be merely a spokes-
man for parsimony. This is an unfortunate and inaccurate
view. Franklin was a practical philosopher who, among
other things, preached true economy because the lessons
of economy were needed in the developing country. Yet his
range of philosophical concern was as broad as it was basically moral. Underlying his pronouncements is a concern for
the betterment of mankind.

135 HARJES, JOHN H. "Discours de Présentation." In Ceremony
Held in Paris to Commemorate the Bi-Centenary of the Birth
of Benjamin Franklin, April 27, 1906. [Compiled by
Theodore Ayrault Dodge.] Paris: Imprimerie Universelle,
English Printers, pp. 49-51.
Tribute to Franklin, France, and the United States by
the man who, more than anyone else, was responsible for
the erection of the statue of Franklin.

136 HARRISON, FREDERIC. "Benjamin Franklin." In Memories and
Thoughts[.] Men--Books--Cities--Art. New York:
Macmillan Co., pp. 119-22.
Franklin was a "typical American patriot" who was also
a great luminary of science and diplomacy. Furthermore,
he was "one of the most complete intelligences and one of
the most all-round personalities" of modern history.
Though self-taught, he became an outstanding literary
figure, and it is an unhappy fact that he has not been
sufficiently honored by his countrymen.

137 HART, ALBERT BUSHNELL. "'Benjamin Franklin As a Commonwealth
Builder.' An Address Delivered Before the Wyoming

Commemorative Association, July 3, 1906." In <u>Wyoming
Commemorative Association</u>[.] <u>Proceedings</u>. Wilkes-Barre,
Pa.: published for the Association by Wm. Puckey & Bro.,
pp. [9]-22.
Franklin's intense desire to leave the world better than
he found it made him a great citizen on every level. He was
an important force in pushing through the Constitution, as
he had been in America's gaining independence, and truly
helped build the United States of America.

138   HART, CHARLES HENRY. "Bust of Franklin Attributed to Ceracchi
the Work of Caffiere." <u>Pennsylvania Magazine of History
and Biography</u> 30, no. 2:241.
Hart corrects a nearly century old error.

139   _____. "Franklin Portraits." <u>Pennsylvania Magazine of History and Biography</u> 30, no. 2:241-42.
Hart tries to discover the whereabouts of Franklin family portraits of Benjamin, Deborah, and Sally referred to
repeatedly in letters.

140   _____. "Franklin Portraits." <u>Pennsylvania Magazine of History and Biography</u> 30, no. 3:379-80.
Discovers where Franklin family portraits are located.
(The portraits were reproduced in the April 1906 issue of
the <u>Pennsylvania Magazine of History and Biography</u>.)

141   _____. [On the 1759 Wilson Portrait of Franklin.] <u>Independ-
ent</u> 60, no. 2995 (26 April):[953].
Recently, in honor of the two-hundredth anniversary of
Franklin's birth, Albert Henry George Grey, fourth Earl
Grey, returned to the United States, the Benjamin Wilson
portrait of Franklin. It had been taken from Franklin's
home by the Earl's ancestor, Major General Sir Charles Grey,
in 1778.

142   HART, SAMUEL. [Address of] "The Connecticut Historical
Society." In <u>Record of the Celebration of the Two Hun-
dredth Anniversary of Benjamin Franklin. . . .</u> Vol. 1.
Philadelphia: printed for the American Philosophical
Society, pp. 259-60.
It is only fitting that so great an organization as the
American Philosophical Society should have as its founder
so outstanding a man as Franklin.

143   HARVEY, JAMES CLARENCE. "Life's Heroes." <u>American Printer</u>
42, no. 1 (March):86.

1906

Tribute to Franklin as the patron saint of printers, who
honor him on the 200th anniversary of his birth. While
Harvey does acclaim Franklin, he actually uses the occasion
to sing the praises of his fellow printers and to reveal
his talents as a versifier and punster, as the following
stanza shows:

Two hundred years have carelessly been <u>pied</u>,
    Since he who wore his hair somewhat like mine,
Sprang from the <u>matrix</u> to become your pride;
    Your <u>type</u> of man with soul almost divine.
How many <u>forms</u> thruout our glorious land,
    Will <u>read the proofs</u> of what you feel tonight,
And chase away the clouds of care to stand
    And toast Ben Franklin in their proud delight!

144   HAWKINS, EDWIN N. "Notes on Franklin Bi-Centenary Recently
Held in Philadelphia under the Auspices of The American
Philosophical Society." <u>Proceedings of the Colorado Scien-
tific Society</u> 8 (November):[186]-91.
A report of the Philadelphia celebration honoring the
bicentennial of Franklin's birth.

145   HAY, JOHN. "Franklin in France." <u>Century</u> 71, no. 3
(January):447-58.
Because the French loved and respected Franklin, he was
able to obtain for the United States the help it needed in
the struggle against England.

146   HEINRICH. [Address of the] "Magyar Tudományos Akadémia."
In <u>Record of the Celebration of the Two Hundredth Anniversary of Benjamin Franklin. . . .</u> Vol. 1. Philadelphia:
printed for the American Philosophical Society, p. 258.
Praise for Franklin.

147   HENKELS, STAN[ISLAUS] V[INCENT], firm. "Franklin Imprint,
Etc." In <u>Valuable Miscellaneous Books[,] Elegant Art
Works[,] Many Rare Items in American History; Franklin and
Other Imprints; Early American Maps[,] Indian Stone Imple-
ments and Other Relics to Be Sold Friday Afternoon, June 22,
1906[,] at 2:30 O'Clock[.] Catalogue No. 955.</u> Philadel-
phia: [Stan. V. Henkels], pp. 30-31.
The one Franklin imprint listed for sale is his 1743
<u>A Confession of Faith.</u> . . .

148   HERWIG. [Address of the] "Deutscher Seefischerei-Verein."
In <u>Record of the Celebration of the Two Hundredth</u>

1906

Anniversary of Benjamin Franklin. . . . Vol. 1. Philadelphia: printed for the American Philosophical Society,
p. 288.
Tribute to Franklin.

149   HESEHUS, N. [Address of] "The Physical Section of the Russian
       Physico-Chemical Society." In Record of the Celebration of
       the Two Hundredth Anniversary of Benjamin Franklin. . . .
       Vol. 1. Philadelphia: printed for the American Philosoph-
       ical Society, pp. 286-87.
           Franklin's name "reminds every one of us of the luminous
       kingdom of Ideals and Understanding. The Russian children
       in one of their earliest books read the biography of
       Benjamin Franklin as a paragon of virtue; the school boys
       learn by the example of Franklin how the brave mind over-
       comes the formidable appearances of nature by its funda-
       mental investigations; the image of the famous leader of
       the great American people rises before the citizens of
       Great Russia at the time of her new stage of the liberat-
       ing evolution."

150   HOLLAND, W[ILLIAM] J[ACOB]. [Address of] "The Carnegie
       Museum." In Record of the Celebration of the Two Hundredth
       Anniversary of Benjamin Franklin. . . . Vol. 1. Philadel-
       phia: printed for the American Philosophical Society,
       pp. 306-7.
           Franklin was "the wisest man of his day and generation,
       a high priest of science, the most famous of all Pennsyl-
       vanians, one of the greatest Americans."

151   HOUSTON, EDWIN JAMES. "Benjamin Franklin Trust Funds to the
       Cities of Boston and Philadelphia." Journal of the Franklin
       Institute 161, no. 5:385-93.
           Houston discusses Franklin's trust funds left to his
       native and adopted cities and the disappointing growth of
       the Philadelphia endowment.

152   ____. "Franklin As a Man of Science and an Inventor."
       Journal of the Franklin Institute 161, no. 4:241-316,
       321-83.
           This is a detailed discussion of Franklin's achievements
       as a scientist and inventor. Houston quotes extensively
       from Franklin and provides copious explanations of many of
       his experiments and concludes that as of 1906 Franklin was
       the greatest man of science America had produced. (The
       discussion has been largely superseded by I. Bernard Cohen,
       the editors of the Papers of Benjamin Franklin, and by
       others.)

1906

153 _____. "Some Important Foundations of Benjamin Franklin."
Electrical World 47, no. 3 (20 January):152-54.
   Franklin founded the Philadelphia Library, the Univer-
sity of Pennsylvania and the American Philosophical Society.
He also established funds in Boston and Philadelphia to
help young married artisans get started in their careers.
His efforts in these areas reflect his concern for learning
and his humanity.

154 IRWIN, AGNES. "The Social and Domestic Life of Franklin."
Journal of the Franklin Institute 161, no. 6:431-38.
   Franklin did many things very well; the mark of genius
was on him. But he is not complex at all. He was thoroughly human and relaxed enough to enjoy life and fellowship
wholeheartedly in the midst of tension.

155 JACKSON, M[ARIE] KATHERINE. "Benjamin Franklin." In Outlines
of the Literary History of Colonial Pennsylvania.
Lancaster, Pa.: New Era Printing Co., pp. 61-79.
   Franklin is an excellent writer, and his Autobiography
will last as long as there are readers. While he lacked
spirituality himself and had no appreciation of spiritual
things, his goodness made him the benefactor of all men.

156 JASTROW, MORRIS. "Frankliniana in the University Library."
Alumni Register 10, no. 6 (March):270-72.
   A list with Jastrow's comments on the items in the
University of Pennsylvania library. (The journal title
later becomes The General Magazine and Historical Chronicle.)

157 JOUKOOSKY, NICHOLAS [YEGOROVICH] (Nikolai Zhokovskii) et al.
[Address of the] "Imperatorskoie Obshchestvo Lubitelei
Iestestvoznania, Antropologii i Etnografii [Imperial society
of friends of the natural sciences]." In Record of the
Celebration of the Two Hundredth Anniversary of Benjamin
Franklin. . . . Vol. 1. Philadelphia: printed for the
American Philosophical Society, p. 285.
   Greetings to Franklin and to the Society.

158 JUSSERAND, JULES J[EAN]. "Reception of the Franklin Medal."
In Record of the Celebration of the Two Hundredth Anniversary of Benjamin Franklin. . . . Vol. 1. Philadelphia:
printed for the American Philosophical Society, pp. 99-102.
   The medal "represents a man ever venerated" in France
as "the scientist, the philosopher, the inventor, the leader
of men, the one who gave to France her first notion of what
true Americans really were."

159 JUSSERAND, [JULES JEAN]. "Remarks." In <u>The Two-Hundredth</u>
<u>Anniversary of the Birth of Benjamin Franklin</u>[.] Celebra-
<u>tion by the Commonwealth of Massachusetts and the City of</u>
<u>Boston</u>[,] <u>in Symphony Hall, Boston</u>[,] <u>January 17, 1906</u>.
[Boston]: printed by order of the Massachusetts General
Court and the Boston City Council, p. 31.
Of all of Franklin's achievements, the most appealing
to the French ambassador is his role in the alliance be-
tween France and America.

160 KENDRICK, GEORGE W., Jr. "Benjamin Franklin." In <u>Proceedings</u>
<u>of the Right Worshipful Grand Lodge of the Most Ancient and</u>
<u>Honorable Fraternity of Free Masons of Pennsyl-</u>
<u>vania</u> . . . [,] <u>at Its Celebration of the Bi-Centenary of</u>
<u>the Birth of</u> . . . <u>Benjamin Franklin.</u> . . . Philadelphia:
Grand Lodge of Pennsylvania, pp. 178-79.
"It is for the broad humanity of Franklin's complex life
that we especially revere him." In no matter what area we
consider him, Franklin "was peculiarly human," and this is
certainly one of the reasons he typifies Freemasonry.

161 _____. "Franklin the Mason, Diplomat, Scientist, Philosopher."
In <u>Proceedings of the Right Worshipful Grand Lodge of the</u>
<u>Most Ancient and Honorable Fraternity of Free Masons of</u>
<u>Pennsylvania</u> . . . [,] <u>at Its Celebration of the Bi-</u>
<u>Centenary of the Birth of</u> . . . <u>Benjamin Franklin.</u> . . .
Philadelphia: Grand Lodge of Pennsylvania, pp. 27-30.
Many of the qualities that made Franklin the great philosopher, founder, diplomat, scientist, and humanitarian
also led him to become a Mason. These are the virtues that
transcend differences in birth and geography, and so it is
not surprising that Washington was also a Mason.

162 KINSEY, JOHN L. [Address.] In <u>Proceedings of the Right</u>
<u>Worshipful Grand Lodge of the Most Ancient and Honorable</u>
<u>Fraternity of Free Masons of Pennsylvania.</u> . . [,] <u>at Its</u>
<u>Celebration of the Bi-Centenary of the Birth of</u> . . .
<u>Benjamin Franklin.</u> . . . Philadelphia: Grand Lodge of
Pennsylvania, pp. 184-90.
Franklin "was the disciple of common sense--the apostle
of applied science," a man so far ahead of his time that it
is accurate to say he had "a last half of the 19th century
intellect set mid way in the 18th."

163 KITTRIDGE [sic], GEORGE LYMAN, and NOBLE, JOHN. [Address of]
"The Colonial Society of Massachusetts." In <u>Record of the</u>
<u>Celebration of the Two Hundredth Anniversary of Benjamin</u>
<u>Franklin.</u> . . . Vol. 1. Philadelphia: printed for the
American Philosophical Society, pp. 304-5.

1906

> Franklin "took all useful knowledge for his province"
> and "was a Citizen of the world . . . , whose chief con-
> cern was the amelioration of mankind."

164   KLINE, BURTON. "Ben Franklin in Boston." New England Maga-
      zine, n.s. 33, no. 5 (January):[546]-54.
      Franklin returns to earth in 1906 and is "grieved" at
      the poor quality of food, at fast transportation, and at
      the neglect of artists, who are as valuable as so-called
      more practical men.

165   KUSENEZOW, N.J. [Address of] "Die Naturforscher-Gesellschaft,
      Dorpat." In Record of the Celebration of the Two Hundredth
      Anniversary of Benjamin Franklin. . . . Vol. 1. Philadel-
      phia: printed for the American Philosophical Society,
      p. 276.
      Sends warm wishes to commemorate the bicentennial of
      Franklin's birth.

166   LACKLAND, R.J., and CUNNINGHAM, A.D. [Address of] "The
      Missouri Botanical Garden." In Record of the Celebration
      of the Two Hundredth Anniversary of Benjamin Franklin. . . .
      Vol. 1. Philadelphia: printed for the American Philosoph-
      ical Society, p. 303.
      The Missouri Botanical Garden acclaims Franklin on the
      bicentennial of his birth.

167   LAMBERTON, JAMES M. "An Account of St. John's Lodge, Philadel-
      phia, and Its 'Liber B.'" In Proceedings of the Right
      Worshipful Grand Lodge of the Most Ancient and Honorable
      Fraternity of Free Masons of Pennsylvania . . . [,] at Its
      Celebration of the Bi-Centenary of the Birth of . . . .
      Benjamin Franklin. . . . Philadelphia: Grand Lodge of
      Pennsylvania, pp. 203-23.
      The "Liber B.," or account book of St. John's Lodge from
      24 June 1731, to 24 June 1738, with one entry for 24 June
      1739, provides information about the Lodge and about
      Franklin's Masonic activities.

168   LANE, WILLIAM C[OOLEDGE]. "Harvard College and Franklin."
      Publications of the Colonial Society of Massachusetts 10
      (January):229-39.
      Reviews the correspondence and records and concludes
      that Harvard and Franklin enjoyed cordial relations for
      many years.

169   LITSON, ELIZABETH J., and CUMMINGS, CARLOS K. [Address of]
      "The Buffalo Society of Natural Sciences." In Record of

the Celebration of the Two Hundredth Anniversary of
Benjamin Franklin. . . . Vol. 1. Philadelphia: printed
for the American Philosophical Society, p. 282.
Greetings.

170 LODGE, HENRY CABOT. "Franklin and His Times." Independent
60, no. 2980 (11 January):72-79.
Franklin was one of the greatest men of a remarkable
century adorned by many great men. Though he was entirely
human enough to have "blemishes in his character," Franklin
stands out among all his contemporaries, indeed stands
high throughout history for his "achievements and services."
During his long life he strove "unceasingly [for] the improvement of man's condition here on earth."

171 LOUDON, J., et al. [Address of] "The University of Toronto."
In Record of the Celebration of the Two Hundredth Anniversary of Benjamin Franklin. . . . Vol. 1. Philadelphia:
printed for the American Philosophical Society, p. 261.
The University honors the memory of Franklin "as a distinguished pioneer in the field of American scientific discovery, and as a founder and organizer of institutions for
the promotion of learning and the advancement of science."

172 MacCALLA, CLIFFORD P., ed. "Masonic Letters of Benjamin
Franklin, of Philadelphia, to Henry Price, of Boston."
In Proceedings of the Right Worshipful Grand Lodge of the
Most Ancient and Honorable Fraternity of Free Masons of
Pennsylvania . . . [,] at Its Celebration of the Bi-
Centenary of the Birth of . . . Benjamin Franklin. . . .
Philadelphia: Grand Lodge of Pennsylvania, pp. 193-202.
The Franklin-Price correspondence proves that Free-
masonry in Pennsylvania is older than in Massachusetts.

173 McCORMICK, ROBERT S. "Discours." In Ceremony Held in Paris
to Commemorate the Bi-Centenary of the Birth of Benjamin
Franklin, April 27, 1906. [Compiled by Theodore Ayrault
Dodge.] Paris: Imprimerie Universelle, English Printers,
pp. 37-38.
The ambassador from the United States delivers in French
a tribute to France and to Franklin.

174 [McCORMICK, ROBERT S.] "Introductory Address." In Ceremony
Held in Paris to Commemorate the Bi-Centenary of the Birth
of Benjamin Franklin, April 27, 1906. [Compiled by
Theodore Ayrault Dodge.] Paris: Imprimerie Universelle,
English Printers, pp. 14-15.

1906

McCormick, the American ambassador to France, expresses
the appreciation of the United States for the honor accorded
Franklin and for the spirit of international cooperation.

175 McGOVERN, JOHN. "Benjamin Franklin and Tom Paine." National
Magazine 23, no. 4 (January):[426]-30.
These pages of a slightly longer piece deal with Franklin
and praise him for his liberalism, humanitarianism, and
wisdom.

176 McKELWAY, St. CLAIR. [Address of] "The University of The
State of New York." In Record of the Celebration of the
Two Hundredth Anniversary of Benjamin Franklin. . . .
Vol. 1. Philadelphia: printed for the American Philosoph-
ical Society, pp. 242-43.
Praise for Franklin's achievements in science and diplo-
macy and for "his services as a patriot."

177 [MAESTRI, VINCENZO?] [Address of the] "R. Accademia di
Scienze, Lettre ed Arti." In Record of the Celebration of
the Two Hundredth Anniversary of Benjamin Franklin. . . .
Vol. 1. Philadelphia: printed for the American Philosoph-
ical Society, p. 222.
Tribute to Franklin as philosopher and statesman.

178 MATHIAS, G. "Adresse Votée par l'Académie ses Sciences,
Inscriptions et Belles-Lettres de Toulouse. . . ." In
Record of the Celebration of the Two Hundredth Anniversary
of Benjamin Franklin. . . . Vol. 1. Philadelphia: printed
for the American Philosophical Society, pp. 231-32.
Praise for Franklin's scientific work.

179 MATSUMURA, JINZO. [Address of] "The Tokyo Botanical Society."
In Record of the Celebration of the Two Hundredth Anniversary of Benjamin Franklin. . . . Vol. 1. Philadelphia:
printed for the American Philosophical Society, p. 297.
Offers the greetings of the Tokyo Botanical Society to
honor Franklin and the American Philosophical Society.

180 MAW, W.H., and LEWIS, THOMAS. [Address of] "The Royal Astro-
nomical Society." In Record of the Celebration of the Two
Hundredth Anniversary of Benjamin Franklin. . . . Vol. 1.
Philadelphia: printed for the American Philosophical
Society, p. 252.
Tribute to Franklin as a scientist.

181 MITCHELL, SILAS WEIR. "The Memory of Franklin." In Record
of the Celebration of the Two Hundredth Anniversary of

1906

Benjamin Franklin. . . . Vol. 1. Philadelphia: printed
for the American Philosophical Society, pp. 193-95.
A poetic tribute to Franklin for his personal qualities
and many services.

182   MITSUKURI, K. [Address of] "The College of Science, Imperial
University, Tokyo." In Record of the Celebration of the
Two Hundredth Anniversary of Benjamin Franklin. . . .
Vol. 1. Philadelphia: printed for the American Philosoph-
ical Society, p. 284.
Franklin is "one of the world's great men."

183   _____. [Address of] "The Tokyo Zoological Society." In
Record of the Celebration of the Two Hundredth Anniversary
of Benjamin Franklin. . . . Vol. 1. Philadelphia:
printed for the American Philosophical Society, p. 298.
The Tokyo Zoological Society pays tribute to Franklin's
memory and to the American Philosophical Society.

184   MONTGOMERY, D[AVID] H[ENRY]. "Part Second." In Benjamin
Franklin; His Life Written by Himself[.] With an Intro-
duction by W.P. Trent. Standard English Classics. Boston:
Ginn & Co., pp. [233]-96.
A continuation of Franklin's life. Montgomery sees
Franklin and the colonists as all good and the Penn family
and, later, England, as completely wrong and evil.

185   MORE, PAUL ELMER. "Franklin in Literature." Independent 60,
no. 2980 (11 January):98-104.
"There is a certain embarrassment in dealing with
Franklin as a man of letters, for the simple reason that
he was never, in the strict sense of the word, concerned
with letters at all." He wrote much, to be sure, and what
he touches he enlarges and clarifies with great intellectual energy and ease, no matter how diverse the topics. "He
had perhaps the most clarifying and renovating intellect of
that keenly alert age. . . . Yet his pen still lacked that
final spell which transmutes life into literature." The
pressure under which he wrote dictated that he address himself to immediate concerns and ignore the more remote powers that make a work literature; therefore, while Franklin's
life is literature, his writings are not. He possessed art
and wit in abundance, but they, like his philosophy, were
often coarse and generally given to a practical rather than
an imaginative turn. The lack of the spiritual element in
his thinking is also reflected in his writings. "In the
end one feels that both in his strength and his limitations,
in the versatility and efficiency of his intellect as in

1906

the lack of the deeper qualities of the imagination, he was
the typical American. If his broad common sense excluded
the thin vein of mysticism which is one of the paradoxes
of our national character, he represented the powers that
have prevailed and are still shaping us to what end we do
not see."

186   MORRIS, CHARLES. "Benjamin Franklin, the Father of the American Union." In Heroes of Progress in America. Philadelphia: J.B. Lippincott Co., pp. 33-43.
The essays in this book seem at times to be written for
children and at other times for adult general readers. The
piece on Franklin reflects this inconsistency. Most of the
essay deals with his life to 1757, the period covered in
the Autobiography, and Franklin's greatest years are covered in less than three pages. Morris is particularly fond
of stressing Franklin's versatility and common sense, attri-
butes which, coupled with his beneficience, make his great
qualities endure for us today.

187   MOUREK, V.E. [Address of the] "Regia Societas Scientiarum
Bohemica." In Record of the Celebration of the Two Hun-
dredth Anniversary of Benjamin Franklin. . . . Vol. 1.
Philadelphia: printed for the American Philosophical
Society, p. 241.
Tribute to Franklin on the bicentennial celebration of
his birth.

188   MÜLLER, SOPHUS. [Address of the] "Kongelige Nordiske Oldskrift
Selskab." In Record of the Celebration of the Two Hundredth
Anniversary of Benjamin Franklin. . . . Vol. 1. Philadelphia: printed for the American Philosophical Society,
p. 257.
Franklin lauded as a "great citizen of the world," and
as "the promoter of civilization and science."

189   MURRAY, DAVID. [Address of] "The Royal Philosophic Society of
Glasgow." In Record of the Celebration of the Two Hundredth
Anniversary of Benjamin Franklin. . . . Vol. 1. Philadelphia: printed for the American Philosophical Society,
pp. 245-46.
Franklin was a "truly great man; great in every department of knowledge that he cultivated, not less than in the
issue of all his undertakings."

190   MUSTARD, WILFRED P[IRT]. "Poor Richard's Poetry." Nation 82,
no. 2125 (22 March):239.
Identifies some of the poems in the almanacs that were
not written by Franklin.

191   MUSY, M. and GOBET, L[OUI]S. [Address of the] "Société
      Fribourgeoise des Sciences Naturelles." In Record of the
      Celebration of the Two Hundredth Anniversary of Benjamin
      Franklin. . . . Vol. 1. Philadelphia: printed for the
      American Philosophical Society, pp. 290-91.
      Praises Franklin for his scientific achievements.

192   NASELLI, [ENRICO?]. [Address.] In Record of the Celebration
      of the Two Hundredth Anniversary of Benjamin Franklin. . . .
      Vol. 1. Philadelphia: printed for the American Philosoph-
      ical Society, pp. 199-201.
      Count Naselli, the minister of the Royal Department of
      Agriculture, Industry and Commerce of Italy, expresses the
      respect the Italian people have for Franklin's abilities
      and humanitarianism.

193   NICHOLS, EDWARD L[EAMINGTON]. "Franklin as a Man of Science."
      Independent 60, no. 2980 (11 January):79-84.
      "In Europe just before the middle of the eighteenth cen-
      tury, there was a passion for dabbling in natural philosophy
      of the lighter sort and especially for playing at electric-
      ity, and nearly every one with pretensions to culture or
      even merely to position in the fashionable world engaged
      in experiments with the electrical machine and the Leyden
      jar." This interest seized Franklin, but he was no dabbler.
      Though his practical side "kept the overhand of Franklin
      the man of science--even while he was most busily employed
      in his investigations--" his work was instrumental in mak-
      ing electrical experimentation a science. He himself, how-
      ever, was more interested in the practical application of
      science than in theory and speculation. He did not under-
      stand fully the implications of electrical studies, but he
      was nevertheless remarkable in the range of scientific
      topics he could handle. Had he been able to devote his
      time to science, he would have become not only one of the
      great scientists of his day, but of all time.

194   _____. "Franklin's Researches in Electricity." In Record of
      the Celebration of the Two Hundredth Anniversary of Benjamin
      Franklin. . . . Vol. 1. Philadelphia: printed for the
      American Philosophical Society, pp. 103-21.
      To appreciate the significance of Franklin's achieve-
      ments in "the science of electricity," one must examine the
      state of scientific knowledge up to his time. This Nichols
      does and then briefly traces Franklin's career in science.
      He concludes that "Franklin contributed nothing of a quanti-
      tative character to the science of electricity, but he was
      an accurate observer of phenomena" and was fond of

1906

speculation. "Speculation is an essential feature of
theory building, particularly in the beginnings of a
science. In Franklin's case it was controlled by practical
common sense, sound logic and a rare definiteness of con-
ception. After any speculative flight the strongly utilitarian side of his nature was sure to assert itself. . . ."
His theory of electricity "comes nearest to our twentieth
century concept," and Franklin possessed "a native endow-
ment unequaled by any of the intellects of his day." Even
science, however, was but one facet in the multifaceted
career of this great man.

195 OBERHOLTZER, ELLIS PAXSON. "The Age of Franklin." In The
      Literary History of Philadelphia. Philadelphia: George W.
      Jacobs & Co.[,] Publishers, pp. 46-58.
          Clearly hostile to his subject, complaining of the "im-
      morality of [Franklin's] youth, and his foolish fondness
      for adulation in his old age," faults which make good peo-
      ple blush "for the honor of our eighteenth century civiliza-
      tion if he be set up as its highest type," Oberholtzer also
      accuses Franklin of "duplicity" in politics and business
      and says that his so-called Yankee shrewdness is no more
      Yankee than German or "recreant Quaker." Moreover, Franklin
      was too liberal and democratic for the author's taste; in-
      deed, he was as unsound a statesman as Paine or Mirabeau,
      while such lesser known contemporaries as Robert Morris and
      James Wilson were more sensibly in the tradition of Burke.
      Finally, Franklin's reputation as an author has been greatly
      exaggerated and rests, as does much of his fame, on his
      happier view of human nature that contradicted the darker
      perception of the world.

196 _____. "Franklin in Europe." Book News 24, no. 281
      (January):[315]-18.
          Franklin is great in many ways, especially as a diplomat;
      however, he has his failings, and these are the failures of
      the self-educated man who is ready to embrace all knowledge
      and theory that is new. Franklin's limited education caused
      him to support French economic theory. He was the darling
      of the people and would surely be so today, were he to re-
      turn to earth. Yet today he would hardly be able to repre-
      sent science or the government in any important way because
      of his lack of education.

197 O'REILLY, MICHAEL FRANCIS [Brother Potamian]. "Franklin and
      de Romas; or the Lightning Kite." Electrical World 47,
      no. 3 (20 January):147-50.

Franklin did indeed conduct his kite experiment, and he
did so a year before M. de Romas performed his experiment
with a kite. The Frenchman had the idea of the "lightning
kite" at least by 12 July 1752, "but he did nothing with it
until 14 May 1753, whereas Franklin undertook his experiment in June 1752 and reported its success to Collinson in
a letter dated 19 October 1752.

198   OVIDI, L[UIGI]. Beniamino Franklin. Ancona: Pastore, 6 pp.
      A sketch of Franklin's life to mark the bicentennial of
      his birth. Ovidi praises Franklin's selfless patriotism
      and goodness.

199   PATTERSON, C[HRISTOPHER] STUART. Benjamin Franklin. A
      Speech . . . Before the Pennsylvania Society of the Colo-
      nial Dames of America, Sixth January, 1906. N.p., 8 pp.
      Franklin was by no means perfect, but his critics ignore
      his high-mindedness, benevolence, generosity, patriotism,
      and his many talents. He was a great and good man and a
      symbol of hope for all.

200   PEACH, BEN[JAMIN] N. [Address of] "The Geological Society of
      Glasgow." In Record of the Celebration of the Two Hundredth
      Anniversary of Benjamin Franklin. . . . Vol. 1. Philadel-
      phia: printed for the American Philosophical Society,
      pp. 280-81.
      Praise for Franklin's role as founder of the American
      Philosophical Society.

201   PEIRCE, ARTHUR W. "Address." In Bicentenary of Benjamin
      Franklin's Birth[,] January Seventeen[,] Nineteen Hundred
      and Six. Franklin, Mass.: Sentinel Press, pp. 49-52.
      Franklin gave books to help found the town's library.

202   PENNSYLVANIA SOCIETY of NEW YORK. Year Book of the Pennsyl-
      vania Society[,] 1906. Edited by Barr Ferree. New York:
      Pennsylvania Society, pp. [16]-65.
      A record of the seventh annual festival of the Society,
      which in this year commemorated the 200th anniversary of
      the birth of Benjamin Franklin. The occasion was marked
      by addresses by J. Hampden Robb, George B. Cortelyou,
      Horace Porter, Frederick P. Fish, George A. Post, and
      Albert H. Smyth. They spoke on such matters as Franklin
      as founder of the University of Pennsylvania, his achieve-
      ments in diplomacy and as postmaster-general, his total
      Americanness and, finally, his career as a man of letters.

1906

203   PENNSYLVANIA, UNIVERSITY of. Bi-Centennial of Benjamin
      Franklin, 1706-1906. Philadelphia: John C. Winston Co.,
      4 pp.
          This is the program of the celebration at which was sung
      a song in honor of Franklin. One stanza of the tribute will
      suffice to indicate the whole:

              A ready blade he often made,
                  Ingenious little toys;
              He built a kite, with great delight,
                  And shocked the little boys!

204   PERCY, HENRY GEORGE [Northumberland]. [Address of] "The Royal
      Institution of Great Britain." In Record of the Celebration
      of the Two Hundredth Anniversary of Benjamin Franklin. . . .
      Vol. 1. Philadelphia: printed for the American Philosoph-
      ical Society, p. 244.
          The Royal Institution of Great Britain "recalls with
      interest and respect the Scientific and Experimental Inves-
      tigations of Benjamin Franklin and their practical utility
      to mankind."

205   PHILADELPHIA CONTRIBUTORSHIP for the INSURANCE of FIRE.
      Franklin & Fires[.] His Interest Therein and His Efforts
      to Protect the Citizens of Philadelphia from Devastation
      Especially in Relation to The Philadelphia Contributorship
      for the Insurance of Houses from Loss by Fire. Philadel-
      phia: published from the Offices of the Company, 16 pp.
          A brief history which notes that Franklin's desire to
      control and help provide insurance against fires was an-
      other important manifestation of his humanitarianism.

206   POLACCO, V., and MEDIN, A. [Address of the Reale Accademia
      di Scienze, Lettere ed Arti in Padova.] In Record of the
      Celebration of the Two Hundredth Anniversary of Benjamin
      Franklin. . . . Vol. 1. Philadelphia: printed for the
      American Philosophical Society, pp. 211-12.
          Tribute to Franklin as scientist and citizen.

207   PORTER, HORACE. "Franklin the Diplomat." In Year Book of the
      Pennsylvania Society[,] 1906. Edited by Barr Ferree.
      New York: Pennsylvania Society, pp. [31]-38.
          Franklin's patience, intelligence, philosophical ways,
      and knowledge of human nature all helped make him an out-
      standing diplomat in France. Moreover, as a diplomat and
      man he won people to his views because he was good. He is
      an example we should all follow.

208   POST, GEORGE A. "Franklin the American." In Year Book of the
       Pennsylvania Society[,] 1906. Edited by Barr Ferree. New
       York: Pennsylvania Society, pp. 54-59.
             Humorous treatment makes two basic points: that Franklin
       was a typical American in his foolishness and faults, and
       that because he believed one should work hard and try to
       succeed on his own merits, he is in this regard no longer
       typical of Americans.

209   PRITCHETT, HENRY S[MITH]. "The Story of the Franklin Fund."
       In The Two-Hundredth Anniversary of the Birth of Benjamin
       Franklin[.] Celebration by the Commonwealth of Massachu-
       setts and the City of Boston[,] in Symphony Hall, Boston[,]
       January 17, 1906. [Boston]: printed by order of the
       Massachusetts General Court and the Boston City Council,
       pp. 41-45.
             The Franklin Fund, which had grown substantially by
       1906, is another expression of Franklin's citizenship and
       generosity.

210   RATHBUN, R. [Address of] "The Smithsonian Institution."
       In Record of the Celebration of the Two Hundredth Anniver-
       sary of Benjamin Franklin. . . . Vol. 1. Philadelphia:
       printed for the American Philosophical Society, pp. 266-68.
             Franklin's scientific and diplomatic efforts reveal "a
       strong, original, comprehensive intellect" as well as
       "keenness of perception and . . . sound common sense."

211   RAY, MAUDE LOUISE. "The Bicentenary Poem." In Bicentenary
       of Benjamin Franklin's Birth[,] January Seventeen[,] Nine-
       teen Hundred and Six. Franklin, Mass.: Sentinel Press,
       pp. 53-57.
             Humor and science joined in Franklin to help make him
       great.

212   RAYLEIGH, [JOHN WILLIAM STRUTT]. [Address of] "The Royal
       Society." In Record of the Celebration of the Two Hundredth
       Anniversary of Benjamin Franklin. . . . Vol. 1. Philadel-
       phia: printed for the American Philosophical Society,
       pp. 219-21.
             The president of the Royal Society praises Franklin as
       a great scientist, philosopher, citizen, and as a testimony
       to the genius of "the Anglosaxon race."

213   REMSBURG, JOHN E. "Benjamin Franklin." In Six Historic Amer-
       icans[:] Paine, Jefferson, Washington, Franklin, Lincoln,
       Grant. The Fathers and Saviors of Our Republic, Free-
       thinkers. New York: Truth Seeker Co., pp. 153-79.

1906

Franklin is depicted as ardently deistic and
anti-Christian.

214   REPPLIER, EMMA. "Franklin's Trials As a Benefactor."
      Lippincott's Magazine 77, no. 3 (January):63-70.
      Franklin's trials as a benefactor were especially acute
      when he was in France, pestered continually by those who
      wished to serve the American cause, or who at least wanted
      some preferential treatment or favors from Franklin.

215   RIBBING, SEVED. [Address of] "The University of Lund." In
      Record of the Celebration of the Two Hundredth Anniversary
      of Benjamin Franklin. . . . Vol. 1. Philadelphia:
      printed for the American Philosophical Society, p. 225.
      Franklin deserves the praise of all mankind.

216   ROBB, J. HAMPDEN. "Address." In Year Book of the Pennsyl-
      vania Society[,] 1906. Edited by Barr Ferree. New York:
      Pennsylvania Society, pp. [21]-22.
      Given the fact that 1906 is the 200th anniversary of the
      birth of Benjamin Franklin, this meeting of the Society
      should focus on Franklin.

217   ROBINS, EDWARD. "Franklin the Man." Book News 24, no. 281
      (January):[305-10].
      This summary of Franklin's career stresses the qualities
      that account for his greatness: his logical and luminous
      mind, his early poverty, his shrewdness in evaluating char-
      acters and situations, and his English heritage.

218   ROCHE, JAMES JEFFREY. "Benjamin Franklin." In The Two-
      Hundredth Anniversary of the Birth of Benjamin Franklin[.]
      Celebration by the Commonwealth of Massachusetts and the
      City of Boston[,] in Symphony Hall, Boston[,] January 17,
      1906. [Boston]: printed by order of the Massachusetts
      General Court and the Boston City Council, pp. 81-82.
      A poetic tribute to Franklin as an international,
      national, and New England sage who had the "first of Yankee
      virtues, Common Sense," and throughout his life bore wit-
      ness to the "lofty message of the Manger-born."

219   ROOT, ELIHU. "Presentation to France of the Gold Medal Author-
      ized by The Congress of the United States, April 27, 1904."
      In Record of the Celebration of the Two Hundredth Anniver-
      sary of Benjamin Franklin. . . . Vol. 1. Philadelphia:
      printed for the American Philosophical Society, pp. 97-99.
      A tribute to France for responding to Franklin's
      "appeals" for help during the Revolution.

220 ROSENGARTEN, J[OSEPH] G[EORGE]. "Franklin and the University."
     Alumni Register 10, no. 5 (February):199-201.
         Franklin was always interested in the University of
     Pennsylvania and dedicated to its welfare. (The journal
     title is later changed to The General Magazine and His-
     torical Chronicle.)

221 ROTCH, ABBOTT LAWRENCE. "Did Benjamin Franklin Fly His Elec-
     trical Kite Before He Invented the Lightning Rod?" Pro-
     ceedings of the American Antiquarian Society, n.s. 18
     (October):118-23.
         Rotch makes the following points: that Franklin "pre-
     pared definite directions for putting rods upon buildings
     as early as 1752"; and that even before this time, certain
     Philadelphia buildings were protected with "points."

222 ROTCH, A[BBOTT] LAWRENCE. "The Lightning-Rod Coincident With
     Franklin's Experiment." Science, n.s. 24, no. 624
     (14 December):780.
         Franklin's own Pennsylvania Gazette for 1752 supports
     Rotch's conclusion published in Science for 21 September
     1906, 24, no. 612:374-76, that "the lightning-rod was in
     use" before Franklin "flew his electrical kite."

223 _____. "When Did Franklin Invent the Lightning-Rod?" Science,
     n.s. 24, no. 612 (21 September):374-76.
         Franklin "drew up definite instructions for erecting
     lightning-rods before the close of . . . 1752," and by this
     time some houses in Philadelphia were equipped with rods
     for either protection or experiment.

224 ROUBIN. [Address of the] "Université de Lyon." In Record of
     the Celebration of the Two Hundredth Anniversary of
     Benjamin Franklin. . . . Vol. 1. Philadelphia: printed
     for the American Philosophical Society, pp. 247-49.
         The University pays tribute to Franklin as a scientist,
     philosopher, and humanitarian.

225 RUGGLES, Le ROY B. "A Few Things Recalled by the Franklin
     Bicentenary." Critic 48, no. 1 (January):40-50.
         A sketch of Franklin's life which concludes that although
     we must admire his genius and achievements, it is for his
     human qualities that we love him. These qualities have been
     paramount in creating the recent revival of interest in
     Franklin.

226 RUPP, GEORGE P. "Franklin--His Masonic Record." In Franklin
     Lodge, No. 134, F. & A.M. Celebration of the 200th

1906

Anniversary of the Birth of Benjamin Franklin[,] January 31,
1906. [Philadelphia?]: pp. 8-12.
Highlights of Franklin's career as a Mason in America,
England, and France.

227   RUTHERFORD, ERNEST. "The Modern Theories of Electricity and
Their Relation to the Franklinian Theory." In Record of
the Celebration of the Two Hundredth Anniversary of
Benjamin Franklin. . . . Vol. 1. Philadelphia: printed
for the American Philosophical Society, pp. 123-57.
Rutherford presents a detailed explanation of Franklin's
single fluid theory of electricity and notes the influence
of this theory on later experimenters. He warns, however,
against exaggerating Franklin's importance or of minimizing
the later efforts of others.

228   SACHSE, JULIUS F[RIEDRICH]. "Franklin As a Freemason." In
Proceedings of the Right Worshipful Grand Lodge of the Most
Ancient and Honorable Fraternity of Free Masons of Pennsylvania . . . [,] at Its Celebration of the Bi-Centenary of
the Birth of . . . Benjamin Franklin. . . . Philadelphia:
Grand Lodge of Pennsylvania, pp. 49-169.
Writing an "exhaustive" account of Franklin's sixty-year
career as a Freemason is complicated by the fact that, very
surprisingly, Franklin's memoirs do not mention his Masonic
activities, and he refers to them very seldom in his letters. This omission is even more startling when we consider
Franklin's "active part" in French Masonic affairs. Franklin
probably became interested in Freemasonry while he was in
London in 1725-1726. When he returned to Philadelphia and
discovered that a lodge had been erected there, he tried to
become a member. He was not accepted, however, because he
was underage and, perhaps more importantly, because Freemasonry both in England and America "was then almost exclu-
sively confined to the nobility and gentry." Franklin kept
trying to be accepted but was unsuccessful. Angered, he
printed in the Gazette an account of the Masons in London,
one which was embarrassing, and preceded the piece with a
sharp comment of his own on the London group and on Freemasonry in general. The piece served Franklin's purpose
and the following year, 1731, as soon as he reached the law-
ful age for membership, he was admitted into the St. John's
Lodge. Freemasonry afterwards received a better press in
the Gazette. Franklin entered fully into the "spirit" of
the organization and, indeed, the junto "was patterned after
the Masonic Fraternity." Franklin's Masonic career and con-
nections were very helpful to him in many of his altruistic
measures and in his personal life. It is, in fact, fair to

1906

say that "it was within the Masonic Lodge at Philadelphia" and later "in the Grand Lodge of Pennsylvania [that] was laid the foundation of Franklin's future greatness as a parliamentarian and a prominent figure in all of the various organizations with which he became identified during his long and active public career." Sachse continues to relate Franklin's quick rise through the ranks of Masons and to detail the ways in which he and the "craft" benefited each other. Much of the remainder of this account consists of anecdotes, documents, and Franklin's writings that bear on his Masonic career, including a very full discussion of the sad case of "Daniel Reese." Though the last Masonic announcement in the Gazette appeared in 1741, Franklin retained his keen interest and involvement in Freemasonry. In France, burdened with the greatest responsibilities and problems of his life, he still took an active part in the Loge des IX Soeurs and in 1782 served as its Worshipful Master. When he returned to Philadelphia for the last time, Franklin was too ill and too busy to assume an active role in Masonry, but he continued to receive the highest regard from his fellow Masons.

229 SACHSE, JULIUS F[RIEDRICH], comp. The Loan Exhibition of Frankliniana. Lancaster, Pa.: New Era Printing Co., 23 pp.
       Exhibit of nearly 500 items in the Philadelphia Mason's tribute to Franklin on the 200th anniversary of his birth.

230 SACHSE, JULIUS F[RIEDRICH]. "The Masonic Chronology of Benjamin Franklin." Pennsylvania Magazine of History and Biography 30, no. 2:238-39.
       Mentioned are the important events of Franklin's sixty-year Masonic career.

231 SANDE BAKHUYZEN; HENDRIK, LEO van de [H.G. vdS. Bakhuijzen]; and WAALS, J[OHANN] D[IDERIK]. [Address of] "De Koninklijke Akademie van Wetenschappen te Amsterdam." In Record of the Celebration of the Two Hundredth Anniversary of Benjamin Franklin. . . . Vol. 1. Philadelphia: printed for the American Philosophical Society, pp. 277-78.
       On Franklin as a great scientist.

232 SCHMIDT, A. [Address of the] "Verein für Vaterlandische Naturkunde in Württemberg." In Record of the Celebration of the Two Hundredth Anniversary of Benjamin Franklin. . . . Vol. 1. Philadelphia: printed for the American Philosophical Society, pp. 264-65.
       Franklin is deservedly famous for his achievements in diplomacy and science.

1906

233 S'JACOB, F.B., and BREMER, G.J.W. [Address of] "Bataafsch
     Genootschap der Proefondervindelijke Wijsbegeerte." In
     Record of the Celebration of the Two Hundredth Anniversary
     of Benjamin Franklin. . . . Vol. 1. Philadelphia:
     printed for the American Philosophical Society, p. 235.
          The "Society feels most honoured, that Benjamin Franklin
     belonged to its first members, and acknowledges with grati-
     tude, that his glory has favoured the rise of the 'Bataafsch
     Genootschap.'"

234 SMITH, EDGAR F[AHS]. "Franklin and the University of Pennsyl-
     vania." In Proceedings of the Right Worshipful Grand Lodge
     of the Most Ancient and Honorable Fraternity of Free Masons
     of Pennsylvania . . . [,] at Its Celebration of the Bi-
     Centenary of the Birth of . . . Benjamin Franklin. . . .
     Philadelphia: Grand Lodge of Pennsylvania, pp. 42-48.
          The University of Pennsylvania is indeed the "child" of
     Franklin, its Masonic founder. Yet Masons numbered at
     least one-fourth of Franklin's cofounders, and the Univer-
     sity's first provost, William Smith, had been made a Mason
     in Scotland.

235 SMYTH, ALBERT HENRY. "Franklin As a Printer." Independent
     60, no. 2980 (11 January):104-8.
          Franklin loved printing and saw it as a more than
     honorable craft. He recognized its social, intellectual,
     cultural, and political importance during his own time and
     for the future. Working at his press, advancing his craft,
     "he heard the tred of the coming generations and saw in
     prophetic vision the swift expansion of the English race
     and the marvelous extension of the English language in the
     New World for whose welfare he planned so wisely."

236 SMYTH, ALBERT H[ENRY]. "Franklin the Man of Letters." In
     Year Book of the Pennsylvania Society[,] 1906. Edited by
     Barr Ferree. New York: Pennsylvania Society, pp. [61]-65.
          Although he did not have time to be a man of letters,
     Franklin has left a treasure. His Autobiography is among
     the greatest literary revelations of character, and his con-
     tributions to the Almanacks and "The Way to Wealth" are
     great works that will endure.

237 SMYTH, ALBERT HENRY. "Franklin's Place in Literature." Book
     News 24, no. 281 (January):[311]-14.
          American literature begins with Franklin, and though he
     lacked the ability to complete works, his literary excel-
     lence assures him of "an enduring place among American
     writers."

238 SMYTH, ALBERT H[ENRY]. "Franklin's Social Life in France."
Putnam's Monthly and the Critic[.] A Magazine of Literature[,] Art & Life 1, nos. 1-4 (October-January 1907):
30-41, 167-73, 310-16, 431-38.
Extensive reprinting of Franklin's correspondence with
Mme. Brillon and Smyth's commentary prove that in spite of
his trials and frustrations, Franklin never lost the ability to enjoy himself.

239 [SMYTH, ALBERT HENRY.] "Oration." In Ceremony Held in Paris
to Commemorate the Bi-Centenary of the Birth of Benjamin
Franklin, April 27, 1906. [Compiled by Theodore Ayrault
Dodge.] Paris: Imprimerie Universelle, English Printers,
pp. 17-36.
Franklin's great qualities made him especially beloved
in France, a country for which he had the kindest feelings.
The cooperation and friendship between France and the United
States today would have delighted Franklin, as would the
general peace prevalent in the world.

240 SPULER, D.A. [Address of the] "Physikalisch-Medicinische
Societät zu Erlangen." In Record of the Celebration of the
Two Hundredth Anniversary of Benjamin Franklin. . . .
Vol. 1. Philadelphia: printed for the American Philosoph-
ical Society, p. 250.
Franklin is praised as a scientist, statesman, and human
being.

241 STORY, R. HERBERT. [Address of the University of Glasgow.]
In Record of the Celebration of the Two Hundredth Anniver-
sary of Benjamin Franklin. . . . Vol. 1. Philadelphia:
printed for the American Philosophical Society, pp. 206-8.
Expresses the "great goodwill" St. Andrews feels toward
Franklin.

242 STRAUS-FRANK, VICTOR. "Influence of Benjamin Franklin Abroad."
Journal of the Franklin Institute 161, no. 6:429-30.
Franklin was "a model-citizen, a great philosopher, [and]
a great statesman," as is attested to by his universal
appeal.

243 TENNIS, EDGAR A. "Franklin--the Lesson His Life Teaches."
In Proceedings of the Right Worshipful Grand Lodge of the
Most Ancient and Honorable Fraternity of Free Masons of
Philadelphia . . . [,] at Its Celebration of the Bi-
Centenary of the Birth of . . . Benjamin Franklin. . . .
Philadelphia: Grand Lodge of Pennsylvania, pp. 31-41.

1906

> While Franklin loved to make money and to teach others
> how to accumulate wealth, he was completely different from
> those money-making scoundrels whose names fill the news-
> papers today. Franklin coupled his desire for financial
> independence not only with exemplary citizenship but with
> the secret of true religion: conduct "which always led him
> to seek the good of each to the advantage of all." Reject-
> ing narrow sectarianism, he dedicated his life to "the hap-
> piness and prosperity of his fellow men," and this is a far
> truer Christianity than we customarily find practiced by
> so-called Christians. Franklin's practical benevolence--
> he was interested in nothing that could not be put to good
> use--makes him typically American.

244   THOMAS, PERCY H. "Benjamin Franklin." Electrical Journal 3,
       no. 6 (June):303.
          Edwin J. Houston's piece in the Journal of the Franklin
       Institute, "Franklin As a Man of Science and an Inventor"
       (1906.152), provides ample reason for people interested in
       electrical science to admire Franklin.

245   [TITUS, ANSON.] "Boston When Ben. Franklin Was a Boy." In
       Proceedings of the Bostonian Society at the Annual Meeting,
       January 9, 1906. Boston: published by order of the Society,
       pp. 55-72.
          The Boston into which Franklin was born and in which he
       spent his youth was an exciting and important city, the
       center of New England intellectual and commercial life.
       Franklin profited from the city in a variety of ways and
       always retained affection for it.

246   TOWLE MFG. COMPANY. The Life and Services of Benj. Franklin,
       With Some of the Proverbs of Poor Richard, and a Catalogue
       of the Benj. Franklin Pattern of Sterling Silver Tableware.
       (5th ser. Colonial.) Springfield, Mass.: Press of Spring-
       field Printing & Binding Co., 98 pp.
          Slightly more than half the book (pp. 3-52) is a narra-
       tive of Franklin's life drawn largely from Bigelow, Parton,
       and Franklin's own writings in Poor Richard's Almanacks and
       the Pennsylvania Gazette. The remainder of the book (pp.
       53-88) displays the Benjamin Franklin pattern of Towle
       silverware and also a mahogany chest with "Metal trimmings
       of Franklin design." This book is interesting because of
       the insight it gives into the way in which Franklin was per-
       ceived by many people in the early twentieth century. There
       is no attempt to make Franklin conventionally religious,
       and his deism is treated approvingly. Poor Richard's max-
       ims appear at the bottom of every page of this narrative,

but those who put together this book for Towle point out
that Franklin was no mean materialist and openly scorn
such people in the name of Franklin.

247   TRENT, W[ILLIAM] P[ETERFIELD]. Introduction to <u>Benjamin</u>
      <u>Franklin: His Life Written by Himself</u>[,] <u>Condensed for</u>
      <u>School Use, With Notes and a Continuation of His Life by</u>
      <u>D.H. Montgomery</u>[.] Boston: Ginn & Co., pp. v-xvii.
           A bibliographical sketch of the <u>Autobiography</u> and praise
      for Franklin's virtues and for his prose.

248   TROWBRIDGE, JOHN. "Benjamin Franklin and Electricity."
      <u>Nation</u> 82, no. 2118 (1 February):93-94.
           Analyzes Franklin's theory of electricity and questions
      tendencies among some modern physicists to turn to Franklin's
      single-fluid theory. Also calls Franklin's achievements
      "luck."

249   TURNER, WILLIAM, and GRANT, L.J. [Address of the University
      of Edinburgh.] In <u>Record of the Celebration of the Two</u>
      <u>Hundredth Anniversary of Benjamin Franklin. . . .</u> Vol. 1.
      Philadelphia: printed for the American Philosophical
      Society, pp. 209-10.
           Franklin's intellectual achievements and his character
      deserve the praise of universities and other centers of
      learning.

250   Van HISE, CHARLES R., and RILEY, E.F. [Address of the]
      "University of Wisconsin." In <u>Record of the Celebration</u>
      <u>of the Two Hundredth Anniversary of Benjamin Franklin. . . .</u>
      Vol. 1. Philadelphia: printed for the American Philosoph-
      ical Society, pp. 270-71.
           Praise for Franklin's "many-sidedness" and "broad
      catholicity of human interests."

251   VINCENT, LEON H. "Franklin As a Man of Letters." In
      <u>Bicentenary of Benjamin Franklin's Birth</u>[,] <u>January Seven-</u>
      <u>teen</u>[,] <u>Nineteen Hundred and Six</u>. Franklin, Mass.:
      Sentinel Press, pp. 58-67.
           Franklin was a master of the pointed, witty remark, a
      device which he used to great effect in all his nonscien-
      tific writing. As a literary man, Franklin improved with
      age, and his <u>Autobiography</u> is his greatest achievement.
      American literature was made distinct and took "a great
      step forward" because of Franklin's efforts; in fact,
      American literature, as such, begins with him.

1906

252 WALCOTT, CHARLES D. [Address of] "The Washington Academy of
     Sciences." In <u>Record of the Celebration of the Two Hun-
     dredth Anniversary of Benjamin Franklin. . . .</u> Vol. 1.
     Philadelphia: printed for the American Philosophical
     Society, p. 308.
         Joins in paying tribute to Benjamin Franklin on the
     bicentennial anniversary of his birth.

253 WALSH, C.M. "Franklin and Plato." <u>Open Court</u> 20, no. 3
     (March):[129]-33.
         In Franklin's ideas concerning the nature of argument,
     virtue, and the plurality of gods, as well as in other
     respects, he was influenced by Plato.

254 WANGERIN, A. [Address of] "Die Kaiserlich Leopoldinisch-
     Carolinisch Deutsche Akademie der Naturforscher." In
     <u>Record of the Celebration of the Two Hundredth Anniversary
     of Benjamin Franklin. . . .</u> Vol. 1. Philadelphia: printed
     for the American Philosophical Society, pp. 223-24.
         Franklin is memorialized as a scientist, patriot, and
     statesman.

255 WEITENKAMPF, FRANK. "Notes on Some Franklin Busts." <u>Bulletin
     of the Metropolitan Museum of Art</u> 1, no. 4 (March):60-61.
         On the basis of findings by Charles Henry Hart (1906.138),
     Weitenkampf corrects his January 1906 piece on Franklin
     busts. Hart had located in France the 1777 Caffieri bust
     presented by Franklin to the French Academy of Science in
     1785. This bust "agrees with the famous Cerrachi bust of
     Franklin" in important ways; however, Caffieri and Cerrachi
     never met, and so "the busts attributed to Cerrachi are in
     reality after Caffieri, the marble ones--such as the one in
     the Pennsylvania Academy--being by John Dixon."

256 ____. "Portraits." <u>Bulletin of the New York Public Library</u>
     10, no. 1 (January):57-83.
         Lists 307 portraits of Franklin and his family.

257 WETTSTEIN, R.V., and VIERHAPPER, F. [Address of the] "K.K.
     Zoologisch-Botanische Gesellschaft." In <u>Record of the
     Celebration of the Two Hundredth Anniversary of Benjamin
     Franklin. . . .</u> Vol. 1. Philadelphia: printed for the
     American Philosophical Society, pp. 274-75.
         Tribute to Franklin as a scientist.

258 WIESSE, CARLOS. "Franklin profeta de la libertad." <u>Prisma</u> 2,
     no. 22 (16 September):10.
         Franklin's wisdom, broadmindedness, and stature were
     important factors in the adoption of the Constitution.

259 WILBERT, M.I. "Benjamin Franklin. His Influence on the
     Progress of the Science of Medicine in America." American
     Journal of Pharmacy 78, no. 5 (May):214-21.
     Franklin helped "introduce the practice of pharmacy into
     America." He also indirectly promoted pharmaceutical edu-
     cation by founding the College of Philadelphia which, in
     turn, later helped in the organization of the Philadelphia
     College of Pharmacy. Medicine and related fields had, in
     fact, been of interest to Franklin since his young manhood.
     As a member of the junto and the American Philosophical So-
     ciety, as a printer and later as a scientist, he encouraged
     medical investigation and training. Understandably, the
     always curious and involved Franklin knew a good deal him-
     self about medical practice and hygiene.

260 WILSON, WOODROW. [Address of] "Princeton University." In
     Record of the Celebration of the Two Hundredth Anniversary
     of Benjamin Franklin. . . . Philadelphia: printed for the
     American Philosophical Society, pp. 229-30.
     Tribute to Franklin as a scientist and man.

261 WOODWARD, ROBERT S. [Address of] "The Carnegie Institution of
     Washington." In Record of the Celebration of the Two Hun-
     dredth Anniversary of Benjamin Franklin. . . . Vol. 1.
     Philadelphia: printed for the American Philosophical
     Society, p. 309.
     Praise for Franklin, "statesman, humanist, seer, scien-
     tist, the wisest and the sanest of Americans."

262 WRIGHT, CARROLL D. "Our Debt to Franklin." In The Two-
     Hundredth Anniversary of the Birth of Benjamin Franklin[.]
     Celebration by the Commonwealth of Massachusetts and the
     City of Boston[,] in Symphony Hall, Boston[,] January 17,
     1906. [Boston]: printed by order of the Massachusetts
     General Court and the Boston City Council, pp. 49-77.
     Franklin is on a pedestal only slightly lower than that
     of the great Washington. This oration recounts Franklin's
     multifaceted career and his numerous accomplishments,
     though it concentrates primarily on his political and
     diplomatic activities. Wright is very full in his praise,
     calling Franklin one of the most remarkable, beloved, and
     best men of all time. His lifelong advocacy of liberty
     and justice particularly unites him with his fellow Amer-
     icans, though he also belongs to mankind.

Undated Material

1   ANON. "Miscellaneous Anecdotes Relating to Benjamin Franklin."
     FCL, no. F414.1.
         Franklin tells a spoiled boy who did not learn his
     school lessons and made excuses for his failure that one
     who excels in making excuses is usually not good at any-
     thing else.

2   ANON. "Miscellaneous Anecdotes Relating to Benjamin Franklin."
     FCL, no. F414.1.
         The fifth page of a fragment dealing with the way in
     which Franklin rid himself of busybodies at public inns.

3   ANON. Aux ouvriers imprimeurs réunis pour célébrer la
     mémoire de Benjamin Franklin. Par un soldat du batallion
     des vétérans. N.p.
         Franklin praised as a patriot, democrat, and benefactor
     to mankind.

4   ANON. Benjamin Franklin. N.p. Columbia University, no. 308
     Z244.
         Franklin, one of the foremost men in American history,
     is the genius-patriot who established the foundation of his
     country's "moral and intellectual as well as material
     growth." His versatility is remarkable: in literature,
     education, politics, science, and diplomacy--Franklin made
     contributions to all these fields. He was perhaps greatest,
     however, as a person, for his large, sympathetic heart led
     him to a lifelong commitment of service to mankind. (This
     piece is the ninth in a bound series of pamphlets.)

5   ANON. Benjamin Franklin (1706-1790). Paris: Centre de
     documentation.
         A brief bibliography of works by and about Franklin.

6   ANON. "Benjamin Franklin." In The Anecdote Magazine: An
     Interesting Collection of Curious Occurrences; and Singular
     and Remarkable Events in the Lives of Eminent Men and Women.
     London: George Harrison, p. 47.
         A fiction in which the young Franklin, who had just
     started his Gazette, teaches a dissatisfied subscriber a
     valuable lesson in values and independence. The subscriber,
     disliking Franklin's vigorous defense of American interests,
     tries to get him to change the newspaper's policies by
     dropping his subscription. Franklin later invited him to
     a very plain dinner to which Benjamin Rush and John Hancock
     were also invited. The four spent many pleasant hours

together, and the former subscriber, having learned the lesson intended, thanked Franklin and took out a new subscription to the Gazette.

7   ANON.   Benjamin Franklin: His Life in Pictures and Stories. N.p.   NYPL.
     This volume is a compilation of materials on Franklin given in 1953 to the New York Public Library from the bequest of Gustavas A. Pfeiffer.   Most of the material inincluded is secondary matter previously published.   Some of it is incomplete and without any identification; however, wherever possible and appropriate the material had been identified and dealt with separately.   There are, for example, a number of attractive reprints of Franklin items with brief introductions, pieces by Butler, Hart, and Oswald, among others, and various clippings and pictures.

8   ANON.   "D[r.] Benjamin Franklin."   Hommes célebres 1, no. 11, unpaginated.   FCL.
     Touches very briefly on some of Franklin's accomplishments and praises him for his successes in spite of having been born in a place so remote from Europe.   A decided advantage he had, however, was that his father's house was one in which the love of God was taught.

9   ANON.   Following Franklin[:]   A Bank-Book Talk.   [Cleveland]: Cleveland Public Library.
     Franklin wrote not only about making money, but also about the benefits derived from libraries.

10 ANON.   "Franklin."   [Periodical not identified] (London) 1: 105-8.   FCL, no. F412.1.
     Sympathetic account of Franklin's career, particularly of his scientific accomplishments and of his role in American independence.

11 ANON.   "Franklin and Governor Burnet."   N.p.   American Philosophical Society, no. BF85x no. 84.   1 p.
     A fictionalized account of a meeting between the young Franklin and Governor Burnet, who is quite impressed by Franklin's love of books.

12 ANON.   Franklin (B)[:] Né à Boston en 1706, mort à Philadelphie. N.p.   FCL.
     Franklin deserved the lovely verses of Turgot.

13 ANON.   "Franklin[:]   Né à Boston en 1706.   Mort en 1790." Musée national 7, no. 27, unpaginated.   FCL, no. F412.1.

This piece is a very brief sketch of Franklin's career.

14 ANON. [Franklin's Writings Relative to Chess: A Scrapbook.] N.p. NYPL, no. 8 MZE7.
Various pieces from The Good Companion Chess Problem Club as well as writings by Jared Sparks, Paul L. Ford and others on Franklin's love of chess.

15 ANON. Jean-Baptiste Nini and the Medallion of Franklin. [Hazlitt Tracts vol. 51, no. 12.] London: Spink & Son, [broadside].
Describes the medallion and offers one of those done by Nini for sale.

16 [ANON?] "Quinzieme leçon. Franklin et l'intervention française en Amérique," pp. [250]-61. FCL.
Evidently a history of America for French readers. This lesson deals with Franklin's life focusing its attention almost entirely on his mission in France and French help in the American cause. The author points out that Franklin's reputation for humanitarianism and his characteristic Americanism made him extremely popular in France.

17 ANON. "The Sun of the Constitution." Family Magazine, p. 5. FCL.
Poem telling the well-known story of Franklin seeing the sun on the back of the chair at the Constitutional Convention and predicting that it was a rising sun, symbolizing an optimistic future for the United States. The poet agrees, saying that the light of that sun "fills the world."

18 ANON. "Une visite au tombeau de Franklin." Nouvelles des sciences, du commerce, de la industrie, etc. N.p., pp. 175-77. FCL, no. F412.1.
The simple inscription and plain tombstone that mark the graves of Benjamin and Deborah Franklin are further testimony to the fact that Franklin was as unassuming and modest as Socrates.

19 ANON. Vie de Franklin, d'apres le notes ecrites par lui-même, suivie de la science du bon-homme Richard, morale philosophique & amusante, tirée des ouvrages de cet apôtre de la liberté. Paris: Bureau de Courrier de la librairie & des ouvrages d'instruction publique, 48 pp.
Much of this life of Franklin is quoted from or is a paraphrase of the Autobiography. Franklin is seen as a great public man and citizen.

20 CHAUVIN, LEON. "Benjamin Franklin, 1706-1790." In <u>Travaileurs</u>
    <u>et hommes utiles</u>. [Paris?]: Librairie Nationale,
    pp. 279-316.
    Nearly all of this sketch deals with Franklin's life
    to 1757, though his later years are dealt with briefly.

21 KRUG, K. "Benjamin Franklin." In <u>Die Männer des Volks</u>.
    Vol. 7. N.p., pp. [68]-132.
    Franklin represents the new world and its potential,
    according to the author of this uncritical biography.

22 MACKENSTEIN-KONIG, J. "Franklin en zijn dagboek" [Franklin
    and his diary]. In <u>Het zondagsboek; twaalf staalgravuren</u>
    <u>met bujschriften, voor jongeres en meisjes</u>. <u>Proza en</u>
    <u>poezy</u> [The Sunday book; twelve steel engravings with in-
    scriptions, for boys and girls. Prose and poetry].
    Schiedam: Roelants, pp. 9-11.
    Biographical sketch stressing Franklin's plan of self-
    improvement and its impact on his life.

23 MAHONY, P., firm. "Franklin, the Greatest of Modern Philoso-
    phers." OIC. . . . Boston: printed for P. Mahony.
    American Philosophical Society.
    A broadside which includes picture writing. Franklin is
    brought in to show that frugality is wise. Then the Mahony
    company calls for people to emulate Franklin's frugality by
    selling their waste paper to the firm, which is in the junk
    business. The "I" in the title is actually a drawn eye.

24 NEW YORK CITY EDUCATION DEPARTMENT, Bureau of Libraries.
    <u>Reference and Reading Lists for School Use</u>. <u>Benjamin</u>
    <u>Franklin</u>. [New York(?): published for the New York City
    Education Department, Bureau of Libraries.]
    Recommends a dozen works about Franklin for students and
    teachers to read and declares that all classroom libraries
    should have copies of the <u>Autobiography</u> and <u>Poor Richard's</u>
    <u>Almanacks</u>.

25 NEW YORK CITY, METROPOLITAN MUSEUM of ART. Huntington Collec-
    tion. Collection of Photographs of Busts, Statuettes, Medals
    and Medallions of Franklin.
    More than three dozen photographs make up this booklet.

26 THE ROYCROFTERS. <u>The Secrets of Benjamin Franklin's Education</u>.
    East Aurora, N.Y. NYPL.
    A pamphlet asserting that Franklin was the best gener-
    ally educated man that America has produced.

27 S[ANTEMINO], L. <u>Verse in English and Foreign Languages</u>: "Sarcastic Sawney, Swoln with spite and hate,/On silent Franklin pour'd his venal prate;/The calm philosopher, without reply, Withdrew,--and gave his country liberty[.]"
    Refers to Alexander Wedderburn's very harsh attack on Franklin and on the equanimity with which the philosopher bore the insult. The experience, though, led Franklin to give up all hope of reaching an accommodation with England.

28 [SOCIETY for the DIFFUSION of USEFUL KNOWLEDGE.] "Life of Dr. Benjamin Franklin." In <u>The Working-Man's Companion.</u> <u>Containing the Results of Machinery, Cottage Evenings, and</u> <u>the Rights of Industry. Addressed to Workingmen.</u> [American ed.] New York: Leavitt & Allen, pp. 130-47.
    Franklin's diligence, perseverance, and dedication should inspire all workingmen to improve their lives.

Index